PLANTS AND ANIMALS IN LATIN AMERICAN CULTURAL PRODUCTION

Edited by Cristina E. Pardo Porto
and Oscar A. Pérez

Plants and Animals in Latin American Cultural Production

University of Florida Press / Gainesville

This book will be made open access within three years of publication thanks to Path to Open, a program developed in partnership between JSTOR, the American Council of Learned Societies (ACLS), University of Michigan Press, and The University of North Carolina Press to bring about equitable access and impact for the entire scholarly community, including authors, researchers, libraries, and university presses around the world. Learn more at https://about.jstor.org/path-to-open/

Cover: Hulda Guzmán. *Under the Flamboyán*, 2020. Acrylic gouache on canvas. 47⅞ × 29½ inches. Collection Pérez Art Museum Miami, museum purchase with funds provided by Suzanne McFayden. © Hulda Guzmán. Courtesy of the artist and Alexander Berggruen, NY.

Published in the United States of America

30 29 28 27 26 25 6 5 4 3 2 1

DOI https://doi.org/10.5744/9781683405535

LIBRARY OF CONGRESS CATALOGING-IN-PUBLICATION DATA

Names: Pardo Porto, Cristina E. editor | Pérez, Oscar A. editor

Title: Plants and animals in Latin American cultural production / edited by Cristina E. Pardo Porto and Oscar A. Pérez.

Description: Gainesville : University of Florida Press, [2025] | Includes bibliographical references and index.

Identifiers: LCCN 2025024456 (print) | LCCN 2025024457 (ebook) | ISBN 9781683405535 hardback | ISBN 9781683405689 paperback | ISBN 9781683405900 ebook | ISBN 9781683405771 pdf

Subjects: LCSH: Plants in art. | Animals in art. | Human ecology in art. | Human ecology in literature. | Arts, Latin American—Themes, motives.

Classification: LCC NX650.P53 P59 2025 (print) | LCC NX650.P53 (ebook)

LC record available at https://lccn.loc.gov/2025024456

LC ebook record available at https://lccn.loc.gov/2025024457

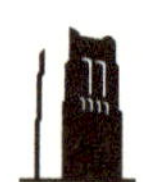

UF PRESS

University of Florida Press / 2046 NE Waldo Road / Suite 2100 / Gainesville, FL 32609 / http://upress.ufl.edu

GPSR EU Authorized Representative: Mare Nostrum Group B.V., Mauritskade 21D, 1091 GC Amsterdam, The Netherlands, gpsr@mare-nostrum.co.uk

CONTENTS

PART III Coloniality and Multispecies Resistance

PART IV The Politics of Plant and Animal Life

FIGURES

ACKNOWLEDGMENTS

This book emerged from an online exchange between the coeditors in August 2022 and our shared interest in a collection about the intersections of animal and plant lives. A brief but lively discussion sparked ideas that were further developed at a conference panel titled "Plants and Animals in Latin American Art and Literature," where the coeditors and some of the contributors came together to explore critical approaches to more-than-human perspectives. The questions raised during those early conversations and that panel helped crystallize the initial framework for this project. We are grateful to those who participated in these exchanges, including Micah McKay, Giannina Reyes Giardiello, and Emily Celeste Vázquez Enríquez; your questions, critiques, and insights resonated deeply, helped shape many of the ideas in this collection, and revealed the depth and urgency of thinking critically about the relationships between animals, plants, and cultural productions in Latin America.

Our gratitude also extends to the many colleagues, collaborators, and reviewers who offered their expertise at various stages of this project. Whether through formal feedback or informal conversations, your engagement has been invaluable. We are especially thankful to the contributors of this volume, who challenged us to refine and broaden our understanding of how plants and animals resist, endure, and thrive in ways that often escape human-centered analysis.

It feels important, too, to acknowledge the animals and plants themselves—not as objects of study but as co-participants in this work: the lilies, ivies, succulents, dogs, cats, and fish who kept us company during long writing sessions, the pines and oaks outside our windows, and the countless living beings who provided loud and quiet reminders of the stakes of this work. This book is, in part, an attempt to honor their presence and consider what a justly shared world would look like.

We would like to equally thank Syracuse University and Skidmore College, which generously helped fund this project. We are also deeply thankful for the enthusiastic support of our editor Stephanye Hunter and everyone at the University of Florida Press. We express our appreciation to the artist Hulda Guzmán, as well as to Pérez Art Museum Miami and Alexander Berggruen, New York, for kindly granting permission to reproduce the painting on the cover of this book. Special thanks to Tess C. Rankin for her assistance with copyediting the introduction.

Finally, we thank our families, friends, and communities in the United States and abroad for their patience and support as we navigated the demands of this project. Your encouragement has sustained us throughout and made this volume possible.

Pushing traditional humanist thought beyond anthropocentrism, animal together with plant thinking is vital to solving the global problems of climate change and anthropogenic extinction.
PATRÍCIA VIEIRA AND SUSAN MCHUGH, "Why Plants and Animals?"

Plants, Animals, and Cultural Criticism from Latin America

CRISTINA E. PARDO PORTO AND OSCAR A. PÉREZ

At the beginning of *De plantas y animales* (2003), Uruguayan poet Ida Vitale relates: "En mi casa, nadie hubiese definido como *útil* la atención puesta en criaturas que no suelen atraerla, pájaros, o esos apenas identificados como *bichos* o plantas poco decorativas que las ciudades erradican al crecer" ("In my home, no one would have defined as *useful* the attention paid to creatures that do not usually attract it, birds, or those barely identified as *bugs* or plants with little ornamental appeal that cities eradicate as they grow") (13). Vitale highlights how tending to other living beings was in itself an act of defiance against traditional practices in her home, a synecdoche for the people closest to her and, perhaps, Montevideo and other urban societies across Latin America. Moreover, the author draws attention to the little regard many humans have for animals and plants that do not serve a utilitarian function in their lives, as well as the distance often placed between humans and other living beings. Birds, bugs, and plants are relegated to categories, classified into isolated boxes of decorative objects, commodities, nuisances, or threats to be eradicated, which strip these beings of relationality. To remedy such neglect, Vitale gifts the reader with *De plantas y animales,* a collection of short essays, poems, and reflections populated by numerous plants and animals. *De plantas y animales* becomes a space where mammals, birds, reptiles, and insects form multispecies communities with rosids, monocots, and asterids. Such life assemblages are central to Vitale's collection and, as Mauricio Cheguhem Riani proposes, her cosmovision is centered on *biocenosis*—a biological community—as an ecological, scientific, and literary paradigm that promotes respect for all species (55).

Plants and animals are deeply interconnected, both biologically and in the context of human and material history. One can point to the plant fibers and animal hide on which most of human history has been recorded. Moreover, as in the case of Vitale's collection, plants and animals have inhabited Latin American cultural productions for centuries. Numerous species in the Plantae and Animalia kingdoms populate Indigenous codices, colonial paintings, odes to the land of the Americas, nation-building novels, and contemporary films denouncing the effects of climate change. Yet, as in Vitale's home, they have not usually received attention as agential living beings.

Despite the inseparability of plant and animal relations, their study in the humanities has been largely compartmentalized. In Latin American cultural criticism, plants and animals are often studied in isolation from each other or within more general humanistic and ecocritical studies of the environment. However, there has been a growing interest in bringing the fields of critical plant studies (CPS) and critical animal studies (CAS) closer together in recent years. Scholars have described these fields' distinct but interrelated origins, noting the earlier attention nonhuman animals received from the humanities and the more recent growth in plant-centered work. *Plants and Animals in Latin American Cultural Production* (*Plants and Animals*) invites readers to reflect on how our cultural understanding of plants and animals changes when we consider them together.

In "Why Plants and Animals?" Patrícia Vieira and Susan McHugh ask themselves, "What can animal studies scholars learn from current plant research and vice versa? How do studies that encompass both plants and animals (and, potentially, other living and non-living forms of existence) enrich our understanding of our planet in all its diversity?" The scholars acknowledge a history of division between the two fields, with critical plant studies initially positioning itself against the prominence of animal studies. However, Vieira and McHugh argue that this perceived rivalry is fading as scholars increasingly work across the two fields and recognize the intertwined roles of plants and animals in ecological and social systems, advocating for breaking artificial disciplinary boundaries and encouraging new pathways for thinking about and with nonhuman life.

The motivation behind *Plants and Animals* echoes that of Vitale's *De plantas y animales* and takes Vieira and McHugh's questions and encouragement as points of departure: We seek to generate a space for plants and animals to be examined, from a humanistic perspective, as part of the communities they form and, by doing so, to bring together two distinct fields devoted to their study—CPS and CAS.[1] In particular, our goal is to explore how Latin American cultural productions can help us reevaluate, in both fields and at their junctures, the "[p]rinciples of ethics, aesthetics, poetics, agency, cognition, intentionality, communication, and language" of all nonhuman life forms (Gagliano et al. xvi).

Plants and Animals takes a powerful stand by putting two fields in conversation and fostering creative contacts between them. There has been no systematic study that explicitly promotes the intersection of the critical study of animals and plants in Latin America. *Plants and Animals* aims to fill this gap and, hopefully, open a dialogue to continue the critical examination of both plants *and* animals in the multifaceted dimensions of current Latin American studies. This includes but is not limited to plant and animal appearances—or representation—in cultural objects, as well as their interactions, oppositions, tensions, and contrasts. The essays included in this volume explore the web of relationships among human and nonhuman living entities in Latin America through a much more radical approach than those employed in existing scholarship. By attending to the moments of intersection between plants and animals in Latin American cultural production, the essays uncover insights into broader societal issues—such as race, gender, care, and labor—but also into other-than-human ways of living, knowing, and communicating. The primary goal of *Plants and Animals* is, then, to scrutinize the relationships, alliances, and conflicts that arise among plants *and* animals, and humans, and how these intertwinements are portrayed in Latin American literature, visual arts, film, and other cultural forms.

Plants have been treated as extractable resources, and animals as exploitable labor. By decentering external agency, we can move beyond such instrumentalizations and genuinely understand their roles in shaping cultural products. In shifting the focus away from anthropocentric views, this volume provides insights for addressing culture and politics through, for example, decolonial and ecofeminist lenses. Examining these intersections enables readers to grasp how human ideologies and actions impact our shared environments and to recognize the profound interspecies entanglements in Latin America's past, present, and future.

Certainly, when we work with plants and animals in cultural objects like artworks, audiovisual media, and literature, which are created for and by humans, they are influenced by how humans see and understand them. However, we aim to challenge the previous position from within our critical scholarship. In *Plants and Animals*, we did not want to invite scholars merely to write *about* plants and animals but to have plants and animals appear in their scholarly works by decentering human perspectives and questioning human mediation of their representation in Latin American cultural production. We believe it is crucial to move beyond the surface of literary and visual languages and delve into what lies beneath the manifestation or presence of a plant or an animal, a complex but essential task. This approach was the result of intentional collaboration, beginning with a conference panel (spring 2023) and a colloquium-workshop (fall 2023) where contributors shared early drafts. Together, we explored how this collaborative process reflects our broader methodology concerning plants and animals—by understanding the challenge of decentering human individualism and emphasizing interconnectedness, even when the collaborators themselves are human. This involved exchanging strategies and acknowledging difficulties, such as the inherent human lens in scholarship and cultural production, to ensure plants and animals were not merely subjects of analysis but central to reshaping how we perceive their roles in cultural production. We propose the study of plants and animals by thinking along with them in their own raw forms of communicating through and appearing in culture. We hope that the works compiled here succeed in demonstrating how animals *and* plants could be—or are, in fact—co-producers of cultural forms (echoing Lesley Wylie). How have plants and animals transformed cultural production in the past and how do they do so today? Plants and animals respond to cultural forms and even interrogate more-than-human ones, creating new inclusive coalitions crucial for resisting environmental devastation and climate change. We must move away from anthropocentrism to address global challenges beyond their impact on the human, such as animal or plant extinction. By paying attention to the shared realms of plants and animals, we can uncover new ways of relating to what is around us and foster more sustainable lives closer to a vegetal and animal way of existing. If we push back against human-centered approaches, maybe it is the plants and animals who will give us the keys to changing the course of ecological decay.

Two Fields Coming Together

If the origins of CAS as a field can be traced to the 1970s animal rights movement, it was in the mid-1980s when scholarship we now recognize as CAS began to emerge (Domínguez 69).[2] The early 2000s saw a definite push toward the establishment of CAS as a defined academic field with the foundation in 2001 of the Center on Animal Liberation Affairs, now the Institute for Critical Animal Studies (Ávila Gaitán 342). Since then, the field has grown exponentially, welcoming a substantial number of works that have expanded it in new and inspiring ways in conversation with other fields, such as gender and sexuality studies, disability studies, film and media studies, and decolonial studies, among many others.[3] Moreover, such interest has driven the emergence of book series exclusively devoted to CAS, anticipating the field's sustained growth in years to come.

If scholarship in the humanities devoted to the study of plants has a long history—one can look at the bibliography compiled by the Literary and Cultural Plant Studies Network and find works going back to the seventeenth century—the origins of contemporary CPS are often located in the early 2000s, when studies that challenged our understanding of plant life had a profound impact on shaping CPS as a thriving transdisciplinary field.[4] As in the case of CAS, there are now entire book series devoted to CPS. As may have become apparent from the previous—limited and incomplete—account, edited volumes have been crucial for the emergence, development, and continuous growth of both CPS and CAS as academic fields. This is no coincidence, as both are deeply rooted in the exchange of ideas, collective efforts, disciplinary boundary breaking, and community building. *Plants and Animals* embraces that tradition and its driving forces.

There have been efforts to draw connections between the theoretical frameworks, intellectual traditions, and activist impetus of CAS and CPS (see, for example, Alessandro Pelizzon and Monica Gagliano's call to expand animal rights to plants through earth jurisprudence). In the scope of cultural criticism, Patrícia Vieira's "zoophytography," Robin Wall Kimmerer's "grammar of animacy," and many other interventions in biosemiotics, posthumanism, environmental humanities, and Indigenous studies have provided tools and necessary new language for critical approaches that decenter human perspectives in favor of both animals and plants.

This book advances Vieira and McHugh's conversation through a threefold intervention in the field, centering scholarship on Latin America through the region's cultural production, its environments, and the often-overlooked lives of its plants and animals. By foregrounding Latin American cultural criticism and research, it challenges the Global North's dominance in the CPS and CAS fields, positioning Latin America not as a peripheral region but as an intellectual and ecological force. Simultaneously, it reframes the region's environments as more than mere backdrops for human narratives and cultural activity, emphasizing the agency of plants and animals within ecosystems shaped by colonialism, historical exploitation, and ongoing extraction. Rather than treating nonhuman life as passive or exotic curiosities, the book highlights their dynamic roles, offering a critical lens that expands the conversation on multispecies entanglements in Latin American studies.

Plants and Animals in Latin American Studies

The convergence of CAS and CPS in Latin American studies is limited. However, the absence of a comprehensive body of scholarly exploration at the intersection of these two fields does not stem from a lack of interest. There is a growing number of works exploring, albeit separately, animal and plant life in Latin American cultural production across different historical periods. Both fields are evolving in parallel with other areas of Latin American studies that possess a more extensive tradition, such as posthumanism, environmental humanities, and ecocriticism. Nevertheless, a seamless dialogue between CAS and CPS is not always present. This propels our own exploration of the intersection that is at the heart of this book. In the subsequent pages, we will try to map independent efforts in each direction, fostering relevant conversations about bringing CAS and CPS closer in Latin American studies and across different historical periods.

Critical animal studies is likely the field that has been explored the most within the context of Latin American studies. Arguably, the first critical works at the intersection of literary studies and CAS emerged in the 1990s.[5] From the mid-2010s onward, the surge in Latin American studies has been substantial, making it challenging to map in detail. The field-defining publication of the book *Centering Animals in Latin American History* (2013), edited by Martha Few and Zeb Tortorici, marks a crucial turning point, initiating a fundamental critique of "antropocentrismo hegemónico"—as Gisela Heffes put it—and advocating for the central consideration of animals not only in historical discourses on Latin America but in Latin American cultural studies more broadly.[6] As highlighted by the editors, the chapters collected in *Centering Animals* aim not to focus on the animal as defining otherness but to emphasize the active participation of animals in shaping the role and trajectory of history as a discipline (Few and Tortorici 3). Few and Tortorici provide an example of bringing nonhuman beings to the forefront of critical inquiry and moving away from the historical instrumentalization of animals as merely providing physical labor or human companionship.

The exploration of animality, or *animalidad*, has gained increasing attention since the publication of Gabriel Giorgi's *Formas comunes* (2014). Works in this line of inquiry explore the impact of nonhuman animal beings on the human experience and the disruptive nature of animality within human contexts and practices, encompassing sociopolitical and biopolitical aspects. In an effort to engage with more-than-human forms of being and existing, in *La letra salvaje* (2015) and later *Biopoéticas para las biopolíticas* (2020), Julieta Yelin proposes a turn away from the animal-as-metaphor, seeking to unravel how writing addresses the "cuestión animal" in terms of literary representation, and introducing the idea of "biopoetics" as a method, applicable to other cultural works. These scholars' interest in displacing the human/nonhuman animal divide, questioning speciesism, and fostering multispecies perspectives is fundamental to CAS and CPS, expanding the horizon of biopolitical studies into the humanities, resisting a linear, superficial definition of "humanism." In *Poéticas de lo viviente, lo animal y lo impersonal* (2020), Matías Ayala Munita introduces the concept of "poéticas de lo viviente," which is clearly influenced by Anglo animal studies and critical ecology. Drawing on the aforementioned works by Giorgi and Yelin, this concept challenges the traditional divide between nature and culture by directing attention to all "formas de vida," an effort shared by most scholars in the fields. Ayala Munita is interested in how *all* forms of life could shape "comunidades (a veces invisibles) que recién comienzan a emerger y a comprenderse a cabalidad al estudiar las dependencias entre vegetales y animales, agua y temperatura, los sustratos minerales y químicos, entre muchos otros" (10) (communities, sometimes invisible, that are just beginning to emerge and be fully understood when studying the dependencies between plants and animals, water and temperature, mineral and chemical substrates, among many others). The idea of a "community" of collective interdependencies between different beings and forms of life—plants and animals included—is one key aspect of exploring the intersection of CAS and CPS.

In the context of cultural studies, works that focus on different forms of representation of animals in literature, film, and other arts are even more exhaustive. From Amerindian and Indigenous studies to colonial, modern, and contemporary regional literatures, the field encompasses a broad range of temporal, geographical, and cultural contexts.[7] We would like to review a couple of interesting examples relevant to *Plants and Animals*, as they touch upon themes aligning with aforementioned trends in CAS and, consequently, are pertinent to CPS. In his work *El otro radical* (2015), Alejandro Lámbarry focuses on the portrayal of animals' voices in literature. Notably, Lámbarry challenges the simplistic inclination to study the anthropomorphizing of the animal voice and, instead, delves into the linguistic agency of animals—a significant aspect when considering the language of plants. He scrutinizes how animals relate to their surroundings and even explores their self-examination as conscious, critical subjects within their literary appearances. Shifting to another perspective, Scott M. DeVries's book *Creature Discomfort* (2016) explores aspects vital to the realm of animal rights, extending beyond the traditional domains of literary studies to shed light on advocacy and animal liberation concerns such as those pertaining to hunting, extinction, exploitation, and the domestication of animals. Furthermore, DeVries also explores philosophical inquiries into animal sentience and the rejection of the human/nonhuman divide, highly relevant within the context of CPS (e.g., plant sentience). DeVries's work functions as a bridge between previously unrelated domains by introducing "fauna-criticism"—another method for conducting CAS within literary analysis. Both Lámbarry's and DeVries's works emphasize the interconnectedness of CAS across different fields and the study of literature, such as activism-driven animal studies and CPS, in addressing shared challenges concerning more-than-human lives. A third recent work, *Vida animal* (2022) by Valeria de los Ríos, extends this line of inquiry into other cultural mediums and representational forms—not confined solely to literature or written works—with a particular focus on the audiovisual domain. In alignment with the principles set out by Giorgi and others in CAS, de los Ríos aims to blur the corporeal hierarchies separating the human and nonhuman, even incorporating the vegetal realm (she works on flowers, for instance), in order to radicalize critical thinking about the life of beings.

Latin American animal studies continues to grow and evolve. The emergence of the Latin American Institute for Critical Animal Studies (Instituto Latinoamericano de Estudios Críticos Animales, ILECA) was crucial in solidifying the field and establishing it as a decolonial project (Ávila Gaitán 341). ILECA's journal, *Revista Latinoamericana de Estudios Críticos Animales* (established in 2014) is now the center of conversations and debates on critical animal studies in the region. Yet, it is not the only venue for such debates. The recent dossier *Paisaje, animalidad y medio ambiente en América Latina y el Caribe, siglo XX* in *Estudios Sociales Contemporáneos*, coordinated by Diana Alejandra Méndez Rojas and Perla Valero, explicitly focuses on contributions that examine nature and nonhuman animals, signaling a broader interest in and expansion of Latin American CAS. New developments also include the emergence of subfields, such as what Sophie Esch has termed "bicho studies." Notably, Esch is actively involved in editing two dossiers: *Critters in the Mexican Imagination: Small Life/Literary Forms* for *Humanimalia* and *Native Fauna in Latin American Literatures: Precolonial to Present Times* for *Hispanic Review*. The special issue of *452°F* on Latin

American and Caribbean entomological and invertebrate aesthetics, coedited by Tomás Bartoletti and Adriana López-Labourdette, also demonstrates the growing interest in and collaborative nature of the study of invertebrate animal life.

The popularity of CPS may appear significantly less pronounced when compared with the prominence of studies attending to animals. This is not exclusive to the context of Latin American studies; it extends to both Latin Americanist and non–Latin Americanist domains. However, Latin American historians have long explored botanical expeditions in early modernity and colonial Latin America. To mention a couple salient and recent examples, in *Plants and Empire* (2004), Londa Schiebinger delves into the geopolitics of plants during the early modern period and underscores their multifaceted role within the transatlantic world. What is remarkable about this work is that Schiebinger chooses to read the involvement of plants in high-stakes politics, emphasizing their participation in exchanges, smuggling, trade, and various forms of movement. The early significance of plants in shaping colonial societies and global Hispanophone relations has also captured the attention of art historian Daniela Bleichmar. She has delved into the visual depiction of the natural world, specifically of Latin American plants and flower specimens, and other forms of vegetal life. In her works, *Visible Empire* (2012) and *Visual Voyages* (2017), Bleichmar argues that images of vegetal life are not merely artistic works or realistic representations; instead, they function as pivotal instruments for the production of knowledge, with global scientific, social, and political repercussions. These titles demonstrate an interest in revealing the agency of plants in shaping Latin American history, a focus that aligns with the concerns of CPS and with the aforementioned *Centering Animals.*

It is crucial to emphasize the significance of new theoretical perspectives, conceptual frameworks, ethical considerations, and modes of engagement and expression that emerge from and within the complexities of plant life. In recent years, there have been advancements in plant theory within the context of Indigenous Latin America. For instance, in literary studies, Juan Duchesne Winter, in *Plant Theory in Amazonian Literature* (2019), employs a transhistorical plant theory framework to delve into Indigenous cosmovisions concerning plant life as portrayed in contemporary literature from the Amazon. Duchesne aims to highlight the productive interactions that the vegetal realm establishes with cultural forms, and even with other species, including nonhuman animals. In this endeavor, Duchesne propels scholarly discourse beyond the confines of solely exploring the organic life of plants, and, instead, he advocates for a broader consideration of the cultural potential embedded in vegetal thinking or the practice of *thinking with* plants, not merely about them—an effort that resonates with us as editors of this collection. Duchesne's intervention aligns with the tradition of Amazonian thought, echoing a rich array of ideas on vegetal metaphysics found in the works of thinkers like Eduardo Viveiros de Castro. *Vozes vegetais* (2021), edited by Joana Cabral de Oliveira, Marta Amoroso, Ana Gabriela Morim de Lima, Karen Shiratori, Stelio Marras, and Laure Emperaire, is also worth mentioning. Arising from a seminar held in April 2019 at the Universidad de São Paulo and the Universidade Estadual de Campinas, and featuring the participation of Amazonian Indigenous thinkers, the cross-disciplinary group of contributing scholars encourages us to attune ourselves to the *voices* of plants and how they manifest—or translate their voices—in texts and cultural artifacts.

Three noteworthy contributions from outside the field of literary or cultural studies are Eduardo Kohn's *How Forests Think* (2013), Marisol de la Cadena's *Earth Beings* (2015), and Micha Rahder's *An Ecology of Knowledges* (2020). Kohn opens *How Forests Think* by powerfully stating that "How other kinds of beings see us matters. That other kinds of beings see us changes things" (1). He draws attention to the perspective of more-than-human beings and questions the way we speak about them. When encountering plants and animals, whether in our daily lives or when reading a novel or watching a film, those encounters are only meaningful when considering them from the perspective of those plants and animals themselves. In Kohn's words: "[S]uch encounters with other kinds of beings force us to recognize the fact that seeing, representing, and perhaps knowing, even thinking, are not exclusively human affairs" (1). These ideas of "seeing," "representing," "knowing," and "thinking" are key aspects that CAS and CPS scholarship has long explored. By ethnographically attending to a series of Amazonian other-than-human encounters in the Runa village of Ávila, in Ecuador's Upper Amazon, Kohn contributes to the posthumanist contestation of "the ways in which we have treated humans as exceptional—and thus as fundamentally separate from the rest of the world" (7). We require a framework, akin to Kohn's, to expand our perspective beyond one-dimensional human interactions with nonhuman entities. The potential solution might involve a radical distinction between humans, and plants *and* animals. De la Cadena's and Rahder's works redirect their attention to nonhuman entities, including the vegetal, but also the animal, challenging the traditional divide between humans and nature. Rahder's examination delves into the profound connections with vegetal species, shedding light on how they influence human conservation practices in Guatemala's Petén. On the other hand, De la Cadena's work engages with the Runakuna cosmovision, such as reading coca leaves, to contemplate "earth beings"—markers of the landscape—to counteract capitalist and state forms of power in Peru.

Alejandro Ponce de León, in "Latin America and the Botanical Turn" (2022), offers a thorough analysis of the recent shift toward the vegetal within Latin American cultural studies, describing it as "an invitation to see, feel, know, and reconnect with botanical forces beyond the narrow parameters of modernity in order to imagine, grow, and foster livable worlds" (130). Ponce de León identifies two key publications within Latin American studies. First, Theresa Miller's *Plant Kin: A Multispecies Ethnography in Indigenous Brazil* (2019), where—despite its being an ethnographic work—she proposes a "sensory ethnobotany framework" to study the affective relations between plants and humans and their interconnected emotional ways of communicating in the context of Canela communities in Brazil. This work is key in proposing the vegetal as sentient. Second, Lesley Wylie's *The Poetics of Plants in Spanish American Literature* (2020), which considers the presence of plants in canonical works of Latin American literature as they communicate through poetic forms of expression, impacting sociopolitical contexts and highlighting the interconnectedness of literature, society, *and* the vegetal. Ponce de León revisits Miller's and Wylie's contributions in defining a "botanical turn" in Latin America and highlighting both books' interventions in centering the "active participation of plants in worldmaking practices in Latin America," following the dialogue initiated by Gagliano, Ryan, and Vieira in *The Language of Plants* (2017), which he also reviews in conversation with Wylie's and Miller's insights (130).

Along with Duchesne's, Wylie's work is arguably one of the most significant contributions to the field of plant studies in Latin American cultural studies, particularly in literary studies. Wylie proposes literature as a "multispecies co-production" and as "plant worlding," asserting that, in Latin American literature from the colonial period to contemporary times, plants have consistently showcased forms of communication and expression critical to understanding the political history of the region. Conducting literary analysis through plants, rather than merely analyzing the presence of plants in literature, sheds light on how plant language and plant poetics are crucial to forms of resistance and decolonial efforts in Latin America.[8] Well-developed more-than-human and multispecies approaches are crucial to the intersection of CAS and CPS. Plant and animal studies challenge human-made hierarchies within specific plant or animal domains. While critical plant and animal studies examine shared issues relating to nonhuman life forms, like communication, sentience, agency, and their roles in ecosystems, multispecies studies adopt a broader framework that explores the interconnectedness of all life forms, emphasizing coevolution and shared ecologies. Both approaches—though multispecies studies to a greater degree—draw from interdisciplinary methods, such as posthumanist theory, to move beyond and actively push back against anthropocentrism, focusing on relationality, multispecies justice, and ethical coexistence.

Understanding ecocriticism as a discipline that examines the relationship between literature, culture, and the environment, this collection joins a rapidly growing ecocritical corpus that explores human-nonhuman relations in Latin American literature and cultural production.[9] Many of these works do so by challenging the passiveness associated with notions such as "landscape," encouraging reflections on how the history of changing—or more accurately, surviving—Latin American landscapes can illuminate the lives of the plants and animals that inhabit such environments.[10] Although these studies often do not approach animal and plant life at the intersection of CAS and CPS, it is worth noting that animals and plants do not go unnoticed by these scholars studying, for example, conquistadors' letters and accounts, the *novela de la tierra or selva*, odes to nature, and other more contemporary works. This group of scholars acknowledges the plants and animals that inhabit the Latin American environment as represented in literature and inquires critically about their relationships with humans to gain a deeper understanding of the natural world and humanity's place in it. By critically examining representations of nature, they contextualize historical environmental degradation, seeking noncapitalist and politically aware modes of reading from the ecological practices hidden in literature.[11]

Structure and Chapters

Composed of sixteen carefully curated chapters and an afterword by Patrícia Vieira, this volume invites readers to make connections within and between its four parts: Part I: Beyond Anthropocentrism, Part II: Language and Knowledge, Part III: Coloniality and Multispecies Resistance, and Part IV: The Politics of Plant and Animal Life. These four sections address key issues central to both CPS and CAS, emphasizing the active co-creation of shared ecosystems and the recognition of agency, rather than merely describing the historical instrumentalization or the othering of plants and animals. In this context, several essays critically reexamine the use of metaphors in literary works that focus on plants and animals, resisting the tendency to treat them as simplistic, one-dimensional symbols. This book's structure challenges traditional approaches by bringing together essays that reflect the interconnectedness of plant and animal lives. Through individual essays on plants or animals and relational ones examining both, we demonstrate that understanding their entanglements requires dismantling long-standing disciplinary boundaries (that are also human-made). Moreover, as the reader will soon realize, the boundaries of the four parts are meant to be questioned. For instance, we have arranged the chapters in such a way that the final chapter of each part is in close dialogue—whether overtly or subtly—with the first chapter of the following part, showcasing how porous the lines that separate CPS and CAS are. In other words, by bridging the gap between CAS and CPS, we aim to demonstrate the rich possibilities that emerge when the two fields intersect, from ontological debates to epistemological questions, shedding light on unexplored dimensions of Latin American cultures and their relationship with the natural world.

Current frameworks in CPS and CAS prove productive in approaching intersections where plants and animals meet. In Part I, authors explore the radical potential of analyzing plant and animal relations by truly highlighting the perspective of the nonhuman. In the essay "Anthropomorphism and Vegetal Life in Sara Gallardo's 'Un césped,'" Micah McKay examines an urban landscape sustaining multiple life forms within an apparently simple patch of grass, challenging established ideas around the anthropomorphism of plant life and proposing that certain anthropomorphisms can, in fact, reveal their own failure. In contrast, Kate Ostrom, in "'They Have Wrapped the Fibers of My Plants around Their Naked Feet,'" focuses on nonhuman-human solidarity and alliances along the US-Mexico border and in the context of the migratory crisis. By analyzing the recent memoir *Solito* (2022) by Salvadoran Javier Zamora, Ostrom underscores the multispecies community inhabiting the border, suggesting that in such a hostile space, solidarity is only found in more-than-human relations. The final two chapters in this part concentrate on well-known vegetal and climate markers of tropical nature, such as palm trees and humidity, as elements that resist human action. In "Tropical Scenery," Cristina E. Pardo Porto argues that tropical plants and animals even when portrayed in photography exhibit resistance within their representation, responsible, as they are, for sustaining the jungle's fragile ecosystem amid relentless exploitation. In "Brazil, the Country of Palm Trees," by Ana Carolina Carmona-Ribeiro, palms take center stage as active agents shaping Brazil's modernity in terms of landscape and its relationship to national identity. Ribeiro explores how palms themselves were able to shape their own narratives of place and country.

Part II includes a series of chapters that propel forward our understanding of animal and vegetal knowledge and sentience, delving into their epistemologies. Language and communication are at the center of "Cattle Intimacies," by Thomaz Amancio, also connecting with the Brazilian focus of the previous section's last chapter. In "Languages of Life," Brian Chandler reads the work of contemporary Mexican poets through the lens of biosemiotics to show how they take up questions of language, communication, and biosemiotic action. With Patrícia Vieira's notion of "zoophytography" as a generative starting point, "Bugs, Plants, and Laboratories," by Oscar A. Pérez, proposes a grammar to describe more-than-human entanglements that centers kinship, intimacy, and intellectual humility. The section closes with Beatriz Rivera-Barnes, who develops a zoopoetic reading of the Mexican film *Amores Perros* (2000) juxtaposed with a medieval Castilian collection of fables to challenge those who discard the fable as a childish or anthropocentric form, setting the stage for the next section focused on colonial contexts.

The chapters included in Part III also investigate plant and animal resistance against the human/nonhuman binary, but in these cases, they also counter colonial violence through Indigenous cosmovisions and multispecies solidarity. Pilar Espitia highlights aesthetic, ethical, and political dimensions of the representations of plants and animals in a cornerstone of female conventual writing in the Viceroyalty of New Granada. Víctor Sierra Matute's "Guamán Poma's Ecocentric Ethos in *Primer Nueva Crónica y Buen Gobierno*" calls attention to the text's unique perspective on the connections among Indigenous worldviews, nonhuman animals, and plants, aiming to expose and respond to the violent consequences of Spanish colonial rule in the region. Emily Celeste Vázquez Enríquez expands upon migration studies to argue that Irma Pineda, a Binnizá/Isthmus Zapotec poet, speaks to the affirmation of migrant agency and the disavowal of deterritorialization through her portrayal of nonhuman animals and plants. To close the section, Jorge Quintana Navarrete explores the interrelation between racialized bodies and vegetal life in representations of *chicle* extraction in Mexico, encapsulating the tensions between plant-human relations and exploitative systems of production.

Part IV addresses the sociopolitical dimensions of multispecies interactions. Authors direct their attention to contexts where plants and animals emerge as active agents influencing extractive systems, like the plantation, and social life throughout the history of the continent and beyond. Niall A. Peach, in "Of Paddocks, Plants, and Cattle," challenges the idea that such spaces are in fact highly controlled by humans. He examines the entanglements of plant and animal life on the colonial hacienda, highlighting alliances among oppressed subjects within these spaces and exploring racial aspects in the contexts of abolitionism and its connections with plants and animals. Continuing with a focus on plantation economies, Mauricio Espinoza, in "'There's Nothing Better Than Giving Life,'" explores the decolonial potential inherent in analyzing the portrayal of coffee in cultural production. Against official narratives that have reduced it to a mere commodity, Espinoza reclaims alternative coffee bean narratives, presenting coffee as an agent, a vehicle for political resistance, and a means of coping with extractive and ecologically devastating practices. Jonathan Mulki then takes us to Alto Paraná, Paraguay, through a critical-collaborative analysis of the documentary *Raídos* (2016), delving into the lives of the *tareferos* who harvest yerba mate and revealing complex interspecies assemblages. Concluding this section, Vanesa Miseres, in "Return to Nature," argues that the international vegetarian movement provides essential insights into the sociopolitical and cultural lives of plants and animals in the transhemispheric Americas. Through the analysis of cookbooks, Miseres illuminates how humans relate to plants and animals, ultimately positing that the Latin American "return to nature" is deeply rooted in early-twentieth-century global and local food politics.

Plants and Animals is a collaborative exploration of Latin American cultural production, engaging scholars from diverse fields such as art history, cultural studies, film and media studies, literary studies, theater and performance studies, and visual studies. This volume breaks disciplinary boundaries, offering an innovative perspective on the intricate interrelationships between plants and animals within the region's rich cultural contexts. With a broad temporal and geographical scope, the collection examines topics from colonial times to contemporary issues, covering works from the Caribbean, Central and South America, Brazil, and the United States, and includes texts written in Indigenous languages. It incorporates analyses of film, documentaries, photography, painting, literary texts, and unconventional formats like cookbooks. The chapters amplify voices often marginalized in cultural discourse: women in colonial contexts, Indigenous communities displaced by climate change, children impacted by migration crises, and environments ravaged by imperialist extraction. Even underrepresented plants and animals, such as yerba mate, are brought into focus. Through decolonial, feminist, and critical race frameworks—alongside interdisciplinary approaches like visual studies and art history—this volume establishes an archive of Latin American cultural production where plants and animals move from the periphery to center stage.

Readers are encouraged to create their own connections across chapters, guided by recurring themes of resistance, agency, ethics, and communication. For example, border studies underpin the analyses of Vázquez Enríquez and Ostrom, while feminist perspectives inform the work of Miseres and Espitia. Pardo Porto and Quintana Navarrete emphasize the jungle as a site of mediation, while McKay and Peach explore the significance of grasslands. McKay and Carmona-Ribeiro investigate the tensions between urban and natural spaces, and Peach and Amancio delve into the cultural history of cattle ranching. Themes of mediation and co-creation emerge through formal readings of visual media in the chapters by Pérez and Pardo Porto, as well as discussions of textual and visual intersections by Amancio and Pardo Porto. Together, these contributions offer a dynamic and multifaceted framework for understanding the roles of plants and animals in Latin American cultural narratives. This collection invites readers not only to appreciate the depth and diversity of these perspectives but also to engage actively with the interconnected threads that weave through its chapters, fostering new insights into the cultural and ecological histories of Latin America.

Notes

1. The gestation of *Plants and Animals* was directly influenced by the undertakings of Patrícia Vieira and Susan McHugh, who have actively promoted bridging CPS and CAS through various endeavors, including the book series they coordinate, Plants and Animals: Interdisciplinary Approaches.

2. This introduction and literature review is not intended to be comprehensive, which would be impossible given the vast array of works on the subjects.

3. CAS scholars are active participants in debates on coloniality (*Colonialism and Animality,* edited by Kelly Struthers Montford and Chloë Taylor, 2020), gender and sexuality studies (*Gender and Sexuality in Critical Animal Studies,* edited by Amber E. George, 2021), race studies (*Animals and Race,* edited by Jonathan W. Thurston-Torres, 2023), disability studies (*Disability and Animality,* edited by Stephanie Jenkins, Kelly Struthers Montford, and Chloë Taylor, 2020), sound studies (Austin McQuinn's *Becoming Audible,* 2021), film and media studies (Claire Parkinson's *Animals, Anthropomorphism and Mediated Encounters,* 2019), and border studies (*Like an Animal,* edited by Natalie Khazaal and Núria Almiron, 2021), to name a few. Recent works also highlight the convergent goals of CAS and the environmental humanities more generally, such

as Nayanika Mathur's *Crooked Cats* (2021), Jeff Sebo's *Saving Animals, Saving Ourselves* (2022), and the collection *Literary Animal Studies and the Climate Crisis,* edited by Sune Borkfelt and Matthias Stephan (2022).

4. Some of these studies include those related to plant intelligence (Anthony Trewavas's "Aspects of Plant Intelligence," 2003), communication (*Communication in Plants,* edited by František Baluška, Stefano Mancuso, and Dieter Volkmann, 2006), autonomy (Matthew Hall's "Plant Autonomy and Human-Plant Ethics," 2009), and senses (Daniel Chamovitz's *What a Plant Knows,* 2012), which expanded the possibilities of humanistic approaches. Foundational works include those by Michael Marder (*Plant-Thinking,* 2013) and Stefano Mancuso and Alessandra Viola (*Brilliant Green,* first published in Italian in 2013) and the collaboration between Monica Gagliano, John C. Ryan, and Patrícia Vieira (*The Green Thread,* 2016; *The Language of Plants,* 2017; *The Mind of Plants,* 2021).

5. See for example Jorge Marcone's "De retorno a lo natural: la serpiente de oro, la 'novela de la selva' y la crítica ecológica" from 1998.

6. In the dossier *Ecocrítica en América Latina,* curated by Gisela Heffes for *Revista de Crítica Literaria Latinoamericana* (2014), notable contributions include articles on animal studies in Latin America by Jorge Marcone, María Esther Maciel (focusing on zooliteratura in Brazil), and others.

7. Virginia DeJohn Anderson's *Creatures of Empire* (2004), John Robert McNeill's *Mosquito Empires* (2010), Miguel de Asúa and Roger French's *A New World of Animals* (2017), and Ana Lucia Camphora's *Animals and Society in Brazil from the Sixteenth to Nineteenth Centuries* (2021) are just a few recent titles of the many noteworthy works that attend to the cultural-historical perspective of animals during early modern and colonial times in transatlantic Spain and Latin America, a field that continues to thrive, as evidenced by Marcy Norton's recent monograph titled *The Tame and the Wild* (2024).

8. Wylie's recent edited volume, *Understories: Plants and Culture in the American Tropics* (2024), continues the line of thought initiated in *The Poetics of Plants,* and is the first collection in CPS to explore the cultural significance of tropical specimens in the American tropics (including non-Hispanophone tropics), centering on plants' perspectives and vegetal ways of thinking from a cross-disciplinary standpoint. There are other significant collaborative endeavors exploring the cultural lives of plants, a drive also embraced by this book, that are noteworthy. The initiative "Pensar desde las plantas" by La Plataforma Latinoamericana de Humanidades Ambientales serves as an example, reflecting the need to center plant perspectives. Additionally, the Latin American Plant Humanities Workshop (2022), led by Elizabeth Chant and organized by the University of Warwick and the Centre for Latin American and Caribbean Studies of the University of London, further highlights the growing interest in the intersection of plants and culture in Latin America.

9. That corpus includes works such as Jennifer French's *Nature, Neo-Colonialism and*

the Spanish American Regional Writers (2005), Beatriz Rivera-Barnes and Jerry Hoeg's *Reading and Writing the Latin American Landscape* (2009), Laura Barbas-Rhoden's *Ecological Imaginations in Latin American Fiction* (2011), Gisela Heffes's *Políticas de la destrucción/Poéticas de la preservación* (2013, and translated in 2023 as *Visualizing Loss in Latin America*), William Flores's *Ecocrítica poscolonial y literatura moderna latino-americana* (2015), and Victoria Saramago's *Fictional Environments* (2021). More recent contributions to this area include Amanda M. Smith's *Mapping the Amazon* (2021), Axel Pérez Trujillo Diniz's *Imagining the Plains of Latin America* (2021), Joanna Page's *Decolonial Ecologies* (2023), Micah McKay's *Trash and Limits in Latin American Culture* (2024), and Carolyn Fornoff's *Subjunctive Aesthetics* (2024).

10. For instance, Jens Andermann has focused his attention on the portrayal of the Latin American natural landscape in literature and visual culture. This effort is crucial in shifting away from the landscape as a mere backdrop to human activity—an approach that aligns with non–Latin Americanist CPS perspectives (Ryan et al. x). His work *Tierras en trance* (2018), along with the volume *Natura* (2018, coedited with Lisa Blackmore and Dayron Carillo Morell), and the recent *Entranced Earth* (2023), position the landscape as having a crucial role in deciphering human and more-than-human relations and agencies.

11. In line with this scholarly ethos, *Plants and Animals* joins a burgeoning collection of contributions reflected in many edited volumes such as *The Natural World in Latin American Literatures* (2010), edited by Adrian Taylor Kane; *Ecological Crisis and Cultural Representation in Latin America* (2016), edited by Mark Anderson and Zélia M. Bora; *Ecofictions, Ecorealities, and Slow Violence in Latin America and the Latinx World* (2019), edited by Ilka Kressner, Ana María Mutis, and Elizabeth Pettinaroli; *Pushing Past the Human in Latin American Cinema* (2021), edited by Carolyn Fornoff and Gisela Heffes; *Literature beyond the Human* (2022), edited by Luca Bacchini and Victoria Saramago; and *Futuros multiespecie* (2023), edited by Azucena Castro. Notably, the *Handbook of Latin American Environmental Aesthetics* (2023), edited by Jens Andermann, Gabriel Giorgi, and Victoria Saramago, includes the itinerary "Multinaturalism/Nonhuman Representation" by Mark Anderson. In this section, Anderson challenges the human/nonhuman divide and highlights a shared cultural network, which he refers to as "multinaturalism." The volume also features contributions such as "Plant" written by Lesley Wylie and "Animal" by Ximena Briceño. We would also like to highlight important recent contributions of academic journals, such as the dossiers *Genealogías latinoamericanas de las Humanidades Ambientales: derivas, cruces y caminos* in *Revista CS,* coedited by Alejandro Ponce de León, Sofía Rosa, and Jesús Alejandro García; *Latin American Environmental Research and Practice* in *Tabula Rasa,* coedited by Lisa Blackmore and Gisela Heffes; and the special issue of the journal *Forma* edited by Timothy Frye, which explores the environmental turn with essays analyzing

extractive practices, toxicity, and other environmental concerns in relation to their entanglements with twentieth-century Latin American literature, film, and visual arts.

Works Cited

Andermann, Jens. *Entranced Earth: Art, Extractivism, and the End of Landscape.* Northwestern University Press, 2023.

Andermann, Jens. *Tierras en trance: arte y naturaleza después del paisaje.* Metales Pesados, 2018.

Andermann, Jens, et al., editors. *Handbook of Latin American Environmental Aesthetics.* De Gruyter, 2023.

Andermann, Jens, et al., editors. *Natura: Environmental Aesthetics after Landscape.* University of Chicago Press, 2018.

Anderson, Mark, and Zélia M. Bora, editors. *Ecological Crisis and Cultural Representation in Latin America: Ecocritical Perspectives on Art, Film, and Literature.* Lexington Books, 2016.

Anderson, Virginia DeJohn. *Creatures of Empire: How Domestic Animals Transformed Early America.* Oxford University Press, 2004.

Asúa, Miguel de, and Roger French. *A New World of Animals: Early Modern Europeans on the Creatures of Iberian America.* Routledge, 2017.

Ávila Gaitán, Iván Darío. "El Instituto Latinoamericano de Estudios Críticos Animales como proyecto decolonial." *Tabula Rasa,* no. 27, 2017, pp. 339–351.

Ayala Munita, Matías. *Poéticas de lo viviente, lo animal y lo impersonal.* Metales Pesados, 2020.

Bacchini, Luca, and Victoria Saramago, editors. *Literature beyond the Human: Post-Anthropocentric Brazil.* Routledge, 2022.

Baluška, František, et al. *Communication in Plants: Neuronal Aspects of Plant Life.* Springer, 2006.

Barbas-Rhoden, Laura. *Ecological Imaginations in Latin American Fiction.* University Press of Florida, 2011.

Bartoletti, Tomás, and Adriana López-Labourdette, editors. *Pulsión entomológica e imaginarios invertebrados en América Latina y el Caribe,* special issue of *452°F,* no. 30, 2024.

"Bibliography." *Literary and Cultural Plant Studies Network,* https://plants.arizona.edu/bibliography/. Accessed 3 Feb. 2024.

Blackmore, Lisa, and Gisela Heffes. "Investigación académica y prácticas artísticas ambientales latinoamericanas." *Tabula Rasa,* vol. 46, 2023, pp. 11–25, https://doi.org/10.25058/20112742.n46.01

Bleichmar, Daniela. *Visible Empire: Botanical Expeditions and Visual Culture in the Hispanic Enlightenment.* University of Chicago Press, 2012.

Bleichmar, Daniela. *Visual Voyages: Images of Latin American Nature from Columbus to Darwin.* Yale University Press, 2017.

Borkfelt, Sune, and Matthias Stephan, editors. *Literary Animal Studies and the Climate Crisis.* Palgrave Macmillan, 2022.

Cabral de Oliveira, Joana, et al., editors. *Vozes vegetais: diversidade, resistências e histórias das florestas.* Ubu Editora, 2021.

Cadena, Marisol de la. *Earth Beings: Ecologies of Practice across Andean Worlds.* Duke University Press, 2015.

Camphora, Ana Lucia. *Animals and Society in Brazil from the Sixteenth to Nineteenth Centuries.* White Horse Press, 2021.

Castro, Azucena, editor. *Futuros multiespecie. Prácticas vinculantes para un planeta en emergencia.* Bartlebooth, 2023.

Chamovitz, Daniel. *What a Plant Knows: A Field Guide to the Senses.* Scientific American/Farrar, Straus and Giroux, 2012.

Cheguhem Riani, Mauricio. "Gramática de la naturaleza: poética y ciencias de lo vivo en Ida Vitale." *Ida Vitale: la escritura como morada,* coordinated by María José Bruña Bragado, Editorial Universidad de Sevilla, 2021, pp. 45–58.

DeVries, Scott M. *Creature Discomfort: Fauna-Criticism, Ethics and the Representation of Animals in Spanish American Fiction and Poetry.* Brill, 2016.

Domínguez, Daisy. "At the Intersection of Animal and Area Studies: Fostering Latin Americanist and Caribbeanist Animal Studies." *Humanimalia,* vol. 8, no. 1, 2016, pp. 66–92, http://doi.org/10.52537/humanimalia.9655.

Duchesne Winter, Juan. *Plant Theory in Amazonian Literature.* Palgrave Macmillan, 2019.

Few, Martha, and Zeb Tortorici, editors. "Writing Animal Histories." Introduction. *Centering Animals in Latin American History,* Duke University Press, 2013, pp. 1–28.

Flores, William. *Ecocrítica poscolonial y literatura moderna latinoamericana.* Fondo Editorial de la UNMSM, 2015.

Fornoff, Carolyn. *Subjunctive Aesthetics: Mexican Cultural Production in the Era of Climate Change.* Vanderbilt University Press, 2024.

Fornoff, Carolyn, and Gisela Heffes, editors. *Pushing Past the Human in Latin American Cinema.* SUNY Press, 2021.

French, Jennifer. *Nature, Neo-Colonialism and the Spanish American Regional Writers.* Dartmouth College Press, 2005.

Frye, Timothy, editor. Special issue of *FORMA,* vol. 2, no. 1, 2023.

Gagliano, Monica, et al., editors. *The Language of Plants: Science, Philosophy, Literature.* University of Minnesota Press, 2017.

George, Amber E., editor. *Gender and Sexuality in Critical Animal Studies.* Lexington Books, 2021.

Giorgi, Gabriel. *Formas comunes: animalidad, cultura, biopolítica.* Metales Pesados, 2014.

Hall, Matthew. "Plant Autonomy and Human-Plant Ethics." *Environmental Ethics,* vol. 31, no. 2, 2009, pp. 169–181.

Heffes, Gisela, editor. *Ecocrítica en América Latina,* special section of *Revista de Crítica Literaria Latinoamericana,* vol. 40, no. 79, 2014.

Heffes, Gisela. *Políticas de la destrucción—poéticas de la preservación: apuntes para una lectura eco-crítica del medio ambiente en América Latina.* Beatriz Viterbo Editora, 2013.

Heffes, Gisela. *Visualizing Loss in Latin America: Biopolitics, Waste, and the Urban Environment.* Palgrave Macmillan, 2023.

Jenkins, Stephanie, et al., editors. *Disability and Animality: Crip Perspectives in Critical Animal Studies.* Routledge, 2020.

Kane, Adrian Taylor, editor. *The Natural World in Latin American Literatures: Ecocritical Essays on Twentieth Century Writings.* McFarland & Company, 2010.

Khazaal, Natalie, and Núria Almiron, editors. *Like an Animal: Critical Animal Studies Approaches to Borders, Displacement, and Othering.* Brill, 2021.

Kimmerer, Robin Wall. *Braiding Sweetgrass: Indigenous Wisdom, Scientific Knowledge and the Teachings of Plants.* Milkweed Editions, 2013.

Kressner, Ilka, et al., editors. *Ecofictions, Ecorealities, and Slow Violence in Latin America and the Latinx World.* Routledge, 2019.

Lámbarry, Alejandro. *El otro radical. La voz animal en la literatura hispanoamericana.* Universidad Iberoamericana Puebla, 2015.

Mancuso, Stefano, and Alessandra Viola. *Brilliant Green: The Surprising History and Science of Plant Intelligence.* Translated by Joan Benham, Island Press, 2015.

Marcone, Jorge. "De retorno a lo natural: la serpiente de oro, la 'novela de la selva' y la crítica ecológica." *Hispania,* vol. 81, no. 2, 1998, pp. 299–308.

Marder, Michael. *Plant-thinking: A Philosophy of Vegetal Life.* Columbia University Press, 2013.

Mathur, Nayanika. *Crooked Cats: Beastly Encounters in the Anthropocene.* University of Chicago Press, 2021.

McKay, Micah. *Trash and Limits in Latin American Culture.* University Press of Florida, 2024.

McNeill, John Robert. *Mosquito Empires: Ecology and War in the Greater Caribbean, 1620–1914.* Cambridge University Press, 2010.

McQuinn, Austin. *Becoming Audible: Sounding Animality in Performance.* Penn State University Press, 2021.

Méndez Rojas, Diana Alejandra, and Perla Valero, editors. *Paisaje, animalidad y medio ambiente en América Latina y el Caribe, siglo XX*, special issue of *Estudios Sociales Contemporáneos*, no. 29, 2023.

Miller, Theresa. *Plant Kin: A Multispecies Ethnography in Indigenous Brazil*. University of Texas Press, 2019.

Norton, Marcy. *The Tame and the Wild: People and Animals after 1492*. Harvard University Press, 2024.

Page, Joanna. *Decolonial Ecologies: The Reinvention of Natural History in Latin American Art*. Open Book Publishers, 2023.

Parkinson, Claire. *Animals, Anthropomorphism and Mediated Encounters*. Routledge, 2019.

Pelizzon, Alessandro, and Monica Gagliano. "The Sentience of Plants: Animal Rights and Rights of Nature Intersecting." *Australian Animal Protection Law Journal*, vol. 11, 2015, pp. 5–13.

Pérez Trujillo Diniz, Axel. *Imagining the Plains of Latin America*. Bloomsbury Publishing, 2021.

Ponce de León, Alejandro. "Latin America and the Botanical Turn." *Journal of Latin American Cultural Studies*, vol. 31, no. 1, 2022.

Ponce de León, Alejandro, et al., editors. *Genealogías latinoamericanas de las Humanidades Ambientales: derivas, cruces y caminos*, special issue of *Revista CS*, no. 36, 2022.

Rahder, Micha. *An Ecology of Knowledges: Fear, Love, and Technoscience in Guatemalan Forest Conservation*. Duke University Press, 2020.

Ríos, Valeria de los. *Vida animal: figuraciones no humanas en el cine, la literatura y la fotografía*. Metales Pesados, 2022.

Rivera-Barnes, Beatriz, and Jerry Hoeg. *Reading and Writing the Latin American Landscape*. Palgrave Macmillan, 2009.

Ryan, John C., et al., editors. *The Mind of Plants: Narratives of Vegetal Intelligence*. Synergetic Press, 2021.

Saramago, Victoria. *Fictional Environments: Mimesis, Deforestation, and Development in Latin America*. Northwestern University Press, 2021.

Schiebinger, Londa. *Plants and Empire: Colonial Bioprospecting in the Atlantic World*. Harvard University Press, 2004.

Sebo, Jeff. *Saving Animals, Saving Ourselves: Why Animals Matter for Pandemics, Climate Change, and Other Catastrophes*. Oxford University Press, 2022.

Smith, Amanda M. *Mapping the Amazon*. Oxford University Press, 2021.

Struthers Montford, Kelly, and Chloë Taylor, editors. *Colonialism and Animality: Anti-Colonial Perspectives in Critical Animal Studies*. Routledge, 2020.

Thurston-Torres, Jonathan W., editor. *Animals and Race*. Michigan State University Press, 2023.

Trewavas, Anthony. "Aspects of Plant Intelligence." *Annals of Botany*, vol. 92, no. 1, 2003, pp. 1–20.

Vieira, Patrícia. "Amazonian Ecopoetics: Paes Loureiro's Shamanic Zoophytography." *Romance Studies*, vol. 41, no. 1, 2023, pp. 54–64.

Vieira, Patrícia, et al., editors. *The Green Thread: Dialogues with the Vegetal World*. Lexington Books, 2016.

Vieira, Patrícia, and Susan McHugh. "Why Plants and Animals?" *Peter Lang Publishing Blog*, 6 Oct. 2022, https://medium.com/peter-lang/why-plants-and-animals-a17cdd872bbe. Accessed 2 Feb. 2024.

Vitale, Ida. *De plantas y animales*. 2003. Tusquets, 2019.

Wylie, Lesley. *The Poetics of Plants in Spanish American Literature*. University of Pittsburgh Press, 2020.

Wylie, Lesley, editor. *Understories: Plants and Culture in the American Tropics*. Liverpool University Press, 2024.

Yelin, Julieta. *Biopoéticas para las biopolíticas: el pensamiento literario latinoamericano ante la cuestión animal*. Ubiquity Press, 2020.

Yelin, Julieta. *La letra salvaje: ensayos sobre literatura y animalidad*. Beatriz Viterbo Editora, 2015.

PART I
Beyond Anthropocentrism

1

Anthropomorphism and Vegetal Life in Sara Gallardo's "Un césped"

MICAH MCKAY

Imagine a patch of grass. It is the kind of small green space that you could find in almost any city you may care to think of, but this one is in Buenos Aires. One of the Argentine capital's busy streets runs right past the patch of grass, so throughout the day there is a steady flow of traffic, both motor vehicles and pedestrians, and traffic lights telling people when to stop and when to go. And there are businesses nearby—restaurants and shops, small grocery stores, men with carts selling ice cream and other treats, and the like. The proprietors of these businesses go through the same steps every day to open and close their businesses, setting up shop, announcing their wares, gathering things up, taking out the trash. Drivers, pedestrians, and workers perform their daily rituals in plain view of the patch of grass. It is always there, but do they notice it?

Along the busy street where the patch of grass is growing, there are also houses and apartments where folks who lead relatively comfortable middle-class lives reside. They come and go to and from work or school, going out to grab a bite to eat or do some shopping. They walk their dogs, meet up with friends, and watch the children play. Perhaps they notice the grass more than the busy shop owners, restaurateurs, and ice cream vendors because they take strolls through this grassy area, they sit down in the grass to rest for a few moments on a pleasant day, they kick a soccer ball around, or they let their dogs exercise their noses and relieve themselves in the grass. But do they ever really *think* about this patch of grass? What if the city government neglected the area, forgetting to send out the groundskeepers to trim it? What if the grass kept growing for weeks, months, or even a year? Would people take notice then? Perhaps the question of what the grass notices is a more interesting—or even disquieting—one. How does it experience what for you or for me are the unremarkable rhythms of daily urban life (traffic, pedestrians, commerce, leisure)? Does it like to be left to grow tall? When the municipal gardeners get their act together and mow the grass, does it lament being cut short? Are such questions actually interesting? Or disquieting? Does thinking about the experience of grass or other plants have any bearing on our very urgent need to take concrete, significant steps to address the various environmental crises that define contemporary life? Or is this all merely some kind of silly exercise that turns our attention away from weightier issues?

These are some of the questions raised by reading Sara Gallardo's 1977 short story "Un césped" ("A Lawn").[1] Running just a few pages in length, this very brief story appears in the Argentine writer's *El país del humo* (*Land of Smoke*), a beautiful collection of cryptic, dazzling tales that offer startling reflections on animality, the blurry indistinction of the human and nonhuman, and the social structures that marginalize and discount the experience of any number of Others.[2] "Un césped" falls into line with this aesthetic project of imagining the experience of what, at first blush, is obviously Other to the human and something that most people would say is insignificant and unworthy of much attention: a humble patch of grass much like the one I invoke above. Gallardo's narrator opens the story by setting the scene: "En los jardines que van de Palermo a la Recoleta hay un cuadro de césped. Cierto año, los jardineros se olvidaron de cortarlo. El pasto creció a sus anchas" (96) ("Among the gardens that run from Palermo to Recoleta there's a square of lawn. One year the gardeners forgot to cut it. The grass grew at its leisure") (151). From there, the story unfolds not by wondering whether or how the people and other creatures who come into contact with the grass notice or think about it, but rather by recounting the grass's experience of its surroundings: the vibrations of street cars that pass by on the half hour like clockwork and shake the grass's roots; the soot and grime from burning trash and car exhaust that leave particles on its blades as they grow ever longer, forgotten and unattended by city groundskeepers; the humans and insects who take refuge in the tall grass's thick, unruly lushness; the birds who search for food there and the dogs who leave their waste there. After some time, the narrator tells us, "Un día, el intendente municipal recorrió todos los jardines que van desde Palermo hasta la Recoleta. Un rey había anunciado su visita" (97) ("One day the city mayor travelled through all the gardens between Palermo to Recoleta. A king had announced his visit") (152). The expected visit of this unnamed king spurs the *jardineros* to action. They mow the grass so that the city can shine brightly and make a good impression on this foreign dignitary, and as they do, Gallardo's narrator tells us that the grass sings a song composed of all the beings with which it had come into contact since it had last been cut: the rain and soot, the worms and dogs, and all the people who had moments of their lives unfold on and around the patch of grass somehow reverberate in what Gallardo calls "esa voz de césped" (97) ("the voice of the grass") (153), as its lush, vibrant verdancy becomes clippings to be disposed of.

With the grass's song, Gallardo's tale comes to an end. This is a beautiful story but a strange one that has stuck with me since I came across it in 2018. It is a very simple tale in which nothing particularly dramatic or memorable seems to happen, but to my mind, despite its humble trappings, it takes a bold stance regarding what matters in literature. It is about as close as you can get to being a story about watching grass grow, and I think it is precisely such an utterly banal premise that makes it a radical statement. Gallardo's attempt to imagine the experience of grass and make that experience bear the weight of narrative storytelling compels us to reflect on both the importance of recognizing our place in the more-than-human world and the key role that literary fiction—an eminently human cultural artifact—can play in helping us apprehend that place.

Many people would balk not only at Gallardo's attempt to narrativize the experience of a patch of grass, but also at the more fundamental notion that grass can be said to have what we might call "experiences" at all. The burgeoning field of critical plant studies certainly gives the lie to such skepticism. Evolutionary ecologist Monica Gagliano, for instance, argues from a scientific perspective that plants exhibit intelligence, make meaning, and communicate their experience of the world, whether human beings attune themselves to that communication or not (6). Plants inhabit their own temporalities that are "marked by their unique and excessive rendering of time through (often) indeterminate growth in space," which means that human attempts to relate "to plants will always involve degrees of distance exceeding the animal world composed through difference" (Margulies 47). For some thinkers operating within critical plant studies, this distance—the utter difference between plant and animal (including human) forms of inhabiting, perceiving, and communicating the experience of time and space—makes processes of vegetal life the key to moving beyond the "totalizing categories of Western metaphysics" and toward "a more open-ended, less instrumental, approach not only to social relations but also to the environment" (Gagliano et al. xv).

If plants have experiences and can communicate them and what they have to say is valuable to human beings who seek to cultivate better relationships with the more-than-human world, how can we conceptualize plant speech with the tools of human thought and perception? As Patrícia Vieira asks, "What would be the parameters of such an utterance? Would we be prepared to listen to flora's paradoxically silent speech? Or would we rather, as Spivak warned in the case of the subaltern, superimpose our thoughts, reasoning, and preconceived ideas, perhaps even in a well-intentioned manner, onto the plant?" (216–217) Vieira's warning against projecting human ways of being and thinking onto plants, even when it is done with the best of intentions, is essential to keep in mind when considering "Un césped." At first blush, this sort of well-intentioned superimposition seems to be precisely what is at play in Gallardo's insistent deployment of personification. In the story, the grass is not only made to sing, as I mention above; it also "abre la boca" (97) ("opens its mouth") (152) to receive refreshing drops of rain, grows "[a] su antojo" (96) ("as it please[s]") (151) when left unattended by the city, and "se [sorprende] con la novedad" (96) ("[is] surprised by the novelty") (151) of autumn juices that soak into the soil. Gallardo clearly attempts to capture the grass's experience and, ultimately, the message it communicates about that experience, in decidedly human terms.[3] In other words, it seems that the figurative language she uses to talk about the grass—personification—betrays a viewpoint that legitimates seeing the world as a reflection of all things human—anthropomorphism. How should we read this translation of the radically Other experience of plants? Is it a reflection of "the human yearning to know the stories of plants" that ultimately reveals "a burning wish to dominate and possess the vegetal world," or can it be seen as something else (Vieira 216)? In what remains of this chapter, I would like to consider the work that personification and anthropomorphism are doing in "Un césped."

Personification and anthropomorphism may certainly be viewed as tropes that shore up the long-standing norm of anthropocentrism in Western culture. As tropes, they turn us away from what the grass *really is* and toward something more legible, familiar, and comfortable, namely, the world of human impulses, emotions, and actions. However, that turn away from the grass as such also marks a limit: the inability of humans to *actually* apprehend (and therefore dominate) something as apparently simple as the way that grass experiences the world. Veering away from the normative notion of personification and anthropomorphism as nothing more than the projection of human schema onto the world is a way of following the unexpected turns that tropes can take and acknowledging literary language's ability to disrupt received modes of thought and swerve into new ones (Cohen and Duckert 2–3). One such turn prompted by rethinking personification as a trope that enacts a limit is the realization that "a careful course of anthropomorphization can help reveal [nonhuman] vitality, even though it resists full translation and exceeds [our] comprehensive grasp" and "chasten [our] fantasies of human mastery, highlight the common materiality of all that is, expose a wider distribution of agency, and reshape the self and its interests" (Bennett, *Vibrant Matter* 122). In other words, anthropomorphism can help us see similarities between ourselves and the nonhuman, which is a key step in reconfiguring our relationship with the nonhuman and forming alliances with other beings (Page 60). But such a form of strategic, carefully cultivated and deployed anthropomorphism requires new, non-anthropocentric modes of seeing and interpreting the world, which includes texts, both literary and otherwise. The very deployment of anthropomorphism in a story like "Un césped" underscores the tension between these competing modes of reading, because the text itself tends to provoke a certain measure of resistance, which I have seen take shape in students' interpretations of the story every time I have used it in an undergraduate or graduate literature course over the last five years or so. Students invariably either want to read it as a prose poem whose natural imagery is symbolic and therefore points toward an underlying meaning that is more significant than any patch of grass could ever be or as a story that is *really* about the daily rhythms of urban life, in which case the titular césped would only amount to something like poetic window dressing that throws into relief the cycles of human life and the ephemerality of the things that preoccupy us from day to day. I recognize and appreciate that these readings can be generative, and I do not mean to critique my students in particular. Indeed, that my students (or anyone else, for that matter) would read Gallardo's use of anthropomorphism as a tool for crafting a literary representation of human actions, desires, and concerns comes as no surprise because that form of reading is symptomatic of our anthropocentric worldview.[4] But it is a reading that fundamentally misunderstands the text. It sidesteps the important fact that the grass is the story's protagonist and that the story's plot, stripped down as it may be, clearly centers on the grass's fate: how it is initially ignored, how it flourishes as it encounters other beings, and how that flourishing is cut short by the groundskeepers' blades.

Some may object to this line of thought and say that the questions of how to classify Gallardo's text (Is it a prose poem or short story?) and interpret it (Does the grass symbolize something that is actually more significant or is this story really about grass?) are minor quibbles and dwelling on them is tantamount to splitting hairs. My point, however, is that these seemingly superficial aesthetic questions are in fact profound because they point toward the essential matter of the ends to which anthropomorphism can be used. On the one hand, it can reflect the hubris of anthropocentrism and normalize hierarchical relationships of domination between humans and nonhumans; on the other, it can be a tool for imagining other modes of relation and "counter[ing] the narcissism of humans in charge of the world" (Bennett, *Vibrant Matter* xvi). The difference between these competing ends comes down to how a given instance of anthropomorphism deals with the limits of human knowledge, vision, and power. It is important to cultivate a form of anthropomorphism that is not the unidirectional projection of human characteristics onto the nonhuman, but rather a gesture that seeks out points of connection and allows the human and nonhuman to become the measure of each other, as opposed to "man" being the sole measure of all things (Page 115). As Joanna Page reminds us (echoing Eduardo Viveiros de Castro), a key part of this is the decoupling of anthropomorphism from anthropocentrism in a way that puts them at odds with each other, because anthropomorphism can be a way of highlighting relationality instead of dominance (131). Through both the utter banality of the type of nonhuman life upon which Gallardo centers her story and the way in which she stages the encounters between human and nonhuman beings, "Un césped" deftly deploys anthropomorphism in a way that exemplifies the limits of the human and the limitations of human beings' ability to know and dominate the vegetal Other.

The notion of "plant blindness" is useful for considering the broader discursive and cultural contexts that make a story that centers such an unremarkable life form as grass a bold statement on the limits of human vision. Plant blindness—a label for a form of cognitive bias coined by the botanists and biology educators James H. Wandersee and Elisabeth Schussler—is the tendency for human beings "to overlook, underemphasize, or neglect plants" despite the fact that they "form the basis of most animal habitats and all life on earth" (82). Wandersee and Schussler chalk this tendency up to a mixture of cultural and natural factors. For instance, they note that, by and large, education in biology tends to focus much more on animals than plants, which leads to a significant knowledge deficit regarding the vegetal world. What is more, plants tend to present a sort of visual homogeneity and their seeming indistinctness makes it hard for us to notice them. Plants are, for the most part, stationary and perceived as static and they typically present little to no threat to humans and can therefore be ignored without causing us much worry (84–86). For Wandersee and Schussler, plant blindness is not merely a metaphor; their invocation of the sense of vision is a key element that grounds the supposedly natural factors that make us blind to plants. In other words, it is tied to the way the human visual apparatus works (86). While this is a compelling account of the limitations of human embodiment vis-à-vis the vegetal world, it is important to (metaphorically) look beyond it so as not to fall into the trap of universality or biological determinism. There are cultural and ideological factors at play as well. Philosopher Val Plumwood, for instance, reminds us of the key role of European colonial ideologies in the development of frameworks for seeing, valuing, and inhabiting the space that we commonly call the natural world. By her account, these frameworks rely on features like radical exclusion "that deny intentionality and subject status to the more-than-human world" and minimize the particularity of a given space in order to more easily subsume it into processes like empire, modernization, or progress (66). Plumwood adds that "In 'backgrounding' particularity, place and narrative as factors in human thought and life, colonizing frameworks make places into mere passive instruments or neutral surfaces for the inscription of human projects" (66). So the *anthropos* in general is not naturally or necessarily blind to plants, but, given the hegemony of Western colonial projects, many of us operate in cultural contexts that conjugate the particularities of our visual apparatus with an exclusionary ideological apparatus in a way that results in us thinking of a patch of grass in a city not as a mutually sustaining interface of multiple life forms and ways of being, but rather as a platform for us humans to assert our will, our being, our priorities.

Gallardo's story stages this sort of dynamic tension between plant blindness and seeing plants through an investment in anthropomorphism. The human characters she places in the narrative are all people who pass by or trod upon the patch of grass: doormen, businesspeople, kids, lovers, dog owners. Because the story is focalized through the grass's perspective and grounded in its experience, we do not know what these people think of this space: do they see it as particular or unique, the bearer of some sort of subjectivity, or is it a feature of urban space that exists to meet their needs, to provide them with a break from all the asphalt and concrete? The story itself cannot answer this question because it does not give us access to these people's thoughts or impressions of the patch of grass, but my hunch is that it is more of the latter than the former. The idea that Buenos Aires's human inhabitants see this particular plantscape through the kind of exclusionary, instrumentalist framework that Plumwood describes is, however, made quite clear by the story's denouement: following the mayor's orders for groundskeepers to cut the lawn ahead of a foreign ruler's visit, "Llegaron los jardineros. Cortaron todo el pasto. De norte a sur, y de este a oeste" (Gallardo 97) ("The gardeners arrived to cut all the grass, north to south, east to west") (153). The combination of the multiple orders of political power (a mayor and a foreign ruler) and the ominous extension of that power over the cardinal points underscores the fact that this seemingly unremarkable political decision (to mow the grass) is intimately connected to deep-seated notions of sovereignty based on the belief in human dominion over the Earth, notions that invariably lead to the relegation of many living beings to a state of exception (Smith 130). If plants, like all living things, are subject to structures of sovereignty, then it is perfectly natural to see the patch of grass as a space that can and must be molded into something useful for humans, as a screen on which to project an image of order and rationality and an anthropocentric aesthetic sense (Smith xiii). In other words, the grass is there *for us.*

But the story indexes another perspective on plants as well, a different way of framing space that destabilizes the anthropocentric thrust of the human characters' modes of interacting with the patch of grass that are condensed in the act of mowing the lawn to prepare for the royal visit. It is a perspective that recognizes nonhuman life's capacity to "refuse to internalise the meanings of human language" and "[rely] instead on their own semiotic interpretations of the environment and [act] accordingly" (Youatt 394). If that human biopolitical framework could be said to perceive the grass as being here *for us,* the more-than-human framework posits that the grass is here *with us* and with a host of other beings. And that framework is made visible to us by Gallardo's use of personification and anthropomorphism. Alongside the human characters' interactions with the grass, Gallardo interweaves those of other creatures, objects, and phenomena. Autumn rain, worms, car exhaust, the multicolored lights of traffic signals, birds, insects, dogs, and dog feces all appear alongside human beings in the story, with none seeming to take precedence over any other (from the grass's perspective, that is), and they are all linked by the kind of shimmering agentic capacity that characterizes anthropomorphism (Bennett, *Vibrant Matter* xvi). The lack of hierarchization among these beings is reflected in the syntax of the story's closing passage: "Y el pasto que moría cantó. Cantó el aliento y el trepidar del tren, el hollín que baja, los jugos del otoño. Las lombrices. Los enamorados. Las luces del semáforo. Los vendedores de helados. Los insectos. Los perros atados y desatados. Y los dueños de los perros. Los pájaros. Los vendedores de café. Los niños crecidos y los que aprenden a caminar. El rocío, el humo de los autos, la lluvia. Cantó, esa voz de césped, ese olor de césped cortado" (Gallardo 97) ("And the grass that died sang. It sang of the breath and rattle of the train, the descending soot, the juices of autumn. The earthworms. The lovers. The traffic lights. The ice cream sellers. The insects. The dogs with and without leashes. The owners of the dogs. The birds. The coffee vendors. The big children and the ones just learning to walk. The dew, the smoke from the cars, the rain. It sang, that voice of the grass, that smell of freshly mown lawn") (153).

The grass's song comprises all the creaturely and material presences with which it has come into contact, human and nonhuman alike, and it is arranged as a list that is almost completely devoid of conjugated verbs, coordinating conjunctions, and relative pronouns. In other words, these presences—whether they be worms, ice cream vendors, dewdrops, or dogs—are part of the same web of materiality. They are different, but that difference does not *necessarily* or *naturally* entail a hierarchy of importance or value. From this perspective, the grass in the story is not an inert stage for human activity or a natural space subject to the sovereign decision, as it seems to be for all of the story's human characters, but rather, as philosopher Emanuele Coccia puts it, an example of "The little green limbs that populate the planet and capture the energy of the Sun [and] are the cosmic connective tissue that has allowed, for millions of years, the most disparate lives to cross paths and mix without melting reciprocally, one into the other" (28). What is more, it is the very anthropomorphic move of making the grass sing that brings this vibrant web of materiality to readers' attention, allowing us to see plant life as beings that "preserve the memory of the Anthropocene, that . . . circulate that memory, its physicality and fluidity, through a becoming that [extends] beyond the human era" (Cortez 189).

That it is precisely the most anthropocentric gesture in the story—the decision to cut the grass to make it conform to human ideas about the beauty of nature—that leads to the clearest expression of story's more-than-human ethos is significant and underscores one of the primary achievements of Gallardo's story, namely, that of showing the consequences of different uses of human faculties. Humans have produced philosophical, ideological, ethical, and political systems that justify intervening in, modifying, and destroying other forms of life for what we humans see as our benefit. Despite its utter banality and seemingly low (or even nonexistent) stakes, the decision to cut the grass at the end of the story exemplifies such systems of hierarchization and exclusion. These systems invariably depend on the foreclosure of the consideration of other possible systems for understanding the ways that different beings can relate to each other. In other words, they depend on the foreclosure of another human faculty, that of imagination. In order to consider a human relationship with a patch of grass that does not assume it to be a "neutral [surface] for the inscription of human projects," to borrow Plumwood's turn of phrase (66), we have to *imagine* what the grass's experience might be like. And this is precisely what Gallardo does in "Un césped." She opts for anthropomorphism and imagines that the grass can grow at its leisure, that it has cravings and desires, that the arrival of rain surprises it, and that it opens its mouth to receive the refreshment that the rain brings. And she imagines that the grass *sings*. We do not know (and I would venture to say that we cannot know) if what Gallardo imagines in "Un césped" actually approximates the experience of grass, but I think there is great value in the anthropomorphic lens through which she sees—and in turn asks us to see—a humble patch of grass. Her story is not, to my mind, a call to leave the grass alone, never cutting it; rather, it is a call to attention, a reminder that human projects and concerns exist alongside those of other beings and life forms, many of which provide us with sustenance, solace, and care. It behooves us to recognize this and expand our notions of dignity and care accordingly.

Notes

1. While originally published by Sudamericana in 1977, the version of Gallardo's story I quote in this chapter is from El cuenco de plata's 2015 edition of *El país del humo*. The English quotations of "Un césped" are from Jessica Sequeira's translation, published by Pushkin Press in 2017. All other translations in this chapter are mine.

2. Gallardo (1931–1988), who wrote novels, short stories, children's literature, and journalistic pieces, achieved acclaim in Argentina during her lifetime but received little critical and popular attention in the years after her death, perhaps because, as Paula Bertúa and Lucía De Leone put it, "El repertorio de sus diferentes apuestas estéticas . . . propende a que su producción literaria no sea fácilmente domesticable por paradigmas críticos, o dúctil para encasillar en colocaciones femeninas consolidadas" (The repertory of her varying aesthetic endeavors . . . tends to make it difficult for her literary production to be domesticated by critical paradigms or pigeon-holed into ready-made constellations of women's writing) (6). Jordana Blejmar and Joanna Page elaborate on the untimely character of Gallardo's narrative, noting that her tendency to portray rural settings and use male narrators confounded a literary establishment that expected women to situate their "fiction in domestic, bourgeois, urban settings" and treat "predictable topics such as childhood or woman's experience." The twenty-first century has seen growing interest in Gallardo's work "because it appears surprisingly fresh, addressing concerns relevant to our own moment," like issues of gender and sexual expression and—of particular interest to readers of this volume—questions of the relationship between the human and the nonhuman (Blejmar and Page). On the

latter question, Gloria Pimpollo reads the figure of the animal in *El país del humo*—whether it be the horses, rats, dogs, tigers, or amorphous monsters scattered across the collection's pages—as a sign pointing toward a form of freedom that exists outside of human-imposed hierarchies and that, with "humor sardónico" (sardonic humor), manages to mock "la solemnidad humana" (human solemnity) (138).

3. The story's use of personification also extends to other nonhuman elements, both living (birds, earthworms, dogs) and nonliving (soot, sparks of fire, cars, water). While I do not give this larger web of life and materiality sustained attention in this chapter, it seems clear to me that the way Gallardo links these disparate elements with the trope of personification is part of the perspective that the story develops. Following Jane Bennett, I would call this perspective one of enchantment vis-à-vis the environment, a shift of affective comportment toward the world "that is necessary if we are to exit the paths of planetary exploitation and destruction" ("Afterward" 495). It is a way of bringing humans and nonhumans back into contact with each other, a way of re-entwining what has been separated by ways of thinking that stem from the Enlightenment project (Page 32–33).

4. Here I use "our" in an exclusive, rather than an inclusive, sense: I am referring to the "we" (including me) who are inheritors of Western, colonialist worldviews that both presuppose a clear separation between human and nonhuman worlds (culture and nature) and assume that the former is inherently and universally more valuable that the latter. Much has been written on the importance of recognizing that recent critiques of such worldviews are not new because many cultures do not subscribe to Western conceptualizations of the nature-culture divide. Where plants are concerned, Matthew Hall very usefully categorizes different cultures' views and practices as tending toward either the exclusion of plants from or the inclusion of plants in structures of moral consideration (4–13).

Works Cited

Bennett, Jane. "Afterward: Look Here." *Environmental Humanities*, vol. 14, no. 2, 2022, pp. 494–498. *e-Duke Journals*, https://doi.org/10.1215/22011919-9712533. Accessed 30 Oct. 2023.

Bennett, Jane. *Vibrant Matter: A Political Ecology of Things*. Duke University Press, 2010.

Bertúa, Paula, and Lucía De Leone. "Prólogo." *Escrito en el viento: lecturas sobre Sara Gallardo*, edited by Paula Bertúa and Lucía De Leone, Editorial de la Facultad de Filosofía y Letras / Universidad de Buenos Aires, 2013, pp. 5–12.

Blejmar, Jordana, and Joanna Page. "Sara Gallardo, recently rediscovered Argentine writer." *European Languages across Borders: Collections in Germanic, Romance and Slavonic Languages at the University of Cambridge*, 15 March 2018, https://

europeancollections.wordpress.com/2018/03/15/sara-gallardo-recently-rediscovered-argentine-writer/. Accessed 26 Oct. 2023.

Coccia, Emanuele. *The Life of Plants: A Metaphysics of Mixture.* Translated by Dylan J. Montanari, Polity, 2019.

Cohen, Jeffrey Jerome, and Lowell Duckert. "Introduction: Welcome to the Whirled." *Veer Ecology: A Companion for Environmental Thinking,* edited by Jeffrey Jerome Cohen and Lowell Duckert, University of Minnesota Press, 2017, pp. 1–15.

Cortez, Beatriz. "The Memory of Plants: Genetics, Migration, and the Construction of the Future." *Timescales: Thinking across Ecological Temporalities,* edited by Bethany Wiggin et al., University of Minnesota Press, 2020, pp. 183–192.

Gagliano, Monica. *Thus Spoke the Plant: A Remarkable Journey of Groundbreaking Scientific Discoveries and Personal Encounters with Plants.* North Atlantic Books, 2018.

Gagliano, Monica, et al. "Introduction." *The Language of Plants: Science, Philosophy, Literature,* edited by Monica Gagliano et al., University of Minnesota Press, 2017, pp. vii–xxxiii.

Gallardo, Sara. "A Lawn." *Land of Smoke,* translated by Jessica Sequeira, Pushkin Press, 2017, pp. 151–153.

Gallardo, Sara. "Un césped." *El país del humo,* El cuenco de plata, 2015, pp. 96–97.

Hall, Matthew. *Plants as Persons: A Philosophical Botany.* SUNY Press, 2011.

Margulies, Jared D. *The Cactus Hunters: Desire and Extinction in the Illicit Succulent Trade.* University of Minnesota Press, 2023.

Page, Joanna. *Decolonial Ecologies: The Reinvention of Natural History in Latin American Art.* Open Book Publishers, 2023, https://doi.org/10.11647/OBP.0339. Accessed 18 Sept. 2024.

Pimpollo, Gloria. "Humanos y animales en los cuentos de Sara Gallardo." *Escrito en el viento: lecturas sobre Sara Gallardo,* edited by Paula Bertúa and Lucía De Leone, Editorial de la Facultad de Filosofía y Letras / Universidad de Buenos Aires, 2013, pp. 131–139.

Plumwood, Val. "Decolonizing Relationships with Nature." *Decolonizing Nature: Strategies for Conservation in a Post-Colonial Era,* edited by William Adams and Martha Mulligan, Taylor & Francis, 2002, pp. 51–78.

Smith, Mick. *Against Ecological Sovereignty: Ethics, Biopolitics, and Saving the Natural World.* University of Minnesota Press, 2011.

Vieira, Patrícia. "Phytographia: Literature as Plant Writing." *The Language of Plants: Science, Philosophy, Literature,* edited by Monica Gagliano et al., University of Minnesota Press, 2017, pp. 215–233.

Wandersee, James H., and Elisabeth E. Schussler. "Preventing Plant Blindness." *The American Biology Teacher,* vol. 61, no. 2, 1999, pp. 82–86.

Youatt, Rafi. "Counting Species: Biopower and the Global Biodiversity Census." *Environmental Values,* vol. 17, no. 3, 2008, pp. 393–417.

2

"They Have Wrapped the Fibers of My Plants around Their Naked Feet"

Plants and Animals of the US-Mexico Borderscape

KATE OSTROM

In August 2020 a gruesome photo surfaced across news outlets: a body was found dead against the US-Mexico border wall. This body was not human. It was a desert mule deer buck, crossing through Organ Pipe Cactus National Monument near the US-Mexico border, along its migratory path between Arizona and Mexico (Kelety 2020). The mule deer is just one of many nonhuman casualties at the hands of border construction and the military industrial border complex in the borderlands. Photos of ensnared birds, dehydrated Sonoran Desert toads, and disoriented javelinas have also made the rounds (Schlyer 2017). These images point to the environmental impact of border construction on both human and nonhuman crossers in an age of accelerated land degradation and climate disruption.

These photos are also disturbing for their parallels to human bodies disappeared in the Sonoran Desert.[1] Human border crossers climb over and tunnel under the border wall, cut through fencing, swim across waterways, and many die in their crossing attempts. According to the International Organization for Migration, the US-Mexico border is the deadliest land migration route in the world, with 686 deaths and disappearances reported in 2022. More than half of these deaths are directly connected to the Sonoran and Chihuahuan Deserts—

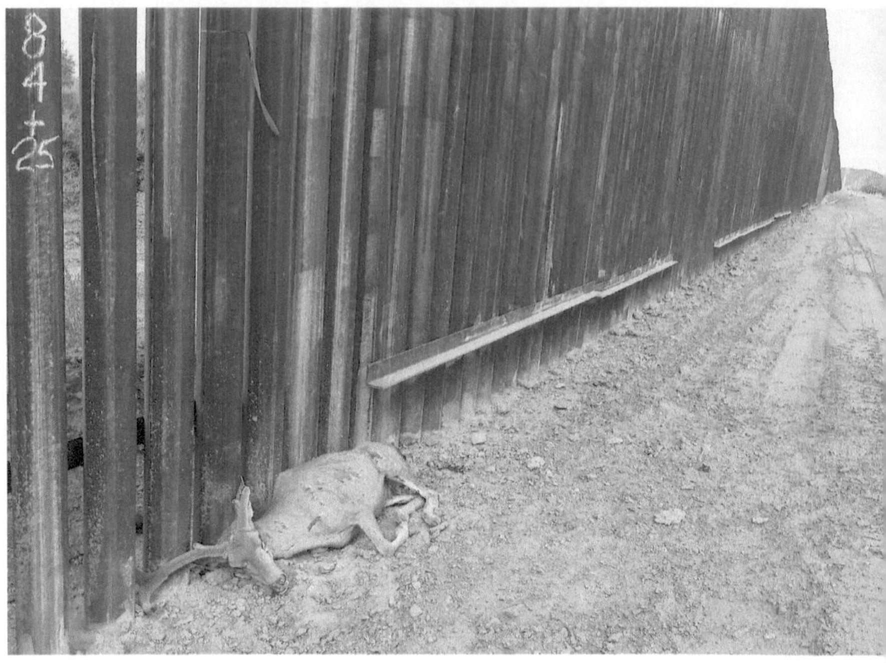

FIGURE 2.1. Dead mule deer buck lying against the side of the US-Mexico border wall. Photo by anonymous, courtesy of Laiken Jordahl.

wildlife hot spots and Indigenous homelands implicated in an alarming human rights crisis ("US-Mexico Border World's Deadliest" 2023).[2] These uniquely biodiverse desert regions are transformed into spaces of death and disappearance, where the 1994 Prevention Through Deterrence (PTD) policy (that continues to define US-Mexico border policy today) pits a hostile "nature" against human crossers, acting as a "natural" barrier and deterrent to undocumented migration.[3] With checkpoints, drones, sensors, and military-like efficiency, the US-Mexico border "wilderness" paradoxically resembles an active war zone; to cross entails a prolonged trek through some of the most remote and dangerous wilderness in the world (*Disappeared* 6).

It is evident there is a multispecies crossing emergency at the border, but to compare human and nonhuman risk is complicated. These "dreaded comparisons" seem wrong.[4] And yet, the US-Mexico border has long conflated the human and nonhuman. Border Patrol uses "signcutting" to "track" migrants.[5] Crossers travel via "La Bestia."[6] Coyotes traffic "sheepish" migrants. Crossers are kept in cages. Highway signs depict border crossers as potential roadkill.[7] Of course, not all comparisons are negative. The monarch butterfly is a symbol for immigration, specifically for Dreamers in the United States—undocumented migrants who arrived as children.[8] But even butterflies—along with other insects, bats, and birds—find themselves at risk of habitat loss due to increased noise and light pollution at the border (McSpadden et al. 2023).

Javier Zamora's 2022 childhood crossing memoir *Solito* does something different. On his journey through Central America, Mexico, and the Sonoran Desert, Javiercito enters into a dynamic relationship with nonhuman crossers, leaving behind all speciesist and anthropocentric views as he braves this unfamiliar desert. By using his childhood imagination inspired by vibrant desert life to recognize the plants and animals as fellow crossers, Javiercito suggests alternative, imaginative ways to read the border. The text speaks to the shared vulnerabilities and (at times) mutually beneficial interactions between species. Border crossers are never solitos, but rather surrounded by plant and animal lives that protect, teach, shelter, guide, and even attack them along the way.

The text maintains species differences *between* and *among* human and nonhuman life (Derrida 2008), while attending to what philosopher Matthew Calarco refers to as "indistinction" among interspecific crossers (*Thinking* 48–49). Rather than limit observations to the purely animal, Javiercito notices sometimes forgotten desert species around him: namely, birds, insects, and plants. Through Lonelies, Spikeys, and Fuzzies, Javiercito envisions radical and transformative kinships among desert life, and writes them into human language.

In this chapter, I highlight multispecies crossing kinships in the US-Mexico borderscape. Human crossing stories are interconnected to—and interdependent on—the nonhuman stories and beings that do their own kinds of crossings through the contested geopolitical terrain of the US-Mexico border. *Solito*, in conversation with plant and animal studies (Gagliano and Calarco), highlights the interspecies entanglements, alliances, and stories that speak to the "slow violence" (Nixon 2011) of the US-Mexico borderscape, while providing alternative readings of both climate disruption and "border crisis." *Solito* rewrites this narrative as one with eco-imaginative and boundless (borderless?) possibilities. Moving beyond "dreaded comparisons" and anthropocentric speciesist thought, and traversing terrain where plant and animal studies meet Indigenous Knowledges, I argue that the US-Mexico borderlands are spaces of shared vulnerability, indistinction, and open possibility between human and nonhuman plant and animal life. Here, survival means forming rebellious and interspecific kinships that seek ecojustice for all border crossers.

"They're Like Us": Animals of the US-Mexico Borderlands

Javiercito begins his 3,000-mile journey as an unaccompanied minor through the US-Mexico borderlands amid the PTD border policy of the 1990s. In a series of three separate crossing attempts (two unsuccessful), Javiercito journeys from El Salvador into "La USA" to meet his parents, waiting for him on the other side. Javiercito gives voice to many collective elements of crossing stories: trickster coyotes, border patrol evasions, detention centers, hunger, thirst, dead bodies. But this text does something different. Along Javiercito's journey through the Sonoran Desert, human and nonhuman animal lives intersect. From burrowing rabbits to swarming bees to *literal* coyotes, the nonhuman animal world crosses too. And like the mule deer, they—along with human border crossers—find themselves trapped in zones of increased vulnerability and violence amid the wide-scale environmental degradation and habitat fragmentation of the US-Mexico borderscape.

Throughout his journey, Javiercito seeks to understand and imaginatively learn from nonhuman crossers. Javiercito does not animalize human border crossers, nor does he anthropomorphize the nonhuman plant and animal world. Instead, Javiercito recognizes the uniquely rich and complex differences of desert species, as well as the shared vulnerabilities among all crossers that must contend with walls, barriers, and increased human disturbances in an age of hardened borders.

In the US-Mexico borderlands, human and nonhuman animal crossers find themselves in what Matthew Calarco refers to as a zone of "indistinction" where "there is no clear-cut ontological difference that bars the possibility of experiments in plasticity with various species" (*Beyond* 37). Borrowed from Gilles Deleuze and Giorgio Agamben, inspired by Donna Haraway, Val Plumwood, and Rosi Braidotti, "indistinction" theory interrogates the limits of both "difference" and "identity" approaches to critical animal studies.[9] Anthropocentric systems and thoughts are dismantled; instead, there are "shared conditions, overlapping experiences, and common fates" across beings (*Beyond* 31). "Indistinction" temporarily suspends anthropological difference(s) to ask new kinds of questions about human and nonhuman beings: "What other possibilities might open up when we no longer take distinctions between human beings and animals as the chief point of departure for thought and practice?" (*Thinking* 51). As disability and animal rights activist Sunaura Taylor asks, "Do animals deserve equal consideration? Do their experiences matter?" ("Beasts" 2011: 207). In US-Mexico crossing stories, they do. In turning the reader's gaze to the nonhuman animal crossing populations through what Alexandra Horowitz and Ed Yong refer to as "informed imaginative leaps" (Horowitz 243; Yong 13),[10] human and animal crossing experiences are intertwined. Not only does the nonhuman animal world teach Javiercito and his fellow crossers to imagine the desert world from a nonhuman perspective, but through informed and imaginative observations attentive to nonhuman animal crossers, humans acquire unique adaptations for survival in the desert.

Javiercito notices the biodiverse nonhuman world as soon as he enters the Sonoran Desert, alongside what he calls the "Centipede" (named for the double line configuration of around fifty human bodies "snaking" through the desert) (Zamora 215). "The adults keep saying 'desert,' but a desert has sand like in *Aladdin*. There's quicksand and pyramids. No trees or cactuses or bushes" (107). This desert is not barren and desolate; it is as Gary Nabhan says, "an enchanted place" with a deep history that embraces "an older way of imagining the desert found in the spiritual traditions of many ancient desert cultures" ("Deep History" 2). As the most biologically diverse desert region in the United States, the Sonoran Desert ecosystem is home to around 130 species of mammals, more than 500 kinds of birds, around 100 reptiles, and as many as 2,500 native plants. Many of these species are endemic to the region—that is, found nowhere else on earth (Nabhan, "Welcome" 1). This is where the jaguar, ocelot, black bear, javelina, desert toads, and a thriving bird community meet (Schlyer 2017). The majestic Sky Islands—mountainous island formations that stretch upward of 3,000–10,000 feet—are biological hot spots and home to more than 7,000 species of plants and animals. Some three quarters of all North American birds have been spotted here ("Sky Islands").

Nonhuman crossers experience their own challenges due to increased human presence in the region. Border wall construction reduces connectivity and quality of habitats, and fragments populations (Flesch et al. 2010; Harrity et al. 2024). Animals are stopped in their tracks. Seed carriers like javelinas can no longer cross, limiting plant migrations. Roads, lights, noise pollution, vehicular traffic, and human activity all contribute to further wildlife displacement, environmental degradation, and habitat fragmentation. The loss of genetic diversity within populations and extinction are very real risks for many species (Peters et al. 741). Under the 2005 RealID Act passed amid post-9/11 heightened anxieties, Congress granted the Department of Homeland Security permission to waive some forty environmental laws in the name of border construction, including the Endangered Species Act, the Clean Air Act, and the National Environmental

Policy Act. This policy has been subsequently invoked to speed up border wall construction along the 2,000-mile stretch (Schlyer 2017).[11] Environmental impact assessments are disregarded in the name of hurried construction projects.[12] Between 2017 and 2021, another 458 miles of border wall were built in the region, leaving more than two thirds of Arizona-Sonora cut off by border wall barriers, further bifurcating traditional migratory paths and access to waterways, and damaging parks, monuments, forests, and wilderness areas, as well as Indigenous lands (Traphagen). Generally, only species the size of a bobcat or smaller can pass through the wall's 18–30-foot tall (5.5–9.1 m) steel bollard fences and 4-inch (10 cm) gaps.[13] For larger species, such as mule deer, it is difficult to find pathways through the wall. They pace the wall, wandering upward of fifty miles, until they exhaust themselves or are struck by the increased vehicular traffic in the region (Meierotto 19).[14] The wall may impact the movement of borderlands species forever.[15]

These nonhuman animal violences may seem trivial alongside those enacted on human bodies in the desert. But, as Mary Mendoza notes, the "immigrant versus nature" debate has a long history in the US-Mexico borderlands. Environmentalists who advocate for nonhuman lives amid border wall construction often fail to acknowledge the human cost of such measures, further reinforcing "the enduring notion in the United States that immigrant bodies are expendable" and secondary to animal and plant life (123). Climate refugees are increasingly blamed for the environmental crisis itself (Banerjee 2).

As Calarco notes, "discriminatory practices aimed at human beings—such as racism, colonialism, sexism, ableism, and so on—tend to bleed into the dominant culture's relationship to animals" (Beyond 21). The addictive anthropocentrism of our "natural" systems of order favors certain privileged humans, while violently excluding the human and nonhuman "other" (21). To approach a borderlands environmental discussion, then, we must consider the human, nonhuman, and greater environmental threats "as one complex web of concerns" (Mendoza 124). "Indistinction" theory is especially useful when considering this multispecies entangled web. Human and animal crossers are trapped together in a zone of "indistinction," that is, a knot of intertwined, shared vulnerabilities and violences. They are co-present victims and witnesses of death and destruction at the border.

Just as animals must cross border fences and barriers, human crossers must as well. Javiercito faces fences in each crossing attempt. Polleros—slang for people who are paid to receive and cross over migrants—use gloves to pull out the sharp wires, but crossers struggle. Some get stuck to the wires, moving the fence back and forth, "like a lizard pinned down by a stick" (Zamora 221). Others slide under "face down, belly flat" (220), are dragged through, or, as in Javiercito's case, are tossed over. Barbs stick to their clothes, backpacks, and skin. As Javiercito observes, "the bunnies must laugh at us jumping, crawling under—they can just run under fast" (224). In later crossings, Javiercito imaginatively channels the animal world in his movements. "The fences are cool. I feel like I'm back home chasing iguanas. I've practiced. ¡It's the most exciting thing we've done all trip! It's a game. ¿Who can make it through the most fences without getting stuck?" (223). In imagining animal crossing experiences, Javiercito learns from the "laughing" bunnies that barriers must be crossed quickly, confidently, and creatively. No barrier is impermeable.

For other animals, these barriers are not so easily crossed. Stressed animals pace for miles in search of openings. Others sense these barriers and communicate them in diverse ways. In *An Immense World* (2022), Ed Yong illustrates how animals experience the world in unique sensorial ways. Though animals share the same physical space with other species, they perceive the vast and multidimensional world through a myriad of diverse sights, sounds, vibrations, textures, smells, and even electric and magnetic fields (5). Crossing animals have spatial awareness, and research suggests they sense the fencing and roads that cut through their pathways.[16] Perhaps there is some passive communication (sight, sound, smell, vibration) that occurs between animal populations, spreading knowledge of wall openings and penetrable border pathways to the other side. While more research is needed to understand the true scale of possible interspecies communication networks, we might imaginatively wonder how animals experience the border, and what they are trying to say. Are there interspecific "conversations" at work? Are there multisensorial warnings in place?

The recent installation of 1,800 artificial lighting fixtures on Arizona protected lands, as well as increased lighting at urban and rural border zones, bring "the devastating habitat fragmentation impacts of the border wall far into the sky" (McSpadden et al. 5). Artificial lighting influences navigation, disrupts migration, and impacts the survival of borderlands birds, bats, and insect populations (7). Javiercito has several encounters with the insect community on his journey. At one point the human crossers stop at the sound of a faint buzzing in the distance. The ground hums, and Javiercito peeks out. "¡Bees! . . . One. Ten. Twenty. Hundreds of bees right on top of us. Huuuuuummmmmmm" (Zamora 314). The cloud swarms around the crossers briefly like a "blanket"—"a single sheet of wings and brown bodies"—and then, gone (314). It is a migrating beehive, a once-in-a-lifetime encounter for the crossers. "They're like us," says one crosser, Patricia. "The bees must be good luck" thinks Javiercito. The hive moves swiftly, deftly through the borderlands, on a mission (314). The bees are "good luck" as Javiercito notes, but not just for the chance encounter. Through this brush with bees, Javiercito comes to realize that safety in the desert comes in numbers. Throughout the journey, Javiercito sticks close to what he calls "the Six," a found family that includes Patricia and her daughter, Carla. The other human crossers realize this too, as they dust themselves off and rejoin the safety of their "Centipede."

As much as humans study the ways in which the animal world might sense these changes in the borderlands, any understanding must come from "informed imaginative leaps" such as those that Javiercito takes upon encountering the nonhuman world in the desert (Yong 17). Javiercito imagines his crossing as a game, a quest, and the animal world as "family"—"mice or bunnies sometimes cross our paths. Bats overhead. If I see them, I say they're my pets. I do the same with strangers: we're all a family" (Zamora 220). It is in their indistinct and shared vulnerabilities, as well as through imaginative, childlike play, that Javiercito finds kinship in the nonhuman animal world—as he observes, learns from, and attends to the ways in which they cross. In taking imaginative leaps into animal experiences, humans undertake perhaps the most profound and human thing we can do amid a changing climate (Yong 9). Indeed, these imaginative leaps into the sensorial experiences of other species may be the very thing we humans have evolved to do.

Many will not witness the full effects of the border wall on wildlife populations in our lifetimes. But humans may sense the looming loss and grieve this legacy for coming generations. In the next section, I explore these "informed imaginative leaps" and shared vulnerabilities with the plant world—who have something more to offer border crossers.

"'*Pequeño pero picoso*'": The Vegetal Border

The plants in *Solito* offer another perspective. Here, the plant world—as guide, shelter, companion—exists in a state of openness, where borders between the human and the vegetal collapse (Gagliano 15–16). Javiercito is struck by the sheer number of diverse plants in the desert and, as he journeys, he imaginatively names each one. The text does not scientifically name the plants, but Javiercito's creative descriptions are lively enough to recognize each species.[17]

"Lonelies" are "fat and with so many hooked needles at the top, sometimes with orange and red flowers—beautiful and paperlike" (Zamora 304). These are the Fishhook barrel cactus (*Ferocactus wislizeni*) or *biznaga* in Spanish. "Spikeys" are the Soaptree yucca (*Yucca elata*) or *palmilla*. Tall plants with silhouettes "like flores de izote because of their spikey leaves," they resemble "big pineapples" at the top. "Sometimes they bend sideways at the top, making them look like they're bursting. Like party poppers. I like them. Spikeys I call them. There's the Lonelies and the Spikeys" (216).

Then there are the "Fuzzies," or the Teddy bear cholla (*Cylindropuntia bigelovii*) or *el cactus saltarín/cholla güera/cholla de oso* (among other Spanish names) (Dimmitt, "Flowering" 205). Javiercito remarks: "My new favorite is a cactus that looks like a small tree, fuzzy all over. At the trunk they're black or dark yellow, at the tips they're bright yellow. From far away, they look like yellow paint rollers. But when we walk close, the needles are longer than my fingers and very pointy. The Fuzzies, I call them" (Zamora 304). Overriding popular naming devices, including the Linnean one (in a deliberately imaginative rebellion on the part of author Zamora), Javiercito relies on "informed imaginative leaps" to see, connect, name, and remember the vegetal in the Sonoran Desert.

Javiercito recognizes these plants as kin. He does not suffer from "plant blindness" nor does he relegate the Lonelies, Fuzzies, and Spikeys to the background of the story.[18] Plants communicate, make choices, compete, and connect (Gagliano 2018). In the desert, it appears they even participate in radical ethics of care, providing shade, shelter, and beds for human crossers along the way.

But these desert plants are also trapped in a zone of "indistinction" alongside the human and nonhuman animal crossers. Due to the construction of walls, fences, as well as increased vehicular traffic, many plants are in danger of losing precious habitat. Mountains are blasted, lands cleared, water sources are dried up, Saguaro are chopped in half (Seukteoma 2020; Main 2020). Plants perform their own migrations, albeit much more slowly than animals. The vegetal world depends on seed carriers, such as birds and javelinas, to carry them across. But if wildlife are limited in their migrations, plants are perhaps even more so (Schlyer 2017).

As Javiercito moves through the desert, he begins to really *see* plants: as protectors, shelters, guides, attackers, healers, and sometimes just a familiar "face." Bushes and trees—in the collective plural—are many things to crossers: shelter, clothing line, bed, guide. Items discarded or left behind in bushes by previous crossers tell Javiercito that he is not alone. Javiercito finds familiarity in the Fuzzies, Spikeys, Lonelies, and People Cactus (the infamous Saguaro or *Carnegiea gigantea*) that he sees in each of his crossings. By his third attempt through the desert, these plants are friends.

Plants also "attack" crossers. Desert vegetation is weaponized as part of the "hostile" terrain used against crossers in PTD policy. At one point, Patricia collides with a Fuzzy and needles cover her "cheeks, forehead lips, nose. Her lips have black liquid all over them" (Zamora 293). Not "fuzzy" at all, this Teddy bear cholla is known for its "sharp and strongly barbed" spines, as well as "joints"—or "short, densely packed horizontal side branches"—that can easily detach "by a slight touch by a passing animal," to be transported over long distances to reproduce (Dimmitt, "Flowering" 205–206). Javiercito and other crossers check themselves for pinpricks, but perhaps some plant pieces and joints remain with human crossers on the move.

Succulent plants of the desert are "spiny, bitter, or toxic, and often all three." Because some animals can work around this armor, "plants must continually improve their defenses" (Dimmitt, "Plant Ecology" 144). Like plants, human crossers must also improve their defenses. After Patricia's Fuzzy attack, Javiercito is more attentive to the plant world. It is not possible to remain blind to plant life when crossing the desert; here, *plant awareness* is a matter of life and death. Later, Patricia points out a new kind of cactus to Javiercito, "small with thick horns like the biggest fish bones" (Zamora 290). It is devil cholla (*Grusonia* spp.). While other crossers carelessly step on it, Patricia and Javiercito cautiously scan the ground. "'Pequeño pero picoso, like me,' Patricia says, as she walks around it" (290).

In *Thus Spoke the Plant* (2018), Monica Gagliano contends that "the plant exists in a state of open communion in which the fiction of personalized boundaries collapses" (15–16). The plant world knows no borders and "is not separate from the exteriority of her milieu" (16). This openness, as Gagliano demonstrates, comes from "listening deeply" and abandoning notions of alterity to "know the other as ourselves" (16). Lesley Wylie suggests that in Latin American literature the human and nonhuman plant world merge, creating continuities between human and vegetal bodies (13). Reading the vegetal world in *Solito* through a lens of openness and continuity between human and plant bodies, borders blur. Javiercito comes to see the Fuzzies, Lonelies, Spikeys, and the People Cactus as fellow crossers, as "people" to whom he has a responsibility to notice, name, and remember. Javiercito writes into language the responsibility all humans have to recognize and relate to the plant world. Like Javiercito, readers literally cannot ignore or remain "blind" to plants in the text—or those in peril at the border.

Comcáac conservation scientist Alberto Mellado Moreno notes that Indigenous peoples have lived in the Arizona-Sonora borderlands since "so long ago that the year of their arrival is incalculable" (57). The plant and animal world are all relations in the "universal family." An iconic example of this is the Saguaro: to Tohono O'odham peoples, Saguaros are not just plants; they are people. As "Heeno"—the word for desert in Comcáac—says: from the beginning, "they have wrapped the fibers of my plants around their naked feet" (57). At the root, the human and nonhuman are not just entangled, but continuous. There is no separation. The image of "naked" human feet moving through the desert (as humans have always done), "wrapped" in the fibers of plants, suggests an interspecific, co-creative relationship of care, as well as the possibility of (or return to) communication, continuity, and openness in the Sonoran Desert ecosystem—of which humans are very much a part.

The openness and continuities of the plant world suggest additional possibilities for plant-human-animal relations in crossing stories. Could human crossers attacked by cactus unknowingly assist in carrying plant seeds across borders, thus aiding in healthier desert ecosystems? Do plants recognize kinships in human crossers through the desert's most remote zones?

Literature is one place for questions such as these—and eco-imaginative answers. Fiction and literary thought already employ devices like "informed imaginative leaps" and "continuities" between the human and nonhuman worlds, as they read the world and its multispecies interactions in imaginative, transgressive ways. Through childlike and imaginative leaps into the crossing experiences of the nonhuman plant and animal world, Javiercito sees the Sonoran Desert—and the border itself—as a multispecies, layered story in this one powerful and enchanted place. As readers, informed of the Sonoran Desert's rich biodiversity and particular environmental challenges, we can utilize this understanding of the physical environment and our uniquely imaginative storytelling capabilities as humans to see the border "crisis" for what it really is—a massive multispecies threat to the survival of ecological life everywhere.

The open possibilities and informed imaginative and *literary* leaps of plant-human-animal kinships in the face of border violences, death, habitat loss, and environmental degradation and destruction are more than just thought-provoking; they are rebelliously hopeful.

Conclusions

There is one more animal that crosses alongside Javiercito in this journey: *el Cadejo*. A dog-like nahual of Mayan-Quiché tradition, this mythological figure passes through stories between generations of Javiercito's family in El Salvador. According to Javiercito's grandfather, *los cadejos* are "like dogs or wolves, but with goat hooves and a goat tail" and both protect and harm humans that cross their path (Zamora 60).[19] The use of this crossing companion for Javiercito throughout the text points to the Indigeneity carried alongside border crossers in US-Mexico crossing stories. Not only does Javiercito cross with these stories in mind, but he comes to the journey already attuned to Indigenous ways of being in the world with plants and animals.

"Indistinction," "imaginative leaps," "openness," "continuities"—as well as imaginative, literary storytelling—are perhaps familiar concepts to Indigenous Knowledge Systems (IKS) and Traditional Ecological Knowledge (TEK).[20] As Calarco himself remarks, many critical plant and animal studies theories have unacknowledged roots in Indigenous cosmovisions (*Beyond* 42). "All my relations" and "seven generations" (to name just two) are concepts present in IKS that encompass the shared web of human and nonhuman beings, as well as the responsibility—to seven generations before, after, and beyond—"we have within this universal family by living our lives in a harmonious and moral manner" (King ix).

If the oppression of human and nonhuman crossers in the US-Mexico borderlands are also entangled (as Sunaura Taylor asks of animal and disability studies), "might not that mean their paths of liberation are entangled as well?" (*Beasts* xv). What stories are possible when humans enter into radical kinships and care for beings around us?

In recognizing the shared vulnerabilities, continuities, and "indistinction" among species—alongside rooted Indigenous ways of being—humans come into being and co-create *with* interspecies coalitions already embedded in the human-plant-animal world. From this "indistinct" and collaborative vantage point, humans can more fully comprehend the climate crisis—the ultimate space of shared vulnerability among species—and search for entangled but viable "paths of liberation" forward. Javiercito's "informed imaginative leaps" into the plant and animal worlds in *Solito* speak to the kinds of eco-imaginative thinking and rebellious and imaginative *literary* leaps our species will need to urgently do as part of our shared responsibility toward the Lonelies, Fuzzies, Spikeys, and *all our relations* amid the collective threat of ongoing climate change.

Notes

1. I use "border crossers" for humans crossing through the US-Mexico borderlands, and "disappeared" for crossers with unknown whereabouts. See "A Note on Language" in *Disappeared.*

2. The Darién Gap—*el tapón del Darién*—has seen an alarming increase in border crossings, with the number of crossers in the region hitting an all-time high of 250,000 in the first eight months of 2023 ("Number of Migrants"). In this "border jungle" between Colombia and Panamá, crossers are subject to both the harsh environment and increasing human violence. Comparing this route to the US-Mexico border is complicated. The IOM's Missing Migrants Project (MMP) suggests that data collection in both Mexico and the Darién Gap is unreliable, due to underreporting and limited accessibility. As the MMP report notes, the overall data in all crossing areas "are best considered as underestimates of the true number of lives lost during migration in the Americas" ("Migration Within").

3. On PTD and the effects on human and animal bodies, see De León 2015.

4. See Spiegel and Socha.

5. See Urrea.

6. See Martínez.

7. From the 1990s to around 2018, the "immigrant crossing sign" in California depicted border crossers running across highways, to warn motorists of potential auto-pedestrian fatalities.

8. As a flagship species for both migrant justice and environmental conservation movements (as well as a vibrant cultural symbol), the monarch butterfly speaks to the collective human and nonhuman right to movement.

9. See Calarco, *Thinking.*

10. See Horowitz for a comprehensive definition of "informed imaginative leaps" (241–43).

11. See also: *"American Scar": The Environmental Tragedy of the Border Wall.*

12. Eamon Harrity, Interview. Harrity oversees Sky Island Alliance's (SIA) *Border Wildlife Study,* which documents border wildlife movement across roughly 100 miles (163.5 km) of the US-Mexico border.

13. Eamon Harrity, e-mail. The Harrity et al. study documents wildlife movement through various types of border barriers (vehicle barriers, steel bollard fencing, and steel bollard fencing with "small wildlife passages"). According to the study, all observed wildlife can cross vehicle barriers, whereas species larger than bobcats are

generally unable to cross through the interstitial steel bollard fencing (though rare crossings of juvenile coyotes and javelinas have been recorded). Small wildlife passages (measuring just 21.5 × 27.8 cm or about the size of A4 printer paper) improved crossing rates for many species and the mere presence of these passages saw more wildlife activity than in other stretches of the wall, but were still much too small for larger mammals such as deer and black bear. The passages are most likely too small for Mexican gray wolves and jaguars as well. Since publication, the authors have recorded American badgers crossing through the interstitial spacing of the steel bollard fencing. The authors have also observed male mountain lions failing to fit through the small wildlife passages, suggesting these passages may be sufficient for female mountain lions (observed crossing frequently) but too small for males. For updates on wildlife and the wall, see SIA's ongoing *Border Wildlife Study.*

14. Meierotto notes that among all causes of borderlands environmental degradation, vehicular traffic is "the most prevalent and damaging" (19). Though vehicle activity is a huge issue, "the wall may forever block movement corridors for species" (Harrity, e-mail).

15. See SIA's *Border Wildlife Study* and Harrity et al.

16. Thanks to Eamon Harrity for pointing this out to me.

17. Many thanks to the Botany Department at the Arizona-Sonora Desert Museum for help in identifying these plants with little more than a shared document and literary clues. I am very thankful, and in awe! Any misunderstandings or errors are my own.

18. See James H. Wandersee and Elisabeth E. Schussler, "Preventing Plant Blindness." For more on the vegetal turn in literary studies, see the introduction in Giovanni Aloi and Michael Marder's *Vegetal Entwinements in Philosophy and Art: A Reader,* 1–10.

19. For more on *los cadejos,* see Efraín Melara Méndez. On the role of dogs as crossing companions see Vázquez Enríquez. For arguably one of the best literary examples of the "nahual" concept, see *Hombres de maíz* (1949) by Guatemalan author Miguel Ángel Asturias.

20. See Kimmerer for more on IKS; see the Nelson and Shilling collection on TEK. For a literary introduction to "all my relations," see King, ix–xvi.

Works Cited

Aloi, Giovanni, and Michael Marder. "Introduction." *Vegetal Entwinements in Philosophy and Art: A Reader,* edited by Giovanni Aloi and Michael Marder, MIT Press, 2023.

"American Scar": The Environmental Tragedy of the Border Wall: The New Yorker Documentary. Directed by Daniel Lombroso, *The New Yorker,* 2022, https://www.youtube.com/watch?v=Cx71C4iguuk.

Asturias, Miguel Ángel. *Hombres de maíz.* Editorial Losada, 1957.

Banerjee, Anindita. "Border Environments: An Introduction to the Special Issue." *Border Environments Special Issue, Latin American Literary Review,* edited by Anindita Banerjee et al., vol. 48, no. 96, 2021, pp. 2–4.

Border Wildlife Study. Sky Island Alliance. https://skyislandalliance.org/our-work/science/borderwildlife/. Accessed 28 Nov. 2023

Calarco, Matthew. *Beyond the Anthropological Difference.* Cambridge University Press, 2020.

Calarco, Matthew. *The Boundaries of Human Nature: The Philosophical Animal from Plato to Haraway.* Columbia University Press, 2021.

Calarco, Matthew. *Thinking through Animals: Identity, Difference, Indistinction.* Stanford University Press, 2015.

De León, Jason. *The Land of Open Graves: Living and Dying on the Migrant Trail.* University of California Press, 2015.

Derrida, Jacques. *The Animal that Therefore I Am.* Fordham University Press, 2008.

Dimmitt, Mark A. "Flowering Plants of the Sonoran Desert." Dimmitt et al., pp. 157–239.

Dimmitt, Mark A. "Plant Ecology of the Sonoran Desert Region." Dimmitt et al., pp. 139–156.

Dimmitt, Mark A., et al., editors. *A Natural History of the Sonoran Desert.* 2nd ed., Arizona-Sonora Desert Museum Press, 2015.

Disappeared: How the US Border Enforcement Agencies Are Fueling a Missing Persons Crisis. La Coalición de Derechos Humanos and No More Deaths, 2016.

Flesch, Aaron D., et al. "Potential Effects of the United States–Mexico Border Fence on Wildlife." *Conservation Biology,* vol. 24, no. 1, 2010, pp. 171–181.

Gagliano, Monica. *Thus Spoke the Plant: A Remarkable Journey of Groundbreaking Scientific Discoveries and Personal Encounters with Plants.* North Atlantic Books, 2018.

Harrity, Eamon. Interview with the author. 28 Nov. 2023.

Harrity, Eamon. Email to the author. 29 Oct. 2024.

Harrity, Eamon, et al. "USA-Mexico Border Wall Impedes Wildlife Movement." *Frontiers in Ecology and Evolution,* vol. 12, 20 Nov. 2024.

Horowitz, Alexandra. *Inside of a Dog: What Dogs See, Smell, and Know.* Simon and Schuster, 2010.

Jordahl, Laiken. Interview with the author. 21 Nov. 2023.

Kelety, Josh. "Ahead of Trump Visit, Deer Found Dead along Border Wall Sparks Outrage." *Phoenix New Times,* 18 Aug. 2023, https://www.phoenixnewtimes.com/news/ahead-of-trump-visit-wildlife-found-dead-along-border-wall-11488269.

Kimmerer, Robin. *Braiding Sweetgrass: Indigenous Wisdom, Scientific Knowledge and the Teachings of Plants.* Milkweed Editions, 2013.

King, Thomas. "Introduction." *All My Relations: An Anthology of Contemporary Canadian Native Fiction,* edited by Thomas King, 1990.

Main, Douglas. "The U.S. Border Wall Is Tearing through Wilderness, Right under Our Noses." *National Geographic,* 2 Nov. 2020, https://www.nationalgeographic.com/environment/article/border-wall-construction-continues-unabated.

Martínez, Óscar. *Los migrantes que no importan.* Debolsillo, 2021.

McSpadden, Russ, et al. *A Wall of Lights through the Wild: 1,800 Stadium Lights on Arizona Conservation Lands Threaten Wildlife.* Center for Biological Diversity, June 2023.

Meierotto, Lisa. "The Blame Game on the Border: Perceptions of Environmental Degradation on the United States–Mexico Border." *Human Organization,* vol. 71, no. 1, Feb. 2012, pp. 11–21.

Melara Méndez, Efraín. *Mitologías cuzcatlecas, o, Los cuentos de mi infancia y otros.* Impresora Pipil, 1979.

Mellado Moreno, Alberto. "Heeno." *The Nature of Desert Nature,* edited by Gary Paul Nabhan, University of Arizona Press, 2020.

Mendoza, Mary E. "Treacherous Terrain: Racial Exclusion and Environmental Control at the U.S.-Mexico Border." *Environmental History,* vol. 23, no. 1, Jan. 2018, pp. 117–126.

"Migration Within the Americas." *The Americas: Missing Migrants Project,* https://missingmigrants.iom.int/region/americas.

Nabhan, Gary Paul. "A Deep History of Everything That Sticks, Stinks, Stings, Sings, Swings, Springs, or Clings in Arid Landscapes." *The Nature of Desert Nature,* edited by Gary Paul Nabhan, University of Arizona Press, 2020.

Nabhan, Gary Paul. "Welcome to the Sonoran Desert." Dimmitt et al., pp. 1–2.

Nelson, Melissa K., and Daniel Shilling, editors. *Traditional Ecological Knowledge: Learning from Indigenous Practices for Environmental Sustainability.* Cambridge University Press, 2018.

Nixon, Rob. *Slow Violence and the Environmentalism of the Poor.* Harvard University Press, 2011.

"Number of Migrants Who Embarked on the Dangerous Darien Gap Route Nearly Doubled in 2022." *International Organization for Migration,* 17 Jan. 2023, https://www.iom.int/news/number-migrants-who-embarked-dangerous-darien-gap-route-nearly-doubled-2022.

Peters, Robert, et al. "Nature Divided, Scientists United: US-Mexico Border Wall Threatens Biodiversity and Binational Conservation." *BioScience,* vol. 68, no. 10, Oct. 2018, pp. 740–743.

Schlyer, Krista. *Embattled Borderlands: Will the Border Wall Strike a Fatal Blow to One of the Most Imperiled Wild Regions in North America?* Center for Biological Diversity, 2017, https://www.biologicaldiversity.org/programs/international/borderlands_and_boundary_waters/story-map/index.html

Seukteoma, Hon'mana. "Standing Together: Our Fight for Quitobaquito." *Center for Bi-*

ological Diversity, 30 Nov. 2020, https://medium.com/center-for-biological-diversity/standing-together-our-fight-for-quitobaquito-ac6ea472f20b.

"Sky Islands." *Sky Island Alliance,* https://sia2023.wpengine.com/our-region/the-sky-islands/.

Socha, Kim. "The 'Dreaded Comparisons' and Speciesism: Leveling the Hierarchy of Suffering." *Confronting Animal Exploitation: Grassroots Essays on Liberation and Veganism,* edited by Kim Socha and Sarahjane Blum, McFarland, 2013, pp. 223–240.

Spiegel, Marjorie. *The Dreaded Comparison: Human and Animal Slavery.* Mirror Books, 1996.

Taylor, Sunaura. *Beasts of Burden: Animal and Disability Liberation.* The New Press, 2017.

Taylor, Sunaura. "Beasts of Burden: Disability Studies and Animal Rights." *Qui Parle,* vol. 19, no. 2, Spring/Summer 2011, pp. 191–222.

Traphagen, Myles. *The Border Wall in Arizona and New Mexico—July 2021.* Wildlands Network, 7 Jul. 2021, https://storymaps.arcgis.com/stories/8532c503c2084293bb88474072452 28d.

Urrea, Luis Alberto. *The Devil's Highway: A True Story.* Little, Brown, 2008.

"US-Mexico Border World's Deadliest Migration Land Route." *International Organization for Migration,* 12 Sept. 2023, https://lac.iom.int/en/node/121866.

Vázquez Enríquez, Emily C. "Companion Species in Border Crossings: 'Mediodía de Frontera' by Claudia Hernández." *Ciberletras,* no. 42, Aug. 2019, 120–132.

Wandersee, James H., and Elisabeth E. Schussler. "Preventing Plant Blindness." *The American Biology Teacher,* vol. 61, no. 2, Feb. 1999, pp. 82, 84, 87.

Wylie, Lesley. *The Poetics of Plants in Spanish American Literature.* University of Pittsburgh Press, 2020.

Yong, Ed. *An Immense World: How Animal Senses Reveal the Hidden Realms Around Us.* Random House, 2022.

Zamora, Javier. *Solito: A Memoir.* Hogarth, 2022.

3

Tropical Scenery

Plant and Animal Resistance in Early Photographs of Panama's Rainforest

CRISTINA E. PARDO PORTO

After a few days of surfing and relaxation at a tourist complex on the Pacific coast of Panama, five Anglo-American tourists on a hike to view breathtaking waterfalls find themselves stranded in the heart of the Darién jungle, the so-called green hell. Their idyllic adventure takes a sinister turn as, one by one, they vanish into the dense foliage, haunted by fleeting glimpses of a mysterious creature—a wild predator that has been stalking them relentlessly. The group had been forewarned about a previous group falling victim to the "Chupacabra." Only two manage to survive until the military arrives to rescue them and bring an end to the Chupacabra's menace.

This formulaic narrative underpins *Indigenous* (2014), a B-movie that encapsulates the clichés surrounding the Darién region.[1] The film's visual representation of the area is rooted in historical stereotypes: an exotic jungle panorama inspired by folklore, perilous coexistence with dangerous native fauna and toxic flora, along with the dehumanization of Indigenous peoples, and the juxtaposition of leisure tourism and military intervention. Portrayals of this kind have endured across centuries, in colonial tales and cartographic depictions by fifteenth-century conquerors, late-nineteenth-century landscape photographs taken by explorers, and more recent media coverage of the migrant crises. The region earned a reputation as a territory to be subdued in order to cross it, exploited for its mineral wealth, and even transformed into an urbanized space. Yet, its history chronicles failed endeavors, from futile attempts to construct the Panama Canal connecting the Pacific, Atlantic, and Caribbean, to the unrealized dream of the Pan-American Highway traversing the jungle. These failures have shaped the contradictory image of the Darién rainforest as both a treacherous route and an ecotourism destination, echoing the dual portrayals of tropical regions as dangerous yet luxurious. Though seemingly navigable, the Darién remains unyielding, defined by its challenging natural features and its sociocultural imagination as an "indomitable" landscape.

Here, I delve into the earliest photographic representations of the jungle. These images constitute perhaps the most comprehensive surviving photographic documentation of any Central American region during the 1870s (Darrah 141). They were captured during the Selfridge Expedition to the Isthmus of Darién from 1870 to 1873, as part of expeditionary surveys exploring Central America. Commanded by Thomas O. Selfridge, Jr., and sponsored by the US Department of the Navy, their objective was to assess the feasibility of constructing a canal connecting the Caribbean Sea and the Atlantic and Pacific Oceans—a plan that was abandoned once the surveys revealed the impracticality of the natural terrain. The expedition's photographers, John Moran (American, born in England, 1831–1902) and Timothy O'Sullivan (American, possibly born in Ireland, 1840–1882), amassed a substantial collection of photographs reproduced as stereographs—an early format that creates an immersive three-dimensional illusion—depicting villages and Indigenous peoples, plants and animals, rock formations, islands, rivers, and waterfalls in the Darién region, which was titled "Tropical Scenery."[2] I analyze this archive from today's perspective and argue that the stereographs of the jungle invite us to speculate on Darién's natural environment's resistance to repeated human attempts to dominate it. I center this resistance, which led to the failure of numerous expeditions (the Panama Canal was ultimately constructed elsewhere), demonstrating the "victory" of Darién's natural environment. I bring together critical plant and animal studies by demonstrating how the prominence of plants and the visual absence of animals in these early Darién photographs underscore the area's impenetrability. After a brief overview of the colonial history of Darién, which has ingrained the visual imagination of the region as untamable, I show how formal details in the stereoscopic views suggest plant and animal resistance. My analysis of "Tropical Scenery" sheds light on the enduring constructed essence of "the tropics" and highlights nature's agency in its self-preservation.

Trekking through the Untamed: From Balboa to Selfridge

The images in the "Tropical Scenery" collection could be viewed as extending ideologies that predate the late-nineteenth-century emergence of photography. The photographers must have been aware of narratives of past journeys through the region. Thus, we can infer that it was this outlook that led them to capture images that portrayed the rainforest as fraught with the unknown. While the region's physical features undeniably contribute to its hostility—evident in the very real challenges migrants continue to face when attempting to traverse it—it is equally important to examine how historical narratives have perpetuated perceptions of the rainforest as untamable. Building on Edward Said's concept of "imaginative geographies," Julie Velásquez Runk delves into the depiction of the Darién region as the "wild Darién," a "taken-for-granted representation of Darién as a rich, dangerous, and backward place" (129).[3] The historical narratives that have gradually solidified the imaginative geography of Darién's natural landscape date back to the fifteenth century and have progressively ingrained the visual culture depicting the region, leading up to the photographs. By situating my analysis within a brief historical overview in the following pages, I underscore how colonial ventures shaped enduring ideas of the rainforest's impenetrability.

The first expedition documented by a non-Native who traversed the Isthmus of Panama was led in September 1513 by the Spanish conquistador Vasco Núñez de Balboa (1475–1519). Balboa has been globally celebrated as a hero for "discovering" the Pacific Ocean or, more accurately, for the first European sighting of it. In an eighteenth-century collection of biographies of "illustrious Spaniards," Balboa's expedition is remembered in the following terms:

> Enormes dificultades embarazaban la empresa. Los Indios, á modo de enxambres, se oponían en las llanuras: los pantanos ocupaban los valles, los torrentes se despeñaban de las cumbres, y las montañas escarpadas, que forman el Istmo, y resisten el embate de los dos mares impracticables por todas partes, no dexaban un momento de descanso á los acosados Españoles. Al cabo de veinte y cinco días de una marcha desesperada, el Océano Pacífico se mostró á los ojos de Balboa. (*Retrato de los españoles ilustres*)
>
> (Huge difficulties burdened the enterprise. The Indians, like swarms, put up resistance in the plains; swamps occupied the valleys, torrents cascaded from the peaks, and the steep mountains, shaping the Isthmus and resisting the onslaught of the two seas, rendered every path impassable. They

allowed no respite for the beleaguered Spaniards. After twenty-five days of a desperate journey, the Pacific Ocean revealed itself to Balboa's eyes.)

As we see, the characterization of Darién's natural space as an impediment to colonizers' progress was already entrenched in eighteenth-century thought. Vegetation is portrayed as a significant obstacle to traversing the space, and Indigenous people are animalized (characterized as an "enjambre"—a swarm). Nature, personified as an unyielding opponent to the Spaniards, is concurrently depicted as resilient against external, human disturbances.

Balboa's enterprise was undeniably driven by the pursuit of gold, mines, and natural wealth, as well as the forceful expansion into Indigenous lands of the region, frequently resulting in the displacement and even extermination of Native communities. As news of Balboa's discovery spread globally by the 1600s, along with the realization of the land's potential for extraction and exploitation and the founding of new Spanish settlements in the region, the Anglo-European focus turned toward to the western coast of Panama. The region's wealth prompted the interest of pirates, who would also journey through the Darién province (Velásquez Runk 132–135).

In 1698, the Kingdom of Scotland sought to establish New Caledonia, a colony on the Caribbean coast of the Isthmus that would link the Caribbean and Pacific coasts overland. Yet, within a few years, the Scottish were met with Spanish attacks, and they failed utterly due to corruption, poor planning, and limited resources, despite mostly blaming factors like the natural landscape and tropical diseases. Scottish accounts consolidated the existing perception of Darién's environment through exaggerated portrayals of nature: "this place affords a legion of monstrous Plants enough to confound all the Methods of Botany ever hitherto thought upon" (qtd. in Velásquez Runk 136). The Darién Scheme came close to bankrupting Scotland, and, by 1700, all settlements were abandoned, coinciding with a decline in Spanish colonial influence. Gradually, the jungle was forsaken, and the center of colonial operations shifted northward to present-day Panama City.[4]

The need for a sea-level canal linking these areas became increasingly apparent during the nineteenth century, reigniting interest in Darién. This was the context for the expedition highlighted in this chapter, framed by the region's entrenched identity as a "no-man's-land worthy of conquest" (S. W. Miller 194). Inspired by the success of the Central New York's Erie Canal in the 1820s, the California Gold Rush in the 1850s, and the construction of the Suez Canal (begun in 1859), the

United States homed in on Central America, resulting in numerous catastrophic expeditions throughout the region (Missal 22–23).[5] In 1869, US President Ulysses S. Grant initiated a series of explorative surveys of multiple countries across the isthmus, all with the goal of finding a viable canal route to facilitate interoceanic communication.[6] Commander Thomas O. Selfridge, Jr. led the Darién expeditions. From 1870 to 1873, he explored and reported on the southern region of Panama, reaching all the way to the headwaters of the Atrato River in Colombia.

Into the Jungle and *through* the Stereoscope

Selfridge's expeditions were pioneering in their use of cameras to assess the physical attributes of jungle trails through Darién. These photographic records not only captured the dense and often treacherous terrain but also provided a visual supplement to textual descriptions, enhancing navigation and planning efforts. The dangers posed by the natural landscape were "reinforced by the new technology of photos, . . . adding dark, foreboding forest images to Darién's largely verbal imagery of wilderness" (Velásquez Runk 139). We see the camera, in its early days, already being used globally, and particularly in the tropics, as an informative tool—one that served empires and fueled territorial expansions by documenting "unknown" cultures, as well as the physical geography of "unexplored" territories and their botanical, zoological, and mineral characteristics.[7] In fact, Joan M. Schwartz's studies reveal that this type of geographical photography also contributed to the creation of imaginative geographies, especially within the framework of the era's Western fascination with positivism, realism, and naturalism (18).

Experienced in capturing geological formations in western-US-based expeditions, the landscape photographer Timothy O'Sullivan joined Selfridge's team on the initial 1870 expedition. It is worth noting that the navy opted not to retain him for the subsequent two missions, potentially influenced by his "murky" but aesthetic photographs of the jungle (Regan). O'Sullivan was also acclaimed for his intentions to elevate landscape photography to an art form (Krauss 312; Missal 86). We can speculate that he probably focused less on the survey's geo-topographical aspects and more on the artistic potential of the tropics. It is also plausible that O'Sullivan, accustomed to the North American landscape, found himself daunted by the dense vegetation of Darién.[8] In 1871, John Moran joined Selfridge as the official photographer for the remaining two surveys (Selfridge 33). Occasional inaccuracies in the notations accompanying the photographs make it unclear which images were taken by which photographer.[9]

Most of the images in "Tropical Scenery" were reproduced and circulated in the stereograph format. This early photographic artifact was designed to be viewed with a stereoscope, a binocular-like apparatus that creates a three-dimensional illusion from two flat, almost identical photos placed side by side, replicating the way our eyes naturally perceive depth. When observed through the lenses of a stereoscope, the photographs merge into a single image, immersing viewers in a lifelike experience, or "perspectival space" through "tunnel vision" (Krauss 314). Simply put, stereographs could be considered the earliest form of 3D technology.

In the late nineteenth and early twentieth centuries, stereographic views emerged as the first mass medium (Fowles 89; Krauss 314). They surged in popularity as collectible souvenirs, aiming to recreate the feeling of travel and engage the emerging middle class as a portable form of "home entertainment" (Pietrobruno 172). Through stereographs issued by geographical surveys, individuals could virtually journey to the most "exotic" locations without leaving the comfort of their homes. These images consolidated photography as "the process by which geographical information was acquired, ordered, and disseminated" thanks to the belief in its power to reproduce reality (Schwartz 17). Alexandre Missal has posited that the photographers behind "Tropical Scenery" sought to evoke motifs reminiscent of the American West or "archetypical" images of the US landscape blended with more "exotic" elements such as palms, mangoes, and coconut trees.[10] According to Missal, the composition created a simultaneously "familiar and foreign" experience for stereograph viewers (87). The archives reveal the potential for these images to circulate on a global scale, thereby deeply embedding the constructed visuality of Darién within the collective imagination associated with tropical regions.[11]

All stereographs from the Selfridge expedition bear the title "Tropical Scenery" and include a title or brief description of the image as a footer, along with the inscription "CMD'R SELFRIDGE. Comd'g." This combination of elements provides the viewer with comprehensive context for the photograph, as in "Tropical forest, Limon River" (fig. 3.1).[12] This stereograph, like most images from the collection that focus on nature, lacks a horizon or perspective, replaced by an infinite depth within the heart of the rainforest landscape. The pair of images captures a dense aura, further intensified when viewed through the stereoscope. They were crafted to create an immersive encounter with the natural environment, evoking a sense of claustrophobia by simulating the sensation of being enveloped by the dense foliage. Evidently, the photographers intended for the global audience to perceive and experience Darién just as Selfridge's team had.

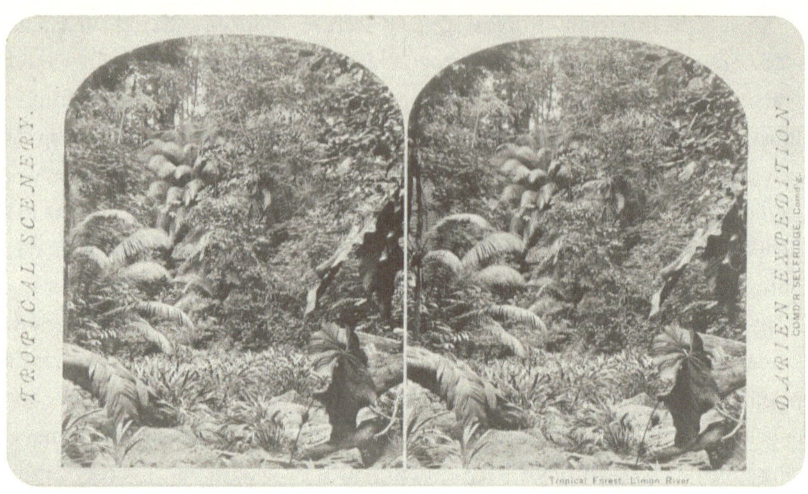

FIGURE 3.1. The Miriam and Ira D. Wallach Division of Art, Prints and Photographs: Photography Collection, The New York Public Library. "Tropical forest, Limon River." 1871. *The New York Public Library Digital Collections*, https://digitalcollections.nypl.org/items/510d47e2-6954-a3d9-e040-e00a18064a99

The formal features of these images, such as focus distance and lighting, reveal the challenges posed by the tropical environment to the technological limitations of the era. In a recent book on one of the photographers, O'Sullivan, it is noted that:

> He proceeded to make his photographs in a forest so thick and humid, so rain-soaked and disorienting that treating a glass plate with chemicals [was] nearly impossible. The tropical humidity would make the coating and drying of photographic plates dismally complex, if not frequently out of the question. For the most part, O'Sullivan's views and angles . . . come across on the Darién survey as cramped and constricted, even run-of-the-mill. (Sullivan)

The technologies of that era were not initially designed to operate in "hostile" environments like the tropics. The formal features of the images seem to suggest that nature in Darién asserts its dominance over human-made devices, such as the camera, potentially limiting their ability to fully capture the environment.

The tropical rainforest is characterized by wet and dry seasons, low light due to tall foliage, 90 percent humidity (owing to abundant water sources like rivers and swamps, sun radiation over the equator, proximity to the ocean, and an average of 130 days of rainfall per year), and elevated temperatures of a median of 82°F (Kricher 4–6, 16–18). Selfridge describes the landscape and wet climate in detail (9), consistently highlighting Darién's "impenetrable growth" throughout (16): "the trees . . . were so interlaced as to give but a peep here and there of the sky" (16). Even when the sun shines intensely during the dry season, "the dense tropical growth does not permit the action of the sun's rays" (39). "Limon River near the beach" (fig. 3.2), for example, captures the dense foliage and low light along the paths the explorers took. The image is dim and lacks detail, making it difficult to identify either the river or other natural features. This recurrent mention of limited light in the report underscores nature's dominion over the explorers' field of vision.

I pose that early photography was marked by a phenomenon now termed "plant blindness." This means a visual bias toward humans and nonhuman animals while overlooking the significance of plant life (Ryan et al., *The Language* viii). While landscape photography was widely employed in scientific disciplines and colonial explorations throughout the nineteenth and twentieth centuries,

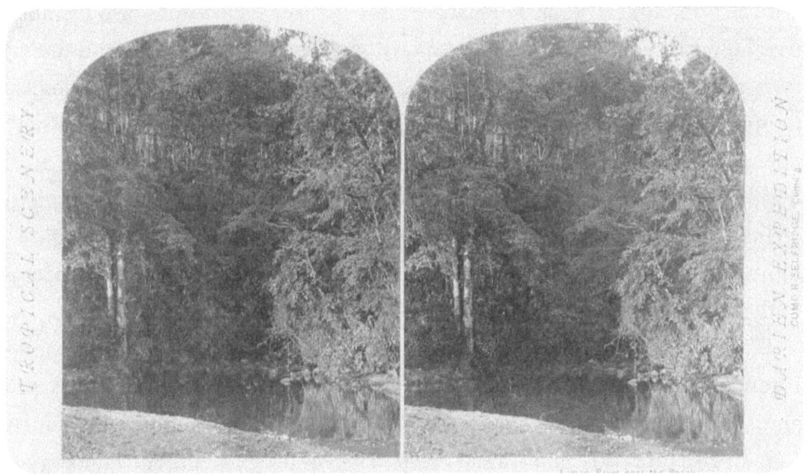

FIGURE 3.2. The Miriam and Ira D. Wallach Division of Art, Prints and Photographs: Photography Collection, The New York Public Library. "Limon River near the beach." 1871. *The New York Public Library Digital Collections*, https://digitalcollections.nypl.org/items/510d47e2-6914-a3d9-e040-e00a18064a99

early photographic practices failed to acknowledge how vegetal life, climate, and natural elements could actively shape the photographic process. This oversight reflects the Western/colonial perspective that reduces nature to a passive backdrop for human activity or an obstacle to urbanization and industrial development (Ryan et al., *The Mind* x).[13] In "Tropical Scenery," we see how Selfridge's enterprise centered on human-driven efforts to "civilize" the tropics, disregarding the ecological roles of plants and their environment, as well as their profound influence on the region's biodiversity.[14] While it is unsurprising that Selfridge's focus aligned with the anthropocentric priorities of his era, the images are noteworthy for the way they unintentionally reveal how Darién's dense vegetation and tropical climate—factors that ultimately contributed to the failure of the canal project—impacted the photographs. Blurred focus, darkness, overexposure, and other visual distortions reflect the challenges posed by the environment, offering subtle evidence of nature's resistance to the colonial project. These formal features allow us to speculate on the extent to which plants and other natural forces asserted their agency, subverting the narrative of human dominion over the land.

Selfridge's team was equipped with the latest technology (Kirkpatrick 211). The account even states that the photographers were "furnished with all necessary apparatuses, including acids" (1), which, apart from being potentially toxic to the natural environment, were quite large, as we see in the photographer's self-portrait, "Photographer at Pinogana" (fig. 3.3).[15] The expeditions also included naval officers, geologists, naturalists, civil engineers, astronomers, and draftsmen, among other technicians, creating an extensive human and technological footprint. Darién's plants and animals were thus confronted by heavy machinery operated by humans. The report even asserts that Selfridge's objectives extended beyond determining the feasibility of just a canal, to include imposing modern civilization upon the nature and peoples of Darién. However, the expedition ultimately fell short of its goal of devising a viable route, despite having access to the most advanced surveying technology of the time.

Building on the earlier discussion of the formal qualities of the photographs, I now turn to the possibility of contemplating the experiences of plants and animals by reinterpreting these formal features as instances of their resistance. Can we visualize plant and animal perspectives as they encounter technology—cameras, machinery, human trespassing, and the creation of trails and routes? How might nature respond to these interactions? By posing these questions, we move beyond analyzing nature as an obstacle or passive background to consider its agency and responses to human intervention.

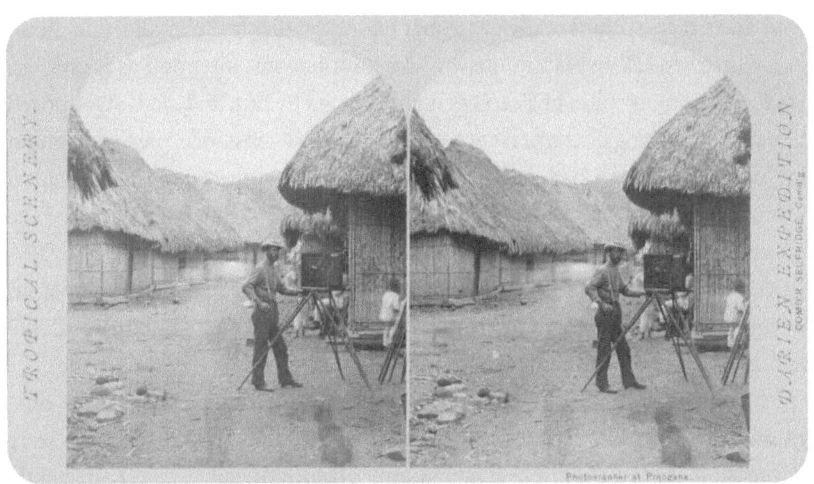

FIGURE 3.3. The Miriam and Ira D. Wallach Division of Art, Prints and Photographs: Photography Collection, The New York Public Library. "Photographer at Pinogana." 1871. *The New York Public Library Digital Collections*, https://digitalcollections.nypl.org/items/510d47e2-68f6-a3d9-e040-e00a18064a99

The stereographs reveal an environment that resists human interference. In these photographs, nature's agency manifests through fading, lack of detail or sharpness, and a sense of movement. Approaching these through the lens of critical plant and animal studies, they can be interpreted as moments where nature actively counters technological intrusion, represented by the camera. The photographs produced during the expedition played a role in the eventual collapse of canal construction plans in the Darién region. In his report, Selfridge explicitly notes that words alone were insufficient to convey the scale of the obstacles posed by Darién's plants and animals; instead, photographs were included to visually demonstrate to his superiors in the United States the impenetrability of the region. Notably, these images were later used as evidence to justify relocating the canal project to present-day Panama City (Missal 91). The portrayal of nature in "Tropical Scenery," coupled with the environmental effects captured in the photographs—such as the impact of humidity—underscored the challenges of navigating and transforming the Darién terrain.

The report celebrates Balboa's renowned route, even noting that "the whole country is almost unchanged since the time of the Spaniards," a reflection of prevailing essentialist narratives about Darién's nature (Selfridge 162). Interestingly, Selfridge simultaneously aims to dismantle these accounts, seeking to "do away with many false notions of danger from noxious reptiles and climatic influences" (14). However, his own account swiftly contradicts this intention as it unfolds. He recounts many tales of sleepless nights caused by rain and challenges posed by swamps but also by the presence of animals. In one instance, men were bitten by "vampire-bats": "I had supposed that the stories of these bat sucking blood was a childish fable; but the numerous occasions . . . on which men would wake up and find their faces covered with blood prove it to be a reality" (52). This particular depiction paints Darién as a realm where fiction and reality coexist, an imaginary that has endured to the present, as seen in the contemporary fictional narrative featuring the Chupacabra in *Indigenous.*

As seen through the stereoscope, the Selfridge expeditions reached the conclusion that the plans for constructing a canal through the Darién jungle were not feasible from a geophysical standpoint. Historian Paul S. Sutter succinctly encapsulates Selfridge's findings by asserting that, at the time, "such an easy route was a chimera," underscoring how this realization contributed to the fading of the proposed Darién canal from historical prominence (3). The construction of the Panama Canal in present-day Panama City, almost two hundred miles from Darién National Park,[16] led to decreased attention to the Darién region until the Darién Subcommittee of the Pan-American Highway was created in 1955—a project that would, once again, fail due to Darién's unyielding nature, contributing to its "long history of confounding outsiders, especially its would-be colonizers" (Sullivan).[17]

Sensing Plants

When viewed in isolation, "Tropical Scenery" might indeed perpetuate the stereotype of Darién's tropical environment as a primitive location with both "exotic" and potentially "dangerous" flora and fauna. Yet, when examined closely through the lens of critical plant and animal studies, the photographs reveal nature's agency. In Selfridge's report, a notable assertion emerges from the section titled "The Geology and Natural History of the Isthmuses of Choco, of Darien, and of Panama," written by Dr. G. A. Maak, the geologist and naturalist of the 1872 expedition (Maak in Selfridge 155–175). He explicitly articulates what I argue is the true essence of the photographs: "we are indeed in a territory where nature alone, untouched and uninfluenced by human work, displays its laws, and where a naturalist will find, of course, a rich field for observation. We feel, therefore, the inability of our pen to express by words what we have seen and witnessed in reality" (169). This not only reaffirms my earlier argument that the natural features of Darién defy written description but also underscores the agency of the plants and animals in the photos in resisting human intervention.

Early photography quickly became intertwined with travel narratives by explorers who had clear anthropological, scientific, and naturalistic interests in the Americas, such as Humboldt, forging a partnership between the visual medium and the fields of Western botany and zoology. Photographs were widely used in the colonial quest to classify and study the tropics' plant and animal species. Dr. Maak states that he collected plant and rock samples, as well as animal specimens preserved in alcohol, to add to the collection of the Museum of Comparative Zoology in Cambridge, Massachusetts. In "Tropical Scenery," we see images titled "Mango Tree," "India-rubber Tree," "Bread-fruit Tree," "Cocoa Grove," "Orchi's Flower," and "Cocoanut [*sic*] Tree," among others. If Selfridge's expedition primarily aimed to evaluate the practicality of a canal, the inclusion of detailed plant close-ups raises questions. These stereographs, along with Dr. Maak's work and methods, like compiling plant lists akin to those used in old colonial herbaria, underline the use of photography to define the nature of Darién. But rather than asking what prompts the photographer to focus on botanical subjects, I seek to explore the narratives these plants might convey.

I want to focus on the stereograph titled "Sensitive plant" (fig. 3.4). It is a close-up of one species prevalent in many locations in Darién, according to Selfridge (129). By adopting a plant perspective, I delve into the plant's awareness through Theresa L. Miller's concept of "sensory ethnobotany." This approach entails exploring the "unfolding knowledge of the sensory systems of humans and plants and the value systems associated with human-plant sensory engagements over time in diverse life-worlds" (T. L. Miller 6). I encourage the viewer to become "plant-minded" or to "attend to plants as they reciprocally attend to us" (Ryan et al., *The Mind* xv), evoking the plant's lived experiences within the context of Selfridge's exploration and the photographers' activities.

Botanical communication relies on tactile experiences and corresponding responses (Karban 46). The sensitive plant is commonly referred to as the "sleepy plant," "touch-me-not," or "shameplant." When touched, its compound leaves delicately fold inward and droop, as if protecting itself from or rejecting outside disturbance. Once it senses "safety," it reopens. In *Plants as Persons,* Matthew Hall explores the sensitive plant as an example of sensation, movement, and plant intelligence. Hall explains that when one of its leaves is touched, not only does the immediate leaflet fold inward, but leaves farther from the source of the stimulus

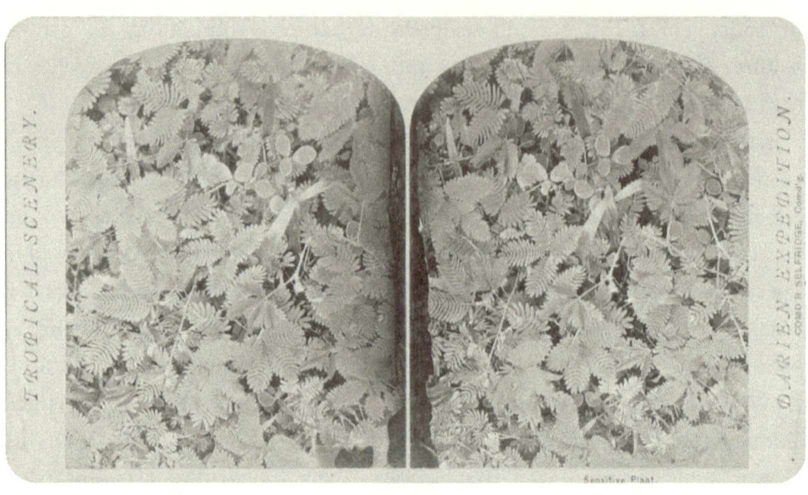

FIGURE 3.4. The Miriam and Ira D. Wallach Division of Art, Prints and Photographs: Photography Collection, The New York Public Library. "Sensitive plant." 1870. *The New York Public Library Digital Collections*, https://digitalcollections.nypl.org/items/510d47e2-6988-a3d9-e040-e00a18064a99

also respond through a process of "signaling and communication" across the plant's entire body (142). This response demonstrates the plant's ability to detect and react to its environment, a behavior that could be interpreted as a form of "intrinsic language" (Ryan et al., *The Language* xvii). By folding its leaves, the plant appears to protect itself from potential harm, illustrating its "perceptual awareness" of external stimuli (Gagliano 3). In this sense, the closing of its leaflets serves as both a defense mechanism and a form of communication. Plants like the sensitive plant rely on movement, color changes, and light sensitivity to interact with their surroundings—behaviors that can be understood as elements of a broader plant language. Considering plant language attributes "greater agency to plants in dynamic relation with their environments . . . [disassembling] the long-standing hierarchies that separate botanical and zoological forms of life" (Ryan et al., *The Language* xiii). Furthermore, the fact that sensitive plants close, from a behavioral ecology perspective, highlights plants' abilities to make decisions, solve problems, and reason (Hall 146; Gagliano 1).

Abundant in the Caribbean, this pantropical specimen is scientifically termed *Mimosa pudica* (Kricher 71). Interestingly, the informal use of *mimosa* in Spanish signifies an affectionate person, while *pudica* in Latin indicates shyness. If the sensitive plant's closure of its leaflets is achieved through a process of "sensing, communication, and action" (Hall 142), then, when approached through an affective lens and considering Hall's invitation to ponder the affective and moral standing of plants, we can perceive this portrait of the sensitive plant as nature manifesting itself as a sentient entity. These ideas align with Indigenous animism, which recognizes plants as relational beings, even "kin," deserving of care and respect (T. L. Miller 5). In the stereograph, the sensitive plant stands fully open, projecting strength and confronting the camera's lens and the photographer's curious gaze. The plant is not protecting herself from the technology; she is not showing herself as shy. The image, however, presents a somewhat unrealistic scenario: when using the stereoscope, it would appear as if the plant were just inches from our eyes. In a real-life situation, the sensitive plant's leaves would be closed due to our breath and proximity. Natural reality has been manipulated by the lens and the photographer, perhaps contributing to the portrayal of Darién as an exotic site for armchair enjoyment. Nonetheless, a plant-perspective analysis suggests that this plant is indeed demonstrating resistance against Selfridge's enterprise by not closing up in front of the camera. The long shutter speed required for early photography may have limited the ability to capture the plant's natural response to stimuli, such as closing its leaves when approached. Nevertheless, the image still invites a speculative reading of the sensitive plant's interaction with its environment and the camera. By remaining open in the photograph, whether due to technical constraints or environmental conditions, the plant appears to assert a form of resilience, presenting itself as unyielding to intrusion. This dual interpretation underscores both the limitations of early photographic technology in capturing ephemeral natural behaviors and the potential agency of the plant as a subject within the colonial visual archive.

Approaching the sensitive plant in this way prompts a consideration of how scientific knowledge and cultural perspectives coalesce in shaping our understanding of plant life and its significance in various contexts. In "Tropical Scenery," the images featuring specific flowers, plants, and tree specimens, when seen through the lens of plant agency, encourage an intimate appreciation of Darién's nature and its distinctive features, challenging both the capitalist mindset of canal construction and the classificatory tendencies of colonial herbaria.

Animals Unseen

The study of animals has traditionally overshadowed that of plants in the sciences. In *The Language of Plants*, Monica Gagliano, John C. Ryan, and Patrícia Vieira argue that this zoocentric bias has reinforced the "privilege of animals as sentient, intelligent, and mobile, at the same time [contributing] to the marginalization of plants as relatively passive life forms" (Ryan et al., *The Language* viii). The "Tropical Scenery" stereographs challenge this bias by foregrounding plants, and my analysis further amplifies this by centering their agency. "Thus far upon this trip we had seen but little of animal life," Selfridge notes (52). However, the lack of readily visible animals in the images does not imply their absence from the Darién ecosystem, as I will demonstrate next. The coexistence of plants and animals in the region points to a more complex interpretation of the photographs. To fully grasp the significance of both plants and animals in these images, it is essential to consider them as part of an interconnected, symbiotic system. This perspective challenges traditional hierarchies in plant and animal studies and highlights the integration of both within a shared habitat, moving beyond one-dimensional representations.

As mentioned, early photography faced a technical challenge, as it required several seconds to capture an image. The extended exposure time or slow shutter speed, along with the difficulty of achieving the right focus distance (for sharpness), made it particularly difficult to photograph everything from small, flitting insects like mosquitoes to larger animals that could hide themselves in nature. Selfridge's report underscores the cohabitation of insects with the lush foliage: "every leaf seems to hold a family of ants" (44), and it also mentions encounters with "ugly-looking" snakes hanging ominously from the overhanging branches of trees, poised to drop into passing boats (100). Such encounters highlight the abundant swamp life, which contribute to the idea of a rich multispecies ecosystem in which plants and animals indeed coexist, and affirming the hidden presence of animals intertwined with the vibrant plant life depicted in the photographs. In this sense, animal camouflage is a recurrent motif throughout the report: "the puma, jaguar, tapir, and tiger inhabit the forests of Darién, but hidden by day in the dense solitudes, are rarely met with" (37). Elusive creatures blend into the natural landscape, making their presence felt primarily through sound—the "roaring of wild animals" (Selfridge 16). For instance, descriptions of black monkeys, whose "ugly head just appearing above the leaves" signals their unseen presence even as their "guttural notes" resound from the treetops, evoking the roar of a "savage beast" (52). The dense foliage then functions as a form of protection, with plants shielding animals from Selfridge's team and the camera's view, potentially demonstrating a form of multispecies solidarity.

Other tiny species such as mosquitoes, ticks, and sand flies, which carry

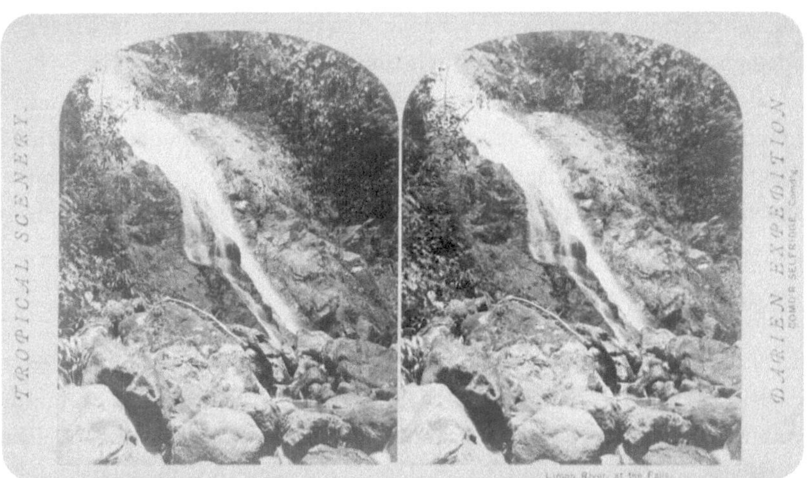

FIGURE 3.5. The Miriam and Ira D. Wallach Division of Art, Prints and Photographs: Photography Collection, The New York Public Library. "Limon River, at the falls." 1871. *The New York Public Library Digital Collections*, https://digitalcollections.nypl.org/items/510d47e2-691c-a3d9-e040-e00a18064a99

tropical illnesses like malaria, are abundant in Darién and incessantly pestered Selfridge's team, who describe these creatures as the jungle's "tiny tormentors" (44).[18] While these insects may not be immediately evident in the photographs, we can *sense* their presence: the report is replete with narratives that vividly illustrate scenes in which mosquitoes take center stage, subjecting the explorers to countless sleepless nights and discomfort. The limiting element of speed in image capture becomes even more visually apparent in photographs of water sources, such as waterfalls and rivers, where the forceful flow appears blurred, such as in "Limon River, at the Falls" (fig. 3.5). The nonvisual presence of mosquitoes and the movement seen in water photos then highlight the ongoing tension between photography and the unyielding forces of nature itself.

A notable example of shutter speed is the self-portrait "Photographer at Pinogana" (fig. 3.3), where a blurred nonhuman animal figure in the lower right corner—possibly a dog or cat—appears to evade capture. With its back to the viewer yet seemingly making eye contact with the photographer, the figure can also be read as an image of nature actively resisting. Its shadowy movement, fading into the horizon, evokes defiance. This blur, likely caused by long exposure, embodies a dual opposition: the animal resists being fully represented by photographic technology while also symbolizing a broader resistance to Selfridge's attempts to impose his enterprise on nature.

Highlighting the limitations of technology and human perception in determining what was visible—or invisible—in these early representations of Darién's nature aligns with my chapter's earlier emphasis on the agency of plants while situating animals as part of the larger ecosystem depicted in the photographs.

Conclusion: Filling in the Gap

The Darién rainforest is popularly known as the "Darién Gap." A "gap" suggests emptiness, but empty of what? "Tropical Scenery" challenges the notion of emptiness, vividly depicting the richness of nature. In another instance of plant blindness, to settlers, colonizers, explorers, and surveyors, the jungle might appear "empty." But from plants' and animals' perspectives, Darién teems with life. Archaeological framings have contributed to the historical "emptiness" of this region, which has traditionally served as a mere pathway or route (Velásquez Runk 131). It is still labeled a gap on maps—and yet Selfridge's reports repeatedly emphasize its fullness: the biodiversity, Indigenous communities, and abundant flora and fauna in the area.

Dr. Maak states that "the natural features of this territory are of a peculiar kind, which bring about a state of things opposed to human settlements in general and consequently to the progress of modern civilization in particular" (Maak in Selfridge 155). The "state of things opposed" to human intervention refers to the autonomy of nature, apparent in both the visible plants and concealed animals captured in the stereographs. As Selfridge stated, "[Darién] will probably remain forever in all its natural wildness" (37). While these stereographs do not document explicit resistance to extractive practices, they are significant as they allow us, from today's perspective, to speculate on the historical resilience of Darién's nature to withstand exploitation and highlight the complexity of its ecosystem.

Indigenous activists like Carlos Doviaza of Darién's Emberá-Wounaan district demonstrate how maps and photography can serve as tools for environmental justice and Indigenous resistance—defending the forest and reclaiming agency for the mutual survival of humans, plants, and nonhuman life.[19] "Tropical Scenery" and its context of production provide early visual evidence of how plants and animals assert themselves within their habitat, offering valuable lessons for the future of tropical rainforests, such as the need to halt logging and ranching, preserve biodiversity, and recognize the interdependence of species. Read this way,

"Tropical Scenery" can be interpreted as nature's call for humans to keep their distance—a call that, despite historical resistance, has largely gone unheeded.

Notes

1. The Darién, located in the Isthmus of Panama, spans Panama's Darién Province and the northern part of Colombia's Chocó Department. In this chapter, "Darién" refers specifically to the rainforest unless stated otherwise.

2. Due to space constraints, I focus on a small selection of images relevant to the chapter's topics. Still, it is important to note that many stereographs contribute to wrongful depictions of Indigenous communities. The peoples of the Darién region in eastern Panama include the Embera, the Wounaan, the Guna (or Kuna), and Afro-Indigenous communities.

3. Velásquez Runk provides a thorough history of Darién and examines how narratives of discovery, intervention, and development have shaped such enduring perceptions.

4. For further information, see Anderson's *Old Panama and Castilla del Oro.* For more on the Darién Scheme, see Edwards.

5. An example is the 1854 Darién expedition led by U.S. Navy Lieutenant Isaac Strain, tied to Lionel Gisborne's "distorted" 1852 map (Dana 136) and later recounted by Todd Balf in *The Darkest Jungle* (2003). For a deeper exploration of Darién's four-hundred-year expedition history, see Kirkpatrick's 1937 survey, covering expeditions from Balboa's era to the 1924 Marsh expedition. Alternatively, Avery's *Picturesque Panama and the Great Canal* (1913) provides an early, albeit U.S.-centric, view of the canal's history, though with exoticizing elements.

6. The expeditions were orchestrated by the chief of the Bureau of Navigation, Daniel Ammen. Survey efforts were undertaken in various regions, such as Tehuantepec, Mexico; Nicaragua; northern Colombia; and Panama, along the railroad line and previously unsuccessful routes (Ammen 193–194). The route chosen for the Panama Canal, which has been operational since 1914, closely resembles the early Panama survey route.

7. For more on this, see Kossoy.

8. For further exploration of O'Sullivan's landscape photographs in geographical surveys, see Kelsey.

9. Selfridge commanded three expeditions in Darién: in 1870, 1871, and 1873. Each expedition's report contains a list of attendees. This document does not account for the change in photographers from O'Sullivan to Moran, although it does mention "two photographers" for the first expedition without specifying the name of the second photographer (Selfridge 1, 6).

10. For an analysis of Panama's stereographs from the perspective of tourism, see

Strain.

11. Identical images can be found in various institutional collections across the United States, such as in the New York Public Library, the Library of Congress, and the Getty Institute. This also suggests the likelihood of additional copies in private collections worldwide.

12. All images are in the public domain, sourced from the New York Public Library.

13. See Raab, "Landscape and the Risk of Metaphor."

14. For more on cultural perspectives and the agency of tropical plants during the era of colonial expansion, see Bleichmar, Schiebinger, and Wylie.

15. In one of the most famous canonical histories of photography, Beaumont Newhall identifies this photographer as Timothy O'Sullivan, describing him as "lean, tough, mustachioed, standing beside his huge camera in a native village'" (96). However, a book on O'Sullivan's life challenges this identification, arguing that the figure is, in fact, John Moran. Other archives also attribute the photograph to Moran. See Sullivan.

16. Before the U.S. construction of the Panama Canal, the French attempted a similar project at the same location from 1881 to 1889, led by Ferdinand de Lesseps, the engineer behind the Suez Canal. The effort ultimately failed due to significant challenges posed by nature. For a historical account of the Panama Canal, see McCullough's *The Path between the Seas* (1977), and for a contemporary cultural history, consult Missal's *Seaway to the Future* (2009).

17. For a historical overview of the Pan-American Highway, emphasizing Darién's environment as the primary impediment, see Shawn W. Miller.

18. For the role of tropical diseases and mosquitoes as instances of nature's resistance to imperial expansion, see McNeill's *Mosquito Empires.*

19. See the films, *Being Emberá: Indigenous Cultures Needed to Protect Forests* (2016) and *The Defenders of the Darién Gap* (2018).

Works Cited

Ammen, Daniel. "Surveys and Reconnaissances from 1870 to 1875 for a Ship Canal across the American Isthmus." *Journal of the American Geographical Society of New York,* vol. 8, 1876, pp. 188–203.

Anderson, Charles Loftus Grant. *Old Panama and Castilla del Oro.* Press of the Sudwarth Company, 1911.

Avery, Ralph Emmett. *Picturesque Panama and the Great Canal.* William C. Haskins of the Canal Record, 1913.

Balf, Todd. *The Darkest Jungle: The True Story of the Darién Expedition and America's Ill-Fated Race to Connect the Seas.* Crown Publishers, 2003.

Bleichmar, Daniela. *Visual Voyages: Images of Latin American Nature from Columbus to Darwin.* Yale University Press, 2017.

Dana, Peter H. "Cutting Across." *Mapping Latin America: A Cartographic Reader,* edited by Jordana Dym and Karl Offen, University of Chicago Press, 2011, pp. 135–138.

Darrah, William Culp. *The World of Stereographs.* National Stereoscopic Association, 1977.

Edwards, Nat. *Caledonia's Last Stand: In Search of the Lost Scots of Darién.* Luath Press Limited, 2007.

Fowles, Jib. "Stereography and the Standardization of Vision." *Journal of American Culture* vol. 17, no. 2, 1994, pp. 89–93.

Gagliano, Monica. "In a Green Frame of Mind: Perspectives on the Behavioural Ecology and Cognitive Nature of Plants." *AoB PLANTS,* vol. 7, 2015.

Hall, Matthew. *Plants as Persons: A Philosophical Botany.* SUNY Press, 2011.

Karban, Richard. *Plant Sensing and Communication.* University of Chicago Press, 2015.

Kelsey, Robin. *Archive Style: Photographs and Illustrations for U.S. Surveys, 1850–1890.* University of California Press, 2007.

Kirkpatrick, Ralph Z. "The First Transisthmian Passageway." *The Military Engineer* vol. 29, no. 165, 1937, pp. 207–211.

Kossoy, Boris. "Photography in Nineteenth-century Latin America. The European Experience and The Exotic Experience." *Image and Memory: Photography from Latin America 1866–1994,* edited by Wendy Watriss et al., University of Texas Press, pp. 18–54.

Krauss, Rosalind. "Photography's Discursive Spaces: Landscape/View." *Art Journal* vol. 42, no. 4, 1982, pp. 311–319.

Kricher, John. *A Neotropical Companion: An Introduction to the Animals, Plants, & Ecosystems of the New World Tropics.* Princeton University Press, 1997.

McCullough, David. *The Path between the Seas: The Creation of the Panama Canal, 1870–1914.* Simon and Schuster, 1977.

McNeill, John Robert. *Mosquito Empires: Ecology and War in the Greater Caribbean, 1620–1914.* Cambridge University Press, 2010

Miller, Shawn W. "Minding the Gap: Pan-Americanism's Highway, American Environmentalism, and Remembering the Failure to Close the Darién Gap." *Environmental History* vol. 19, no. 2, 2014, pp. 189–216.

Miller, Theresa L. *Plant Kin: A Multispecies Ethnography in Indigenous Brazil.* University of Texas Press, 2019.

Missal, Alexandre. *Seaway to the Future: American Social Visions and the Construction of the Panama Canal.* University of Wisconsin Press, 2009.

Newhall, Beaumont. *The History of Photography, from 1839 to the Present Day.* 4th ed., revised. Museum of Modern Art, 1964.

Pietrobruno, Sheenagh. "The Stereoscope and the Miniature." *Early Popular Visual Culture* vol. 9, no. 3, 2011, pp. 171–190.

Raab, Jennifer. “Landscape and the Risk of Metaphor.” *American Art*, vol. 31, no. 2, 2017, pp. 56–58.

Regan, Margaret. “The Life of Timothy H. O’Sullivan: The Story of the Irishman Who Helped Shape American and Arizonan Photography.” *Tucson Weekly*, 13 Mar. 2003, https://www.tucsonweekly.com/tucson/the-life-of-timothy-h-osullivan/Content?oid=1071872

Retrato de los españoles ilustres con un epítome de sus vidas. Madrid: Imprenta Real, 1791.

Ryan, John C., et al., editors. *The Language of Plants: Science, Philosophy, Literature*. University of Minnesota Press, 2017.

Ryan, John C., et al., editors. *The Mind of Plants: Narratives of Vegetal Intelligence*. Sinergetic Press, 2021.

Schiebinger, Londa. *Plants and Empire: Colonial Bioprospecting in the Atlantic World*. Harvard University Press, 2007.

Schwartz, Joan M. “The Geography Lesson: Photographs and the Construction of Imaginative Geographies.” *Journal of Historical Geography* vol. 22, no. 1, 1996, pp. 16–45.

Selfridge, Thomas Oliver. *Reports of Explorations and Surveys to Ascertain the Practicability of a Ship-Canal between the Atlantic and Pacific Oceans by the Way of the Isthmus of Darién*. Department of the Navy, 1874.

Strain, Ellen. “Stereoscopic Visions: Touring the Panama Canal.” *Visual Anthropology Review*, vol. 12, no. 2, Fall/Winter 1996/1997, pp. 44–58.

Sullivan, Robert. *Double Exposure: Resurveying the West with Timothy O’Sullivan, America’s Most Mysterious War Photographer*. Farrar, Straus and Giroux, 2024.

Sutter, Paul. “The Isthmus of Panama and the Knowledge Anthropocene.” *Springs: The Rachel Carson Center Reviews* vol. 3, 2023, pp. 1–8.

Velásquez Runk, Julie. “Creating Wild Darién: Centuries of Darién’s Imaginative Geography and its Lasting Effects.” *Journal of Latin American Geography* vol. 14, no. 3, 2015, pp. 127–156.

Wylie, Lesley, editor. *Understories: Plants and Culture in the American Tropics*. Liverpool University Press, 2024.

4

Brazil, the Country of Palm Trees

A Study of the Arecaceae in the Work of Tarsila do Amaral

ANA CAROLINA CARMONA-RIBEIRO

In Brazil's artistic and literary tradition, the Arecaceae—or palm trees—are the most-often represented and a widely valued plant family. Before the arrival of the colonizers, the Indigenous word Pindorama, or "place of palms," designated the native land. Arriving in 1500, Portuguese were impressed by the vast palm groves found in the newly *discovered* lands, and associated them with the Edenic character of the so-called New World. Nineteenth-century naturalists featured the Arecaceae in drawings that expressed the Europeans' desire for tropical nature alongside their yearning for economic exploitation. Carl Friedrich von Martius, for example, dedicated the second volume of the grandiose *Historia naturalis palmarum* (1823–1850) entirely to Brazilian palm trees. In a similar direction, the French neoclassical landscape painters who landed in Rio de Janeiro in 1816 chose the palm tree as a representation of Brazil itself. Around 1850, the imperial palm tree (*Roystonea oleracea*) spread from the Botanical Garden to the coffee plantation zones, highlighting the connection between imperial power and coffee-grower's wealth. In the Romantic movement, artists continued to praise the plants, helping to consolidate the "crowned place of the palm tree" in literary tradition (M. Andrade as qtd. in J. Cunha 104). In the Republican period at the end of the century, palm trees were planted in the urban reforms that transformed

Brazilian cities, next to buildings or parks designed by foreign urbanists, where, amid well-manicured lawns, they became a "nationality index" served in "the French way" (M. Andrade, *Poesias* 248).

Palm trees constantly appear in the São Paulo–based modernist movement of the 1920s and 1930s. Emerging from the transformations brought by the wealth of coffee and industrialization, this artistic movement intended to bring national culture on par with modern times, seeking new and authentically Brazilian forms of expression. These plants became a fixture in the modernist gardens and in the works of artists and writers. Their drawings and poems emphasize the plants' morphology, and they are characterized as "thorny," "thin," or "leafy." Individually or in groups, palms stand out for their effect on the landscape, gain attributes usually associated with animated beings, and even acquire social status—"literature in my land is as official as the palm trees," writes the poet Carlos Drummond in 1926. Invariably, all these characteristics can be summarized under a single epithet: they are palm trees "from Brazil," plant symbols that reaffirm or call into question the ideas of *national identity* and *tropical civilization* (Carmona-Ribeiro, *Guide Book* 58–59).

■

In this sense, this chapter discusses the meanings acquired by the palm tree in the works of Brazilian painter Tarsila do Amaral (1886–1973)—encompassing mainly the artist's points of view but also pointing to the plant's increasing *agency*. It is part of a broader investigation, our doctoral thesis, in which we did not depart from critical plant studies or other similar standpoints—back then unknown to us, since, in Brazil, few academic groups have these approaches—but from the traditional perspectives of art history and cultural studies, seeking to build our argument by a thorough analysis of the modernist works in conjunction with the reading of the sociocultural conditions of the 1920s and 30s. Toward the end of the PhD we became acquainted with these approaches and their potential as theoretical constructs that could enrich the interpretation of works that, a hundred years ago, already had plants at their center.[1]

Tarsila was one of the key figures of Brazilian modernism, born in a family of rich coffee growers and educated in São Paulo and Paris. She represented palm trees in many paintings and drawings, demonstrating the intimate relationship between country (in French, *pays*) and landscape (*paysage*).[2] In the *Pau Brasil* (Brazilwood) phase of her work, prevails an appreciation of vegetation and the quest for new ways of representing it, but plants—palm trees included—are still treated in a conventional way, in the sense of an anthropocentric approach that sees them as "objects." In the Anthropophagic phase, however, plants assume an animated nature, an active role, embodying and questioning the colonial condition of Brazil and its contradictions. They become beings capable of (re)(de)forming "humanity" itself, in addition to offering forms of resistance to the European invasion (although, as we know, this is often a losing battle).

The *Pau Brasil* Phase (1924–1925): Palm Trees and National Unity

In 1923, in Paris, Tarsila notes that the French capital was tired of Parisian art. While studying with avant-garde artists Albert Gleizes, André Lhote, and Fernand Léger, she claims to be feeling "increasingly Brazilian" and declares her intention to become "the painter of my land" (Amaral 101). After returning to São Paulo in 1924, she joins the group that had promoted the Modern Art Week of 1922. This launches a new phase in her work, known as *Pau Brasil*—an analytical moment in which, drawing on cubism and based on a critical and lyrical perspective, she attempts to decode the constituent elements of "our environmental and human landscape" (Campos, *Tarsila* 111). Vegetation turns into an index of locality in her production, qualifying the countryside, the metropolis, and the suburbs as *Brazilian* and *tropical.* Black and mixed-race characters, and popular cultural manifestations demonstrate the search for the most "authentic" roots of the nationality, in recognition of their musical, culinary, and linguistic contributions.

A synthesis of her production in the mid-1920s comes about in her drawings for the poetry book *Pau Brasil* (1925), by Oswald de Andrade, then Tarsila's partner. The figures, together with the cover, the page layout, and the "plastic penchant" of Oswaldian poetry are decisive for the "physicality" of the book. Tarsila's pieces function simultaneously as visual advertisements of the poems and as autonomous elements, overcoming the function of mere illustrations (Campos, *Uma poética* 36).

The first part of the book is titled "História do Brasil" (History of Brazil). Here the *ready-made* poems originate from the writings of colonial chroniclers. By poetically recreating the voice of the European invader (Fonseca 134), de Andrade exposes how, from the desire for Indigenous women to the greed for the tropical fruits, concupiscence permeated the imaginary about the New World. Thus, the poet unveils the idea of the country as an exploitable paradise, in an implicit criticism of Brazil's identification with "natural nature," its exclusion from "culture"

(Perrone-Moisés 42), and its relegation to the role of a commodities exporter. The poems highlight the relationship between the country and its nature, as in "Paisagem" (Landscape), where the newly discovered land is summarized as "palm groves of large coconuts" facing the sea.

Tarsila's ink drawing is characterized by synthetic lines. The profile of the Sugar Loaf Mountain stands out alongside a leafy and thick-stemmed palm, possibly a coconut tree (*Cocos nucifera*). The diversity of the Brazilian flora is obfuscated: the entirety of the local vegetation is summarized by the coconut tree, characterizing Brazil as a domain of tropical nature. Meanwhile, by shifting the moment of the "discovery" of Brazil from Bahia to Rio de Janeiro, Tarsila fuses imaginaries linked to two distinct epochs: the time of the arrival of the Portuguese colonizer, and the twentieth century. The painter references her work in Brazilian historical painting, which had often represented these scenes, and in postcards from the 1920s—which are invariably centered on Rio de Janeiro's mountains and palm trees, attesting to the centrality of nature in the city's rise as a central tourist destination. In this sense, if Oswald's poems have a fragmentary and critical character, Tarsila's well-resolved drawings fall short of any problematization of stereotypes, emptying history of its elements of conflict and reiterating the myth of "discovery" and the perspective of the colonizer (or tourist). In this characterization, the Brazilian landscape becomes an image of unbridled consumption, a mere commodity.

In "Poemas da Colonização" (Poems of Colonization), three thick palm trees stand alongside a horizontal building with many windows, surrounded by livestock and undefined human figures. In its relationship with the poems, this rural scene appears to reference the forgotten, "old" sugarcane farms of the colonial period, different from the "modern farms" in which native trees were being replaced by coffee plantations. Oswald reconstitutes the ambience and sociability of rural Brazil by giving voice to multiple characters, addressing slavery and its violence. In a meaningful absence, however, such tensions are nowhere to be seen in Tarsila's drawing—where even the local plant diversity (so well represented by other artists, such as seventeenth-century landscape painter Frans Post), is subsumed in the single synthetic palm tree. This operation confers the plant with a central place in the colonial context, and the drawing becomes a kind of generalistic *summary* of an entire historical period.

"São Martinho" addresses a context familiar to the modernists, since São Martinho was one of the main properties of the influential Prado family. In the drawing, the archaism of the old cycles of exploitation of natural resources is replaced by the iconic image of the modern coffee farm of western São Paulo. The attention to the architectural details of the main house allows an accurate identification of the farm. Flanking the house, the palm trees reinforce its monumentality. They are leafy, with rectilinear stems that resemble the shafts of classic columns, indicating an important change: these are no longer representations of coconut palms, but rather of imperial palms.

The drawing can be analyzed in conjunction with *Palmeiras* (1925), a painting by Tarsila that represents coffee rurality: hills covered with plantations, settler houses, train tracks and generic shrubs, and, in the center of the composition, a group of five slender palms. Thick brown lines form both their stems and the metallic parts of the railway path, as if they were made of the same material. According to the neoclassical tradition, their verticality orders tropical nature, breaking "the voluptuous force of the curved forms of the scenery" (M. Andrade as qtd. in J. Cunha 101). The palm trees function as pictorial and symbolic mediations, and the nature-artifice paradox unfolds into other paradoxes, such as sensuality-rationality and tradition-modernity. Imperial palm trees become signifiers of coffee, and coffee itself becomes a ubiquitous force across the landscape, as exemplified by Oswald's synesthetic verse: "in the framed silence, a smell of coffee." And like coffee plants—but with more elegance and *tropicality*—the palm tree becomes the link between ancient and contemporary times and spaces.

The drawing "Postes da Light" (Light's Lamp Posts) makes reference to Cia Light, a Canadian company that since the beginning of the twentieth century monopolized the provision of public services in São Paulo. It emphasizes the modernizing significance of imperial palm trees, a trait that becomes even clearer when the drawing is compared with other paintings that address urbanization, such as *Gazo* (1924). These works dialogue with Léger's Mechanical period (1918–1923), as Tarsila shares with the French painter an appreciation for the *decorative* aspect of painting—qualifying the urban environment with figurative symbols of modernity and city life. However, her approach has an important difference: gone is the explicit reference to *labor*, and nature-referenced objects are introduced. At first glance, these objects seem to oppose the artificiality of the symbols of modernity—buildings, trams, automobiles—which might lead to the interpretation that they would be signs of nature's *resistance* in the city. But in the "tropical-mechanical" landscapes of Tarsila, natural objects—most notably plants—cannot be seen as "pure nature," as a *denaturing* operation is underway. The palm trees, subjected to modern civilization and made equivalent to artificial elements, do not seem to have any agency.

The drawing provides a synthetic approach to the thematic of the city in the process of modernization. The palm trees, the only "natural" objects represented, are formed by a single vertical line surmounted by small strokes, in a "maximum reduction of almost ideogrammatic graphic elements" (Amaral 177). Transfigured into lamp posts, they become signifiers of a modern *and* tropical city. In the *Gazo* painting—which shows an industrialized town with some of its old buildings—a second tree is included. Both trees have perfectly cylindrical trunks that stand in striking similarity to metal pipes. The crown of the palm and the canopy of the other tree sit neatly atop their respective trunks, almost like autonomous parts of a mechanical object; still, they do refer to the morphology of the plant, by maintaining the naturalistic chromatic reference. While this procedure of *mechanization* of vegetation is reminiscent of Léger's work, it is important to note that while Léger makes use of the principle of *equivalence* with the machine (enabling the mechanical element to give rise to a new pictorial logic), Tarsila operates by *similarity,* elevating the machine to condition of a formal model for all other objects.

Comparing these scenes with photos of downtown São Paulo in the 1920s, it becomes clear that Tarsila closely followed the urban embellishment works of the time, and the radical change in the city's identity. While the inauguration of new buildings, transport networks, and street lighting erased the memory of the colonial past, the creation of boulevards, parks, and gardens erased the memory of pre-existing nature. Imperial palm trees played a central role in this context, which made them the exact opposite of a symbol of nature's resistance in the city. They gave the Republic the attributes of distinction to which the *Roystonea oleracea* had been associated since being first introduced in Brazil, in imperial times—and represented the ideals associated with the opulence and prosperity of coffee, now transmuted into industrial advancement. Urban renovations transformed the city center into an elegant scenic panorama with "touches of European *décor*" (Sevchenko 115–116), and imperial palm trees conferred the remodeled spaces a note of controlled, official, and superficial tropicality. They replaced the ancestral araucaria pines and humble banana trees, contributing to transforming the last remaining patches of native forest into well-ordered gardens.

The Anthropophagic Phase (1928–1929)

Between 1928 and 1929, in the Anthropophagic phase, Tarsila's work undergoes significant transformations. Her paintings now represent the "theater of nature," shifting toward Brazil's violent history of greed and exploitation of nature by the colonial enterprise (Salzstein 15). These "subconscious landscapes" (Amaral 282) are modeled after psychoanalytic processes, such as deformations, displacements, projections, and condensations. *Pau Brasil* localities are replaced by *wild* environments, and signs of culture or civilization seem absent. The paintings still dwell on the nation's ethnic bases, but any remnants of nineteenth-century nativism are overcome. The Brazilian landscape is the jungle, and the Brazilian becomes the savage, a "pre-Judaeo-Christian civilization man" (Amaral 286), in dialogue with psychoanalysis and surrealism.

Plants turn into *protagonists,* characters that exhibit an *artificial naturalness.* Reinforcing this, Salzstein (15) states that in Tarsila's anthropophagic painting everything, including the supposedly natural forms, is subject to "hybridity, adaptation, artifice." While in some works the human is made vegetal—as the "planted man" of *Abaporu* (1928) demonstrates—in others it is the plant that is humanized: in *A lua* (The moon) (1928), for instance, a solitary cactus acquires a human silhouette. Even though the "theater of nature" rejects anthropocentrism, it is still deeply affected by human beings. Human beings and plants meet through unconsciousness, and vegetation plays a key role in the lifting of repression in the Freudian sense (*Verdrängung*). Some plants will turn into archetypical forms, generative of the landscape and of other plants, minerals, and animals. Three vegetable groups stand out: the succulents (especially cacti), the banana tree, and the Arecaceae.

Reminiscent of the Garden of Eden, *O lago* (*The Lake*) (1928) inaugurates Tarsila's "theater of nature." Urban, suburban, and rural Brazil vanish together with the signs of industry. Even human beings are absent. The pale blue sky, the mountains and the water act as a backdrop; what truly qualifies the scene are the plants that vigorously sprout, bloom, and fructify all around. The identification of these vegetable figures as characters in a play is striking, given their lively nature and the way they dynamically interact within the pictorial space. There is a great diversity of shapes, and flashes of pink, red, orange, and yellow stand out from the greens.

Such figures have little similarity with the representation of vegetation in the *Pau Brasil* phase. Now plants are subjected to radical pruning, fertilization, grafting, and hybridization. Such horticultural experimentation generates a varied flora, such as the group of *plant-flowers* in the left corner (formed by the metonymic action of isolating parts of known species and re-presenting them as species in and of themselves); the gigantic succulent in the lower right (obtained via the same procedure, plus a change of scale); or the exuberant plant that occupies the right side (whose structure resembles that of a cactus, to which an epiphyte is attached). These operations of selection and assemblage relate to the psychoanalytic phenomena of displacements and condensations.

Tarsila's horticultural experiments enable the identification of her plants as *inventions,* in a radicalization of the artistic procedure of abstraction and recreation of natural things. In this sense, she establishes dialogues with Mário de Andrade's *Macunaíma* (1928), where individual trees are capable of generating fruits of many different species; with the propositions of the manifesto *The Futurist Flora* (1924), by Fedele Azari (155), who upholds the creation of a "plastic flora / completely original / totally invented / completely colorful / wonderfully perfumed // and above all inexhaustible, given the endless variety of the samples"; and with the fanciful re-creation of tropical vegetation by the French painter Henri Rousseau (1844–1910). The most important reference for these brand-new plants, however, are primitive, extinct specimens, intertwining past and future in the "completely original" flora of *O Lago.* The word *original* here has two uses—it refers not only to *newness,* but also to something that *relates to the origin.* History is momentarily suspended, and human beings are made absent. However, turning to nature is only a momentary withdrawal, so that *humanity* can, from afar, see itself in greater depth—and, in return, experience the multitude of forms of the *other* (including nature).

The palm tree is perhaps the only plant to remain morphologically recognizable. The green stem lacks differentiation from the leaves, but the figure is not subjected to radical changes in shape or size. Discreetly positioned on the upper left corner of the painting, it is equivalent to the other species, and one gets the impression that the artist wanted it to be reintegrated into the totality of the flora. It is as if the other plants—untethered by wealth, urbanity, or tradition; more colorful, inventive, anonymous, and ancestral than the palm tree—were nothing more than projections of the palm tree's repressed desires. Abandoning extraneously imposed forms and behaviors, the palm tree would, maybe, be able to return to its past self (in the luxuriant jungle of the Tertiary Age, or in the forests of precolonial Brazil).

Even in its title, *Distância* (*Distance*) (1928) confirms that the conciliatory attitude of *Pau Brasil* is now problematized by Tarsila. The structure of the composition clarifies the title. Horizontally, the bowed skyline is the axis that divides earth and sky—surfaces on which successive lines reverberate like waves. An ellipsoidal green field emerges, overlapped by a pink patch on the right side.

Vertically, the vegetable figures form a pair: a palm tree on the upper right and a group of cacti on the left. Such figures are more than inert elements, being elevated to the status of *characters.*

Tarsila is not seeking to convey to these characters personal traits, but rather to present them as *models.* The palm tree assumes the role of the mother (or ultimate descendant) of all Brazilian palm trees, unifying them in its figure. Considering the meanings assumed in the painter's previous work, one could point out that, even here, this plant continues to symbolize Brazil as a cultural identity, or as a *tropical civilization.* The cactus, in turn, symbolizes the inverse of the modern nation: a precolonial, poor, and largely unknown Brazil, savage and *barbaric*—a notion that, in the nineteenth century, referred to the "non-European and non-white" peoples whose exploitation was justified by imperialist "civilizational catechization" (Zilly 8). In Brazilian modernism, however, the notion of barbarism will take on different contours, by the appreciation of the transformative potential of primitive *brutality.* The figures of the palm tree and the cactus, therefore, are both congenerous and antithetical, a notion that is reinforced by their relative positioning and the pictorial treatment that shapes them.

At first, the figures seem to effectively *distance* themselves, for two reasons: first, the monumentality of the cacti in the foreground, which reinforces the contrast with the tiny palm tree on the horizon line, and second, the fact that the cacti are presented as a group, while the palm tree is an individual. However, it is also possible to identify an inverse movement of *approximation.* This occurs through correspondences of shape: the two figures assume a soft and liquefied aspect. Moreover, both are painted in the same shade of green, as if they were of the same substance and matter. The use of this dark opaque green that Tarsila termed "barbaric green" (Amaral 297) reveals changes in her palette; heavier greens and nocturnal blues replace the "chromatic exoticism" of the *Pau Brasil* phase (Amaral 289).

Having clarified the constitution of the figures and their interrelationship, our attention turns to the vast green field, key to the comprehension of the work. The place it occupies in the composition, its design and color (a gradient between the "barbaric green" and the vivid green of the previous phase) are indicators of its multiple and contradictory meanings. It reinforces the figures' propensity for successive distancing and approximation, and can be associated with an aquatic surface, in which throwing a stone generates waves that form concentric circles. Although, physically speaking, waves carry energy but not matter, in *Distance* the phenomenon is intense enough to carry away both cacti and palm trees, in a centrifugal movement. But there is another possible association: that of the green field as a whirlpool, undergoing a centripetal motion that pulls everything to the center of the painting, precisely where a sinkhole is located—a place where objects are usually lost, but where cacti and palm trees could meet. In this sense, the field can also be thought of as a plantation, or rather as a coffee plantation, the verdant monoculture that crushes and transforms everything that stands in its way.

This brings us to the painting's dilemma: it is centered on the two contradictory, mutually exclusive elements of the composition—the palm tree and the cactus—but the coffee field and the pink patch also play a significant role. The work advances a dualistic representation of Brazil, in a reading of the nation's "vacillating character" and of the "hybrid" physiognomy of its culture. The coffee plantation situates itself between these two mutually exclusive premises as a great *active void*, a motor that perpetuates the dilemma and the continuous oscillation of the cactus and the palm tree between a state of *being* and *not being*, or between the *same* and the *other*. This movement expresses the dominant regime in Brazilian cultural formation: a "borderline regime," as Pasta Jr. (18–21; my translation) puts it, always operating in ambiguity and alternation. Hypothetically, the coffee plantation *could* bring together the two plant symbols and even resolve the contradictions between the two "Brazils." However, this would require the socialization of wealth, and of its material and spiritual outcomes, such as urbanization, industrialization, and modernism itself.

But this would only happen if, nourished by coffee, the palm tree and the cactus could together generate fruit, originating a new plant. From that new plant an entire pioneer flora would emerge, creating the conditions for the reestablishment of Brazil's autochthonous nature and culture. At the same time, realistically, coffee seems to constitute an obvious impediment to the reemergence of such an autochthonous culture, insofar as it depletes the soils and reiterates, in the twentieth century, the vicissitudes of centuries of colonialism. As such, despite their momentary proximity, the palm tree and the cactus are unable to effectively meet, let alone generate any fruits. Eternally uprooted, floating on the surface of the plantation, the two become monumental symbols of the *impossibilities* underlying Brazil's formation, in its subjection to the ups and downs of coffee, sugarcane, rubber—or even, in an irresistible anachronism, of the soy monoculture that nowadays annihilates the nation's savannas and forests.

Even so, Tarsila insists on achieving that very impossibility: the strange patch that invades the plantation emerges as a sign of a potential interruption in the alternation between the *same* and the *other.* Looming surreptitiously behind the cacti, its lively pink color suggests the search for alternatives for the palm tree, for Brazil and for her own work. This color, here, is no longer a signifier of the country of *Pau Brasil* and of the artist's "luminous" painting as an expression of the triumphal "rise of coffee" (Pagu as qtd. in Amaral 91)—for now, in the Brazil of 1928, mountains of coffee would soon be burned as famine hit the masses of workers, and the signs of the 1930 Revolution were already being felt. In this sense, the pink patch becomes a negative sign, indicating *disruptions* in the context surrounding the work: crisis in coffee production, in the modernist movement, and in Tarsila's personal life (her partnership with Oswald was falling apart and her estate was fading). Like every crisis, this one pointed to uncertain consequences. It could mean the institution of both a cultural desert, or new possibilities for Brazil: for some artists, the magical, for others, the unconscious, for others still, social revolution.

Floresta (*Forest*) (1929) maintains the structure of *Distance:* the bowed line of the horizon, the vertical elements in opposition. The chromatic reference remains, consisting of roses, greens, and darker blues; a glimmer of pink insinuates itself on the horizon, creeping toward the center of the work. Tarsila now turns her attention to the coffee plantation's *other,* the forest, and continues to meditate on the previously presented dilemma. The kind of nature that emerges is nature *at the limit,* through which the painter meets the writer Euclides da Cunha. At the beginning of the twentieth century, da Cunha had denounced the action of Brazilian "desert makers" and the *barbarism* inherent to *civilization:* "We have been an element of terribly barbaric antagonism [against the] very nature that surrounds us." (Cunha, *Fazedores* 134) Formed by nature, nonetheless man was seen as responsible for the (de)formation of the environment. In *Floresta,* this relationship between man and nature remains valid, and men, although absent, are recognized by the vestiges of the destruction they have left behind.

The plants, again, are the protagonists, essential elements of the landscape. In the foreground, a large multistemmed specimen, the result of a hybridization of palm and tree, cactus and tree, or palm and cactus: there are several possibilities, and it would be more adequate to consider all of them intermingled—because, in this plant, Tarsila summarizes her horticultural-pictorial procedures. The figure of the palm tree now disappears completely. If before it was one of the premises of the dilemma of *being* and *not being,* here the hybrid plant is the dilemma itself. It becomes the *other*—thus arriving at the formula that, as Pasta Jr. (19) points out, is experienced at various times in Brazilian literature, as a response of the characters to a problematic and slavery-based nationality that requests from them simultaneously recognizing "difference" and "the absence of difference."

The roots of this plant are a continuation of the stems and leaves and embrace a nest of pink fruits or eggs, over which it bends, as a "mother plant" protecting its offspring. The appearance of this nest is curious, considering that, in *Distance,* it seemed clear that the palm tree and the cactus would never bear fruit. Here, with the metaphor of eggs, Tarsila insists on the search for a solution to the dilemma, which manifests itself in this archetypal *total plant* that fantasizes or projects a possibility of a future for Brazil and for modernism itself.

But the dilemma is greater than the painting, and insists on renewing itself: on the left side of the canvas—in dialogue with the "mother plant"—a profusion of prisms suggests severed trunks. In addition to being dark and glossy (referring to charred logs, bones, minerals, or mechanical parts), such figures demonstrate a return to volume. In the context of the deformation of the landscape, they indicate that the forest, once verdant and diverse, is now approaching the picture of drought in the Brazilian Northeast, described by Cunha in *Os sertões* (41); or even approaching a war scenario, in which the *barbarity* of green and pink things (which insist on surviving) is fought by the agents of the so-called *civilization.* Thus, in this landscape, everything seems to indicate that the logs would be the future of the "mother plant." In these extreme conditions, when the forest became desert, merging the *same* and the *other* implied a replacement of the dilemma: if the *same* equals the *other, being* can equal *not being.* And this is what the logs reveal: they are the "mother plant," in a hypothetical future—the severed trunks as its own *non-being* or annihilated form.

■

The review of Tarsila's work and the comparison with her contemporaries' production reveal that the palm tree is an object of great interest to Brazilian modernists, as well as an object of constant experimentation. Throughout her drawings and paintings, the palm tree assumes the role of one of the main symbols of "Brazilianness." Initially, in the *Pau Brasil* phase, the painter accepts and reinforces this role, aligning with the national artistic and literary tradition and focusing on the coconut tree and the imperial palm tree. The coconut tree expresses an acceptance of the idea of Brazil as "natural nature" (although permeated by a popular character, differing in this from the nineteenth-century trends that emphasized the *nobility* of the palm tree). The imperial palm tree, on the other hand, conveys a positive vision of Brazilian modernization, generated mainly by the coffee production cycle. In this context, plants are seen as objects, occupying a subordinate and dependent place in relation to humans.

In the Anthropophagic phase, the notion of a homogeneous and conflict-free nationality is questioned. Tarsila begins to problematize the symbols of this nationality, incorporating more radically—in a less conciliatory way—the contributions of Black and Indigenous peoples, the working classes, and local nature itself, to "Brazilianness." She critiques the place the palm tree, and especially the imperial palm tree, had represented in this tradition, in association with the ideas of *civilization* and *progress.* The tree is pictorially liquefied or deformed, losing its monumentality, rationality, and order; the plant naturalizes itself once again, blending with the rest of the flora, on equal terms with other plants of the forest. This allows Tarsila to see the palm tree not as a univocal symbol, but rather as a contradictory element—which represents what Brazil *is* and also what it *is not,* with the potential to actively participate in the Anthropophagic project of searching for an original culture (of which, undeniably, nature would be a part).

This transformation brings an artistic and political opening for the agency of plants. The palm tree, abandoning its role as a *symbol,* a representation of something *external to itself,* can then emerge as an agent—a living being capable of formulating the answers of the "peripheral culture" to centuries of colonialism and destruction of nature (Salzstein 15). Its character as a contradictory element brings to light the cultural and environmental potentialities of Brazil, and simultaneously the nation's conjunctural and structural impossibilities. Its ambiguous and hybrid constitution expresses well what Pasta Jr. (11) defines as a "negative formation," or the radical non-formation of Brazil, "at the level of the subject, artwork and society." In this sense, both Tarsila and the palm tree are at their limits: the artist, at the limit of an artistic project that was on the verge of exhaustion, and the palm tree at an even more dramatic limit—that of its own survival, in ecological terms[3] and also at a metaphorical level, as a depleted symbol incapable of producing fruit, or new symbols, due to the inhospitable conditions of the environment.

Notes

1. There are many examples of this, such as the Amazonian trees in Raul Bopp's poetry, animated and feminine beings who guide the dynamics of the forest; or the cacti of Flávio de Carvalho and Manuel Bandeira, monumental and mythical warriors, offering resistance to the bourgeois lifestyle and capitalist modernization. We recom-

mend *The Guidebook of Modernist Botany* for a more detailed understanding of the modernist relationship with plants.

2. Due to copyright and licensing issues, it was not possible to reproduce the images of the works discussed here, but most of them can be found in the Itaú Cultural online encyclopedia: https://enciclopedia.itaucultural.org.br/pessoas/300-tarsila-do-amaral/obras?classificacao_id=60

3. The 1920s was a period of marked degradation of the Atlantic Forest; between only 1854 and 1920, with the expansion of coffee farming in the state of São Paulo, it lost 35 percent of its forestry cover (Victor 15–26). A hundred years later, the Official List of Threatened Species of Brazilian Flora, published by the Federal Government, listed nineteen species of Arecaceae in the categories "vulnerable," "endangered," or even "critically endangered (probably extinct)" (Portaria MMA no. 148, June 7th 2022).

Works Cited

Amaral, Aracy. *Tarsila: Sua Obra e Seu tempo.* Edusp, 2003.

Andrade, Carlos Drummond de. "Minha Terra Tem Palmeiras." Handwritten poem, 1926. Instituto de Estudos Brasileiros da Universidade de São Paulo (IEB-USP).

Andrade, Mário de. *Poesias Completas—Volume 1.* Record, 2013.

Andrade, Mário de. *O Turista Aprendiz.* IPHAN, 2015.

Andrade, Oswald de. *Pau Brasil.* Au Sans Pareil, 1925.

Azari, Fedele. *The Futurist Flora and the Plastic Equivalents of Artificial Odors* (1924). Translated by Fernando Marcelino, *Revista de História da Arte e Arqueologia,* no. 13, 2010, pp. 145–156.

Campos, Haroldo de. "Uma Poética da Radicalidade." *Cadernos de Poesia do Aluno Oswald,* by Oswald de Andrade, Círculo do Livro, s.d.

Campos, Haroldo de. "Tarsila: Uma Pintura Estrutural." *Tarsila Anos 20,* organized by Sônia Salzstein. Sesi, 1997, pp. 111–114.

Carmona-Ribeiro, Ana Carolina. *The Guidebook of Modernist Botany.* Ed. da Autora, 2020.

Carmona-Ribeiro, Ana Carolina. *Botânica Modernista e a Natureza do Brasil Rredescoberto.* 2023. University of São Paulo, PhD thesis, https://doi:10.11606/T.16.2023.tde-11122023-112427.

Cunha, Euclides da. "Fazedores de Desertos." *Contrastes e Confrontos.* 1907. Rio de Janeiro, Fundação Darcy Ribeiro, 2013, pp. 133–138, https://fundar.org.br/wp-content/uploads/2021/06/contrastes-e-confrontos.pdf

Cunha, Euclides da. *Os Sertões.*1902. Fundação Darcy Ribeiro, 2013.

Cunha, Jakeline. *Mário de Andrade Paisagista em "O Turista Aprendiz."* 2016. University of São Paulo, PhD thesis, https://teses.usp.br/teses/disponiveis/8/8151/tde-09082016-095734/en.php

Fonseca, Maria Augusta. "Taí: É e Não ÉCancioneiro Pau Brasil." *Literatura e Sociedade,* vol. 9, no. 7, 2004, pp. 120–145, https://doi.org/10.11606/issn.2237-1184.v0i7p120-145

Pasta Jr., José Antonio. "Volubilidade e Ideia Fixa (O Outro no Romance Brasileiro)." *Sinal de Menos,* no. 4, 2010, pp. 5–25, https://sinaldemenos.net/2011/02/24/sinal-de-menos-4/

Perrone-Moisés, Leyla. *Vira e Mexe Nacionalismo: Paradoxos do Nacionalismo Literário.* Cia das Letras, 2007.

Salzstein, Sônia. "A Saga Moderna de Tarsila." *Tarsila Anos 20,* organized by Sônia Salzstein. Sesi, 1997, pp. 9–17.

Sevchenko, Nicolau. *Orfeu Extático na Metrópole: São Paulo, Sociedade e Cultura nos Frementes Anos 20.* Cia das Letras, 2014.

Victor, Mauro A. M. *Cem anos de devastação: revisitada 30 anos depois.* Ministério do Meio Ambiente, 2005.

Zilly, Berthold. "Sertão e Nacionalidade: Formação Étnica e Civilizatória do Brasil Segundo Euclides da Cunha." *Estudos Sociedade e Agricultura,* vol. 7, no. 1, 1999, pp. 5–45, https://revistaesa.com/ojs/index.php/esa/article/view/144

PART II
Language and Knowledge

5

Cattle Intimacies

Animal Voice and Literary Speech in João Guimarães Rosa and Marília Floôr Kosby

THOMAZ AMANCIO

At the beginning of João Guimarães Rosa's story "Conversa de bois" ("Oxen Talk"), the narrator ponders whether animals can talk. He initially concedes that "once upon a time" animals were able to speak, but then he asks if that is still the case: "Que já houve um tempo em que eles conversavam, entre si e com os homens, é certo e indiscutível [. . .] mas, hoje-em-dia, agora, agorinha mesmo, aqui, aí, ali, e em toda parte, poderão os bichos falar e serem entendidos, por você, por mim, por todo o mundo, por qualquer um filho de Deus?!" ("That once they talked, among themselves and with men, cannot be argued . . . but what about today, now, right now, here, there, and everywhere, could critters talk and be understood, by you, by me, by everybody, by any child of God?!"[1]) (*Sagarana* 325). The way the question is formulated poses a sequence of specifications, as the animals' ability to speak is treated not simply as binary yes-or-no, but defined by a multiplicity of conditions related to temporality ("um tempo" vs. "hoje-em-dia"), geography ("aqui, aí, ali, e em toda parte"), and interlocution ("por você, por mim, por todo o mundo, por qualquer um"). It is not simply a matter of *being able* to speak, but of when, where, and by whom one can be understood ("falar e serem entendidos"). Such declination of conditions amounts to an epistemological inquiry into the animal voice. If they speak, under which conditions might it be possible for us to understand it?

This chapter takes up Rosa's framing question—and the answer he offers to it—as an invitation to consider the specificity of literary mediation of animal voices. What are the conditions in which one encounters the animal voice in a literary text? How does aestheticized speech afford contact with the animal voice, and how does it interfere with that voice? To the extent that literature and other cultural objects become vessels for thinking *about* and *with* animals and other nonhuman beings, the operation of such mediums must be made explicit. Rosa's story, together with Marília Floôr Kosby's 2017 poetry collection *Mugido*, are privileged occasions to consider those questions, as both texts make the mediation of animal voices by literary speech a central concern. Because they belong to the same tradition—literary representations of the world of cattle ranching in Brazil—we can read them against the background of that cultural history. Although Kosby and Rosa are not alone in centering animals in depictions of cattle ranching life in Brazil (Carlos Drummond de Andrade, Graciliano Ramos, and Ana Paula Maia come to mind), they stand out by both centering animal perspectives *and* making explicit their own role as mediators of those perspectives. Such a thematization of the literary text as "go-between" connecting, as it were, animals and readers, makes Rosa's and Kosby's texts invaluable documents for the theorization of the literary mediation of animal voice. As we will see, they have distinct but overlapping ethico-aesthetic programs: Rosa's one of fabulation as temporary suspension of normative reality, Kosby's one of translation as ethical practice.

By animal voice, I refer to the assumption that the text conveys some kind of truth about the life of an animal, in its phenomenological and ethical dimensions. This assumption can be found, for example, in Patrícia Vieira's notion of "zoophytography," defined as "the inscription of animal and plant modes of expression in human texts, thus integrating the specific forms of existence and of articulation of non-humans into human culture" (56). As Vieira notes, such inscription entails "the risk of merely ventriloquizing non-humans"—in other words, of passing someone else's voice for the nonhuman's—a risk that inheres in the very process of representation. Because of its symbolic and aesthetic nature, literary speech is always in excess of whatever may be construed as its referent. Moreover, as Robert R. McKay observes, representation is a concept at variance with itself, as it implicitly or explicitly invokes its political, legal, and aesthetic connotations. In animal and plant studies, that is a particularly vexing issue, as the "key meanings [of] portrayal and advocacy" are equally important to the broader project of the field (McKay 308). How to think, then, about the mediation of the animal perspective in texts that are about animals, but not by or for (nonhuman) animals?

Rosa and Kosby help us answer this question by addressing representation as both aesthetic and political problem. Their texts offer a double pedagogy that invites readers to think about animals as it concomitantly seeks to teach them how to read a text about animals. "Conversa de bois," first published in *Sagarana* (1946), attributes articulate speech to a group of cart oxen, generating a fable-like discursivity that is framed as the account of a cowboy to an erudite interlocutor, thus portraying the discourse of the animals as impossible to untangle from human speech. Kosby's poetry collection, in turn, makes this entanglement the point of departure for its lyric address to the reader. The first poem in the collection—fulfilling a similar framing function to the opening paragraph of "Conversa de bois"—challenges the reader to "translate the *mugido,*" establishing a demand not only for translation (and thus interpretation), but also for recognizing translation as such. These inaugural gestures highlighting mediation establish the conditions in which the reader will encounter what comes after, portrayals of everyday life in multispecies rural communities that explore the often-violent relationships between humans and animals in the context of ranching systems.

As portraits of everyday life, both the story and the poetry collection have a realistic orientation, in the sense that they envision to represent nuanced and detailed scenes of social reality. Within this context, they can be read as a literary variety of multispecies ethnography, concerned with the representation of human and animal lives situated in the socioeconomic systems which constitute them. In fact, both Rosa and Kosby performed some kind of field research before they wrote about life in the ranching system. While Rosa traveled with cowhands as they traversed the landscape to bring the cattle from ranches to train stations and back, Kosby worked as an anthropologist, doing ethnographic work in pastoral communities.[2] Both also had familiar intimacy with those worlds, having been raised in close contact with cattle in rural areas, which added a personal dimension to their writing. However, the texts they wrote in the wake of such experiences do not take for granted either the immediacy of experience or their own ability to communicate it.

While maintaining a realist orientation, these texts foreground their own mediating function, and thus face the ethical and aesthetic questions of representation head-on. How to capture the situated perspectives of the people and the animals involved in cattle raising systems? How to fabricate a language that does justice to those perspectives, in terms of both aesthetic sensibility and ethical interpellation? The intersection of rural labor—organized along gender lines—and animal life, which their authors encountered in the field, made them face class, species, and gender divides at the same time. Such a conundrum, instead of silencing expression, becomes for them the occasion to turn the literary text into a site of encounter, but also of *desencontro*, to use the Portuguese word chosen by Michael Marder to describe interspecies contact. For Marder, this word evokes the "narrowly missed meeting, a crossing of paths that was about to happen but ended up not taking place" (13). If the literary text can "bridge the divide" between forms of life, as Vieira contends, Marder suggests that such a bridge is hurled into space with no guarantee to take one where one hoped to arrive. Rather, such acts of bridging embed a utopian disposition, indicative more of a desire to understand the voice of nonhuman beings than of any success in actually doing so.

Rosa and Kosby grapple with the utopian *desencontro* in the critical ethico-epistemological moment of representation, when literary speech risks betraying the animal voice. Fellow poet Angélica Freitas, who coauthored the afterword of Kosby's book, explicitly articulates this question: "Uma vaca faz um baita esforço para mugir. Como se traduz 'muuuu?' Como se faz para não trair, mais uma vez, a vaca?" ("A cow makes a great effort to 'moo.' How do you translate 'moo'? How do you not betray the cow once again?") (*Mugido* 107). To address this possibility of "betrayal," the works of Rosa and Kosby advance distinct aesthetic and ethical programs for the mediation of animal voices in literature, each imagining in different ways animals' capacity for self-expression as well as literary speech's capacity for capturing such expression. I synthesize Rosa's as a program of fabulation and suspension, and Kosby's as a program of translation and interruption. In what follows, I elaborate on the meaning of those terms.

Bovine Dialogues

Sagarana is a collection of stories set in the Cerrado, a tropical savanna historically and culturally connected to cattle ranching. In the twentieth century, the region was conceived as an agricultural and populational frontier in the Brazilian interior. The nine stories of *Sagarana* depict the life of that region's cowboys, which involves the habitual but dangerous work of driving cattle through the landscape, but also its political, religious, and sexual institutions, often marked by violence. Rosa's writing incorporates the rhythms and vocabularies of oral expression in the Cerrado, as well as the minutiae of the landscape. Any given page will be punctuated both by the lexicon of the region and by constant references to the local fauna and flora. Rosa collected this archive of minutiae in several travels undertaken through the Cerrado alongside the region's cowhands, in which he carefully jotted down their language and his impressions of the landscape.

Rosa's immense critical reception has gone through many phases, alternatively emphasizing his work's relation to regionalism, Brazilian history, or narratological theory, to give a few examples.[3] More recently, his interest in mediating nature has become central in the work of ecocritical scholars like Victoria Saramago and Ashley Brock, whose readings of Rosa emphasize how the materiality of his language is part of the ethical injunction produced by his work. Such readings focus on Rosa's later masterpiece *Grande Sertão: Veredas* (1956), which dominates discussions about Rosa's work. Nevertheless, his longform stories—and "Oxen Talk" in particular—have started to receive more attention in debates related to animal studies. Works informed by the anthropology of science and philosophy of animality have emphasized the mediating potential of literary language, claiming for it a "hybrid power" (Freitas and Carvalho 76) capable of capturing and expressing what I have been calling the animal voice.[4] While I appreciate these authors' centering of literary speech in the work of mediation, I diverge from them in drawing attention to the possibility of betrayal inherent in such work.

Among the stories of *Sagarana*, two of them center the perspective of the animals that participate in the multispecies environment of cattle ranching in the Cerrado. "O burrinho pedrês" ("The beige donkey") and "Conversa de bois" adopt different strategies to represent the life of animals. "O burrinho pedrês" utilizes a third-person narrative focus to suggest the phenomenological experience of a humble donkey as he goes along with a group of cattle drivers who end up victims of a flood. Although the story attributes great dignity to the character of the donkey, it never intrudes in what might be construed as his inner life, keeping instead a respectful distance. The donkey serves, on the one hand, as an observer of the dynamics among the cowhands that play out in that story, and on the other as survivor of the tragedy that befalls them. But, because he doesn't speak, this lone escapee cannot tell the story of that tragedy.

By contrast, "Conversa de bois" is organized around the titular "talk" among cart oxen, who are auxiliary narrators of the story. The fact of this conversation is what justifies the introductory paragraph mentioned above, in which the narrator ponders about the animal's ability to speak. In response to that question, the narrator's interlocutor, a bird catcher named Manoel Timborna, emphatically affirms: "Falam, sim senhor, falam! [Os bois] são os mais! . . . Boi fala o tempo todo" ("They do! They do! . . . Oxen most of all. They talk all the time") (*Sagarana* 326). Timborna then shares with the narrator a story about oxen's talking, the story which is presented to the reader as the fulcrum of "Conversa de bois." In this story, a young oxcart driver named Tiãozinho is briefly able to partake in a conversation among oxen, an event which produces a shift in the boy's fate, as I explain in more detail below. If on the level of the plot becoming privy to the bovine dialogue is a climactic incident, on the level of reading it is the whole point, as the title itself suggests.

The stories in *Sagarana* are difficult to summarize, since they are usually composed of long sequences of scenes that extend the kernel of the plot through multiple digressions. In "Conversa de bois," the core narrative is the story of Tiãozinho, a young boy who is helping an oxcart driver lead his vehicle through the landscape. As the story unfolds, we discover that the cart holds a coffin containing the corpse of Tiãozinho's father and a load of *rapadura* (unrefined sugar blocks). The driver, Agenor Soronho, has been courting Tiãozinho's mother since before the sickly father's death, and he constantly mistreats the boy and the oxen. Deep in unelaborated grief, Tiãozinho resents the mother and hates Agenor. At some point along the way, both Tiãozinho and Agenor start to fall asleep. Half-asleep, Tiãozinho engages in a conversation with the oxen in which their individual personalities are mingled, and in which he/they manifest the wish that Agenor would die. Tiãozinho wakes up startled, startling the oxen in turn and making them go faster. The abrupt movement makes the sleepy Agenor fall off the cart and be crushed under its wheels. The story ends with Tiãozinho driving the cart—which now carries two corpses—by himself.

This core narrative is extended and punctuated by other micro episodes, usually involving the encounter with other oxcart drivers traversing the landscape. More importantly, the core narrative runs parallel to the "oxen talk" that gives the story its title. This subplot follows its own structure, which converges with the story of Tiãozinho at the climactic moment of Agenor's death. It is a kind of Platonic dialogue in which each one of the eight oxen driving the cart—carefully described as individual animals when they first appear—alternate sharing their impressions about being an ox driving a cart through the landscape in the company of two men. Their dialogue revolves around issues of identity and difference between oxen and men, and culminates with the story, or fable, of Rodapião, an ox who plays the role of tragic hero in his quest to think for himself and submit the landscape to his wishes (in other words, to become a man). The dialogue between the oxen offers the privileged perspective into

Tiãozinho's story. As the story progresses, it is through their speech that we come to learn much about Tiãozinho's actions and even feelings. In this sense, their speech is mixed up with that of the narrator, whose work of narration they share. To give an example, in their conversation one of the oxen recalls the time he saw Agenor—whom he describes phenomenologically as "homem-do-pau-comprido-com-o-marimbondo-na-ponta," in reference to the pointy stick used to drive the cattle—"correr de uma vaca," a mention that helps characterizing the older human as cowardly and somewhat pathetic ("The-man-of-the-long-stick-with-a-hornet-at-the-tip . . . running from a cow") (*Sagarana* 331).

In fact, the oxen's dialogue, which mediates Tiãozinho's story, is presented to us as already mediated, not once, but three times. Initially skeptical, the narrator agrees to hear Timborna's story if, and only if, he can later tell it again, reviewed and expanded ("diferente, enfeitado e acrescentado ponto e pouco" ["different, embellished, expanded here and there"]), presumably the story we are now reading. As the story begins, it is initially focalized from the point of view of an *irara* (*E. barbara,* a mustelid found across South and Central America) who observes the scene being set for the main plot, from the details of the landscape to the characters of Agenor, Tiãozinho, and the oxen. Only a few pages later do we learn that the *irara* (who is called Risoleta) is the one telling herself the story to Manoel Timborna, who captured her and demands a story in exchange for her freedom. Thus, in sum, the story of Tiãozinho is overheard from the oxen and observed by the *irara,* who tells it in exchange for her freedom to Manoel Timborna, who tells it in exchange for the right to retell it to the narrator, who writes it down for the readers. This series of exchanges and shifts in perception is as much the subject of "Conversa de bois," if not more, as the story of Tiãozinho. This complex structure of mediation is reflected in the texture of the language used by Rosa's narrator, who abundantly resorts to onomatopoeia to register the soundscape of the story.

Indeed, in the climax of Tiãozinho's story, the superposition of voices that characterizes this style becomes part of the plot, as Tiãozinho, falling asleep, starts to lose himself in the oxen talk. At this point, the talk overcomes the narrator completely, as their voices—indicated by long dashes—alternate in describing what is happening to Tiãozinho and Agenor. Tiãozinho, who had already been ontologically approximated to the oxen (they call him "bezerro-de-homem," "man calf"), now is grammatically equated to them. In a sequence of alternating direct speech, the individual identities of the steers and of Tiãozinho become lost in a confusion of names, pronouns, and onomatopoeia: "Mhú! Hmoung!

. . . Boi . . . Bezerro-de-homem . . . Mas, eu sou o boi Capitão! . . . Moung! . . . Não há nenhum boi Capitão . . . Mas, todos os bois . . . Não há bezerro-de-homem! . . . Todos . . . Tudo . . . Tudo é enorme . . . Eu sou enorme! . . . Sou grande e forte . . . Mais do que seu Agenor Soronho! . . . Posso vingar meu pai . . ." ("Moo! Moo! . . . Ox . . . Man-calf . . . But I am the ox Capitão! . . . Moo! . . . There is no ox Capitão . . . But every ox . . . There is no man-calf! . . . Everyone . . . Everything . . . Everything is immense . . . I am immense . . . I am big and strong . . . Stronger than Agenor Soronho! . . . I can avenge my father . . . !") (*Sagarana* 359). As the sequence proceeds, Tiãozinho-turned-oxen decides to stop the cart and make Agenor fall to his death. At this point, the identification between Tiãozinho and the oxen is complete—ontological, grammatical, and agentive—but lasts only for a second, as Agenor's death brings him out of his dreamy state.

Briefly guilty about what happened, Tiãozinho asks the virgin for forgiveness, but ends the story happy with his triumph. Having taken upon himself the strength of the steers, Little Cowboy Hamlet was able to kill the stepfather and dreamed of becoming himself the ranching patriarch: "Quem manda agora na nossa cafua sou eu . . . Eu, Tiãozinho! . . . Sou grande, sou dono de muitas terras, com muitos carros de bois, com muitas juntas . . ." ("I rule our den now . . . Me, Tiãozinho! . . . I am large, I am the owner of much land, with many oxcarts, many yokes . . .") (*Sagarana* 360). Thus, Tiãozinho's communion with the oxen can be read as a final foray into the world of infancy before he steps into violent male adulthood for good. By infancy, I invoke here the nexus of childhood, animality, and speechlessness that Rosa himself alludes to more than once in the story. In the initial dialogue with Manoel Timborna, the erudite narrator quotes a passage from the *Georgics* in Latin, in which Virgil refers to the "obscure night in which the cattle talked," and characterizes the event as "Infandum!," which means "unspeakable" in both the epistemological and the moral sense. Later, as Tiãozinho begins to lose himself in the steer talk, the oxen "quote" Virgil in their description of the human kid as closer to them than the adults: "O bezerro-de-homem sabe mais, às vezes . . . Ele vive muito perto de nós, e ainda é bezerro . . . [. . .] Quando está meio dormindo, pensa quase como nós bois . . . [. . .] Se encosta em nós, no escuro . . . No mato-escuro-de-todos-bois . . . Tenho medo de que ele entenda a nossa conversa . . ." ("The man-calf knows more, sometimes . . . He lives close to us, he is still a calf . . . When he is half-asleep, he thinks almost like us . . . He comes near in the dark . . . In the dark-bush-of-all-the-oxen . . . I'm afraid he understands our talk . . .") (*Sagarana* 358).

The steer's fear of being understood is justified by the outcome of Tiãozinho's entanglement of languages, as he is able to master the bovine will into killing Agenor. This element of the plot represents the betrayal of the animal voice in Rosa's story. The plot of "Conversa de bois," like much of *Sagarana*, revolves around male jealousy. Tiãozinho is resentful of his mother and blames her, incapable of sympathizing with her own predicament. By killing his "uncle," he stands alone as master of animals and women and can lose the "inho" that defined his minority (in the middle of the mixed speech he says, "Sou Tião!"). Tiãozinho's flight into animality resolves into the familiar plot of heteropatriarchal masculinity. The story also ends there, as Tião is apparently joined in his joy by the oxcart itself, whose sound celebrates his victory: "E talvez até dois defuntos deem mais para a viagem, pois até o carro está contente—renhein . . . nhein . . .—e abre a goela do chumaço, numa toada triunfal" ("And perhaps two corpses even contribute with the journey, for even the oxcart is joyful—renhein-nhein—and opens the throat on a triumphant melody") (*Sagarana* 362). This final sentence ironically encapsulates the dangers of language and interpretation, as the noise of the oxcart straining under the weight of two corpses *sounds as* a triumphant celebration.

Although we never learn of the narrator's reaction to Manoel Timborna's story, the story we are reading presumably encapsulates that reaction. By beginning with the extended account of how the story was passed along, Rosa highlights that the account is always of another account, and it is stories all the way down. By emphasizing his own fabulation—how he told Timborna he would retell the story "different, embellished, and expanded here and there"—he underlines his role as mediator of someone else's story, and his own unreliability as a witness. Indeed, the story's title word, "conversa," can be understood in the double meaning of "conversation, dialogue" and "lie, tall tale." Finally, by ending with the ironic description of the oxcart's behavior, Rosa foregrounds the ambivalence of sound, and thus of language itself. All these stances amount to a commentary on the story's own mediating power. Like Tiãozinho, the reader partakes in the "steer talk," but unlike him, we are not able to channel this entanglement of languages into efficacious action—at least not immediately. Should we be able to do it, would we, like Tiãozinho, use this entanglement to "say" what we would have said anyway? Would we betray the intimacy with the thoughts and words of the oxen? Rosa's story warns against the danger of such entanglement while his fictional artifice saves the voice at the moment of its betrayal, when it will be condemned to repeat the already-existing story. Through fabulation and irony, he keeps the story—the voices—at a remove from the reader, and thus suspended in the realm of undecidability of fiction.

A Closed Throat

Marília Floôr Kosby's poetry collection *Mugido* (2017) adds a new chapter in the cultural history of the cattle ranch in Brazilian literature. Drawing from her personal and professional experience as anthropologist and the daughter of a veterinarian that took care of farm animals in Rio Grande do Sul, Kosby reconstructs the existential space of small towns in the south of Brazil, where family-owned ranches raise and sometimes kill animals for the meat plants that supply the city. Although the South is a different ranching system from the one in the Cerrado, it shares with it a similar social and cultural history premised on the frontier as political and imaginary space. While the work of Rosa—one of Brazil's most important mid-century writers—can be seen as the culmination of the secular interest, on the part of Brazilian artists and intellectuals, in the aestheticized life-worlds of *vaqueiros*, Kosby is a contemporary poet whose work challenges and renovates the regionalist tradition of cattle literature by centering on women and animals, instead of the heroic figure of the male cowboy. While some of these elements can be found in Rosa's work, the writing of Kosby invites a renewed attention to such matters, unsettling previous reading habits and unquestioned assumptions. Most importantly for us, the assumption of the univocity of the literary text.

Kosby's work departs from the point where Rosa had led us, the equivocality of language. Her investment in heterogeneity and equivocation is visible in many aspects of the book, starting with the full title, *Mugido: ou diários de uma doula* ("Cow bellow; or the journals of a doula"), which combines a signifier of cattle expression—the bellow—with the archetypical genre of written human selfhood—the journal. This ambiguity characterizes the texts in the book, which present themselves both as raw feeling (defamiliarized through the intervention of poetic language) and collected observation. Kosby combines the perspective of the local, tied to the ranching landscape by kinship, and of the ethnographer, whose sharp discourse carefully describes how the practices of manhood in the area are molded in relation with women, horses, and cows; how practices of womanhood constitute themselves in relation with figures of masculinity, femininity, and care toward animals; and how this bundle of gender and species relations are connected to the food industry, which in its turn links small towns to the big city, in a large territorial distribution of positions and effects. While centering both the body and the embodied experience in her evocations of the life and death of human and nonhuman animals, she always engages with embodiment as traversed, on the one hand, by systems of relations and affects, and as producing, on the other, discourses that elaborate and rationalize its own phenomenology.

Besides this intensive combination of aesthetics and analytics, Kosby also makes polyvocality explicit by alternating the poems—which presumably all have the same speaker or voice—with a narrative in prose that ties the book together and focuses on the daughter of a veterinarian who follows her father to a farm, to attend to a cow that is having trouble giving birth. There she finds Jaqueline, the wife of the owner, who suffers herself because of the animal, while her son and husband mock her for feeling that for a cow. In the difficult birth, "daughter" and "wife" support each other, as well as the cow. This narrative serves as background for the poems, which observe "from the inside" experiences of pain, violence, and discomfort. Similarly, the book ends with an afterword by poet Angélica Freitas, who also interviews the author about her personal experience in the Southern ranching system. Far from being a fungible paratext, this afterword integrates the project of *Mugido.* It concludes the series of ambivalences that mark the work—between vocal bellow and written journal, embodiment and discourse, lyric mimesis and narrative explanation, individual authorship and collective participation—and opens it up to the "outside" of the text. Like Rosa, Kosby institutes dialogue—the fact that an utterance always takes place in a potential responsive structure—as the framework of her text, but unlike him she does not subsume dialogue in the single discourse of the author. Where Rosa begins with a dialogue he is solely responsible for, she ends with a dialogue that brings in another voice.

The aforementioned opening poem of *Mugido,* like an epic preface, establishes the plan of the ensemble:

"mmmmmm"

mais ou menos que um livro,
isto é um êxodo
de uma tal condição
humana
o mugido foi a ação escolhida para essa desarticulação
parem para ver uma vaca mugir
já nem digo ouvir
ouvir é difícil, o mugido de uma vaca
parem pra ver e procurem a próxima nota
em que palavra daria

aquela melodia
aquele esforço todo
de guela, olho, bucho, língua, rúmen
que fecunda epifania valeria
aquele esforço todo?
Traduzam
o mugido
(*Mugido* 11)

The poem's title, "mmmmmm," suggests through the repetition of the letter "m" the low and prolonged sound of the bellow. The first four lines describe what the reader has in hand: "more or less than a book, / this is an exodus / of such a so-called / human condition. / The *mugido* was the action chosen for this disarticulation." In these lines, the work, which looks like a book, is performatively unequated with a book: it is either more or less, and not exactly the same thing. This quantum of difference—this *desencontro* between being and not being—is what sends the human condition on an exodus, an escape, a fugue. However, in Portuguese, "exôdo de uma tal condição humana" can mean that the "condição humana" is either that which is going away itself or that *from* which one runs away. The word used to describe this movement is disarticulation, which can refer both to the articulations that allow a body to move and to the articulation that enables speech. This sequence of ambiguous constructions right at the beginning establish *Mugido* as in-between book and bellow, body and speech. If the *mugido* is what disarticulates the human condition, it is not only because animal sounds are not considered speech, one of the ontological seats of the so-called human condition, but also because the *mugido* is right in the middle of the word "humana." One cannot say "condição humana" without producing a quick *mugido.* The *mugido* meddles in the words. Therefore, the *mugido* is not in stark opposition to human speech, but is part of it in a surprising way. Only by going through the *mugido* can "human condition" wind up.

The second stanza in the poem-exordium changes from the descriptive mode to the exhortative. It invites us to: "stop and watch a mooing cow. / I won't even say listen /—listening is difficult—to the moo of a cow: / Stop and watch and look for the next note, / in which word would / that melody end up, / all that effort / of throat, eye, tripe, tongue, rumen." Here, again, Kosby plays with binomials. Watching and listening as two modes of apprehending a certain reality. The reader cannot listen to the cow because the cow is not present, but transformed into text, which can only be seen. However, the nature of text is such that, even if the visual element predominates, it is connected to the phonic basis of verbal language. In the case of written poetry, visuality and sound participate both in a strong manner. In this poem, rhymes and alliteration intervene to make the sonic dimension explicit.

However, if sound and vision can be in opposition, they also share the quality of being senses that allow for the transmission of information through a distance. The poetic speaker urges the reader to watch and maybe listen to the *mugido,* but we cannot touch it, let alone feel with our internal senses the production of the *mugido,* as the cow does with her "throat, eye, tripe, tongue, rumen." It is this body full of organs that, through "effort," emits a "melody" that can end up in a word that signifies the human condition. The body participates in the production of the *mugido,* and if our body can also produce a *mugido,* maybe we are not that different from the cow, after all. Nevertheless, the meaning of the *mugido* is not reducible to the performance of a sound. It is a bodily function expressing some kind of deep feeling not easily translated into human language. Before we translate, before we even listen, we must "stop to watch." It is a break in discourse and reasoning, a moment of silence and attention. Kosby brings to the contact with cows an ethnographic sensibility that recommends prudence with the displacing powers of language. Knowing that every translator must be a betrayer, she performs an ethics of untranslatability founded on the *breaking up* of discourse. The *moo* "disjoints" the so-called human condition because it (*mmmmmm*), the humming low-pitch sound made by cows, is right there, in the middle of the word "human."

The poem ends with a question and a last exhortation: "what fruitful epiphany / would all that effort be worth? / Translate the *mugido.*" The mention of an epiphany inevitably recalls the idea of the sublime, that which transcends human condition, that which is defined, in Longinus, Kant, and the romantics, as the expansion and annihilation of human perceptions and consciousness. However, if the sublime transcendence moves in the direction of an absolute without reference, the transcendence of the *mugido* is that of an exchange from a particular point of view to another, limited in the same manner, but not in the same intensity. That is why the poetic speaker tells us to "translate the mugido." Her goal is not to convert human language into the language of God, but into the language of a cow. The movement between woman and cow is analogous to, and actually goes through, the movement between languages. In other poems in the collection, Kosby will play with the border between languages, especially that between Portuguese and Spanish, so relevant in the south of Brazil. This procedure stands as a correlative for the translation of the animal voice. Therefore, Kosby approximates the experience of listening to the bellow to that of learning a foreign language, which is always partial and effacing. There's no forgetting the mother tongue just like there's no abandoning the human condition for good. But there's learning a new language just like there's listening to the cow's bellow.

In another poem in the collection, Kosby imagines a dog gnawing the discarded spinal bone of a sheep in the patio of a meat factory. While the sheep "mal esperneou pra morrer" ("barely fidgeted about dying"), the dog spends the whole night "escarrando a espinha" ("spittling the spinal bone") (*Mugido* 45). In other words, his throat is closed by the bone which, just like the letter m, "tem três pontinhas / fininhas" ("has three slim / tips"). He is compelled to keep that memory (of violence, of animality), ruminating on its meaning. This image figures *Mugido* as a project of mediation of the animal voice—and of what it says about the violence visited on human and nonhuman bodies. It signifies the procedure of interruption of previous discourses (on gender), concepts (of animality), and genres (of regionalist literature) that the collection performs, and thus makes the reader *stay with the trouble* of the untranslatable animal voice.

Conclusion

Both partial (because recognizing that human condition cannot be abandoned for good) and aspirational (because enjoining the reader to translate anyway), Kosby's program for the literary mediation of the animal voice complements Rosa's as a model of the utopian *desencontro.* While Rosa recommended irony and reserve in the face of the equivocality of language, Kosby advances a discourse ethically committed to animals while highly conscious of its own in-betweenness. These alternative models of mediation are, I contend, useful critical tools for the analysis of texts concerned with animals and other nonhuman beings. To the extent that a literary text is able to mediate, however utopianly, the voice of nonhumans, critical attention must be paid to the modes of its expression and the context of its circulation. If, as McKay suggests, representation is ambiguously situated between aesthetic and political implications, its critical mediation should highlight the limits and possibilities of literary expression in each case, without resorting to generalities which, in the worst case, betray the specificity of nonhuman voices.

Notes

1. All translations are mine.

2. For more on Kosby's fieldwork, see her article "Mulheres, vacas e partos na pecuária do extremo sul do Brasil." Rosa's most famous field trip happened in 1952, as registered in *A Boiada.*

3. For each of these themes, see Candido, Bolle, and Merrim.

4. Besides Freitas and Carvalho, see also Bühler and Melo, Hermann for similar positions.

Works Cited

Bolle, Willi. *Grandesertão.br: o romance de formação do Brasil.* Livraria Duas Cidades, 2004.

Brock, Ashley. *Dwelling in Fiction: Poetics of Place and the Experimental Novel in Latin America.* Northwestern University Press, 2023.

Bühler, Andréa Morais C., and Jorrana Ferreira de Melo. "A contação dos bois: uma leitura sobre as vozes bovinas no conto 'Conversa de bois,' na obra Sagarana." *Revista Estação Literária,* vol. 17, 2016, pp. 114–134.

Candido, Antonio. "Jagunços Mineiros de Cláudio a Guimarães Rosa." *Vários escritos.* Livraria Duas Cidades, 1977.

Freitas, Gabriela Pereira de, and Rhaysa Novakoski Carvalho. "Imagens de um devir-animal: entre literatura e ilustração no conto 'Conversa de bois,' de Guimarães Rosa." *Revista Mídia e Cotidiano,* vol. 15, no. 2, 2021, pp. 75–98.

Hermann, Victor. "Poderão os bichos falar? A biologia do linguajear em 'Conversa de Bois,' de Guimarães Rosa." *Anuário de Literatura,* vol. 28, 2023, pp. 1–15.

Kosby, Marília Floôr. *Mugido: ou diários de uma doula.* Garupa, 2017.

Kosby, Marília Floôr. "Mulheres, vacas e partos nas pecuários do extremo Sul do Brasil: relações transespecíficas a partir do encontro entre antropologia e epistemologias feministas." *Tessituras,* vol. 7, no. 1, 2019, pp. 94–105.

Marder, Michael. *Plant-thinking: A Philosophy of Vegetal Life.* Columbia University Press, 2013.

McKay, Robert R. "Representation." *Critical Terms for Animal Studies,* edited by Lori Gruen, University of Chicago Press, 2018, pp. 307–319.

Merrim, Stephanie. "Sagarana: A Story System." *Hispania,* vol. 66, no. 4, 1983, pp. 502–510.

Rosa, João Guimarães. *A Boiada.* Nova Fronteira, 2011.

Rosa, João Guimarães. *Sagarana.* Nova Fronteira, 2001.

Saramago, Victoria. "Birds, Rivers, Book: Material Mimesis in João Guimarães Rosa's Grande Sertão: Veredas." *Luso-Brazilian Review*, vol. 57, no. 1, 2020, pp. 125–149.

Vieira, Patrícia. "Amazonian Ecopoetics: Paes Loureiro's Shamanic Zoophytography." *Romance Studies*, vol. 41, no. 1, 2023, pp. 54–64.

6

Languages of Life

Biosemiotics and Living Systems of Plants and Animals in Contemporary Mexican Poetry

BRIAN T. CHANDLER

Plants and animals have long featured prominently in Mexican cultural imaginaries, from the Mexica foundational myth of the eagle atop the *nopal* cactus, itself subsumed into the modern nation-state's iconography, the cosmic ceiba as world tree of the Maya, the scent of marigolds on the Day of the Dead, to the assertion that *mexicanidad* (Mexicanness) is best portrayed in the amphibious axolotl and its capacity to inspire metaphors of metamorphosis and melancholy (Bartra 25). Such anthropocentric treatment of flora and fauna over the years is captured in the verses of poet Alberto Blanco who assesses, "Extraño destino el de las plantas / . . . / Quedan ligadas indeleblemente a los avatares del sueño humano" (Strange destiny that of plants / . . . / They are linked indelibly to the avatars of human dream)[1] (113). Similarly reflecting a growing awareness of the problematic anthropocentric treatment of animals and plants in literature, in recent years there has been a proliferation of lyrical works by Mexican writers that attempt to reorient the relationships between humans, plants, and animals. In particular, many of these authors engage plants and animals through a special focus on communicative and relational systems in the more-than-human world. A generation of poets including Marco Antonio Rodríguez Murillo, Elisa Díaz Castelo, Karen Villeda, Isabel Zapata, and Maricela Guerrero are looking to plant, animal, fungal, and microbial networks to lyrically portray interrelations between all living things while depicting potential models of human existence that contrast with those that have driven the ecological crises of the Anthropocene. Central to many of these works of poetry is the question of language, both in its representational and symbolic function in human and animal communication as well as a more expansive understanding of language as biosemiotic action in and among all living systems, including those of plants, fungi, and microbes. As we will see in an analysis of these features in Maricela Guerrero's *El sueño de toda célula* (*The Dream of Every Cell*) and Isabel Zapata's *Una ballena es un país* (*A Whale is a Country*), these poets blur the distinctions between a human-centered model of semiosis and the more-than-human biosemiosis in order to highlight interrelationality and interdependency both within human society as well as in and among organisms in the more-than-human world, illustrating and imagining ethical responses to contest and counter extractivism and anthropocentrism.

While anthropomorphism has long been a feature in conceptions of nonhuman organisms in Latin American and Mexican literature, their depiction frequently reflects the region's heterogeneous positioning of plants, animals, and humans. As in the case of literary engagement with plants we see that often these conceptualizations are not simply repetitions of Western tropes, but rather signal relationships and connectivities between humans and plants that are actually fundamental to counterhegemonic identities (Wylie 4). The region's heterogeneity regarding human and more-than-human relationships is shaped in part by Indigenous cosmologies, its diverse ecologies, as well as a history of resistance to environmental degradation, all of which "provide fertile ground for dialogues about divergent visions of progress, selfhood, ecology, and society" (Ponce de León 130). As such, Latin American authors are uniquely positioned to depict, challenge, and imagine both current and potential human and more-than-human ecologies, yet their works often are not considered in scholarship on animal and plant studies produced outside the region. Far from being a recent phenomenon, for centuries Latin American authors have advocated for the interest of animals and explored the agency of nonhuman beings, engaging questions of animal ethics through novels, poetry, and fictional works (DeVries 2). Mexican literature features these same legacies of human and more-than-human entanglements, yet in the late 2010s a further turn began to emerge in lyrical works that engage the relational connections between plants, animals, and humans in innovative ways. The publication of Maricela Guerrero's *El sueño de toda célula* (*The Dream of Every Cell*), Elisa Díaz Castelo's *Principia*, Jorge

Gutiérrez Reyna's *El otro nombre de los árboles* (*The Other Name of the Trees*), and Marco Antonio Rodríguez Murillo's *Tal vez el crecimiento de un jardín sea la única forma en que los muertos pueden hablarnos* (*Maybe the Growth of a Garden Is the Only Way the Dead Can Speak to Us*) in 2018 as well as Isabel Zapata's *Una ballena es un país* (*A Whale is a Country*) in 2019, among others, signal a clear shift in Mexican lyrical production toward the more-than-human world, taking up the activity of *poeisis*, that is the creation of or emergence of something that did not previously exist, along with *biosemiosis*, the meaning-making processes that feature in all living systems. Undoubtedly, these works are a subset of what Carolyn Fornoff identifies as "planetary poetics" in recent Mexican poetry, where poets transcend the limits of the nation-state or themes of *mexicanidad*, mapping alternative geographies and timescales to "broach matters of planetary concern in ways that reach beyond national borders and even the bounds of species. These spatial, temporary, and ontological jumps are a defining characteristic of contemporary Mexican poetry concerned with environmental themes" (232). Within the context of ecological crisis, plants and animals feature prominently in these poems through a presence and portrayal that overtly problematizes traditional anthropomorphic inscriptions upon flora and fauna, reversing conceptual movement to resituate humans and notions of human subjectivity within greater more-than-human systems, processes, and relations.

While all differ in their subject matter and lyrical and thematic treatment of plants and animals, these works share three common characteristics. The first is a concerted engagement with the social and ecological impacts of extractivism and human activity on the more-than-human world, often offering speculative imaginings that ethically engage interspecies interconnectivity and coexistence. Second, these works problematize anthropocentric notions of human subjectivity by placing humans and all living organisms within deeper evolutionary timescales and more expansive ecological systems, highlighting interdependence and interconnectivity. Finally, these poems frequently appropriate scientific knowledge and concepts, portraying biosemiotic communication as a feature of all living systems. As we will see in Isabel Zapata's and Maricela Guerrero's representative works, these poets utilize these strategies to lyrically interface with plants and animals within their ecologies, focusing on concepts of communication within and across organisms, species, and their environments.

Central to the idea of communication in the poems is an expansive understanding of languages, sign relations, and semiosis. Contrary to the more widely held view that semiosis—the process in which a sign stands for, represents, and communicates a meaning that is not the sign itself—is somehow a unique attribute of human language and culture, the activity of sign processes and relations both between and within all organisms is actually a ubiquitous and central feature of the biological world (Favareau 2). In their treatment of plants, animals, and other organisms, these poets lyrically portray many features of biosemiotics, a multifaceted approach to semiosis in living systems built upon the central idea "that all life—from the cell all the way up to us—is characterized by communication, or semiosis" (Wheeler 270). Contemporary biosemiotics has its beginnings in Charles Sanders Peirce's logic of relations which posits that all biological systems are relational and these relations themselves also become representable as signs (Favareau 40–41). Through this web of signs, Peirce avers, "all this universe is perfused with signs, if it is not composed exclusively of signs" (394). In a similar manner, biologist Jakob von Uexküll articulates how all organisms function within their *Umwelten* (216), signifying worlds that emerge from the continual cycling between their external semiotic environments and their inner semiotic worlds with "each making each in a ceaseless living ecological process" (Wheeler 272). Incorporating the work of von Uexküll and Peirce, Thomas Sebeok first articulates zoosemiotics, famously refuting the capacity for human language in nonhuman animals while at the same time expanding our understanding of the semiosphere to encompass the entire biosphere, arguing that, "the process of message exchanges, or semiosis, is an indispensable characteristic of all terrestrial life forms" (22). Biosemiotics has branched out and expanded from these first conceptualizations to examine semiotic processes in areas as diverse as genetics, biological and chemical signaling, informational exchange between species, and evolutionary development. Central to all of these is the key notion that all organisms and life processes—animal, vegetal, or otherwise—feature semiosis in signs, codes, interpretations, and other communicative processes.[2] This more expansive understanding of language challenges anthropocentric notions of subjectivity, wherein coordinated actions of communication are not "the mechanical result of an individuated living subject (plant or otherwise) but as an ecology produced by organisms in an interdependent and multispecies interrelation" (Gagliano et al., xviii).

Such insights from biosemiotics into animal, plant, and human communication, language, and ecology are paradoxically occurring at a time when the impacts of human activity on the environment and ecosystem continue to propel the world into deeper social and ecological crisis. In engaging in these themes, contemporary Mexican poets frequently eschew the prior apocalyptic registers regarding extinction and planetary fragility (Fornoff 235), to instead offer clear-eyed assessments of the present-day environmental situation alongside hopeful imaginings and speculative worlds, reflecting a trend of "ecological imagination" in works of Latin American literature that "recuperate a sense of place" and "posit an ecocentric agenda that valorizes nonhuman nature" (Barbas-Rhoden 2). These poets frequently tap into scientific knowledge and discourse to draw attention to the complexity of more-than-human life, highlighting examples of interdependence and interconnectivity in ecological systems. At the same time, these works reflect the complex ways that science, scientific knowledge, and science writing have been generated and deployed in the region throughout the last five centuries, frequently transculturating the very same scientific discourse to depict in equal measure how the natural sciences and technology can be used for either destructive or life-affirming ends.

Biosemiotic Bodies and the Question of Animal Language in *Una ballena es un país*

In Isabel Zapata's *Una ballena es un país,* historical and scientific depictions of extinct animal species as well those in danger of extinction are intercalated with poems that examine the mythic jackelope or offer a litany of reasons why we humans should not step on snails. Throughout, the poet is aware of her anthropocentric positioning yet at the same time works to upend and challenge anthropomorphic conceptualizations, as when she vacillates in the poem "Espermaceti" between affirmations that whales resemble humans in many ways and statements echoed in the final verse of the poem that assert that "Las ballenas no se parecen a nosotros" (Whales do not resemble us) (26). She observes how "Sus dientes son troncos: / si cortas uno a la mitad puedes leer en él la edad de la ballena. / Las ballenas se parecen más a las secuoyas de California que a nosotros" (Their teeth are trunks: / if you cut one in half you can read in it the age of the whale. / Whales are more like the redwoods of California than us) (26). While these verses at first appear as yet another metaphoric inscription upon the body of a whale, when the poet holds together the teeth and the redwoods in synecdochic relation, a plurality of interconnectivities open up between the animal and the plant, evoking their respective existence and evolution over timescales of magnitudes that tower above the human. These transspecies and transtemporal configurations constitute an example of what Astrida Neimanis and Rachel Loewen Walker term "thick time," "a transcorporeal stretching between present, future, and past, that foregrounds a nonchronological durationality" (561). Bringing together species across diverging temporalities and timescales demonstrates the many concentric nested semiotic systems that are active within and among living entities, human and nonhuman. Likewise, the explorations of language in *Una ballena es un país* encompass not only animal communication, but also a biosemiotic model of evolutionary systems in which all organisms feature embodied, stratified communicative systems that have evolved with each layer over time increasingly rich in communication (Wheeler 272):

> Las ballenas fueron animales terrestres,
> caminaron en tierra firme en forma de pakicétidos:
> zorritos peludos con pezuñas y cola gruesa
> que podían escuchar debajo del agua.
> . . .
> Así como nosotros tenemos muelas de juicio,
> tenemos apéndice, se nos pone la carne gallina,
> ellas tienen un hueso donde estuvo alguna vez
> la pelvis de sus peludos antepasados. (25)
> (Whales were terrestrial animals,
> they walked on dry land in the form of Pakicetidae:
> little furry foxes with hooves and a thick tail
> that were able to hear underwater.
> . . .
> Just as we have wisdom teeth,
> we have an appendix, we get goosebumps,
> they have a bone where once there was
> the pelvis of their furry ancestors)

These thick time depictions of evolutionary change through vestigial organs and behaviors in both humans and whales demonstrate the lyric's "capacity to put multiple temporalities and scales within a single frame, to 'thicken' the present with an awareness of other times and places" (Farrier 9). Whales both resemble and differ from humans in their communicative language as well as in the semiotic systems embodied within their organism. Holding both ideas together, the poet positions humans and whales within common, ongoing evolutionary biosemiotic flows, examples of these features that transcend species and epochs.

Likewise, in the poem "Pulpos" (Octopuses) the poet considers what these cephalopods have in common with humans, beginning with a common ancestor that lived more than 600 million years ago of which the poet confesses the limits of our knowledge through the repeated epiphora “no sabemos más” (we don't know more) (37). In contrast, through a paradoxical configuration the poet here juxtaposes the tangible and the intangible, describing observable factoids about octopuses, their behaviors, their intelligence, and even their exclusion from protocols against animal cruelty, while marveling at their amorphic form and pigment-filled chromatophores. By fusing scientific descriptions of these cells and how they function underneath the cephalopod's skin with lyrical descriptions of its changing appearance, the poet depicts processes of biosemiosis that occur both within the octopus as well as among the matter and other organisms in its surroundings:

> Un cuerpo de pura posibilidad: sin distancia,
> ángulos, esquinas, huesos, recovecos.
> Carne libre de empalmes y articulaciones:
> hongos, pasteles, asteroides,
> manojos de lenguas afelpadas,
> tupidos jardines submarinos,
> tréboles de amor vegetal. (40)
> (A body of pure possibility: without distance,
> angles, corners, bones, nooks.
> Flesh free of joints and articulations:
> mushrooms, cakes, asteroids,
> bunches of plush tongues,
> dense underwater gardens,
> clovers of vegetal love.)

The poetic voice frames the octopus's ability for mimicry in spite of not having a nervous system like that of humans within evolutionary timescales that incorporate common ancestors, upending anthropocentric conceptions of subjectivity, sentience, and communication. The octopus is able to respond to other organisms as well as its environment in remarkable ways, through a nervous system that evolved almost separately from that of humans and noncephalopods, given that “the octopus is suffused with nervousness; the body is not a separate thing that is controlled by the brain or nervous system . . . [it] lives outside the usual body/brain divide” (Godfrey-Smith). With this depiction in mind, the octopus challenges our common conception of cognition as being of the mind, as when the poet remarks, “por eso sienten con el cerebro y piensan con los pies”

(39). Through its engagement with other organisms and its surroundings, the octopus demonstrates how biosemiosis and nonlinguistic sign relations bridge subject-dependent experience with "the inescapable subject independent reality of alterity—an alterity that *all* organisms have to find some way to successfully perceive and act upon in order to maintain themselves in existence" (Favareau 6). In showing the ways communication in humans and other animals converges and diverges, these poems underscore different responses of organisms to their *Umwelten* as well as those evolutionary, nested semiotic systems that are still active within all organisms, transcending species across deep timescales.

The final poem of *Una ballena es un país,* "La voz de las ballenas" (The Voice of Whales), consists of fifteen numbered stanzas that range from scientific and historical facts to musings and subjective observations that have the feel of aphorisms. An example can be found in the second stanza where the poet again overtly challenges anthropomorphic signs ascribed to animal communication, stating that blue whales are known for producing repetitive sounds "con distintas frecuencias que consideramos *cantos*" (with different frequencies that we consider *songs*) (88). The use of the first-person plural along with the italicization of the word *cantos* denoting the poet's doubts stand in stark contrast to a later stanza where the poet counters that "el canto de las ballenas sigue siendo un misterio para los científicos" (the song of whales is still a mystery to scientists) (88). Instead the poet argues that "Esperamos encontrar en los animales virtudes que escasean en nosotros mismos" (We hope to find in animals virtues that are lacking in us) (88), scolding us for projecting human conceptions of language and culture onto animal communication, repeating playfully in several stanzas the idea that "Nada sugiere que las ballenas estén tratando de comunicarse con nosotros" (Nothing suggests that whales are trying to communicate with us) (88). Instead, the lyrical subject contemplates how the activity of communication and semiosis in whales is neither a less-evolved form of human language nor an attempt at interspecies communication, but rather the activity of living organisms that becomes a sort of proof of life in spite of the impacts of human activity. After observing how the tonal frequencies of whales are changing each year possibly due to sound pollution or changing ocean temperatures, the poet states simply that "Sabemos que cantan y esto basta" (We know that they sing and that's enough) (90). *Una ballena es un país* closes with a final stanza that offers a hopeful future for whales, and metonymically all other organisms, as the processes of biosemiosis will continue as long as there is life, closing with the words, "La voz de las ballenas nos sobrevivirá" (The voice of whales will outlast us) (90).

Communication and the Flow of Life in *El sueño de toda célula*

The question of language also serves as a thematic thread that connects the forty-three poems that make up Maricela Guerrero's *El sueño de toda célula.* In this collection the poet fuses childhood memories and conversational registers with scientific discourse and biological concepts to depict networks of interdependency and communication that span diverse spaces, epochs, and species. By utilizing spatial jumps that go back and forth from the level of the cell to entire ecosystems, often within the same verse or stanza, the poet contemplates the lessons about the more-than-human world that she learned as a child which stand in stark contrast to present-day threats and dangers to all living things including plants, animals, and humans due to ongoing extractivism, biological destruction, and economic and political systems that devalue life. In accordance with overarching themes of equilibrium in the collection, Guerrero balances these fear-inducing events ripped from current headlines with real-world examples of hope where humans have practiced care for each other and the more-than-human world. The poet interweaves these actions with depictions of the activity of cells, ecological cycles, and organic networks, demonstrating the interconnectivity and interdependence between humans, plants, and animals. Through the lyrical portrayal of these biosemiotic processes that are a feature of all living organisms, *El sueño de toda célula* presents an overall hopeful and life-affirming tone, underscoring how communication and cooperation are essential to the activity of life.

Many of the poems revolve around some iteration of the phrase "el sueño de toda célula es devenir células" (the dream of every cell is to become cells)[3] (16). Contrary to its anthropomorphic phrasing, the poet's depiction of cells and the activity of cells in these poems is deeply rooted in biology and the careful observation of the more-than-human world. This phrase, as well as much of the content of the poems, is formed around the poetic voice's fond recollection of her childhood science teacher, Maestra Olmedo (Ms. Olmedo), who teaches her students how science can be used to get closer to the more-than-human world through careful and ethical study. It is through her lessons in science and care that the poet learns of ecological systems, interdependent networks of organisms, and the importance of seeing plants, animals, and humans as interconnected through our common vital processes and ecologies. The poet fuses science and sentimentality in "La maestra Olmedo" (Ms. Olmedo) in which she remembers how her teacher "con su voz de subida y bajada nos llevó al lenguaje de humus de nitrógeno de nutrientes y de la canción de cuna bajo los lentes del microscopio" (led us with her rising and falling voice into the language of humus of nitrogen of nutrients and lullabies under the microscope lens) (17). Movement is key in these poems as we can see here in the rising and falling of the teacher's voice, the image of students drawing near to hear of the "language" of humus, and the nurturing, rocking motion of lullabies sung to newly created organisms. Moreover, as in this poem's reference to "language of humus," that nutrient-rich organic matter in soil formed of the decomposition of organisms, the poems of *El sueño de toda célula* speak of communication and language as part of the movement or flowing of life, the vital activity of organisms interdependent on other organisms, matter, and their surroundings, propelling potential life cycles and the ability for a cell to become cells.

In contrast to these languages of life in *El sueño de toda célula,* the poet positions what she calls "la lengua del imperio" (the language of empire) to represent colonial human languages such as Latin, Spanish, and English as well as the capitalistic and consumeristic paradigms that shape contemporary society's treatment of the more-than-human world. Moreover, the language of empire harnesses scientific knowledge and technology in a race to perpetually increase flows of data, resources, and capital at the expense of all living things. As such, it represents the cultural, political, economic logic of neoliberal capitalism, which justifies its own rationality through what Irmgard Emmelhainz calls the "tiranía del sentido común" (tyranny of common sense), conditioning our current way of seeing and inhabiting the world through "una forma de reingeniería ecológica, social y cultural que ha destruido el medio ambiente al tiempo que ha reproducido la cultura de consumo, estupidez y analfabetismo" (a form of ecological, social, and cultural reengineering that has destroyed the environment while it has reproduced the culture of consumption, stupidity, and illiteracy) (Emmelhainz 18). Likewise in *El sueño de toda célula,* the language of empire stops the flows of life through scarcity, partition, accumulation, and extraction as seen in the poem "Datos": "El imperio habla en monedas y talentos que absorben y cercan ríos que destrozan territorios y extraen minerales y ríos y personas: que disuelven, trozan, acumulan. Intervienen procesos metabólicos: sustraen" (The empire speaks in currencies and talents that absorb and fence in rivers that demolish land and strip-mine minerals and rivers and people: that dissolve, cut up, accumulate. They intervene in metabolic processes: they subtract) (67). The language of empire conditions how we see plants, animals, and even ourselves within entire ecosystems, all with an air of naturality baked within the semiotic system itself, resulting in what the poet defines as "una carrera por la incomunicación" (a race for incommunication) (61). It facilitates flows of capital, data, and currencies by inhibiting and smothering flows of life in a race that continues to distance ourselves from each other and the more-than-human world. Similar to Emmelhainz's assertation that neoliberalism "confunde la información por el conocimiento, a la comunicación con la información" (confuses information with knowledge, communication with information) (41), the poetic voice observes in "Hidrocarburos" (Hydrocarbons) the transforming power of vast flows of information that turn us into "una masa de datos engaños coloridos y ajenos que abren abismos de comunicación entre comunidades, que determinan atributos y arrojan personas, plantas y animales de su casa" (a mass of data deceits colorful and external to us that open abysses of communication between communities, that determine attributes and expel people, plants, and animals from their homes) (84). Through its transformative capacity to define attributes in plants, animals, and people, the language of empire conditions a rationality that justifies biopolitical domination and degradation in the name of technology, progress, and development. In effect, it demonstrates the capacity for human semiosis to condition how we inhabit the world, impacting the activity of biosemiotic processes in human and more-than-human life.

In writing *El sueño de toda célula* Guerrero found inspiration in how as a child "parecía que me podía comunicar con la naturaleza: al ver cómo bailaban los árboles, sentir el aire" (it seemed that I could communicate with nature: seeing how the trees would dance, feeling the air) (Paz Avedaño). The poetic voice combines this childlike approach of seeing plants and animals with the wonder inspired by studying biology for the first time, approaching organisms as they are, not how we are conditioned to see them through the language of empire. Instead, in "Lenguaje" (Language) she searches for language "hecho de manos y viento y nutrientes" (made of hands and wind and nutrients) (78), which feature in other communicative systems. Incorporating Indigenous languages, transcorporeal communication between plants and animals, and biosemiotic processes in all organisms from the cellular level up, the poet in "Introducciones" (Introductions) looks to what she terms "lenguas vernáculas" (vernacular languages) to identify ways of being outside of the language and logic of empire:

> Devenir lengua en agua que fluye:
> sílabas, sonidos, fonemas que en combinaciones
> inusitadas y variables

resuenan
como un conjunto de árboles:
alamedas, pinales, plantaciones, bosques, selvas:
el baldío de al lado:
. . .
expandir el corazón: brotan manantiales en difusas y posibles lenguas en químicas orgánicas e inorgánicas y los pulmones y el baldío de al lado habitan:
aire compartido:
células soñando con células (22–23)
(Becoming words in flowing water:
syllables, sounds, varied and unusual combinations
of phonemes
resounding
like a group of trees:
poplars, pine groves, crop fields, jungles, forests:
the vacant lot next door:
. . .
your heart expanding: springs springing forth in hazy and possible languages in organic and inorganic chemicals and lungs and the vacant lot next door inhabit:
shared air:
cells dreaming of cells)

Instead of the typical anthropocentric treatment of metaphoric movement from the human onto the more-than-human, here we see how the poetic voice establishes analogous relationships between components of human and vegetal languages. In particular, this reversal of metaphoric movement highlights how syllables, phonemes, and morphologies as markers of human language possess the potentiality, unrealized so far, to approximate the more expansive communicative capacity of the more-than-human world here portrayed through plant systems. Akin to Enrique Leff's call for a new "racionalidad ambiental" (environmental rationality), an ethic of *otredad* (alterity) that can only come from a "diálogo de saberes" (dialogue of knowledges) that transcend current ontological and epistemological suppositions (xv), the poet affirms that the only possible way out of current social and environmental crises is through regrounding culture in alternative forms of living, modeled in communication and interdependence found in subjugated human and more-than-human languages. In this way, in "Anotar con Cuidado" (Taking Careful Notes) the poet affirms that "un día de estos reconoceremos en lenguas vernáculas cómo aligerar la lengua del imperio y sacudirla" (one of these days we'll recognize in vernacular languages how to lighten the tongue of empire and shake it out) (25).

In the poem "¿El abedul y el abeto?" (The Birch and the Fir?) the poet depicts the intrinsic language of plants, "the modes of communication and articulation used by vegetal species to negotiate ecologically with their biotic and abiotic environments" (Gagliano et al. xvii–xviii), privileging the perspective of plants and their communicative capacity to utilize organic and inorganic materials to go about the activity of life. Here the poet embeds within her verses direct quotes from Canadian ecologist Suzanne Simard regarding the research she and her team have made regarding plant communication (see Chapman), discovering that birch and fir trees not only speak through the language of carbon, "sino en nitrógeno y fósforo y agua y en signos defensivos, en alelos químicos y hormonas a través de redes de hongos diminutos y bacterias" (but also nitrogen and phosphorous and water and defensive signs, in allelochemicals and hormones through networks of tiny mushrooms and bacteria) (39). Through the repetition of the phrase "resulta que" (as it turns out), the poet elides these depictions of intrinsic vegetal language with extrinsic imagery, speaking of "familias de árboles" (families of trees) that through their language of molecules "se reparten nutrientes, que se cuidan su crecimiento y se procuran" (distribute nutrients to each other, that they take care of and tend to each other as they grow) (39). Unlike in many conventional anthropomorphic descriptions of plant and animal life, the poet here conscientiously vacillates between intrinsic and extrinsic language to present the ubiquity of actions of communication and interdependence found in living networks in the more-than-human world. This crossing over and elision between plants and human culture can be seen as an example of a new type of "'cross-cultural' dialogue" possible through an immersion into the beingness of all organisms (Gagliano 96). In this manner, Guerrero engages with plants and animals not to project notions of human subjectivity or metaphors of meaning onto them, but rather to illustrate how biosemiotic communication functions in all living beings and systems, offering up examples of cooperation, interdependence, and communication through other ways of being in a more-than-human world.

The current turn in contemporary Mexican poetry to explore alternative forms of living through plants and animals is undoubtedly part of a larger pattern in

Latin American literature that draws upon subjugated knowledges and ways of being to explore emergent alternatives in "life otherwise" (Gómez-Barris). In particular, these works of contemporary Mexican poetry look to language and communication in plants and animals to challenge an anthropocentric worldview that distances humanity from the more-than-human world while at the same time driving environmental and ecological destruction. Much like the image that Guerrero evokes of the cell as an open space or a page yet to be written (11), these works imagine alternative futurities that emerge from knowledge of the more-than-human world. These futurities imagine a human and more-than-human coexistence outside the extractivist paradigm, questioning the role that our language itself plays in naturalizing and propelling destructive social and economic systems. Instead of projecting and inscribing the human onto plants and animals, these works seek to identify spaces and possibilities to consider human and nonhuman organisms within their ecologies.

The final words of the respective collections invert anthropocentric positioning of humans within a more-than-human world, underscoring the urgency of articulating postextractivist futurities in the face of a future in which even humans will become an extinct species. In Zapata's collection we are reminded that "La voz de las ballenas nos sobrevivirá" (The voice of whales will outlast us) (90), while the poetic voice in Guerrero's book holds humans and packs of wolves in physical and relational proximity, reminding readers in the final poem "Partidas" (Beginnings) that "A veces detenerse es otra forma de fluir. / Una manada a nuestro lado duerme bosque arriba" (To stop can be another way to flow. / A pack besides us sleeps on the mountainside) (115). Through examples of interconnectivity, cooperation, and communication in plants and animals as well as through depictions of biosemiotic processes, these works of contemporary Mexican poetry open up the concept of language as being a feature of all organisms and the activity of living. They demonstrate that the coordinated actions of communication found in organic networks and ecological systems are in themselves the activity of life, a space where semiosis drives *poiesis* in the creation and continuation of life that flows through the dreams of cells becoming cells.

Notes

1. All translations from Spanish, unless otherwise indicated, are mine. In translating poetry, I have emphasized comprehensibility for non-Spanish readers over lyrical form, rhyme, and meter.

2. I provide this very brief overview of a handful of key ideas in biosemiotics to contextualize how these poets portray semiosis in the biological domain. For a concise and informative introduction into the expansive field of biosemiotics, see Favareau, Donald. "The Evolutionary History of Biosemiotics." *Introduction to Biosemiotics: The New Biological Synthesis,* edited by Marcello Barbieri, Springer, 2007, pp. 1–68.

3. All English translations from *El sueño de toda célula* are from Myers, Robin, translator. *The Dream of Every Cell / El sueño de toda célula.* By Maricela Guerrero. Cardboard House Press, 2022.

Works Cited

Barbas-Rhoden, Laura. *Ecological Imaginations in Latin American Fiction.* University Press of Florida, 2011.

Bartra, Roger. *La jaula de la melancolía: Identidad y metamorfosis del mexicano.* Grijalbo, 1987.

Blanco, Alberto. *A la luz de siempre.* Fondo de Cultura Económica, 2018.

Chapman, Leonora. "Científicos hablan con árboles." *Radio Canadá Internacional,* 3 May 2017, https://www.rcinet.ca/es/2017/05/03/cientificos-que-hablan-con-arboles/. Accessed 30 Nov. 2023.

DeVries, Scott M. *Creature Discomfort: Fauna-Criticism, Ethics and the Representation of Animals in Spanish American Fiction and Poetry.* Brill, 2016.

Díaz Castelo, Elisa. *Principia.* Tierra Adentro, 2018.

Emmelhainz, Irmgard. *La tiranía del sentido común: La reconversión neoliberal de México.* Paradiso, 2016.

Farrier, David. *Anthropocene Poetics: Deep Time, Sacrifice Zones, and Extinction.* University of Minnesota Press, 2019.

Favareau, Donald. "The Evolutionary History of Biosemiotics." *Introduction to Biosemiotics: The New Biological Synthesis,* edited by Marcello Barbieri, Springer, 2007, pp. 1–68.

Fornoff, Carolyn. "Planetary Poetics of Extinction in Contemporary Mexican Poetry." *Mexican Literature as World Literature,* edited by Ignacio M. Sánchez Prado, Bloomsbury, 2021, pp. 231–245.

Gagliano, Monica. "Breaking Silence: Green Mudras and the Faculty of Language in Plants." *The Language of Plants: Science, Philosophy, Literature,* edited by Monica Gagliano et al., University of Minnesota Press, 2017, pp. 84–100.

Gagliano, Monica, et al. "Introduction." *The Language of Plants: Science, Philosophy, Literature,* edited by Monica Gagliano et al., University of Minnesota Press, 2017, pp. vii–xxxiii.

Godfrey-Smith, Peter. "The Mind of an Octopus." *Scientific American,* 1 Jan. 2017, https://www.scientificamerican.com/article/the-mind-of-an-octopus/. Accessed 24 Oct 2023.

Gómez-Barris, Macarena. *The Extractive Zone: Social Ecologies and Decolonial Perspectives.* Duke University Press, 2017.

Guerrero, Maricela. *El sueño de toda célula.* Antílope, 2018.

Gutiérrez Reyna, Jorge. *El otro nombre de los árboles.* Universidad de Guadalajara, 2018.

Leff, Enrique. *Racionalidad Ambiental: La reapropiación social de la naturaleza.* Siglo XXI, 2004.

Myers, Robin, translator. *The Dream of Every Cell / El sueño de toda célula.* By Maricela Guerrero. Cardboard House Press, 2022.

Neimanis, Astrida, and Rachel Loewen Walker. "Weathering: Climate Change and the 'Thick Time' of Transcorporeality." *Hypatia,* vol. 29, no. 3, 2014, pp. 558–575.

Paz Avedaño, Reyna. "Debemos cambiar nuestra relación con la naturaleza: Maricela Guerrero." *Crónica,* 19 Feb. 2020, https://www.cronica.com.mx/notas-debemos_cambiar_nuestra_relacion_con_la_naturaleza_maricela_guerrero-1146243-2020. Accessed 10 Oct. 2023.

Peirce, Charles Sanders. *The Essential Peirce: Selected Philosophical Writings, Vol. 2 (1893-1913).* Indiana University Press, 1998.

Ponce de León, Alejandro. "Latin America and the Botanical Turn." *Journal of Latin American Cultural Studies,* vol. 31, no. 1, 2022, pp. 129–140.

Rodríguez Murillo, Marco Antonio. *Tal vez el crecimiento de un jardín sea la única forma en que los muertos pueden hablarnos.* Universidad de Guadalajara, 2018.

Sebeok, Thomas A. "Communication." *A Sign Is Just a Sign.* Indiana University Press, 1991, pp. 22–35.

Uexküll, Jakob von. *A Foray into the Worlds of Animals and Humans* with *A Theory of Meaning.* 1934, 1940. University of Minnesota Press, 2010.

Wheeler, Wendy. "The Biosemiotic Turn: Abduction, or, the Nature of Creative Reason in Nature and Culture." *Ecocritical Theory: New European Approaches,* edited by Axel Goodbody and Kate Rigby, University of Virginia Press, 2011, pp. 270–282.

Wylie, Lesley. *The Poetics of Plants in Spanish American Literature.* University of Pittsburg Press, 2020.

Zapata, Isabel. *Una ballena es un país.* Almadía, 2019.

7

Bugs, Plants, and Laboratories

A Grammar for/of More-Than-Human Entanglements in Alexis Gambis's Science New Wave Films

OSCAR A. PÉREZ

A series of colorful images fills the screen before the audience hears any dialogue lines. Extradiegetic sounds signal an urban space. Soon, a chrysalis in a petri dish takes over the center of the frame. Iris scissors and dissection forceps carefully separate the organism while the thoughtful eyes of a scientist look through the lenses of a microscope. A sudden change occurs. The audience is transported to a forest inhabited by thousands of monarch butterflies. This is a sequence of contrasts and continuities that are emphasized through lighting and the use of verbal and visual language. Rays of sunlight filter through the treetops to highlight the orange parts of the insects in flight while shadows cover the butterfly roosts hanging from the oyamel fir trees. On the ground, two children move between the lights and shadows, carefully interacting with the butterflies. In these first minutes of Alexis Gambis's *Son of Monarchs* (2020), the laboratory and forest are connected by the on-screen presence of the monarchs, unsuspecting participants in the fiction film. The monarchs on the screen experience their lives—sleep, fly, reproduce, die—oblivious to any director's notes. The same can be said about the multiple plant species that inhabit the forest. While the camera maintains control of what the audience sees, from what angles, through which frames, and at what pace, once the plants and animals are on the screen, they inscribe themselves in the film in ways that surpass the will of the humans creating it. Monarchs, oyamel fir trees, and other living beings invite spectators to take a look into their existence, their connections to the environment, and their interspecies alliances. These plants and animals are co-creating the film. In this respect, what theoretical tools can we use to examine such a co-creation process? Furthermore, what role do plants and animals play in a film in which science—as a form of human knowledge—takes center stage (such as *Son of Monarchs* and other films by the same director)? Does looking at the film as a co-created text open a window into plant and animal participation in (human) knowledge production and, more broadly, more-than-human knowledge?

In this chapter, I center my attention on Alexis Gambis's feature films *The Fly Room* (2014) and *Son of Monarchs* (2020), as well as the short film series *The Monarch Triptych*, which consists of *La que sueña* (2017), *Los mimos monarcas* (2018), and *Mi hermano* (2018), which are part of the Science New Wave, a cinematographic movement that encourages experimentation and individual expression in science films—over more traditional conventions of the genre. I interrogate the presence of insects and plants in these films, focusing on issues related to communication and knowledge. Informed by Robin Wall Kimmerer's discussion on the grammar of animacy and three crucial concepts of plant and animal inscription in human texts—Patrícia Vieira's zoophytographia, Joela Jacobs's work on phytopoetics, and the various scholars studying the notion of zoopoetics—this chapter describes how a grammar for/of more-than-human entanglements provides tools to interrogate issues of other-than-human agency, language, expression, and knowledge in Gambis's films.

A Grammar for/of More-Than-Human Entanglements

The notion of other-than-human agency has become a point of convergence between scholars in political ecology, critical plant and animal studies (CPS and CAS, respectively), posthumanism, science and technology studies, and the environmental humanities. Specifically, scholars in CAS and CPS have devoted significant attention to the role that language plays in how humans think of nonhuman beings, nonhuman participation in (human) knowledge production, and the nature of relationships that humans establish with nonhumans.[1]

Research on animal and plant communication has raised key epistemological and ethical questions, particularly about the consequences of organizing and categorizing the world from an anthropocentric perspective inherited from the Enlightenment. In response, new ways of thinking about language in human-nonhuman relations have emerged. For instance, Monica Gagliano, John C. Ryan, and Patrícia Vieira propose two modes to think about the language of plants: extrinsic and intrinsic (xvii). On the one hand, extrinsic language refers to the language used by humans—from scientists to writers—to talk about plants. The authors remind us that extrinsic language used without ethical concern "is imposed upon plants as a means of dissecting, ordering, or consigning them to the background" (xvii). Nevertheless, the careful use of extrinsic language can serve as a doorway into plant lives and inspire us to conceive what thinking, being, and acting as plants would be. On the other hand, intrinsic language refers to the ways plants communicate among themselves with other living beings in their environment—a research area in continuous expansion. Thinking about these two language modes when it comes to animals and other nonhuman life—in addition to plants—provides a generative entry point into the limitations and possibilities of the language used by humans to articulate the more-than-human world and its complexities.[2]

Scholars like Patrícia Vieira, Joela Jacobs, John Charles Ryan, Robin Wall Kimmerer, and others have given us theoretical tools to reflect on and describe human-nonhuman entanglements, particularly when it comes to the co-creation of cultural texts. Patrícia Vieira proposed the notion of zoophytographia as a form of interspecies writing (*States* 70). Vieira first developed this notion with respect to plants (phytographia) and later expanded it to plants and animals (zoophytographia). In its initial conceptualization, phytographia referred to "the appellation of an encounter between writings on plants and the writing *of* plants, which inscribed themselves in human texts," a concept that also "stands for the literary portrayal of plants that is indebted both to the ingenuity of the author who crafts the text and to the inscription of plants in that very process of creation" ("Phytographia" 215). To clarify this concept further, Vieira compares it to photography. While photographs can be conceptualized as material things interacting with light to create an imprint of reality filtered by the photographer (the writing of light), plants leave impressions of themselves (the writing *of* plants) in human cultural productions (the writing *on* plants) ("Phytographia" 216). Heavily influenced by perspectivism, as described by Eduardo Viveiros de Castro, zoophytographia expands such co-creation of cultural texts into non-human animals, resulting in interspecies writing that widens the boundaries of literature in an encounter between animals, humans, and plants that "does not involve conquest but operates through a give and take, transforming each party in the process and resulting in a novel literary language" (*States* 71). Indeed, human-nonhuman co-creation not only produces a new language but also requires new critical language to scrutinize such a process.

The notions of zoopoetics and phytopoetics are two other theoretical frameworks crucial for thinking about plant and animal agency in human cultural productions. Many scholars have examined textual animal interventions through the notion of zoopoetics. As Driscoll and Hoffmann relate, contemporary discussions related to zoopoetics emerge from and expand the work of Kafka and Derrida (2). Despite the variety of zoopoetic approaches and examples, one commonality remains: "zoopoetic texts are not—at least not necessarily and certainly not simply—texts about animals," they are texts in which reflection "on questions of writing and representation, proceeds via the animal" (Driscoll and Hoffmann 4). Further exploring this concept, Joela Jacobs has proposed a "grammar of zoopoetics," which consists of "the particular linguistic creativity enabled by anthropomorphized animal language that questions its own presuppositions" (74). Jacobs's favorable position with respect to anthropomorphized animal language—a contested subject in animal studies—aligns with that of other scholars who advise not to "fear or mistrust the metaphorical, symbolic, and allegorical meanings embodied by literary animals, so long as we do not make the mistake of reading these nonhuman presences *only* or *simply* as metaphors" (Driscoll and Hoffmann 4). Based on this work, Joela Jacobs and, later, John Charles Ryan have discussed phytopoetics with slightly different but confluent implications. Jacobs understands phytopoetics as a parallel concept to zoopoetics, entailing "both a poetic engagement with plants in literature and moments in which plants take on literary or cultural agency themselves" ("Phytopoetics" 1). For Ryan, phytopoetics "denotes a praxis that aims to integrate distinctly vegetal modes of being, including embodied cognition and systems intelligence" (119). The emphasis on cognition and other intelligences is important when considering the agency of plants and animals in representations of scientific knowledge and the possibilities of other-than-human knowledges.

On their part, scholars of Indigenous studies have pointed out how Indigenous communities already have languages in which "we use the same words to address the living world as we use for our family" (Kimmerer 55). Robin Wall Kimmerer talks about a "grammar of animacy" in the Potawatomi language. Kimmerer, a member of the Citizen Potawatomi Nation, describes "grammar of animacy" as language that extends animacy to plants, animals, and other nonliving beings. In contrast to European languages that tend to organize the natural world into categories and dichotomic states, many Indigenous languages encompass a grammar of animacy that reminds us of our kinship with all the animate world, "a communion of subjects, not a collection of objects" (56). For non-Indigenous communities, embracing a grammar of animacy would provide multiple opportunities; in Kimmerer's words: "Imagine the access we would have to different perspectives, the things we might see through other eyes, the wisdom that surrounds us. We don't have to figure out everything by ourselves: there are intelligences other than our own, teachers all around us" (57). In this way, the grammar of animacy traces a pathway for more inclusive ways of thinking about and understanding our connections as humans to other living and nonliving beings, including plants and animals.

With the previous considerations in mind, I suggest a grammar *for/of* more-than-human entanglements. Such grammar is informed by Kimmerer's grammar of animacy and Vieira's zoophytographia and speaks to both the extrinsic language (*for*) we humans use to talk about nonhuman living beings and the intrinsic language (*of*) associated with nonhuman communication. This grammar provides language attentive to the wide range and changing nature of relationships in which humans and nonhumans participate—language that strives to distance itself from anthropocentric worldviews while emphasizing modes of interdependence that transcend utilitarian associations between species as the default paradigm. This grammar for/of more-than-human entanglements is underpinned by (i) the recognition that all living and nonliving beings are connected at multiple levels (*interconnectedness*) and that our shared connections are ontological (*kinship*), (ii) a worldview that embraces commonalities rather than differentiation and categorization (*continuity*) and processes rather than stagnation (*fluidity*); (iii) the revalorization of care and closeness as a site of connection (*intimacy*), and (iv) the humbleness to recognize the limitations of human understanding and to embrace multiple ways of knowing (*intellectual humility*). In this sense, a grammar *for/of* more-than-human entanglements provides a set of critical tools to describe and interrogate expressions of zoophytographia, zoopoetics, and phytopoetics in texts co-created by plants, animals, and other living beings.

Bugs, Plants, and Science on the Screen

Alexis Gambis, a French-Venezuelan biologist and filmmaker, is a promoter and leading representative of the so-called Science New Wave. This movement is associated with Imagine Science Films, an initiative supported by The Rockefeller University. The same institution also hosts the annual Imagine Science Film Festival (renamed Science New Wave Festival since its 2023 edition). Many of the films associated with this movement are distributed through the Labocine platform, which provides wide access to a collection of films that come in many different formats, genres, and subjects. These films, however, have in common their alignment with the six traits listed in the Science New Wave Manifesto, which highlight a movement that welcomes experimentation, multiple perspectives, and interconnectedness, seeing science as inseparable from culture, and dismissing the potential opposition between science and narrative.[3] The sixth trait is particularly relevant, as it states: "WE ARE ALL MESSENGERS." But who are "we" in this sentence? I argue that, at least in the case of Gambis's films analyzed in this chapter, the first-person plural pronoun has broad boundaries and includes the plants and animals on the screen.

According to the filmmaker, more than a specific genre, science new wave films take different forms and are interested in a wide variety of issues in order to understand the world of which we are part:

> A science film follows the creative deconstruction of nature and evolution. A science film is not genre-specific. A science film is an alchemy of real-life events and experiences. A science film is about understanding human existence. Above all, a science film explores the same fundamental questions about the world that are asked at the beginning of any scientific study. ("Narrative" 48)

Although the centrality of scientific work is a constant, these are films that highlight subjectivity in knowledge generation: creativity, deconstructions, explorations, and inquiry. This inquisitive and critical aspect, combined with the desire not to limit oneself to specific genres and their limitations, fosters an environment open to diverse knowledge and ways of knowing.

Gambis's filmography includes a combination of short and feature films of fiction, documentary, and experimental forms. Insects have a prominent place in Gambis's films, including his debut feature film *The Fly Room,* the lauded film *Son of Monarchs,* and the short film series *The Monarch Triptych.* As the director has stated: "Mis películas siempre tienen una perspectiva animal, porque me gusta la metáfora del animal para hablar de la condición humana" (My films always have an animal perspective, because I like the metaphor of the animal to talk about the human condition) (Musi). Gambis's reference to the metaphor in connection to animal life as the source of inspiration for his films illuminates the potentiality of this rhetorical figure, inviting the audience to pay particular attention to the presence of metaphors in his films. As anticipated by the director, metaphorical representations play an essential role in his filmography, an aspect that becomes more salient when examined in conjunction with other forms of science films. Traditional science films frequently take the form of expository documentaries with voice-overs that fulfill a pedagogical function and foster a sense of credibility based on detachment, neutrality, impartiality, and omniscience (Nichols 169). This authoritative voice uses diverse explanatory strategies—such as metaphors—to clarify and expand the public's understanding of complex scientific ideas, concepts, and processes (Van Dijck 8). I will show that Gambis uses some of these techniques with different results. Moreover, echoing Jacobs's attention to figurative language that brings together human and nonhuman animals—such as anthropomorphism—metaphors in Gambis's films open a space for human-nonhuman co-creation.

Gambis's fascination with invertebrate living beings is connected to his own research as a biologist studying photoreceptors in fruit flies. The close relationship between his work as a filmmaker and a scientist is evident in the dedication of his doctoral dissertation to Imagine Science Films (*Cell* iii), but also in *The Fly Room,* a film that incorporates documentary and docufiction elements to examine the legacy of biologist Calvin Bridges. *The Fly Room* aligns with recent efforts to draw attention to the "ways insects have conceptually co-shaped the geographies of knowledge production throughout history" (de Carvalho Cabral and Freitas 137).

Through the perspective of Calvin Bridges's daughter, Betsy, *The Fly Room* brings attention to the history of Columbia University's renowned "Fly Room," a laboratory at the center of significant developments in genetics and evolutionary biology from 1910 to 1928.[4] Despite what the title might suggest, the camera ventures outdoors on many occasions. In these instances, it assumes an "insect gaze" intermittently, navigating through long leaves of grass as if attached to a flying insect (a perception reinforced by mimicking extradiegetic sounds). But *The Fly Room*'s zoophytographic impulse goes beyond this obvious technique. Perhaps more compelling are the scope of multispecies connections we witness and the revalorization of intimacy in scientific spaces proposed by the film.

Latimer and López Gómez have talked about the role of intimacy in the production of scientific knowledge. In their words: "The scientific ethos reproduces the differentiation between public and private spheres, and relegates intimacy to the private sphere, locating it as something that can potentially jeopardise scientific settings" (251). These critics encourage us to reconsider the role of intimacy in science and think about it "not as a prefigured property of relations" among various actors, "but as an effect of material entanglements that may cross and reshape differences of kind" (253). From this perspective, "[i]ntimacy is thus revealed as a site of connection through which a sense of belonging and alterity might arise in relation to human and more-than-human others" (254). *The Fly Room* echoes such a proposition, blurring the lines not only between the public and private spheres of science but also between the human and the more-than-human. The laboratory itself invites such a reading. Portrayed with a warm color palette as an intimate and messy space where fruit flies, bananas, and humans coexist, it resembles a workshop more than a space we currently associate with the scientific enterprise.

Toward the end of the film, after Calvin and Betsy get into an argument, we see the scientist looking through a microscope on his desk. The camera is positioned at a low angle to evoke a sense of intimacy and vulnerability, showing the protagonist's pursuit of scientific knowledge amid personal challenges. This angle also accentuates the insects' significance within the narrative, as it coincides with the location of the jars full of fruit flies on the desk. The insects have a front-row seat to what is about to happen. The laboratory has changed. Translucent curtains cover the windows. On the other side, insects of a more-than-human scale seem to wander around. Calvin's body—now on the floor—makes insect-like movements. An extreme close-up shot of one of his eyes confirms that a transformation is happening. The boundaries between the scientist and the fruit flies, human and other-than-human, have been removed. The scene exhibits the intricate relationship between the insects and the character. The fruit flies' role as generators of scientific knowledge is unveiled, effectively illustrating the interplay between the microcosm of scientific exploration and the macrocosm of human-nonhuman relationships.

Butterflies and Flowers in an Interconnected World

Gambis's attraction to invertebrate living beings continues in the three short films that constitute *The Monarch Triptych* and the feature film *Son of Monarchs*. As suggested by their titles, monarch butterflies are the most visible common thread between all these four productions; nevertheless, there are many more commonalities. *The Monarch Triptych* short films anticipate many themes further developed in *Son of Monarchs,* including loss, mourning, individual transformation, and knowledge.

The first film of the triptych in chronological order of production is *La que sueña* (She Who Dreams). In it, a scientist goes through a metamorphosis that results in her becoming a monarch butterfly. The camera captures the protagonist's gradual transformation in appearance and behavior. Gambis relies on a delicate balance between anthropomorphism and animalization to challenge the audience's perception of the transformation occurring before their eyes. Both processes are constructed with a combination of extreme close-ups, evocative makeup, costume design, and sound effects that, taken together, make the film's zoopoetic impulse obvious. The images on the screen show a woman slowly going through various stages of a monarch's life cycle, almost as if her human state corresponded with that of a larva. The protagonist explicitly refers to her transformation as a process that brought liveness to her existence, especially after the death of her father: "Antes, cuando yo tenía completamente forma humana, estaba como en un sueño, un poco como adormecida, no estaba viviendo realmente" (Before, when I had a completely human form, I was in a dream, a bit drowsy, I wasn't truly living). The space connected to this sense of incompleteness and the calling for change is very telling. The protagonist's transformation begins in a laboratory, where the scientist examines some dead butterflies through a microscope. When the transformation is complete, the scientist-turned-butterfly wanders through New York City, interacting with other butterflies and plants on her path. Knowledge lies beyond the walls of the laboratory. The scientist cannot rely on butterfly corpses to awaken from a somnolent life.

The final scene is particularly thought-provoking. The voice-over that guides the audience throughout the film talks about reaching a state of fulfillment. The camera shows an extreme close-up of the protagonist with a left profile angle. The composition of the frame emphasizes the connection between the living beings taking over the screen. A New York aster inhabits the background and the left foreground with its characteristic lavender flowers. A monarch rests on one of the flowers, laboriously drinking nectar. The human-monarch occupies the right foreground. By visually aligning the three, this shot points to the interspecies interconnectedness and the deeper level of such connection, a kinship that fosters self-knowledge. A sense of fulfillment is reached when the human-monarch embraces other living beings in her environment and recognizes herself as one of them.

Mi hermano (My Brother) transports the audience to the mountains of Michoacán, one of the Mexican states where monarchs spend the Northern Hemisphere's winter. The film begins with a scene in an elementary school classroom. Children work on an assignment when another kid peeks through the window. One of the boys in the class recognizes him, and then both kids walk on the street of a town immersed in the mountains. The two kids reach a wooded area and talk about the upcoming seasonal arrival of the monarch butterflies. The younger boy suddenly loses track of the older one, named Simón. As he makes his way back to his house, he meets a woman who explains to him how the souls of the departed become monarchs. At this point, the audience realizes that Simón, the older brother, has been dead since the beginning. The characterization of this community highlights its multispecies nature. The people of this town constantly move through wooded areas, living in community with plants and animals. Wide shots are prevalent, showing the human characters in an environment of a more-than-human scale dominated by the forested mountains. Connections between multiple species occur at various levels, from local legends and school festivals where kids wear animal costumes (butterflies, bears, and rabbits) to extradiegetic sounds that constantly remind the audience of the presence of birds and other living beings. This interspecies communion is reinforced in the final scene. A wide shot captures hundreds of monarchs flying in between trees. The younger boy is sitting on a rock surrounded by the monarchs and the multiple plant species living on the mountain. He wonders if his brother is back—perhaps his soul now resides in the body of a butterfly—and expresses how much he misses him. The seamless integration of human and nonhuman elements underscores the multispecies nature of the intimate moment. As the younger boy grapples with the absence of his brother, the final scene captures the essence of interspecies communion through the boy's contemplation of life's interconnectedness and the enduring bonds that transcend the limits between species.

Los mimos monarcas (The Monarch Mimes) is the third film in *The Monarch Triptych* and the most experimental of the three. There is no dialogue, as the main characters are two mimes. The film begins with one of the mimes dressed as a monarch emerging from a casket while breathing through a plastic tube connected to what looks like a terrarium. Suddenly, she is in a wooded area. A group of children wearing orange and black butterfly wings moves along her until they encounter the body of the other monarch mime, lying on the ground. She helps him recover, and soon after, they are both living together in a building in ruins. As in *Mi hermano,* wide shots are common. This technique, combined with high angles, shows the small scale of human-made structures compared with the surrounding mountains. Additionally, it likens in scale the world of the two mime monarchs (the human world) to the insect world.

Los mimos monarcas is a film of human-nonhuman interconnectedness, material and emotional continuities in a changing world, and intimate encounters, characteristics depicted throughout the film and confirmed in the last scene. The film ends with a shot of a gravestone on the ground, surrounded by flowers, food, and *papel picado*, elements associated with traditional celebrations of the Day of the Dead in Mexico. The gravestone reads: "En recuerdo de los millones de mariposas monarca que murieron congeladas por la gran tormenta de enero del 2002" (In remembrance of millions of monarch butterflies that froze to death during the great storm of January 2002). The gravestone in Angangueo's cemetery points to a multispecies community sustained by mutual care, a richly interconnected world in the mountains of Michoacán. Through the focus on loss and mourning, the film explores themes of grief and the transcendence of the human experience, themes found across many of the works discussed in this chapter.

Metaphors and Bidirectionality

Gambis's *Son of Monarchs* continues and deepens the director's exploration of many themes that appeared in *The Monarch Triptych*. Media critics paid significant attention to the film after its screenings at the 2020 Morelia International Film Festival and the 2021 Sundance Film Festival, where it won the Alfred P. Sloan Award for a feature film focused on science and technology. Reviews frequently noted the authenticity with which science-related issues were portrayed, its treatment of migration between the United States and Mexico (and the monarchs as a symbol of movement across human-made borders), and the protagonist's personal turmoil and ultimate journey of self-discovery (Andaluz).

The film follows Mendel, a Mexican biologist split between New York City—where his entomology research work takes place—and Angangueo—his hometown in the Mexican state of Michoacán. This is a film about loss but also about how loss becomes the common element in a network of interspecies entanglements. Mendel lost his parents during a flood when he was a child. In the present, he mourns the death of his grandmother. However, loss and grief surpass the protagonist's individual experience.

Mendel, the people from Angangueo, the monarchs, and the plants in the surrounding forest see their ecosystem being destroyed due to the expansion of mining activities and illegal logging. One could read the environmental devastation as a metaphor that speaks to the protagonist's unresolved grief. Yet, reading the film through a grammar for/of more-than-human entanglements would challenge the directionality of the previous metaphor. What if Mendel's grief is a metaphor for the loss experienced by the monarchs and other living beings due to the destruction of the forest? If human metaphors are often unidirectional due to conceptual maps where "more animate entities tend to be described in terms of less animate ones and less prototypical entities in terms of more prototypical ones" (Gil and Shen 2), challenging the directionality of a metaphor questions animacy hierarchies that often result from anthropocentric worldviews.

Bidirectionality (and even pluridirectionality) in figurative language allows for an interrogation of hierarchical assumptions in relations of similarity, making such assumptions explicit. For instance, what are the implications of thinking about the monarchs' journey as a metaphor for human migration *and*, simultaneously, considering histories of human migration—like Mendel's—as metaphors for the struggles faced by the monarchs? What meanings do we assign to the mime-butterflies in *Los mimos monarcas* if the metaphor is meant for the oyamel fir trees? What happens when we reflect from the butterflies' point of view on the legend that says monarchs are the souls of the departed? Or if we analyze the scientist's metamorphosis in *La que sueña* from the perspective of the New York aster flowers? How would fruit flies perceive their presence in the laboratory of *The Fly Room?* For one, we are quickly forced to recognize multispecies interconnectedness and kinship. We are all part of a network that makes meaning and knowledge possible, a possibility not exclusive to humans. When the animals and plants on the screen co-create the text, they are participating in an epistemological process that challenges anthropocentrism. Bidirectional metaphors also make evident the commonalities, shared liveness, and joint materiality of multiple species—continuity—and the constant changes that affect all of us—fluidity.

Science, Knowledge, and Intimacy

Like *The Fly Room, Son of Monarchs* asks questions related to knowledge, intimacy, and care, but in this case, multiple ways of knowing become more prominent. While *The Fly Room* recovers a passage from the canonical history of biology, in *Son of Monarchs,* there is an explicit effort to understand science as one among many domains of knowledge. In this respect, the film uncovers the strong bond between ancestral knowledges, oral traditions, and Western science from a position of intellectual humility.

Diálogo de saberes (dialogue of knowledges) has emerged in the Latin American context as a framework that questions hegemonic epistemic models and opens a bridge between modern Eurocentric Western science and Indigenous ways of knowing. *Diálogo de saberes* challenges the perception that only universalizing, quantitative, and experimental perspectives are legitimate, especially among scientific communities in the Global South (Delgado and Rist 48). This position appears as part of efforts to decolonize knowledge. Elsewhere, I have described how *Son of Monarchs* echoes this position through sound codes—subjective perspectives that build emotional ties and privilege plurality—and representations of scientific and traditional knowledge in symmetrical power relations ("Pérdida" 210).

The intention to represent diverse ways of knowing in symmetrical power relations can be seen clearly in the scenes of *Son of Monarchs* that evoke nahualistic rituals. In the first of these scenes, the participants gather around a campfire. Attendees wear masks, move their bodies, and make sounds that evoke animals. This ritual highlights the continuity in the ties that unite human and nonhuman beings. This scene takes on new meanings when it is analyzed in light of another scene near the end when Mendel talks about the nahuales—people with the ability to transform into animals—and confesses how, as a child, he pretended to be a bear. This intervention makes a connection between the rituals that we see on screen and ancestral knowledge, in particular with the figure of the nahual/nahualli, which is "a nodal element in the Mesoamerican worldview" (Martínez González 431). A similar ritual is repeated in the final sequence of the film. In the center of a medium shot, the biologist is seen with a naked torso preparing for the ritual. We can see a pair of antennae protruding. The scientist has a tattoo of butterfly wings on his back. Visually, Mendel has been transformed into a butterfly. This ritual underscores the continuity and interdependence between human and nonhuman beings. It also highlights the fluidity of identity and the transformative power of ancestral knowledge. Moreover, the scientist's visual and symbolic metamorphosis into a butterfly encapsulates the annual transformative journey of monarchs themselves.

The visual metaphors in *Son of Monarchs* function as conduits for reimagining epistemic hierarchies, blurring the boundaries between scientific and ancestral knowledge. The film's invocation of the nahual illustrates a human-nonhuman continuum. This interplay between human and nonhuman, between ancestral tradition and Western science, reveals a relationship where each mode of knowing informs and enriches the other, and both are being shaped by humans and nonhumans. Mendel's transformation into a butterfly is emblematic of this reciprocity, embodying a form of knowledge that is at once individual and collective, human and nonhuman. In this sense, the film enacts a *diálogo de saberes* not as a mere juxtaposition of perspectives but as an interwoven, metamorphic process—one in which knowledge itself, like the monarch's migration, moves across borders, shifting and adapting with each crossing.

Final Remarks

The previous analysis draws attention to interspecies connections, the human-nonhuman co-creation of cultural texts, and the various theoretical frameworks that help us understand such processes. The five films at the center of this chapter have a well-defined zoophytographic intentionality. Hence, a grammar for/of more-than-human entanglements provides critical tools for analyzing the co-creation of these films by plants, animals, and humans. Given that this grammar emphasizes interconnectedness, kinship, continuity, fluidity, intimacy, and intellectual humility, it challenges anthropocentric perspectives on these cultural products. Moreover, it highlights the multifaceted nature of relationships, including those that result in artistic production, in which humans and nonhumans participate.

Furthermore, the analysis pushes us to rethink readings of metaphorical language that privilege anthropocentric hierarchies of animacy. In the case of Gambis's films, where themes of loss, migration, and interconnectedness are intertwined with scientific inquiry and ancestral wisdom, the bidirectionality of metaphors allows for a more meticulous examination of interspecies relationships and the defiance of hierarchical assumptions inherent in anthropocentric worldviews. By acknowledging the interconnectedness, kinship, and continuity of all living beings, we are prompted to embrace a more inclusive worldview that transcends human-centeredness.

Shifting our critical approach to films such as Gambis's Science New Wave films allows us to access more diverse perspectives and modes of knowing, deepening reflections on the intersections of agency, knowledge, and intimacy. The analysis advocates for a reconsideration of our relationships with the beings with whom we share the natural world and embracement of a more holistic understanding of human-nonhuman entanglements, a new grammar that recognizes all human and nonhuman entities as active participants in knowledge production.

Notes

1. See, for example, Gagliano et al., *The Language of Plants,* Jacobs's "The Grammar of Zoopoetics," and Meijer's *When Animals Speak.*

2. By more-than-human world I understand "the open spectrum of the interrelationships between the worlds of living and non-living beings and human societies," recognizing that "there are other 'selves' with corporally distinct centers of experience that take place in a vast intersubjective and inter-corporeal horizon" (Bernardes de Souza Júnior 2–3).

3. The Science New Wave Manifesto lists the following traits: "1) Culture is Science. Science is Culture, 2) Diversity feeds the ecosystem, 3) Experiments become Cinema, 4) Structure dictates function, 5) Science & Story never collide, 6) WE ARE ALL MESSENGERS" ("Science New Wave Manifesto").

4. See chapter 4, "The Fly People," of Robert E. Kohler's *Lords of the Fly* for a detailed description of the workings of the laboratory.

Works Cited

Andaluz, Diego. "Sundance Review: Son of Monarchs is a Lyrical Portrait of Fractured Identity." *The Film Stage,* 3 Feb. 2021, http://thefilmstage.com/sundance-review-son-of-monarchs-is-a-lyrical-portrait-of-fractured-identity/. Accessed 15 March 2023.

Bernardes de Souza Júnior, Carlos Roberto. "More-Than-Human Cultural Geographies Towards Co-Dwelling on Earth." *Mercator,* vol. 20, no. 1, 2021, pp. 1–10.

de Carvalho Cabral, Diogo, and Frederico Freitas. "Placing Insects in Histories of Science." *Isis,* vol. 115, no. 1, 2024, pp. 136–140.

Delgado, Freddy, and Stephan Rist. "Las ciencias desde la perspectiva del diálogo de saberes, la transdisciplinariedad y el diálogo intercientífico." *Ciencias, diálogo de saberes y transdisciplinariedad: Aportes teórico metodológicos para la sustentabilidad alimentaria y del desarrollo,* edited by Freddy Delgado and Stephan Rist, AGRUCO, 2016, pp. 35–60.

Driscoll, Kári, and Eva Hoffmann, editors. *What is Zoopoetics?: Texts, Bodies, Entanglement.* Palgrave Macmillan, 2018.

Gagliano, Monica, et al., editors. *The Language of Plants: Science, Philosophy, Literature.* University of Minnesota Press, 2017.

Gambis, Alexis R. "Narrative Alchemy: From Vision to Visual." *Hollywood Chemis-*

try: *When Science Met Entertainment,* edited by Donna J. Nelson et al., American Chemical Society, 2013, pp. 47–56.

Gambis, Alexis R. *Cell Death Mechanisms in Drosophila Differentiated Photoreceptor Neurons.* 2010. The Rockefeller University, PhD dissertation.

Gambis, Alexis, director. *La que sueña.* Imaginal Disc/Labocine, 2017.

Gambis, Alexis, director . *Los mimos monarcas.* Imaginal Disc/Labocine, 2018.

Gambis, Alexis, director. *Mi hermano.* Imaginal Disc, 2018.

Gambis, Alexis, director. *Son of Monarchs.* Imaginal Disc/Labocine, 2020.

Gambis, Alexis, director. *The Fly Room.* Imaginal Disc, 2014.

Gil, David, and Yeshayahu Shen. "Metaphors: The Evolutionary Journey from Bidirectionality to Unidirectionality." *Philosophical Transactions B,* vol. 376, no. 1824, 2021, pp. 1–7.

Jacobs, Joela. "The Grammar of Zoopoetics: Human and Canine Language Play." Driscoll and Hoffmann, pp. 63–79.

Jacobs, Joela. "Phytopoetics: Upending the Passive Paradigm with Vegetal Violence and Eroticism." Catalyst, vol. 5, no. 2, 2019, pp. 1–18.

Kimmerer, Robin Wall. *Braiding Sweetgrass: Indigenous Wisdom, Scientific Knowledge and the Teachings of Plants.* Milkweed Editions, 2013.

Kohler, Robert E. *Lords of the Fly: Drosophila Genetics and the Experimental Life.* University of Chicago Press, 1994.

Labocine. "The Science New Wave: Reimagining Science in Cinema." *YouTube,* 11 June 2021, https://youtu.be/MRQqd9Tx-so

Latimer, Joanna, and Daniel López Gómez. "Intimate entanglements: Affects, more-than-human intimacies and the politics of relations in science and technology." *The Sociological Review,* vol. 67, no. 2, 2019, pp. 247–263.

Martínez González, Roberto. "Nahuales, nahualismo y nahualólogos." *Iniciaciones, trances, sueños . . . Investigaciones sobre el chamanismo en México,* coordinated by Antonella Fagetti, Plaza y Valdés, 2010, pp. 413–440.

Meijer, Eva. *When Animals Speak: Toward an Interspecies Democracy.* New York University Press, 2019.

Musi, Alejandra. "Alexis Gambis levanta el vuelo hacia Sundance." *El Universal,* 28 Jan. 2021, https://www.eluniversal.com.mx/espectaculos/alexis-gambis-levanta-el-vuelo-hacia-sundance. Accessed 15 March 2023.

Nichols, Bill. *Introduction to Documentary.* 3rd ed., Indiana University Press, 2017.

Pérez, Oscar A. "Pérdida y duelo en *Hijo de monarcas* (*Son of Monarchs*): una aproximación desde las humanidades médicas." *Hispanic Issues On Line,* vol. 33, 2024, pp. 202–217.

Ryan, John Charles. "Phytopoetics: Human-Plant Relations and the Poiesis of Vegetal Life." *The Routledge Companion to Ecopoetics,* edited by Julia Fiedorczuk et al., Routledge, 2023, pp. 117–126.

"Science New Wave Manifesto." *Science New Wave,* https://www.sciencenewwave.com. Accessed 15 Feb. 2024.

Van Dijck, José. "Picturizing Science: The Science Documentary as Multimedia Spectacle." *International Journal of Cultural Studies,* vol. 9, no. 1, 2006, pp. 5–24.

Vieira, Patrícia. "Phytographia: Literature as Plant Writing." *Environmental Philosophy,* vol. 12, no. 2, 2015, pp. 205–220.

Vieira, Patrícia. *States of Grace: Utopia in Brazilian Culture.* SUNY Press, 2018.

8

In the Beginning Was the Fable!

Textually Transmitted Beasts and Commodities in Amores Perros *and* Calila e Dimna

BEATRIZ RIVERA-BARNES

The fable is textually transmitted and linguistically determined. It is inhabited by beasts and sovereigns, nonhuman and human animals. But who came first? The animal, or the antagonist whose presence *is* the absence of the animal and who always feels he has the right to kill? The fable: useless in daily life according to Franz Kafka, to be avoided according to Jacques Derrida, and possibly as hollow as the vixen's drum.[1] For Burkhard Müller, to interpret the fable always means to do the wrong thing (101) because fables strive for something impossible (105) and if they are attractive, it is because they are cheap and simple and they cut things short (106). Enter a fox, no need to explain; this knowledge comes from the cradle. Enter a wolf, no need to explain either. In his study of the animal presence in Franz Kafka's stories, the comparatist Kári Driscoll calls attention to the fact that the protagonist of "Erinnerungen an die Kaldabahn" (Memories of the Kalda) falls victim to an incursion from the surrounding landscape in the form of an illness known as Wolfshusten (whooping cough). The illness is called Wolfshusten because the cough—in other words the symptom and the sign—sounds like the barking of a wolf. Driscoll adds that once the narrator's condition has been given an animal name, the condition itself becomes linguistically determined. Tongue in cheek, Driscoll concludes that Wolfshusten is therefore a "textually transmitted disease" (2011, 31). Hence, the disease has been named, the result being a contagion that carries an animal name or trait. Such memories of the Kalda present all the elements of the fable, but then again fables are nothing but stories.

Wolfshusten is not the only instance of a disease being given an animal name: lupus, for example, refers to the wolf's face. There is also the butterfly rash of lupus, because the rash has the irregular shape of a butterfly. Other examples include cat's scratch fever, bird flu, swine flu, mad cow, acariasis (infestation of the hair follicles with acarids, a.k.a. mites), tinea cruris (a.k.a. ringworm), elephantiasis, and even cancer because the malignant cells resemble a crab. Entering the realm of zoopoetics, with the idea of text, language, and contagion, and keeping in mind that the fable is often met with incredulity because it is deemed either childish or anthropocentric (of no value and of no use to animals because they fail to provide any information about real-life animals), but that there may be no reversing anthropomorphism or even the damage done, I propose a zoopoetic reading of the 2001 film *Amores Perros* in light of the third chapter of a medieval Castilian collection of fables, *Calila e Dimna.* I argue that these and other fables remain at the cradle of Latin American cultures. Like *Calila e Dimna, Amores Perros* presents a main narrative, an embedded narrative, and a third dimension that points to a new story frame. The film also presents different points of view and a recurrent car crash seen from different angles. The film was directed by Alejandro González Iñárritu and written by Guillermo Arriaga. It is a modern-day fable rated R for violence, sex, nudity, gore, profanity, alcohol, drugs, smoking, and frightening and intense scenes such as car crashes and dog fights.

The term zoopoetics was first used by Jacques Derrida in *L'animal que donc je suis,* in allusion to Kafka: "Le chat dont je parle n'appartient pas à l'immense zoopoétique de Kafka" (20) (The cat I am talking about does not belong to Kafka's immense zoopoetics). Derrida's cat does not belong to Baudelaire's family of cats either. Nor is it the cat who talks in *Alice in Wonderland.* The cat Derrida is talking about is his own cat, a little cat, the cat that saw him naked and embarrassed him. As a result, Derrida asks himself, "qui je suis au moment où, surpris nu, en silence, par le regard d'un animal, par exemple les yeux du chat" (18) (Who am I (or who I follow) at the precise moment when I am taken by surprise naked, in silence, by the gaze of an animal, for example the eyes of the cat). Driscoll and Hoffmann interpret this experience of seeing oneself being seen through the eyes of an animal as the starting point of thinking (2). Derrida's cat, at the origin of zoopoetics, the gaze of the nonhuman animal upon the human animal, and the human returning the gaze, turned both inward and outward, the structure of fables, asking if there *is* reversing the quick of the fable.

An allusion to the first lines of the Gospel According to John: Paul Valéry's exclamation, "Au commencement était la fable!" (I, 966) (In the beginning was the fable!). Valéry explains, "Ce qui veut dire que toute origine, toute aurore des choses est de la même substance que les chansons et que les contes qui environnent les berceaux" (I, 966) (Which means that every origin, every genesis is of the same substance as the songs and the stories that surround the cradle). Such an interpretation suggests that fables are the hand that rocks the cradle and, ultimately, civilization, and implies that fables are not minor or lesser because they are good enough for children. For Gérard Farasse, the fable manifests itself through a gradual shift of the register. "Le terme de parabole, d'où dérive parole, dit le pèlerinage vers les origines, en même temps qu'il conserve le sens qu'il avait en grec ecclésiastique de comparaison entre le propre et le figuré: Parler, c'est toujours fabler, paraboler (. . .), cela vient de fari, la fable c'est la parole" (3) (The term parable, from which comes [the word] parole, tells of the pilgrimage to the origins, while retaining the meaning it had in ecclesiastical Greek: To speak is to tell a fable, to parable [. . .] it comes from fari, the fable is the word). Farasse's vision of the fable justifies the place that fables hold in the collective psyche as well as in the canon.

"Masters take after their dogs," says El Chivo (Emilio Echevarría) toward the conclusion of González Iñárritu's film *Amores Perros.* El Chivo (the Goat) (an animal nickname for a human) is a former teacher turned terrorist (for the love of humankind), then turned hitman turned vagrant. "Ese cabrón era como tú y yo, una gente normal" (That son of a bitch used to be just like you and me, normal people), says Leonardo, a corrupt detective to his buddy who is looking for a hired hitman to kill his brother. In this world, the corrupt Leonardo considers himself as normal as the young man wanting to kill his brother, as normal as you and me for that matter. Deirdra Reber points out that *Amores Perros* has been accused by critics as reading like a sequence of visual bullets, with a commodification of violence that impedes narrative evolution or moral transcendence and argues that the narrative content makes this film more than a case of commodified violence. In other words, Reber sees *Amores Perros* as "love as politics," and considers it emblematic of a new kind of political discourse (281). By definition, commodification is the act of turning something (a commodity) into an item that can be bought or sold; a commodity being an economic good or raw material such as water, time, or a body. The root word for commodity, however, is the Latin *com-*

modus which means appropriate, satisfactory, and as convenient as a commode that points to comfort. So I would disagree with the suggestion that violence is being commodified in this film, for the viewer never feels comfortable with it. The violence is never watered down. it is very difficult to watch *Amores Perros,* it even takes several tries to get through the opening scene and there is no respite. Cheap perhaps, but the commodity comes at a very high price.

El Chivo used to be a husband and a father, now his daughter thinks he is dead and he goes by an animal name: the Goat. Goats have been important symbols throughout the ages. In Greek mythology, while the female goat is viewed as nurturing, the male is viewed negatively. Pan is a virile ruler who is always ready to mate and appreciates the ladies. In the film *Pan's Labyrinth,* the goat is a trickster and the viewer is never sure if he is looking after the innocent girl's interests or paving the way for her to burn in hell. Mary Jo Hazard writes that everything about Pan is magical, including his voice, because his screech could make an enemy cover his ears and flee in disgrace, hence the word *panic.* In the Bible, the goat was the first animal to have been sacrificed (Genesis 22:13). Mark Davoren writes that if goats have come to be associated with the devil and Satanism, it is because of their behavior. Goats are lascivious, they like to butt heads, their eyes are slanted because of their lust, and their nature is so hot that they can dissolve diamonds. Medieval bestiaries, however, also see the goat as a symbol of Christ. El Chivo in *Amores Perros* could very well tick *all-of-the-above* descriptions.

Amores Perros was translated into English as *Love's a Bitch,* as if this were a romantic comedy with a happy ending. Sooner should it be *Love Doggone,* or *Dog Days of Love,* or simply *Love Gone Wrong,* for *perros* in *Amores Perros* is an adjective describing three distinct love stories that failed. These stories are all about nasty love, awful, hurtful love, if love there is. Perhaps it is only about dogs, not about love. *Un día perro* is a day gone to the dogs. Although a symbol of fidelity, man's best friend Fido has negative connotations both in English and in Spanish: to be treated like a dog, to be as sick as a dog, the dog days, to work like a dog, dog-eat-dog. Burkhard Müller argues that Kafka uses his dogs to uncover the repulsiveness of everything that is social. "No dog, that is quite certain, will ever share the tiniest morsel of food with another dog; in this respect, dogs might as well live in complete solitude. They even surpass mere egotism: they snatch away the food even when they are full and even from their malnourished neighbors, not out of greed but for reasons of principle. Which principle could that be: Probably the same one that makes us collect even the tiniest debts of others, although we do not need or even want the money" (109). Similarly,

Amores Perros presents the world of the dog in the manger who is not hungry yet does not allow others to eat. Cofi is Ramiro's dog, yet Ramiro (Marco Pérez) only wants his dog back when he becomes Octavio's (Gael García Bernal) dog.

Once upon a time there was a dog named Cofi who lived with human beasts: Octavio and his lusty, cruel brother Ramiro, Ramiro's confused wife Susana (Vanessa Bauche), and a bitter grandmother who didn't want to look after her grandchild. It is a triptych, three narratives, three couplings or pairings: Octavio and Susana, Daniel (Álvaro Guerrero) and Valeria (Goya Toledo), and El Chivo and his daughter Maru. However, many more pairings can be discerned throughout this fable that spills over with dogs: Octavio and Cofi (his dog), Octavio and Ramiro (brothers), Valeria and Richie (her dog), Daniel the unfaithful husband and his family, Susana and Ramiro (husband and wife), El Chivo and all his adopted street dogs (La Gringuita, Frijolito, etc.), endless possibilities for the pairings of beasts and sovereigns.

The story behind the fables of *Calila e Dimna,* in turn, much resembles the twisting rhythm of the parables: a Castilian collection of exemplary tales translated from the Arabic *Calila wa-Dimna* in either 1251 or 1261, that itself was translated from an eighth-century Persian version that itself was translated from the Sanskrit Panchatantra that dates to 300 CE.[2] Most of the versions available, however, are for children. The reason for this is that stories with animals that talk and mirror human traits and vices are usually relegated to children's reading lists. If the Panchatantra is available for kindergarten through sixth grade, it must have everything to do with the fact that fables are false; they are also naive, and they lack gravity. They are not *for real:* from old French *fable,* story, tale, lie, falsehood, from Latin *fabula.* Children are told imaginary tales to hold their attention. In the real world, however, crabs do not take pity on aging herons (*Calila e Dimna* 143), oxen do not experience loneliness (134), lynxes are not ambitious (125), neither are jackals, nor are lynxes thrown in prison for plotting against the anxious lion (chapter 4) who is not really a sovereign, nor a political animal. Moreover, fables never refer to real animals, and real animals never use human language. Now the question is whether fables can go beyond this obvious limitation and recuperate value. Paul Valéry suggests that *indeed* they could, but then again perhaps not, and this has everything to do with the fact that they stand at the origin, beside the Word, at the very beginning of *once upon a time,* of the myth, of the fable itself, the fable that, according to Paul Valéry, could not exist or subsist without the word as cause (I, 964). In this case, being the cause would imply that the word is also the beginning, the origin. However, Valéry reminds us that every beginning is a consequence (I, 864). Something always causes and precedes the beginning, just as something, anything, be it nothingness as in *Amores Perros,* will always come after the end.

Exemplary tales, parables, and fables are also about the art of teaching. In the second half of the thirteenth century, many Castilian translations of exempla appeared: *Calila e Dimna,* Sendebar, *Poridat de poridades, Disciplina clericalis,* and *Libro del Caballero Zifar,* just to cite a few examples. According to J. M. Cacho Blecua and María Jesús Lacarra, as a collection of exemplary stories *Calila e Dimna* deals with the ability to adapt to concrete circumstances, to apply general rules to a situation, and to recognize the intentions of the Other even if these intentions seem to be in contradiction with reality. "En definitiva, se trata de un movimiento dialéctico entre lo abstracto y lo concreto, entre las verdades generales y los ejemplos de aplicación particular" (21–22). (In fact, this is about a dialectic movement between the abstract and the concrete, between general and individual truths.) Cacho Blecua and Lacarra add that on a social plane the stories of *Calila e Dimna* teach how to know the Other, while on an individual plane they recommend measured conduct, as opposed to hastiness and impulsiveness. There is, however, doubt as to whether the teaching is effective, because, in fact, the protagonists in *Calila e Dimna,* be they animal or human, make many errors, and the rogue lynx Dimna does not heed the exemplary stories being told to him. In fact, the fables from *Calila e Dimna* do not appear to have a moralistic function or even moralistic success. Nor does *Amores Perros,* for what is there to learn?

Amores Perros begins with a car chase. The driver, Octavio, is drenched in sweat and cursing. He and his friend are being chased like animals. There is a dog bleeding to death in the back seat. "Is he dead?" asks Octavio, he who is being hunted. The scene culminates in a horrific car accident. The first twelve minutes present short, agonizing scenes. The viewer suddenly enters the world of dog fights, cut to a young woman opening the front door to a building and a black dog escaping, cut to a kitchen scene with a resentful grandmother washing dishes, cut to a street scene with El Chivo and his stray dogs. The viewer is taken from the dog fight, to the street, to Cofi the black dog roaming the streets, back to the dog fight, to a close-up of El Chivo's gun because he is about to kill someone, to eggs frying, to an assassination, back to fried eggs to a recurring image of a model on a billboard, to persistent telephone calls in which the caller does not speak when the call is answered. Nineteen minutes into the film, Ramiro has held up a drugstore and Susana has told Octavio that she is pregnant again. Twenty-five minutes in, there is yet another dog fight, Octavio listening to Susana and Ramiro having sex, Octavio interrupting the act under a pretense of a phone call and then trying to rape Susana when she enters his room to take the call.

Now the question is whether these animals, these political animals, the gentle ox, the conniving, storytelling lynx, the undecided lion, the Mexican street dog, Octavio, Ramiro, and Susana are representative of the human or whether the human is representative of the animals. What came first, the human or the animal? In *L'animal que donc je suis*, Derrida suggests that the animal came first. The title is a play on words, and although it is translated as *The Animal that Therefore I Am*, it can also be understood as *The Animal that therefore I follow* since *je suis* can either mean *I am* or *I follow.* Consequently, Derrida is either the animal, or he comes after the animal, an ambiguity that he maintains throughout the essay. An example of this deliberate doublespeak would be, "Si jamais un jour l'animal que je suis devait écrire une autobiographie . . ." (16) (Possible translations: *If ever the animal that I am were to write an autobiography*, or *If ever the animal that I follow were to write an autobiography.*) In the next paragraph, Derrida alludes to "l'animal autobiographique" (17) (the autobiographical animal), and he begins the paragraph after that with the conditional *if*, if he is what came after, then he needs to determine not only what it means to follow, to come after, but also what he is doing when he says *I am* or *I follow.* Obviously, since *je suis* can mean either *I am* or *I follow*, Derrida also has to determine what he is doing when he says *I am* and *I am* and *I follow* and *I follow* (17). Furthermore, Derrida asks himself who he is or whom he comes after just as he notices that he is being seen naked by his cat. Here, a new cogito is being established; it is not so much the Cartesian *Am I?* but rather *Whom do I come after?* It could also be *I am seen, therefore I am.* Who comes first, the one who sees or the one being seen?

While in the Panchatantra and in the Arabic version, the brothers Calila and Dimna are jackals who represent tricksters, in the Castilian version they are lynxes or servals, representative of keen vision and hearing. The Spanish word for lynx is *lobo cerval*, which introduces a canine element to the feline lynx, the word lobo meaning *wolf.* In this sense, the lynx would be a combination of a canine and a feline. Jacques Derrida would describe them as being *entre chien et loup* (between dog and wolf) (neither this nor that) with *une faim the loup* (the hunger of a wolf) (their ambition), and figures of the zoo-political (2008, I, 23), an allusion to the *homo homini lupus.* In this case, the animal can be considered the human of other animals. As symbols, both the jackal and the lynx can be rendered negative, the jackal often being associated with death and destruction because it feeds on the bodies of dead animals, and the lynx with cunning and fierceness. Consequently, the nonhuman animals are being associated with the human and given human traits. The reverse can also be done when humans are associated with nonhuman animals. In his ecocritical reading of Shakespeare's play Titus Andronicus, Simon Estok cites many examples of this association, "No less so are Aaron and Tamora othered with images fairly standard for the day in their bestializing gestures. Aaron and Tamora are both tigers (5.3.5; 5.3.195, respectively); Aaron is an adder (2.3.35) for his vengeful nature, a 'hellish dog' (4.2.78) for his miscegenatory (and, according to the times, monstrous) relationship, and is 'like a black dog, as the saying is' (5.1.122) for his hellish deeds" (68). Hence, Dimna, Cofi, El Chivo, Ramiro, and Octavio can be either the nonhuman animals associated with the human, or the human associated with the nonhuman animal.

Recently, there has been an effort on the part of scholars to shed the anthropocentrism of the fable and trade it for an anthropo(ex)centrism and to read animal behavior and natural history into the fable. Sebastian Schönbeck argues that our theoretical premises are crucial for understanding and evaluating literary animals but also wonders if we can learn something from the fable about animals and the environment (112). Does Kafka's fable "Jackals and Arabs," for example, tell us anything about jackals, Arabs, a desert oasis, and the foreigner who came from the North? Perhaps. For one, the jackals smell bad, nonetheless they seem to hate uncleanliness, and they like carrion so much that they keep on eating even while being lashed by their sovereigns the Arabs, whom they disdain for killing animals for food. It is a symbiotic relationship; the beast needs the sovereign and the sovereign needs the beast. Powell writes that "The parabolic narrative is nothing more than a vehicle to transport meaning. It is hollow at its core. It possesses no value unless it is interpreted, unless a meaning is realized by the reader" (270). For Schönbeck, in turn, the fable is a prime example of zoopoetics and ecopoetics, "because the fable problematizes and theorizes the relation of texts, animals, and environments. Another reason for the yet undiminished interest in fables is that theoretical key texts of ecocriticism and animal studies include fables both as a method and an object of research" (270). Does such an argument suggest that a reading of *Calila e Dimna* and a viewing of *Amores Perros* would teach us something about the fabled animals? Does the crow telling the lynx that she wanted to peck the serpent's eyes out for having eaten her chicks tell us anything about the crow and the serpent? Does it tell us anything about the lynx who advises the crow to refrain from being like the heron who wanted to kill the crab who felt sorry for her and ended up dead herself? Do dog fights tell us anything about dogs and humans? To approach the question or questions, I return to Derrida's, "pas de loup" (I, 23) (no wolf, the step of the wolf) and "la bêtise est le propre de l'homme" (I, 104) (Stupidity is intrinsic to man).

After having tried to rape Susana, Octavio confides to his friend that he simply wants her to come and live with him. In hopes of convincing her, he takes Ramiro's dog and enters him in a dog fight. A product of his environment, this is the only way Octavio knows how to manifest the love he feels for his brother's wife (if this is love). He gives her money, money that they will accumulate and save until they have enough to run away together. Unfortunately, Susana ends up running away with her own husband with the money that Octavio gave her, making Octavio feel stupid. Dimna, in turn, feels just as stupid so he listens to the fable of the heron and the crab; perhaps there is something to learn, some way to earn back the favor of the king. To make a long story short, the crab who felt sorry for the heron and tried to help her ends up killing the heron who was getting ready to kill him. After telling the story to Dimna, Calila says, "Et non te di este enxenplo sinon por que sepas que las artes fazen por ventura algunas cosas que la fuerça non puede fazer" (145) (I only gave you this example so that you know the arts accomplish some things that force alone cannot). Calila adds that were Sençeba to be strong but of an unsound mind, so would it be, but that Sençeba appeared to be brave, good, and wise (as does Octavio). But there is no convincing Dimna as there is no convincing anyone in *Amores Perros.*

Once upon a time in Mexico there were two brothers, Octavio and Ramiro, who somehow managed to render the story of Cain and Abel quite innocuous. When Ramiro (mom's favorite) was not at home beating his wife, he was either working the cash register at a supermarket, chasing skirts like a goat, or robbing pharmacies. Since Octavio happened to be in love with Ramiro's battered wife, he entered Ramiro's Rottweiler, Cofi, into the world of dog fighting in hopes of making much money and thus winning Susana's heart. For Terrie Waddell, it is the energy of canine figures in Aztec myth that filters through the narratives of *Amores Perros.* These canine figures evoke hellhounds associated with Xolótl, the human/dog that guided the dead to the underworld, and the trickster Tezcatlipoca, known as "the enemy of both sides" (123). This canine energy, however, is not unique to Aztec myth; the belief that dogs guard or guide entry into the underworld is universal. Waddell points to Cerberus and Anubis, black dogs (like Cofi) who signify death, depression, guardianship, the trickster (129). In reference to the protagonists/antagonists of *Amores Perros,* Waddell observes that as they slide into and out of personal underworlds, "their passage is magnified, reflected, and eased by canine child surrogates" (123). Waddell adds that "As they begin to emotionally merge with the animals they've adopted it's impossible to tell whether these pets are 'written on' by the owners, the owners are 'inscribed' by their pets, or this hybridization represents a more psychological twinning" (124). The canine guiding the dead to the underworld becomes the animal that is followed, as is the trickster, and this impossibility of knowing who writes on whom and who inscribes whom harkens to the animal that therefore one is, or one follows. Not quite as threatening as Cofi, but just as ominous, is Valeria's dog Richie who disappears under the floorboards and thus leads the couple Valeria-Daniel into their own personal underworld.

On the other hand, although Dimna's lynx eyes do observe, he refuses to follow, words go in one lynx ear and out the next. He does not learn and such a refusal to learn places him beyond the allegory and possibly challenges the didactic goal of the parable being told to him in hopes of quelling his reckless ambition. Is his resistance that of a human or nonhuman animal? Again, he follows not. And neither does Chivo who leads the dogs in *Amores Perros*. Time and again, Dimna's reaction upon hearing an exemplary tale is, "Entendido he lo que dexiste. Dizes verdad en quanto dizes, mas . . ." (130) (I heard what you said. You tell the truth with what you say, but . . .) If we were talking to Octavio, Ramiro, Susana, and all the other characters of *Amores Perros*, they would say the same. They would not hesitate, they would agree, but the agreement would be shadowed by the conjunction *but*. Thus, Dimna negates everything he just said and indicates that what matters is the argument that comes after the contrastive conjunction. In this instance, the fable fails to satisfy a didactive and moralistic role, it fails to tame both the animal and the human. This calls for a novel interpretation of the fable's value and function. For Kafka, as Matthew Powell argues, the parable may state a fact, but these facts do not mean what they state and they refer, instead, to some fabulous beyond. "Parables reproduce the words of the wise, but these words prove useless in daily life. Inevitably all that one can take from a parable is that the incomprehensible is incomprehensible, and that we already knew" (272). Hence, *Calila e Dimna* and *Amores Perros* could very well point to the possibility of something other than the conventional anthropocentric and narcissistic knowledge produced by the reading of fables. As Akira Mizuta Lippit reflects, the animal brings to language something that is not part of language and remains within language as a foreign presence (165–166). In other words, because the animal lacks language capacity, its function in language is a metaphor that originates elsewhere (165–166). Any attempt to reverse the limitations of the fable would have the human bringing to the animal world something that is not part of the animal world and that can remain there as a metaphor that originates elsewhere.

It is precisely in that "elsewhere" that zoopoetics "thinks through" the text. For Walter Benjamin, animals in Kafka's stories are "repositories of the forgotten" (810). Driscoll and Hoffmann add that it is not because Kafka's texts are about animals that his poetics is a zoopoetics, but because the animals that inhabit his texts serve as a necessary means to a poetic end. "Without them, it can't be done. But what is 'it'? We may never know, and indeed, the answer will be different each time, but whatever 'it' may be, it contains the whole of zoopoetics" (2018, 3). Accordingly, without Calila and Dimna and all those who inhabit the Mexican film including the dogs, and regardless of whether they listen or learn, "it" cannot be done.

Rather than teaching and telling a moral, *Calila e Dimna* and *Amores Perros* resemble opportunistic vegetation, the stories spread and ramble. A story frame, an embedded narrative, and a third dimension that points the way to a new story frame, the dialectic of the fable. Once upon a time (story frame) there was an ox named Sençeba who fell into a ditch while pulling a wagon and as a result was abandoned by the rich merchant's prodigal son who entrusted him to a lazy servant who left him for dead. Once upon a time there was a magical dog named Cofi who could kill several dogs at a time and who was entered in a dog fight because his master's brother wanted to run off with his master's wife. Once upon a time there was a pretty woman named Valeria who owned and loved a dog named Richie and who was in love with a married man whose wife suspected him of cheating. Sençeba enters the scene with a fall that is symbolic, according to Estrella Ruiz-Gálvez Priego, precisely because Sençeba is an ox, in other words an incomplete and amputated being (297). Valeria also enters the scene with a symbolic fall from beauty and grace, a car accident that damages her. This time it is not the loss of manhood, but of its opposite. The streets of Mexico City are strewn with images of Valeria's beauty on billboards. Valeria looks out her window and sees herself when she was beautiful. As for Sençeba, he managed to survive, he limped out of the ditch, and ventured onto a pasture where he thrived and fattened. Valeria also limped out of the hospital, onto the wheelchair, only to fall under the floorboards following her dog who was being attacked by a rat, and she ended up losing her leg because of all that.

Both Valeria and Sençeba were lonely, which explains Sençeba's bellowing and

Valeria's silent calls, the phone constantly ringing in the house of her married lover. On Sençeba's pasture there happened to be a man (embedded narrative) who was afraid of a wolf who wanted to bite him. Knowing well that wolves hate water, the man jumped into a river and would have drowned had he not been rescued and taken to a nearby village where he met his death after leaning up against a flimsy wall that fell on him ("Si tu veux vivre, il faut que l'autre meure" (Foucault 227)) (If you want to live, the other must die). If you want to keep your leg, someone else must lose theirs. Valeria loses her leg and Daniel starts to regret having left his own wife for this one-legged woman who won't stop yelling at him. Now he is the one making the silent calls to his own wife. All the while (new story frame), there was a lion king terrified by Sençeba's bellowing and rogue lynx (or jackal) brothers, Calila and Dimna, standing on the outside looking in, political animals and vassals of the apprehensive lion king, the sovereign, debating the exemplary story of the monkey, the wedge, and the carpenter (embedded narrative) that Dimna does not want to hear.

The animal figures of the political: the ox, the lion, the man who is afraid of the wolf, the lynx/jackal/fox, the monkey, the wolf, the carpenter out to lunch, and Cofi the killer dog. For Ruiz-Gálvez Priego, these are stories of default and treachery (295). The rich merchant's prodigal son, the lazy servant, both defaulting on the ox, castrated, amputated slave of the human, dumb as an ox, an ox-in-the-ditch who is not as strong as an ox but does have the constitution of an ox. If there is natural history in the fable, the ox demonstrates what humans do to oxen and this neighborhood of Mexico City to its children and animals. Such human domination of nonhuman animals would point the way to the ethics of such domination, as Simon Estok does in his reading of Titus Andronicus: "At times, so poignant are the representations of the general theme of the ethical intertwining of human and nonhuman animals and so complex are the involvements of the natural physical environment in the drama that it is virtually impossible to avoid a political reading" (66). The human animal grants himself power over the nonhuman animal. The human grants himself the right to decide whether the animal will live or die and whether the animal species will be annihilated by virtue of death or castration. In *Il faut défendre la société*, Foucault presents the notion of biopower, the sovereign's power to decide who would live and who should die being replaced by the power to let live and let die. Foucault cites as an example of this conjecture the death of Spain's Francisco Franco that he describes as a joyful event because he who had the right to decide over life and death, "ne s'était même pas aperçu qu'il était déjà mort et qu'on le faisait vivre après sa mort" (221). ([He] had not realized that he was already dead and that they were making him live after his death.)

Once upon a time signifies that these animals are no longer among us, as dead as Franco. "Pas de loup," as Jacques Derrida suggests (I, 23) (*pas de loup* meaning either no wolf, or the step of the wolf), an absence that bespeaks power, a certain caution, a required absence that points Derrida's fable theory in two directions: the direction of humans and their animalistic politics, and the direction of the nonhumans and their zoopolitics (Schönbeck 122). Such directions steer clear of the moralistic function of the genre and possibly contribute to an effort at reversal of anthropomorphism. "We have made the louse in our image; let us see ourselves in his," (7) Michel Serres writes in *Le Parasite*. This would argue for focusing on animal-like behavior of humans instead of the human-like behavior of animals and to explore the parasitic relations demonstrated in fables, as opposed to the moral or to the evident anthropomorphism. Indeed, if fables are to be a subject worthy of study in ecocriticism, they therefore deserve an effort at a reversal, their own right, a mitigation of the anthropomorphic taming. Once upon a time, the lynx brothers Calila and Dimna stood at the entrance to the lion's kingdom in hopes of being welcome. They wanted to guard the entry to the kingdom, as some canines guarded the entry to the underworld. Are they representative of the human? Are they only props describing the political animal that is the human? Dimna, the trickster, more akin to "the enemy of both sides," and Calila the hopeful moderator who sees no harm in killing, unless of course, "Si tu pudieres matar a Sençeba sin daño del león, fazlo" (147). (If you can kill Sençeba without harming the lion, do so . . .) The "enemy of both sides," however, is a god, enter the anthropo-zoo-theological. Lynxes are also known as servals, a word that comes from the Iberian *lobo cerval*, in other words wolf serval, so we remain in the canine underworld. This cat/dog is ready to lead the lion, his sovereign, to his dark places, just like Octavio leads Cofi and Cofi leads Octavio, and even the adorable Lhasa Apso Richie lures Valeria under the floorboards where he is being attacked by rats. In her effort to rescue her dog, Valeria steps on her broken leg (a result of the car crash) and further damages it. Dog-eat-dog, the betrayed who betray who are betrayed, *homo homini lupus*, wolf is the human to other wolves. Valeria the homewrecker, Octavio the broken-wannabe-homewrecker, driving fast, being chased by Jarocho, the leader of a dog fighting gang whom he had just stabbed in the abdomen for having shot Cofi who was winning too many dog fights. The chase culminates in a horrific car accident that, for Amit

Thakkar, is of more importance than the dogs because it permeates all layers of the film and connects all the characters (12). The crash is re-enacted from different perspectives and repeated four times. Can we say that had there been no dogs there would have been no car crash? Had there been no humans, perhaps.

Most of what Derrida has written about animals touches on the ways that philosophers and theorists have tried to separate human beings from animals using traits such as the hand, spirit, nudity, awareness of death, while other traits such as language and reason are discussed only in passing. For Matthew Calarco, it is clear that Derrida is suspicious of the classical formulations of the human-animal and that he is seeking to rethink the differences in a nonhierarchical way (105). I argue that fables were thinking this *difference* or *thinking otherwise* from times immemorial and that fables serve as an example of this *thinking otherwise.* Far from being anthropocentric, they are anthropo(ex) centric, they do not want to teach, they do not seek a moral, for they are as immoral as nature. Certainly, this leaves us unsatisfied. Chapter 4 of *Calila e Dimna* was not part of the original, it was added on by the Arabic translator who wanted to make up for the amorality of the story of the lion and the ox where the culpable remained unpunished. There was a similar effort in Iñárritu's death trilogy. *Amores Perros,* a Mexican product, constitutes the first panel of the triptych. The next two panels, *21 Grams* and *Babel,* created by Hollywood, want a didactive raison d'être, a moral, and a relatively happy ending. But fables are tricksters. *Calila e Dimna* and *Amores Perros* are amoral. El Chivo the hitman steals money from the dead and the wounded and walks into the horizon with his killer dog. This is not an acceptable ending. Moreover, such denouements are contrary to Muslim and Christian precepts, because God's creation, the ox, cannot be scorned by a manipulator who gets away with the ox's death. Gilbert Fabre explains that in the Hindu version of *Calila e Dimna* (The Panchatantra) the cosmic order is threatened by the friendship between a carnivore and an herbivore, thus calling for an adviser (311). The lion alludes to this when arguing with Dimna, "ca él comme yerva et yo commo carne" (151–152).[3] (He eats grass and I eat meat.) This is how and why Dimna gets away with it in the original. These can be humans in animal clothing or animals in human clothing developing, like Derrida, "a thought of the Same-Other relation where the Same is not simply a human self and where the Other is not simply a human Other" (Calarco 106). Like the political, human is human by exclusion, but the human can be defined in negative terms, neither rock nor animal nor god. Fabre argues that these talking animals that appear to be a mere literary convention were quite something else for the Hindi because their language was symbolic of the continuity between the human and the animal implied by the belief in reincarnation (309). By contrast, in the Koran the animals never speak a human language, only the initiated can understand them.

Is there reversing the limitation and rendering a lost value? The answer is yes, there isn't, or it is too late because the fable was at the beginning and, "Il fallait éviter la fable" (Derrida 2006 60). (The fable should have been avoided.) Derrida subsequently explains why, "L'affabulation, on en connaît l'histoire, reste un apprivoisement anthropomorphique, un assujettissement moralisateur, une domestication. Toujours un discours de l'homme, mais pour l'homme, et en l'homme" (60). (The fable, whose history we know well, remains an anthropomorphic taming, a moralizing subjugation, a domestication. Always a discourse about man, for man, in man.) However, Derrida also wonders how he can either welcome or liberate so many "animots" in him, for him, like him. "Animots" is a play on words, its homonym is animaux (animals); *mot*s, however, means *words,* so the made-up word is *aniword* as opposed to *animal:* we have come full circle, back to the beginning, the fable, the word. Dimna did try to avoid the moralizing subjugation, as did the dogs and their masters; Cofi begins by leading Octavio to the underworld, and ends by leading El Chivo, the goat. Without the Jackal, the Serval, the Wolf, the Dogs, and all those people it cannot be done. Once upon a time there was an implication of fault in this effort to make animals think and talk. What appeared to be innocent was not innocent at all, it was culpable. Then time passed and the textually transmitted beasts became commodities, raw materials, something useful, cheap, comfortable, and cheap enough to produce money. The wolf of thrown to the wolves, fighting for his life and surrounded by human wolves eating each other alive, for the sake of profit, in this case for a handful of Mexican pesos, oblivious of the high price that was paid for all this cheap stuff.

Notes

1. Reference to the fable of the vixen and the drum in *Calila e Dimna,* p. 135.

2. Calila and Dimna are lynxes in the Castilian version, Jackals in the Arabic version, and foxes in the Panchatantra.

3. In note 66, page 152 of the *Calila e Dimna,* the editors cite R. Llull, "los animals que comen carne significan a los nobles; y los que comen yerba a los plebeyos." (The animals who eat meat represent the nobles and the ones who eat grass the plebeians).

Works Cited

Amores Perros. Directed by Alejandro González Iñárritu. Altavista Films S.A. de C.V. / Z Film S.A. Studio Home Entertainment [distributor], 2000.

Anonymous. *Calila e Dimna.* Castalia, 1984.

Benjamin, Walter. *Selected Writings.* Vol. 2, 1931–1934. Belknap Press, 1999.

Biaggini, Olivier. "Quelques enjeux de l'exemplarité dans le Calila e Dimna et Sendebar." *Cahiers de Narratologie,* https://doi.org/10.4000/narratologie.28.

Cacho Blecua, J. M., editor. *Calila e Dimna.* Castalia, 1984.

Calarco, Matthew. *Zoographies.* Columbia University Press, 2008.

Davoren, Mark. "Biblical Beasts: Goat." https://www.english.op.org/godzdogz/biblical-beasts-goat/.

Derrida, Jacques. *L'animal que donc je suis.* Galilée, 2006.

Derrida, Jacques. *Séminaire La bête et le souverain I* (2001–2002). Galilée, 2008.

Derrida, Jacques. *Séminaire La bête et le souverain II* (2002–2003). Galilée, 2010.

Driscoll, Kári, and Eva Hoffmann, editors. *What is Zoopoetics? Texts, Bodies, Entanglements.* Palgrave, 2018.

Driscoll, Kári. "The Enemy Within: Zoopoetics in Erinnerungen an die Kaldabahn." *Journal of the Kafka Society of America,* vol./issue 35–36, 2011, pp. 23–31.

Estok, Simon C. "Theory from the Fringes: Animals, Ecocriticism, Shakespeare." *Mosaic: A Journal for the Interdisciplinary Study of Literature,* vol. 40, issue 1, 2007, pp. 61–78.

Fabre, Gilbert. "L'archilexie OMNE dans le *Calila e Dimna.*" *Cahier d'Etudes Hispaniques Médiévales,* vol. 25, 2002, pp. 307–318.

Farasse, Gérard. "Au commencement était la fable," https://www.ecriture-art.com/comment_fable_farasse.pdf

Foucault, Michel. *Il faut défendre la société.* Seuil/Gallimard, 1997.

Hazard, Mary Jo. "Goat Symbolism." https://www.palosverdespulse.com/blog/2022/6/11/goat-symbolism-by-mary-jo-hazard.

Kafka, Franz. *The Complete Stories.* Schocken, 1971.

Lucht, Marc, and Donna Yari, editors. *Kafka's Creatures: Animals, Hybrids, and Other Fantastic Beings.* Lexington Books, 2010.

Lippit, Akira Mizuta. *Cinema without Reflection.* Milwaukee: University of Minnesota Press, 2016.

Middelholf, Frederike, Sebastian Schönbeck, Roland Borgards, and Catrin Gersdorf, editors. *Texts, Animals, Environments.* Rombach Verlag, 2019.

Müller, Burkhard. "Consolation in your Neighbor's Fur: On Kafka's Animal Parables." *Kafka's Creatures: Animals, Hybrids, and Other Fantastic Beings,* edited by Marc Lucht and Donna Yari, pp. 101–118.

Powell, Matthew T. "From an Urn Already Crumbled to Dust: Kafka's use of Parable and the Midrashic Mashal." *Renascence Milwaukee*, vol. 58, issue 4, 2006, pp. 269–287.

Reber, Dierdra. "Love as Politics: Amores Perros and the Emotional Aesthetics of Neoliberalism." *Journal of Latin American Cultural Studies*, vol. 19, no. 3, 2010, pp. 279–298.

Ruiz-Gálvez Priego, Estrella. "Calila e Dimna: conte du Moyen Âge et récit primordial." *Cahier d'Etudes Hispaniques Médiévales*, vol. 25, 2002, pp. 293–306.

Schönbeck, Sebastian. "Return to the Fable: Rethinking a Genre Neglected in Animal Studies and Ecocriticism." *Texts, Animals, Environments*, edited by Middelhoff et al. pp. 111–125.

Serres, Michel. *Le Parasite*. Grasset, 1980.

Thakkar, Amit. "Crash and Return: Choque, Allusion and Composite Structure in Alejandro González Iñárritu's *Amores Perros* (2000)." *Quarterly Review of Film and Video*, vol. 31, no. 1, 2014, pp. 11–26.

Valéry, Paul. *Œuvres, I*. La Pléiade, 1957.

Waddell, Terrie. *Wild/lives: Trickster, Place and Liminality on Screen*. Routledge, 2009.

PART III
Coloniality and Multispecies Resistance

Those hordes of vital statistics, those hysterical masses, those faces bereft of all humanity. Those distended bodies which are like nothing on earth, that mob without beginning or end, those children who seem to belong to nobody, that laziness stretched out in the sun, that vegetative rhythm of life,—all this forms part of the colonial vocabulary

FRANTZ FANON, *The Wretched of the Earth*

9

"He wanted me to be his little dog"

Imagery of Nature, Gender, and Colonial Powers in Jerónima Nava y Saavedra's Spiritual Autobiography

PILAR ESPITIA

The spiritual writing of Jerónima Nava y Saavedra (1669–1727), *Autobiografía de una monja venerable,*[1] is crucial to examine female conventual writing in the colonial territory of New Granada. Its importance stems from two primary aspects: First, it reveals the writing contexts for women during colonial times. Second, it showcases how religious women could construct through writing and experience a multifaceted spiritual world that occasionally challenged the prescribed obedience and orthodoxy. I would add that a third aspect—a fairly new one, due to current events related to climate emergencies—comes from the abundant references to plants and animals in Jerónima's mystical visions. Although not rare within mystical discourse, Jerónima's lively and dynamic images allow for an alternative reading of how these existences are not mere allegories of human spirituality. Owing to feminist and historiographical revisions, the colonial and women's history of the Americas is undergoing a process of reconsideration, and this perspective can be nurtured by intersecting critical studies of plants and animals. Part of the critical achievements of a feminist revision has been to identify that many of the spiritual writings were wrongfully attributed to men. This is the case for Jerónima's writing: It was erroneously believed that Jerónima's spiritual life was penned by her confessor, Juan de Olmos y Zapiaín. Ángela Inés Robledo, the editor of the first modern version of Jerónima's writings, identified the misattribution (8).

While feminist perspectives have highlighted the indispensable roles played by women during the colonial period, delving into critical studies of plants and animals opens a captivating avenue for reconsidering colonial history in the Americas. This book chapter proposes how an integrative study of plants and animals should be intersected with gender, postcolonial, and posthumanist discussions, and how the mystical writings of Jerónima Nava y Saavedra could be enlightening when considering a critical genealogy of the nature/culture paradigm. I delve into the imagery of nonhuman beings—plants and animals—by focusing on their material and symbolic manifestations in Nava y Saavedra's spiritual writings, a line of study that has not been fully addressed by previous studies. Such an approach will pave the way for an exploration and problematization of the aesthetic, ethical, and political dimensions of the colonial world's relationship with nature. Zeb Tortorici, in his insightful work on marriages, baptisms, and funerals of dogs in Bourbonic New Spain, asserts that "colonialism was relational and highly dependent on alterities not only of language, race, class, gender, and sex, but of species as well" (113). If we are to grasp colonialism in the New World as a complex tapestry of ideological entanglements and interconnections between humans and nonhumans, what theoretical and methodological shifts and adjustments are necessary to center[2] animals and plants within these human-constructed, historical texts? Can the study of female mystical texts expand the understanding of colonial relationships that humans forged with nature during the early modern period? Fanon's opening quote reminds us of nonhuman and human forms of existence—women, children, Indigenous and Black people, animals, plants, etc.—that have been erased, misinterpreted, diminished, or exploited by colonial powers, and yet, they were always on the margins of the texts, always coexisting and interacting with hegemonic narratives. Hence, revising the fissures within the texts and the shadows where marginal lives exist necessarily takes new hermeneutical and methodological postures. I would affirm that female mystical textualities of the Americas—and especially Jerónima's spiritual autobiography—due to their polysemic and ambiguous nature, provide an alternative framework of analysis that problematizes and alters the perception regarding plants and animals.

To address these questions, I will first examine the existing scholarship on Jerónima's spiritual life, especially some that mention nature. Subsequently, I will contextualize the comprehension of the relational concepts of nature within Hispanic colonial societies to elucidate the reevaluation of animal and plant representations within female mystical discourse. This exploration will not only reaffirm these colonial structures but also challenge or alter them. The discussion will consider the relevance of methodology and theoretical frameworks when it comes to considering other nonhuman forms of life. Finally, I will examine Jerónima's spiritual experiences from a perspective of natural consciousness, selecting specific vocabulary and mystical visions in which animals and plants play a prominent role.

Historians like Robledo, Osorio, and Herrera have considered the sensuous descriptions of Jerónima's mystical discourse and the multifaceted construction of female subjectivity and language within the confines of conventual life. In the studies authored by María Piedad Quevedo (*Un cuerpo para el espíritu*; "La imagen del jardín")—which I consider the most relevant to my proposal—representations of plants and animals in conventual life and mystical writings of Neogranadine nuns (including Jerónima) are studied to comprehend the significance of their symbolism within colonial political orders. Quevedo asserts that the appearance of certain natural landscapes, such as gardens, or the visions of sin epitomized by "disgusting" creatures like serpents or worms, are part of broader historical and discursive categories of taste and disgust. These categories guided the orientation of the body as a religious and spiritual site within Christianity in the New World (*Un cuerpo* 103). She acknowledges the prominence of animal imagery in the representations of spiritual life among nuns, dedicating some brief sections of her book to discussing the "bestiaries" of taste and disgust featured in the nuns' spiritual visions (*Un cuerpo* 161–167; 201–204). Animals such as doves and lambs—which are present in Jerónima's visions—represent a positive and tasteful aspect of spiritual transcendence, while serpents, worms, and vermin represent a sinful and disgusting degradation of the soul.

Vegetal imagery also emerged as a potent symbol in mystical writings, reflecting the soul's yearning for perfection, its communion with the divine, and the societal projection of women and convents as embodiments of the colonial order. As Quevedo's study demonstrates, this religious and political botanical symbolism permeated the spiritual narratives of these nuns ("La imagen" 77). Echoing this notion, Cañizares-Esguerra's work underscores the discursive construction of nature in support of Creole patriotic projects within the Pan-American territory. Feminine convents were "walled gardens, not ramparts: beautiful plantations with hedges to keep assailants and weeds out" (Cañizares-Esguerra 178).

The garden imagery drew upon a long-standing tradition within Christianity (the Garden of Eden or the *Songs of Songs*). Vegetal symbolic language extended to the naming of virtuous women and saints in the Americas (Saint Rose of Lima or Mariana de Jesús, known as the Lily of Quito). Within the pictorial tradition of *monjas coronadas* (crowned nuns), Jerónima is depicted at the time of her death with a crown of flowers. This reminds us of the importance of vegetal life within the Christian symbolism of the soul. For Jerónima, this language takes preponderance on a more intimate level. In one of her visions, she makes a very personal comment on how fond she is of plants: "Y io e sido y soi afisionadísima a las flores (And I have been and I am a great enthusiast of flowers)" (100).[3] The biographical information provided by her confessor does not mention that Jerónima worked as a gardener in her convent or why she loved flowers,[4] but because of her comment, we can imagine the influence that the materiality of the garden had on her spiritual writing.

Animality can represent the mystical scale or levels of the soul within Christian spiritual practices. Animals embody moral virtues or defects that move the nuns to imitate or despise them (Quevedo, *Un cuerpo* 162). Similarly, a spiritual analogy can be traced between plants and gardens: Flowers and fruits represent the desired state of the soul, while barren gardens or weeds are associated with sin. The sensitive grade of the soul was related to the internal/external senses and the (sexual) appetite, a commonality between humans and animals. It was humankind's duty to overcome this spiritual level to ascend to God, achievable only through reason and God's grace. Otherwise, the soul could descend to its brutal or vegetative state, which symbolizes the devil (Quevedo, *Un cuerpo* 163). Women, more than men, were considered prone to lust and animal-like behaviors, as per Christian religious and medical discourses from older Western traditions.[5] That is why fear and insecurities are constantly present in Jerónima's writing, as she consistently asks her confessor to verify her visions and ensure that her "womanly" condition does not lead to mistakes (55). This underscores the importance of subjecting women's actions and writing to vigilance, though we will reveal Jerónima's strategies to legitimize her scriptural production and subjectivity.

The representation of animals and plants inscribed in mystical writing is also linked to a dualist view prevalent in the Western world: Among different binaries that help build the "proper" orders of the world we can find "human against animal" (Quevedo, *Un cuerpo* 171). I would argue that plants could also be inscribed within this binary. However, they were regarded as inferior entities to animals due to Western culture and Aristotelian thinking, and this also demonstrates why plants have been less studied as historical or conscious agents, and more as commodities.[6] These binaries and hierarchies solidified the desired colonial orders: white Catholic Spaniards or Creoles were recognized as the rightful divine orders of the world. In contrast, Indigenous people, African slaves, mestizos, and mulatos were placed lower in the hierarchy and deemed in need of evangelization. It becomes evident that a significant part of colonial and early modern ideology involved fabricating a racialized fiction of the world and promoting an anthropocentric perspective. Additionally, representation of nature has often revolved around the paradigm that nature is closer to women. Carolyn Merchant notes two main feminine allegories of nature during the early modern period: a nurturing, kind mother (2), or a rebellious woman, a witch, associated with a wild nature that needs to be tamed (127). These aesthetic and moralistic proposals align with colonial strategies to dominate and exploit nature and women in both Europe and the New World.

While Quevedo's work is vital for understanding the baroque dynamics of the body and soul within colonial mystical discourse, I aim to shift the focus to the plants and animals in these textualities. I defend that these nonhuman elements are symbolic or rhetorical reiterations of the correct social orders, and they represent suspensions or alterations of those orders. To recognize and problematize the intersections between nature, women's mystical writing, and colonialism, it is essential to dismantle the Western perspective of (white male) domination that has reinforced the paradigm of nature/culture. This process involves articulating and integrating critical studies about plants and animals, as well as other living natural elements. To maintain the same classifications and disparities assigned by humans to other living beings is to obscure the overall tensions and complexities of life. I align with Neil L. Whitehead's approach and proposition of two anthropological, non-Western perspectives that have emerged from Amerindian thought: "perspectival quality" and "multinaturalism." These perspectives are recognized as cosmological systems within Indigenous cultures and have been acknowledged through the ethnographic works of several anthropologists from a decolonial and posthumanist point of view.[7] Whitehead affirms that this could be an escape from the dominance of the culture/nature divide and it might serve to shed light on how to "center animals" (333).

"Perspectival quality" entails viewing the world as inhabited by different subjects or persons, both human and nonhuman, each apprehending reality from distinct points of view (333). This would include plural perspectives of all existing beings.[8] The second approach, multinaturalism, challenges the anthropocentrism of Western "multiculturalism" and questions the nature/culture divide (Whitehead 333). Multinaturalism seeks to overturn imposed hierarchies constructed by rigid ontological systems where humans and then animals are considered superior in their existence. In doing so, multinaturalism dismantles this power system, allowing all beings to exist and interrelate in a continuum.

A second approach to centering beings other than humans involves acknowledging the historical limitations of the sources we study: "How do we come to terms with the anthropocentric nature of historical sources?" (Tortorici 113). It is undeniable that the documents produced by mystical nuns were created for human purposes. In these texts, animals and plants serve as symbolic representations within a human system of language production. The animals or plants in mystical visions often signify moral/spiritual abstractions of entire species rather than specific entities. While these texts and their readability are constrained by specific forms of communication, it is relevant to identify that these animals or plants transcend their capacity to represent something else. Drawing on Walter Benjamin's insights about Kafka's animality, Driscoll and Hoffmann argue that "we need not fear or mistrust the metaphorical, symbolic, and allegorical meanings embodied by literary animals, so long as we do not make the mistake of reading these nonhuman presences only or simply as metaphors—as arbitrary and interchangeable ciphers for the 'real' or 'intended' meaning" (4).

The recognition of intersections and entanglements between a semiotic and material world (the *animot*[9]), humans and nonhumans, body and soul, requires a methodological approach that is highly detail-oriented and allows imagination and poetry to take over. We can only begin to comprehend Jerónima's visions of animals and plants when we surpass the allegorical significance of the source. If we also acknowledge the oxymoronic nature of mystical discourse[10]—its penetration within a supernatural world where the loving/erotic presence of the divine is transformative, indecipherable, and unspeakable—the representation of nature within Jerónima's writing experience is also one where human/divine capabilities are questioned and transformed through plants and animals. Although Jerónima's visions can be separated into animal and plant visions—an artificial divide of the world where species do not interact—I consider that animals and plants are equally meaningful in her visions. They allow for human bodies to transform and transcend human intelligibility and sensuality.

Jerónima's Mystical Writing: The Paradoxical Grammar of Fierce Meekness

It is critical to reconstruct and imagine Jerónima's early life before she became a black-veiled nun of the Order of Saint Claire in Santa Fe in 1683. Born in Tocaima, a town some seventy-one miles southwest of Santa Fe (modern-day Bogotá), Jerónima entered the world in a rural area profoundly affected by the Hispanic colonization project. This encompassed the exploitation of natural resources, the genocide of Indigenous people (particularly the Panches and Pantagoros) living in the territories of the Patí River (nowadays Bogotá River), and the subjugation of African slaves. The distinctive experience of nature evident in her visions may have been influenced by the colonial processes that shaped her native territory for more than a century. To illustrate this, one can highlight the story of Juan Díaz Xaramillo (known as The Rich), a founder of the city of Tocaima in 1544. Many chronicles of the Indies recognize him as a greedy man who embarked on a mission to discover El Dorado (Suárez Guava 234).

Díaz's settlement on the hillsides along the Patí River was made possible through his participation in an expedition that systematically destroyed Indigenous communities. This brutal process involved the use of dogs to devour people, treachery, ruthless killing, and deprivation of lands (Suárez Guava 237). During his life, Díaz's house was renowned, but when Jerónima was born he was all but a legend: his house and much of Tocaima were devastated by the flooding of the Patí River in 1581. Many believed that Díaz's downfall was a result of a pact he had made with the devil to amass wealth. Following this tragedy, Tocaima was restored in 1621, and it was in this second settlement that Jerónima was born.

While Olmo's depiction of Jerónima's early life is brief (he recounts how Jerónima and her sister lived in their father's sugarcane plantation in Tocaima for only five years, before moving to Santa Fe) and focuses more on her virtues within the convent, it is important to recreate how this experience might have shaped Jerónima and her mystical exercises. What predominates in Jerónima's visions concerning nature is a paradoxical *grammar of fierce meekness,* reflected in the vocabulary and adjectives she employs to describe herself and Christ. Perhaps, her violent subjugation to Jesus reflects the systematic violence used to dominate Indigenous people, slaves, and nature, a situation she might have witnessed as a child. However, the initial structure of her spiritual experience takes on a transformative character, obscuring the initial reproduction of colonial orders.

In her first visions, Jerónima portrays herself as a vile, brute, ignorant, or pusillanimous creature in stark contrast to Christ, who is depicted as a meek yet demanding master. Jerónima recounts how God calls her to follow a righteous path, but she ignores the calling due to her "fiera grosería (fierce rudeness)" (59). Consequently, God sends messages indicating that her steps are leading her to hell rather than heaven (59); the only solution to mend her soul is through a terrible illness. When examining the terms used by Jerónima in Covarrubias's *Tesoro de la lengua* such as fierce (*fiero/a*), rude (*rudo/a*), pusillanimous (*pusilánime*), vileness (*vileza*), and brute (*bruto/a*), all these suggest a word choice associated with a presumed "primitive" and "violent" state of nature that must be overcome.

This vocabulary is expansive and seems to interconnect moral, formal, and aesthetic values associated with the things they name. For example, the definition of the word brute (*bruto/a*) in Covarrubias's *Tesoro* is as follows: "comúnmente se toma por el animal irracional, cuadrúpedo, tardío, grosero, cruel, indisciplinable [. . .] En lengua Toscana bruto vale sucio, feo (commonly it is taken as the irrational animal, quadruped, slow, rude, cruel, undisciplinable [. . .] In Tuscan language brute is equal to dirty, ugly, bad)" (Covarrubias vol.1, 154). These terms also encompass the vegetal world; the definition of rude (*rudo/a*) uses a simile comparing the rude subject to an uncarved piece of wood, rough to the feeling (Covarrubias vol.2, 16).

In contrast, one of the terms Jerónima uses to describe Christ is meekness (*mansedumbre*). After receiving a severe illness, she evokes an image of Nazarene Jesus (an iconographic representation of Christ carrying the Cross on his back), depicting him as meek (62). In the definition of meek (*manso*), it seems like the term needs to be defined by how nature should ideally be: "Se dice lo que es apacible, y sin violencia, como correr el agua o el río manso (It is what is peaceful and without violence, like the running of water or a gentle river)" (Coavarrubias vol.1, 538).

The iconography of Nazarene Jesus associated with meekness becomes a behavioral model for the black-veiled nun. In an *Imitatio Christi*, Jerónima is tasked with emulating the figure of a defeated and humble man, which also serves as a model for a body that has transcended its "brutal" or "violent" tendencies; a subjugated and passive body that reproduces the desired body of colonial orders. As Jerónima accepts the pain and suffering of her illness as a means of correcting her spirituality and "nature," the visions begin to replicate this model through various images of animals and plants.

However, the complete subjugation of Jerónima's life and visions to the presence of Christ becomes increasingly paradoxical. As Jerónima becomes meeker and more obedient, the oxymoronic nature of mystical discourse begins to operate: her body and Christ's acquire a transformative quality that allows them to assume the forms of animals or plants. It becomes paradoxical that, in representing the correct orders of the world, the nun and Jesus are displaced from their human bodies into animal or vegetal forms to render their spirituality intelligible. As observed in other visions, Jesus transforms from an authoritative figure into more of a lover or equal.

The remarkable aspect of Jerónima's visions is that she not only observes external images as representations to be interpreted as abstractions of her inner world, but she also physically embodies parts of the visions that are not entirely decipherable. The mystical experience of the dog—the vision that gives title to this chapter—is particularly intriguing. On one occasion, Jerónima is by the Choir of the Church, and she sees Jesus in the shape of a shepherd with a crook in his hand. He asks the nun to be "mi perrillo y as de andar siempre cabe mí (my little dog and you must always walk next to me)" (72).

Jerónima does not comprehend this request; the typical imagery of Jesus dressed as a shepherd would traditionally allude to his role as a guide and his followers as sheep. However, Jerónima must seek clarification and asks the Lord: "Yo me admiré de que, en ves de querer que fuese su obeja, quisiese que fuera perro; y Su Magestad dio respuesta a mi duda, porque me dio a entender que quería que le resguardase su perzona (I was admired that, instead of him wanting me to be his sheep, he wanted me to be his dog; and His Majesty answered my doubt because he made me understand that he wanted me to safeguard his person)" (72).

Even though the transformation in this vision only takes place through conversation, we can perceive the paradox of nature within mystical discourse. On the one hand, common references or allegorical Christian meanings regarding nature become suspended, and even to Jerónima's understanding, the vision is unforeseen (she expected to become a sheep, but instead, she is asked to be a *perrillo*). Additionally, in the case of the dog as a symbol of Christianity, the image can be ambivalent, which is common with other zoological forms in the world of religion. In particular, the image of the dog can be interpreted as a sign of loyalty and service (Cirlot 364), but there are instances where the dog can represent the devil (Quevedo, *Un cuerpo* 163). On the other hand, it is noteworthy how the vision erases the contradiction of nature seen as a violent force that needs to be tamed or controlled. In this case, the potentially violent nature of the dog is viewed as a virtue, if it is used to defend the master (Jesus).

We can also acknowledge the ambivalent reality of dogs in the New World. As

Tortorici has studied in the case of New Spain, we find "working dogs," animals brought from Europe for war or working purposes (Thomas in Tortorici 98–99) that did not receive any affection from humans. However, new sensitivities regarding dogs and other animals began to appear during the sixteenth and seventeenth centuries: "the humanism that expressed itself in the civil usage of and bonds of affection with 'pets'" (Tortorici 99). Jerónima's vision aligns with this evolving perspective: In a subsequent vision where Jerónima displays more power and agency, she sees Jesus as a child entering her heart. Jerónima feels ashamed that he is entering this place of her body, considering it "indecent." However, Jesus goes into her heart and says with kind words: "Mis esposas son afisionadas a perritos y a criar avesitas; pudieran aplicarse a tenerme a mí en su compañía, como tienen estas cosas ¡Qué poco ruido les diera! (My wives are fond of little dogs and of raising little birds; they could get used to having me as a company, as they have these things. How little noise I would make!)" (157). This passage challenges the colonial discourse prevalent in the previous visions.

First, Jesus entertains the possibility of becoming a little dog—he compares himself to birds or dogs as companions to nuns—inverting the previous vision where Jerónima was incarnating the animal. This suspends the hierarchical relationships previously established, giving Jerónima agency in her relationship with Jesus, or becoming a partner. Second, it highlights the affective relationships that could be formed between nuns and their "convent pets," a more horizontal relationship that partially dissolves hierarchies. This raises questions about the animals Jerónima and her partners possibly cared for inside the convent walls,[11] which allows readers to go beyond the allegorical meaning of dogs and think about their existence in everyday life. A particular vision in the text reaffirms the power Jerónima has gained through her fierce meek transformation: in an exchange of hearts, she steals the heart of Jesus and refuses to give it back. Jerónima claims: "No quise. Me salí con la mía (I did not want to. I got away with it)" (104). After this passage we see the nun gaining more influence in the convent and even proposing to become a preacher. This passage also emphasizes Jerónima's transformation into Jesus, which highlights the metamorphic capabilities of mystical discourse.

Similar to the first vision of the dog is the vision of the bull. Jerónima initially observes a bull being chased by a hunter (Jesus) and his vassals. Suddenly, the scene transforms from a hunting scenario into what appears to be a bullfighting arena, where the Celestial Court, including the Virgin Mary, watches the spectacle. What is surprising is the shift from an external, third-person narrative to a first-person perspective, where Jerónima becomes the chased bull. She, incarnating the bull, perceives the imprisonment as a gift from her Chaser (90). The oxymoronic qualities of mystical discourse become evident here: Jerónima embraces the suffering and imprisonment of herself as a bull, finding pleasure in the pain typical of mystic love. The change in perspective is intriguing, allowing Jerónima to momentarily embody a bull and recreate the thoughts and feelings of this creature, even if from a human perspective. It is also noteworthy to consider the material influences on Jerónima to construct the vision. The painting of Saint Francisco Solano (1549–1610) hanging from the convent walls—currently in the Museo Santa Clara in Bogotá—which depicts a miracle of the saint taming a bull, could have played a role. Additionally, the proximity of Jerónima's convent to the main square of Santa Fe, where bullfighting arenas were temporarily built for secular or religious festivities, might have contributed to her vision (Gómez Rondón).

Similarly, vegetal visions undergo an evolutionary progression as the nun deepens her relationship with Christ, encapsulating allegorical representations of the desired social orders and, at the same time, other types of sensual responses. In Jerónima's narrative, Christ is depicted entering the nun's heart as a gardener tasked with restoring a somewhat devastated and disorganized garden: "Tenía, a mi pareser, este huerto la serca muy ruin; a trechos estaba como a pique de yrse toda al suelo. Las plantas y flores qu avía estavan como confusas; con que su Magestad lo primero que reparó fueron los muros. Vi que los levantó mucho y después que hizo esto desía 'ortuz conclusus' [*sic*] (It had, as it appeared to me, this garden the fence very shabby; some stretches were about to all go to the ground. The plants and flowers that were there were all confused; so His Majesty first repaired the walls. I saw that he made them very high and then he said this: 'ortuz conclusus' [*sic*])" (83). In this vision, Jerónima's heart transforms into the landscape tended by a Divine Gardener, symbolizing his efforts to define and organize. The garden becomes a representation of human structures (architecture) striving to contain and restrict nature (Cirlot 267). *Hortus conclusus* or the enclosed garden is a conventional topic of Christianity and art. It represents an idyllic state of the soul: ordered nature is the perfect locus for a pure and mystical union with Christ. Hence, Jerónima is not only the lover but a piece of land requiring organization by the Gardener, which represents the desired gendered and anthropocentric orders of colonial powers.

However, Jerónima's plant visions also present some instances of ambiguity and sensuality. In one of them, she compares Christ to various flowers, referring to him as her narcissus, jasmine, carnation, and orange blossom. Remarkably, in this same vision, Jesus transforms, embodying an orange tree that produces a delightful fragrance (100). Subsequently, Jerónima envisions her soul transforming into a basil plant,[12] with Jesus explicitly instructing the confessor to take good care of this special herb (147). It is conceivable that Jerónima was familiar with these plants not only through their symbolic significance in literary tradition but also because they were part of the convent garden. In these visions, the focus seems to transcend the mere desire to reiterate orders, giving way to a more sensual experience of mystical love.

Conclusion: Mystical Discourse and Poetics of Nature

My chapter has provided a dedicated exploration of Jerónima's mystical visions, offering an exemplary foundation for a broader examination of multinaturalism and quality perspectives within mystical discourse. It confirms how this discursive modality allows for an integrative centering of plants and animals, not only in their allegorical meaning but also beyond their "paper" existence. It highlights the importance of intersecting critical studies of animals and plants with questions about postcolonialism, gender, and posthumanism. This analysis can be extended to other mystical female writings throughout the colonial history of the Americas. Such a comparative and comprehensive study would not only render visible the potential allegorical and metaphorical meanings attributed to nature in this genre, but also shed light on the historical and material specificities of nonhuman existences, along with the cultural production of women, within the colonial context.

The enigmatic and shape-shifting nature of mystical writing, characterized by its resistance to suffice rational comprehension and the constant perturbation of language, makes the sensuous appearance of natural figurations, such as animals or plants, a rich field for exploration. Animals and plants in mystical experiences have the potential to problematize and redefine the assumed relationships that humans have established with nature, and, at the same time, they alter the desired colonial and gendered orders of the Western world. In the realm of the supernatural and the spiritual imagination, realities can be reshaped; the tangible embodiment of other existences such as animals, plants, and deities expands the vision of how human and more-than-human life should be perceived. The selection of poetic resources in Jerónima's visions contributes to an alternative epistemology of heterogeneous forms of living existence. Feminine mystical discourse becomes a gateway to what Derrida identified as an alternative to mainstream Western philosophical thinking—the discourse of poets and prophets: "who admit taking upon themselves the address of an animal [or plant, or mineral, or river] that addresses them, before even having the time of the power to take themselves off [*s'y dérober*]" (383).

Notes

1. The term "spiritual autobiography" or "visions" is a fitting descriptor for Jerónima's manuscript. Angela Inés Robledo's contribution in naming and editing the manuscript is significant, as it shapes the way the work has been received and referred to by scholars and readers alike (Janiga-Perkins). The absence of new editions since Robledo's highlights the need for continued scholarly attention and exploration of Jerónima's mystical visions.

2. As defined by Tortorici and Few: "In this vein, we want to pose the question of what Latin American stories look like if we choose as the standpoint of our observation a focus not only on the human-animal interaction but also on the experiences and histories of the nonhuman actor in the unfolding of history [. . .] the transforming of nonhuman animals into *central* actors in the historical narrative" (3).

3. Quevedo mentions how the *Regla, constituciones y ordenaciones de las Religiosas de S. Clara de la Ciudad de Santa Feê de Bogotâ* refer to the importance of the gardener within the convent. They stipulate that the gardener must have virtues such as strength and temperance, as gardening is solitary. This would imply that being alone in the garden could be a temptation ("La imagen del jardín" 79–80).

4. The translation of Jerónima's text strove to reproduce the language in English as it appears in Spanish, minus some orthographic errata found in the source.

5. See Robert Archer's work, *Misoginia y defensa de las mujeres: Antología de textos medievales*.

6. "It's as if by a tacit agreement religions, literature, philosophy, and even modern science promulgate in Western culture the idea that plants are being endowed with a level of life (not to speak of 'intelligence,' for the moment) lower than that of other species" (Mancuso and Viola 9).

7. Whitehead reviews several ethnographic studies regarding Amazonian cosmologies where kingship and certain forms of culture and human behaviors are present and recognized in animal cultures.

8. This expansive perspective is possible if the materiality and ecologies of objects, or the presence of other existing beings can be considered when they are transformed by/interact with human life. See, for instance, the dossier of *postmedieval*, "Ecologies of things and texts: Nature, matter, and material culture in the Middle Ages" (Khanmohamadi and Schulz, eds.).

9. See Jacques Derrida's essay "The Animal that Therefore I Am (More to Follow)" (trad. David Wills).

10. Mystical experience can be understood as the intimate, direct, and loving experience of God. In this sense, the practices of mysticism for women within the Church were extremely dangerous and, to some extent, they were a direct affront to the orthodox of the Counter-reformist Church. The latter sought to establish that the experience of God was only possible through the intervention of the Church, the mediation of the clerics, and the sacraments. See Michel de Certeau, *La fábula mística: Siglos XVI–XVII.*

11. It was common for nuns to keep pets, but different convents throughout the Middle Ages in Europe prohibited this practice. For instance, a set of rules of a nunnery located in Langendorf, Saxony, from the early fifteenth century mentioned that "cats, dogs and other animals are not to be kept by nuns as they distract from seriousness" (Walker-Meikle 34). More attention needs to be paid when studying the material realities of animals and plants within colonial convents. From an archeological point of view, some studies have taken place, such as the study of zooarchaeological remains in the convents of San Francisco and Santo Domingo in Quito (Gutierrez and Iglesias).

12. The flowers and plants mentioned in Jerónima's vision are particularly colorful and produce different fragrances. The basil plant represents humility as it is a small plant with no flowers, but the more it is crushed, the more fragrance it produces (Hoess in Quevedo "La imagen del jardín," 80). From a symbolic point of view, garden plants are related to the virtues or different stages of Christ's life and refer to remote and various traditions (Añón Feliú 26).

Works Cited

Añón Feliú, Carmen. "El claustro: jardín místico-litúrgico." *El lenguaje oculto del jardín: jardín y metáfora. Cursos de verano de El Escorial,* edited by Carmen Añón Feliú, Universidad Complutense, 1996, pp. 11–36.

Archer, Robert. *Misoginia y defensa de las mujeres: Antología de textos medievales.* Ediciones Cátedra, 2001.

Cañizares-Esguerra, Jorge. *Puritan* Conquistadors.

Iberianizing the Atlantic, 1550–1700. Stanford University Press, 2006.

Certeau, Michel de. *La fábula mística: Siglos XVI–XVII.* Universidad Iberoamericana, 2010.

Cirlot, Juan Eduardo. *Diccionario de símbolos.* Siruela, 2019.

Covarrubias Orozco, Sebastián de. *Tesoro de la lengua castellana o española,* Luis Sánchez impresor del rey, 1611. *Biblioteca Digital Hispánica,* https://bdh-rd.bne.es/viewer.vm?id=0000178994&page=1. Accessed 30 Nov. 2023.

Derrida, Jacques. "The Animal that Therefore I Am (More to Follow)," translated by

David Wills. *Critical Inquiry,* vol. 28, no. 2, 2002, pp. 369–418. *JSTOR,* https://www.jstor.org/stable/1344276. Accessed 30 Nov. 2023.

Driscoll, K., and E. Hoffmann. "Introduction: What is Zoopoetics." *What is Zoopoetics? Texts, Bodies, Entanglements,* edited by Kári Driscoll and Eva Hoffmann, Palgrave Macmillan, 2018, pp. 1–13. https://doi.org/10.1007/978-3-319-64416-5_1. Accessed 30 Nov. 2023.

Fanon, Frantz. *The Wretched of the Earth.* Grove Press, 1963.

Gómez Rondón, María Fernanda. *De costumbre a perdición: corridas de toros desarrolladas en el virreinato de la Nueva Granada—Siglo XVIII.* 2015. Universidad de los Andes, Masters Thesis. https://repositorio.uniandes.edu.co/bitstream/handle/1992/12961/u713481.pdf?sequence=1&isAllowed=y. Accessed 30 Nov. 2023.

Gutiérrez Husillos, Andrés, and José Ramón Iglesias Aliagas. "Identificación y análisis de los restos de fauna recuperados en los conventos de San Francisco y Santo Domingo de Quito (siglos XVI–XIX)." *Revista Española de Antropología Atnerhxina,* 26, 1996, pp. 77–100. *Dialnet,* https://dialnet.unirioja.es/servlet/articulo?codigo=143054. Accessed 30 Nov. 2023.

Herrera, Clara. *Las místicas de la Nueva Granada: tres casos de búsqueda de la perfección y construcción de la santidad.* Paso de barca, 2013.

Janiga-Perkins, Constance. "Editing the Life Story of Jerónima Nava y Saavedra: Colonial Female Spiritual Autobiography and the Twentieth-Century Editor." *Letras Femeninas,* vol. 37, no. 2, 2011, pp. 117–138. *JSTOR,* https://www.jstor.org/stable/23346744. Accessed 30 Nov. 2023.

Khanmohamadi, Shirin A., and Vera-Simone Schulz, editors. "Ecologies of things and texts: Nature, matter, and material culture in the Middle Ages." *postmedieval* 13, 2022, pp. 163–166. https://doi.org/10.1057/s41280-022-00230-6. Accessed 30 Nov. 2023.

Mancuso, Stefano, and Alessandra Viola. *Brilliant Green: The Surprising History and Science of Plant Intelligence* (Foreword by Michael Pollan). Island Press, 2015.

Merchant, Carolyn. *La muerte de la naturaleza: Mujeres, ecología y Revolución Científica.* Editorial Comares S.L., 2020.

Nava y Saavedra, Jerónima. *Jerónima Nava y Saavedra (1669–1727): Autobiografía de una monja venerable,* edited by Ángela Inés Robledo, Centro Editorial Universidad del Valle, 1994.

Osorio, Betty. "La escritura religiosa de Jerónima Nava y Saavedra: Juego entre afirmación y obediencia." *Cuadernos de Literatura,* vol. VI, no. 12, 2000–2001, pp. 71–80. *Editorial Universidad Javeriana,* https://revistas.javeriana.edu.co/index.php/cualit/article/view/8027. Accessed 30 Nov. 2023.

Quevedo, María Piedad. *Un cuerpo para el espíritu: Mística en la Nueva Granada, el cuerpo, el gusto y el asco (1680–1750).* ICAH, 2007.

Quevedo, María Piedad. "La imagen del jardín en la vida conventual femenina de la

Nueva Granada." VII *Jornadas internacionales de arte, historia y cultura colonial: Vida y cultura conventual*, August 13–15, 2013, Bogotá, pp. 76–93.

Robledo, Ángela Inés. "La autobiografía espiritual de Jerónima Nava y Saavedra: Historia de un yo fragmentado." *Cuadernos de Literatura*, vol. VI, no. 12, 2000–2001, pp. 81–89. *Editorial Universidad Javeriana*, https://revistas.javeriana.edu.co/index.php/cualit/article/view/8028. Accessed 30 Nov. 2023.

Suárez Guava, Luis Alberto. "Juan Díaz engañado por la riqueza. Un artífice de la fortuna y la tragedia en el mundo colonial." *Maguaré*, 22, 2008, pp. 223–289. *Repositorio Universidad Nacional*, https://repositorio.unal.edu.co/handle/unal/29276. Accessed 1 Dec. 2023.

Tortorici, Zeb, and Martha Few. "Introduction: Writing Animal Histories." *Centering Animals in Latin American History*, edited by Zeb Tortorici and Martha Few, Duke University Press, 2013, pp. 1–31.

Tortorici, Zeb. "'In the Name of the Father and the Mother of All Dogs': Canine Baptisms, Weddings, and Funerals in Bourbon México." *Centering Animals in Latin American History*, edited by Zeb Tortorici and Martha Few, Duke University Press, 2013, pp. 93–123.

Walker-Meikle, Kathleen. *Cats in Medieval Manuscripts*. The British Library, 2019.

Whitehead, Neil L. "Conclusion: Loving, Being, Killing Animals." *Centering Animals in Latin American History*, edited by Zeb Tortorici and Martha Few, Duke University Press, 2013, pp. 329–345.

10

Guamán Poma's Ecocentric Ethos in *Primer Nueva Crónica y Buen Gobierno*

VÍCTOR SIERRA MATUTE

Felipe Guamán Poma de Ayala's *Primer Nueva Crónica y Buen Gobierno* (*The First New Chronicle and Good Government*) is a rich repository of knowledge on the nature of plants and animals, as evidenced by the index of "flora and fauna" terms with more than 500 entries in the 2017 edition of the Colección Bicentenario: Biblioteca del Perú (Guamán Poma, *Corónica* 617–669).[1] However, what makes this chronicle truly remarkable is Guamán Poma's depiction of plants and animals as active participants in the shaping of the history and culture of Perú, challenging the prevalent anthropocentric worldview of the early seventeenth century.[2] Written as a letter addressed directly to King Philip III of Spain with the explicit aim of confronting the violence of colonization, the *Primer nueva corónica* provides a unique perspective on the complex connections among humans, nonhuman animals, and plants, aiming to expose the dramatic consequences of Spanish colonial rule in the region. In addition to shedding light on the history and culture of the Andean native communities, the chronicle engages with the ethics of human treatment of the natural world.

My chapter critically examines the significant contributions of *Primer Nueva Crónica y Buen Gobierno*, using interdisciplinary and transhistorical methodologies to explore its cultural implications. I argue that Guamán Poma de Ayala's notion of "buen gobierno" ("good government") is ultimately fueled by what I call an "ecocentric ethos," that is, a worldview that places nature and the environment at the center of ethical, aesthetic, and epistemological concerns. Guamán Poma de Ayala's ecocentric ethos portrays nature as a complex multispecies web, where humans, nonhuman animals, and plants possess equal agency and importance. This challenges Eurocentric perspectives on Indigenous epistemologies and nature, and it criticizes the imposition of a Western anthropocentric worldview and the consequent disruption of Indigenous ways of coexisting with the environment.[3]

Guamán Poma de Ayala positions himself as a mediator between nature and humans, as well as between the Spanish king and the Andean communities, but he does so by blurring the boundaries between human and nonhuman agents in his depictions of history and culture. Furthermore, the *Primer nueva corónica* presents a critique of the colonial extractivist mindset that views nature as a resource to be exploited for economic gain. Instead, Guamán Poma advocates for a more harmonious relationship between humans and the environment, one that acknowledges the agency of nonhuman entities and the interdependence of all life forms, thus promoting the idea of a multispecies society. Guamán Poma de Ayala portrays the diverse roles of animals and plants in Andean communities, including their medicinal, ritual, and cultural significance. Moreover, he sheds light on the experiences of marginalized groups in relation to nonhuman animals and plants, thereby raising important questions for the fields of critical plant and animal studies, while simultaneously challenging anthropocentric perspectives within these scholarly frameworks. Ultimately, Guamán Poma's ecocentric ethos carries significant implications for how we perceive our place in the world and our relationship with the environment.

Centering Ecology in *Primer Nueva Crónica y Buen Gobierno*

Coined by the German biologist Ernst Haeckel in 1866, the term "ecology" has its origins in the combination of the Greek words *oikos* and *logos,* that is, "home" and "study," meaning the "study of the relations of plants and animals with their environment" (Onions 300). In Guamán Poma's *Primer nueva corónica,* we encounter an ecological manifesto that surpasses the boundaries of the canonical definition of "ecology," infusing *oikos* with a deeply affective component by intertwining it with his native concept of *wasi* (also "home" in Quechua).[4] Guamán Poma not only staunchly defends Peru's natural habitats against the threats of the Colonialocene (Echazú Böschemeier et al. 158), but also, in a deeper etymological sense, immerses the reader in an emotive exploration of the region he affectionately calls home.[5]

The emotional depth with which Guamán Poma delves into his exploration of the ecosystem as *wasi* not only reverberates in his defense of both natural *habitats* and their *habitants* but also finds expression in the ongoing revitalization of the *Primer Nueva Crónica y Buen Gobierno*, utilized in contemporary times for various purposes, ranging from cultural promotion to political resistance.[6] Ultimately, the world inhabited by Guamán Poma, though temporally distant, remains our planet and continues to grapple with the challenges imposed by coloniality today. In alignment with Guamán Poma's advocacy, I contend that his work holds the potential to act as a catalyst for reflections in dialogues aimed at centering plants and animals within discussions encompassing the energy crisis, climate change and other forms of "terracide,"[7] the so-called sixth mass extinction (Ceballos et al.), and the critical examination of nature as merely a resource exploited by multinational corporations—an extractivism that perpetuates the colonizing gaze of the Western world upon the territories of the Global South.[8]

Ecocentrism, described as "the broadest term for worldviews that recognize intrinsic value in all lifeforms and ecosystems themselves," has recently been shown to be the sole pathway to achieving sustainability and an essential solution to addressing the ongoing environmental crisis (Washington et al. 35). If we keep in mind that "every species and every organism living today got here through the same long struggle for existence" (Washington et al. 39), then we come to understand the interconnectedness and interdependence of all life forms on earth.[9] Plants, nonhuman animals, and humans "exist on the same ontological continuum" (Tortorici 113). In this context, Guamán Poma's ecocentrism transcends mere appreciation for nonbiological natural elements like *huacas*, ancestral Andean entities manifested in rock formations, lakes, and landscapes (Echazú Böschemeier et al. 172). It embraces the intrinsic value of both human and nonhuman lives as central to its ethos, thus qualifying for the classification of "bioecocentrism" (Heffes 32)

Guamán Poma adopts the fundamental principles of ecocentrism—understood as bioecocentrism—in the *Primer Nueva Crónica y Buen Gobierno*. Silvia Rivera Cusicanqui and Rolena Adorno, alongside other activists and Guamán Poma scholars, have underscored the central role of the concept of "mundo al revés" (upside-down world) within the chronicler's narrative (Rivera Cusicanqui, *Ch'ixinakax* 21; Adorno, *Guaman* 142). This inverted or chaotic world emerges as a direct consequence of the conquest and colonization processes.[10] Guamán Poma's mission to expose abuses represents an endeavor to reinstate ethical underpinnings within societal structures through his unique linguistic expression (Rivera

Cusicanqui, *Ch'ixinakax* 14). Here, the concept of good government emerges at the core of the *Primer nueva corónica*, embodying Guamán Poma's firm intention to restore—within the political sphere—an ethos rooted in absolute respect for the ecosystem and its biodiversity.

Guamán Poma unites the plant and nonhuman animal worlds to counteract the impacts of the Colonialocene, which has marginalized their significance as legitimate knowledge sources. By bringing together plants and animals, Guamán Poma critiques the highly compartmentalized practices enforced by the conquest and colonization of Latin America/Abya Yala upon the nonhuman world, segregating the functions of plants and animals and thereby stripping them of their inherent agency.[11] One approach Guamán Poma employs to rectify this worldview is to accentuate the pervasive presence of plants and animals in his text through descriptions and enumerations, and in his drawings, through depictions of living beings actively intertwined with natural landscapes.

Let's examine a dual example of this approach. The last section of the first half of the book is devoted to the characterization of the months (*Nueva* 556–576), chapters "which provide minute details of human interactions with celestial bodies, climate, the soil, native and introduced crop plants, domestic and wild animals, disease, and even excrement, during the course of the agricultural and ritual year" (Cushman 90). The most prominent features defining each month include the flourishing flora, the agricultural tasks required, the types of animals that emerge during both day and night in that season, and the interactions these animals have with the plants of the month and with humans. For instance, when explaining the characteristics of the month of March, Guamán Poma presents a drawing titled "Travaxos: Zaramanta oritota carcoy mitan, marzo, Pacha Pocoy Quilla" (*Nueva* 561) (Labor: Time to expel the corn crows, March, month of the earth's ripening).[12] In the image, we are presented with a richly detailed depiction of a crop field teeming with life (fig. 10.1).

The scene is vibrant with various plants, animals, and human activity, illustrating the interconnectedness of these elements within the ecosystem. At the center of the image, we see cultivated fields, indicating human agricultural practices. Surrounding these fields are diverse plant species—maize, trees, shrubs—emphasizing the biodiversity of the environment. Adding to the complexity of the scene is the presence of several animals, both "free" and domesticated.[13] Birds fly overhead, while a female fox, known as an *atoc*, walks among the vegetation. Another *atoc* is carried on the back of a human figure identified as a "*parian arariua, oxeador*," or a "watching sparrow-scarer" (*Nueva* 561). This interaction

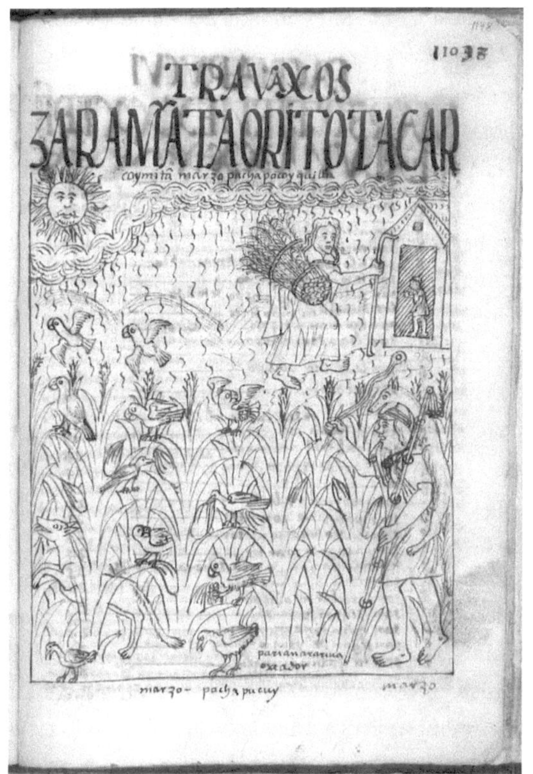

FIGURE 10.1. "Travaxos: Zaramanta oritota carcoy mitan, marzo, Pacha Pocoy Quilla." Royal Danish Library, GKS 2232 kvart: Guamán Poma, *Primer Nueva Crónica y Buen Gobierno* (c. 1615), p. 1148.

highlights the symbiotic relationship between humans and animals in the vegetal setting. Furthermore, the presence of the *parian arariua* and the *atoc* together, as one entity, exemplifies the symbiotic interaction between humans and nonhuman animals in shaping the landscape, as they are actively safeguarding crops from avian and other wildlife consumption.

The drawing representing March is accompanied by a rich description of the tasks depicted (*Nueva* 560). The main task is that "este dicho mes se an de ocupar los yndios de oxear de los loritos y de otros paxaros y de los zorrillas y zorras y de los perros y de los yndios negros mestizos que hurtan los chocllos" (*Nueva* 560) (during this month, the Indigenous people must be occupied with watching over the parakeets and other birds, as well as the skunks, foxes, dogs, and black mestizo Indians who steal the corn). What adds intrigue is the closure of this section with a Quechua enumeration of key terms, predominantly comprising the fauna and flora representative of the month. The enumeration in Quechua includes terms such as "*pacha puquy killa*" ("middle of the rainy month"), "*chuqllu*" ("corn"), "*chuqllu suwa*" ("corn thief"), "*araríwa*" ("guardian of the harvest"), "*churu*" ("furrow"), "*llullucha*" (a type of corn), "*wanaku*" ("guanaco," a type of llama), "*wik'uña*" ("vicuña," a species of camelid native to South America), "*purutu*" (a bean), "*chichi*" ("meat"), and the type of mushroom known as "*quncha*" (*Nueva* 561). This extensive list serves to identify the various types of animals and vegetation depicted in the drawing; because of its sketchy nature, it may be difficult for the reader to discern the differences. It is in this combination of words and images that Guamán Poma vividly portrays lush landscapes teeming with diverse flora and fauna, emphasizing the interconnectedness of the natural world. These landscapes are never depicted as passive scenery but instead as active participants in shaping the ecosystem depicted by Guamán Poma. They engage in a dialogue with Andean ritual practices of mutual nurturing and collaboration between humans and nonhumans, some of them enduring to this day.[14]

In addition to visual and textual accumulation, the underscoring of the presence of plants and animals is achieved through their positioning as a central part of the discourse. With his Quechua surnames "Guamán" (derived from Quechua *waman*, meaning "falcon") and "Poma" ("puma" in Quechua), signing his full name beginning with the Spanish "Felipe" and ending with "de Ayala," Felipe *Guamán Poma* de Ayala distinctly emphasizes animality by literally placing it at the center of his identity.[15] Nonetheless, the material inscription of his name is not the only approach deployed by Guamán Poma to center more-than-human life. In the following pages, I analyze the two strategies utilized by Guamán Poma in his ecocentric-infused reclaim of a good government. First, I explore Guamán Poma's textual accounts, which offer detailed portrayals of the ecological landscape, highlighting the complex interdependence between plants and animals, a relationship imperiled by colonization. Second, I delve into Guamán Poma's illustrations, wherein he employs visual imagery to illustrate the complex network of ecological relationships. While text and images are inseparable in the chronicle, as I have already shown, they pursue distinct yet complementary approaches to emphasize the centrality of animals and plants in Guamán Poma's vision of a sustainable future between humans and the natural world. As Rolena Adorno has argued, these supplementary approaches highlight the distinctions between textual and visual modalities, which at times come into conflict (*Guamán* 116). Guamán Poma's text clearly carries a nostalgic tone of past times and offers a stark denunciation of colonial abuses, yet it consistently acknowledges the authority of the king (Adorno, *Guamán* 117). In turn, the visual rhetoric adopts a more raw and direct approach, juxtaposing contrasting images of both an orderly Incan society and a world turned upside down by the process of colonization (Adorno, *Guamán* 116).

An Ethics of Biological Coexistence in Guamán Poma's Text

"Coexistence begins in place—the places we come from and call home, the places we care for and struggle over, the places that sustain us, the places we share" (Larsen and Johnson, "Introduction" 1). Guamán Poma negotiated the coexistence between Europeans and Indigenous peoples with diplomacy. In his plea to the king to address the critical situation arising from the violence of colonization in his homeland, he avoids embracing a confrontational stance toward royal authority. Instead, Guamán Poma accepts it, yet fails to comprehend the logic behind justifying such barbaric acts, and thus, requests the king's explicit intervention. In essence, he seeks not opposition but collaboration between colonial authorities and native cultures to rectify the destruction caused by the conquerors' cruelty. In Guamán Poma's own words, what he ultimately demands is an "emienda de vida" (*Nueva* 33) (to mend their ways [of living]; *New* 9) from the colonizers themselves.

The *Primer nueva corónica* has been described as a work that exemplifies various forms of formal mixing: it blends languages, incorporates diverse media, and integrates multiple philosophies (López-Baralt 405). It can be interpreted as a manifesto promoting the idea of harmonious coexistence among cultures and species.[16] Guamán Poma "was in the borderland/borderline between Andean (and not only Inca) cosmology and Castilian cosmology" (Mignolo in López-Calvo 181), embodying a synthesis of Indigenous Andean and Spanish colonial worldviews, thus epitomizing the concept of cultural coexistence.[17] It should come as no surprise, then, that Guamán Poma ardently advocated for the ethical cohabitation of humans, plants, and nonhuman animals within colonial Peru. This advocacy for a multispecies society stemmed not only from his ties to Indigenous beliefs in respect for nature but also from his promotion of cultural coexistence and his own lived experience as a product of biological cohabitation. However, in aligning with Guamán Poma's perspective, we must navigate his discourse while avoiding the risk of falling into the "stereotypical representation of Indigenous cultures as essentialized ecological natives" (Schmidt 413). As emphasized by various Indigenous critics, the oversimplified classifications of Indigenous peoples arise from a teleological viewpoint of modernity—a trajectory extending from Hobbes to Marx, through Locke, Rousseau, and Hegel—that seeks to compartmentalize politics and nature as mutually exclusive spheres (Cadena 101). Modernity has been influenced by a hierarchical perspective of humanity, positioning it in relation to its distance from the nonhuman.[18] Echoing Marisol de la Cadena's perspective, examining Indigenous politics requires a broader framework than Western political discourse: it entails recognizing the political foundations of Indigenous practices, often relegated by the West to the domains of the spiritual, the magical, the shamanic, and the natural, precisely to depoliticize them; it also entails acknowledging that Indigenous societies have not only been influenced by non-modern ontologies but also strategically adapted to modern institutions (Cadena 105).

Indeed, understanding Guamán Poma's ecocentric ethos can shed light on how Indigenous societies navigate and adapt to the challenges posed by modern ontologies. One of the places where we can observe Guamán Poma's ecological consciousness is in his textual reinterpretation of biblical passages. Critics have approached Guamán Poma's text with skepticism, particularly in contrast to his drawings, suspecting that his "colonial ego" speaks on his behalf, driven by the desire to present himself as an exemplary subject to the King of Spain (Rivera Cusicanqui, "Pensando" 213). However, from my perspective, it is precisely in the subtle textual derivations from canonical discourse that he seeks to reconcile different cosmologies without falling into the risk of appearing heretical, while also making clear how they diverge from his own ecocentric principles.

A clear example of Guamán Poma's reinterpretation of biblical narratives is his reexamination of the biblical flood myth (Genesis 6–9), positioned within his sequence of the "Edades del mundo" (Guamán Poma, *Nueva* 42) (Ages of the World; *New* 17) precisely amid the transition from the First to the Second Age. For Guamán Poma, this global event serves as the culmination of the First Age of the World, marking the inception of what he terms "El segundo mundo, de Noe" (43) (The Second Age of the World, of Noah; 19). In the biblical narrative, God's wrath leading to the destruction of humanity is attributed to the wickedness of men. Although Guamán Poma reflects this idea, highlighting humanity's unforgivable sins, what is truly striking is his emphasis on an aspect absent in the canonical biblical narrative: according to him, God destroys humanity because "estubo el mundo lleno de hombres que no cauia" (43) (The world was overflowing with people; 19). This emphasis on global overpopulation underscores Guamán Poma's concern for the consequences of uncontrolled human expansion, likely experienced through the arrival and massive reproduction of colonizers.[19] It also reveals his ecological awareness of the delicate balance between humans and other biological entities. At this point in Guamán Poma's discourse, an intriguing disparity emerges between the visual portrayal of Noah's Ark in his drawing, which emphasizes the presence of animals, and the textual narration of the episode, which underscores the role of plants. As the floodwaters recede and Noah is finally able to exit his ark, his action is not to consume the animals, but rather, "noe salio del arca y planto uina y de ello hizo uino y biuio del dicho uino y se enborrachó" (43) (Noah went out of the ark, planted a vineyard, made wine, drank of the wine, and became drunk; 19). In both Guamán Poma's and the canonical biblical narrative, Noah celebrates the end of the flood with wine. However, the Bible primarily emphasizes God's act of celebration through the display of a vast rainbow, without explicitly highlighting Noah's act of planting a vineyard. In contrast, Guamán Poma emphasizes the vital role of the harvest in rebuilding the global ecosystem. This distinction not only sets his interpretation apart from the biblical narrative but also underscores his ecocentric perspective on the relationship between living organisms and the post-flood world. Guamán Poma's dual portrayal complements the prominence of animals in his visual depiction of the Ark. When viewed from a reader's standpoint, the combination of text and image offers a holistic defense of plants and animals as central to the reconstruction of a sustainable ecosystem, fostering an ethics of interspecies coexistence. By foregrounding a residual anecdote in his narrative, Guamán Poma reframes the biblical event, thereby materially centering the importance of plants and animals in a foundational myth within his chronicle.

Visualizing Ecocentrism through Guamán Poma's Drawings

As previously mentioned, Guamán Poma extends his narrative from textual reinterpretation to visual representation, employing various strategies to symbolically center plants and animals within his drawings. Scholars such as Mercedes López-Baralt and Rolena Adorno have examined the impact of Andean spatial symbology on Guamán Poma's images.[20] It is agreed that Guamán Poma incorporates a grid-like pattern into his drawings, characterized by two diagonal lines crossing the square to form an X at its center: [x]. In every image found within the *Primer nueva corónica,* the depicted figures consistently establish a hierarchical relationship. The central part, or *chawpi,* serves as the focal point of the drawing, representing Guamán Poma's deliberate emphasis (Adorno, *Guamán* 123). This focal point is followed, in descending order of significance, by the upper (*hanan*), left (*paña*), right (*pata*), and lower (*urin*) triangles (Adorno,

Guamán 124). In the following pages, I analyze how these visual hierarchies are translated into the drawings depicting plants and animals. I anticipate that depending on the message Guamán Poma intends to convey, there are two types of depictions: those that represent the harmony of "the good government" and those that portray the world turned upside down by colonization.

In examining the first category of images, let's consider the depiction titled "El Primer Mundo [de] Adán [y] Eva" (Guamán, *Nueva* 22) (The first age of the world, Adam and Eve; *New* 18), which portrays the primal inhabitants within an Andean landscape (fig. 10.2).

The sun is positioned in the upper left corner, representing the passage of time (Cushman 91), while the moon occupies the right. Representing masculinity and femininity, respectively, both the sun and the moon oversee the Andean-like Eden. The indigeneity of paradise is emphasized through various visual elements: Adam is depicted wielding a *taki chaclla*, a specialized digging stick used for sowing, while Eve, seated on the ground, embraces their children. Alongside them, several birds, including a rooster and a dove, share the space. However, the focal point of interest lies in the center of the image, where two doves, symbolizing animality, are situated alongside the hand grasping the *taki chaclla*, emblematic of the act of planting. Guamán Poma, thus, centers the harmony between humans, nonhuman animals, and plants, portraying them as integral components of a balanced and sustainable existence in the very origins of the world.

In the representations of conquest and colonization, the pictorial spaces convey a distinct message, employing symbolic value to illustrate the disorder resulting from the Colonialocene. Within these images, the center may either remain vacant, symbolizing the absence of order, or be occupied by figures that are out of place: a suffering Indigenous individual, a corrupt Spanish colonizer, or an impious religious figure. A quintessential example of this illustrative style is found in the drawing titled "Pobre de los indios: de seis animales que temen los pobres de los yndios en este reyno" (Poor Indian: six animals feared by the poor Indians of this kingdom), depicting a native surrounded by six violent animals (fig. 10.3).

The unique aspect of this image lies in the association of each animal with a colonial figure, serving as a pointed critique by Guamán Poma: the royal administrator represented as a serpent, the itinerant Spaniard conquistador as a tiger, the *encomendero* as a lion, the parish priest as a fox, the notary as a cat, and the cacique as a rodent. In a simultaneous attack, all these animals assail the distressed Indian.[21] Within the context of drawings portraying the upside-down

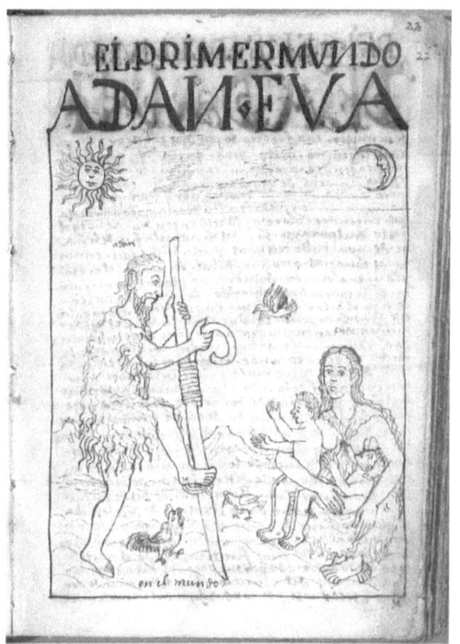

FIGURE 10.2. "El Primer Mundo, Adán, Eva." Royal Danish Library, GKS 2232 kvart: Guamán Poma, *Primer Nueva Crónica y Buen Gobierno* (c. 1615), p. 22.

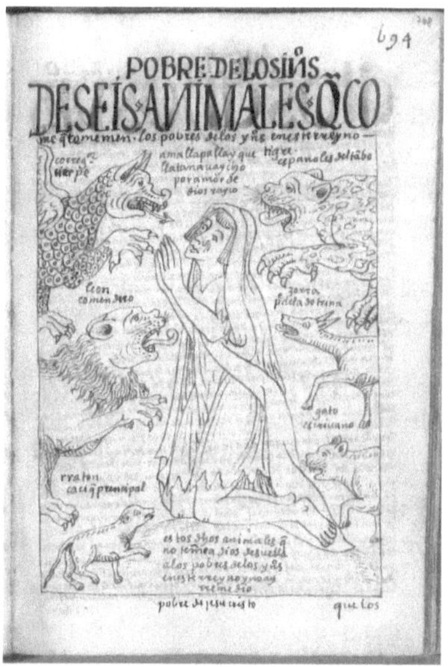

FIGURE 10.3. "Pobre de los indios: de seis animales que temen los pobres de los yndios en este reyno." Royal Danish Library, GKS 2232 kvart: Guamán Poma, *Primer Nueva Crónica y Buen Gobierno* (c. 1615), p. 708.

world, Guamán Poma highlights the consequence of decentralizing animality from the ecosystem, revealing how colonial powers exploit and dominate native society.

Conclusion

Engaging with the *Primer Nueva Crónica y Buen Gobierno* invites us to explore a work that critics once viewed as a missed opportunity, with its potential to drive meaningful change seemingly lost to history (Araníbar 7). However, rather than being a lost cause, Guamán Poma's thought is proving to be more relevant than ever.[22] Recent studies reveal that his ideas remain vital, as scholars increasingly turn to his work to reshape contemporary discussions on race, coloniality, and the environment.[23] The *Primer nueva corónica* retains its critical importance not only in historical narratives but also in ecocritical discourse, a field that it will undoubtedly continue to shape for years to come.

For Guamán Poma de Ayala, a "buen gobierno" is an ecocentric government: one that places the environment and all living beings at the core of governance. The ecocritical urgency conveyed in the *Primer nueva corónica* resonates through both its text and its images, reflecting Guamán Poma's ethical and aesthetical praxis in defense of plants and nonhuman animals. Just as Guamán Poma directed his chronicle to the King of Spain in hopes of provoking change, our responsibility in interpreting this private document is to act and respond with decisive action, particularly in matters concerning ecology, environmental stewardship, and the responsible coexistence of humans with plants and nonhuman animals. This responsibility includes recognizing the critical biological consciousness of Guamán Poma as part of an overlooked ecocritical Latin American tradition by literary and cultural critics (Heffes 12). Guamán Poma's insights in the *Primer Nueva Crónica y Buen Gobierno* must be reclaimed to gain a more comprehensive understanding of Latin American ecocritical thought (Heffes 31), as his environmentally centered perspective could significantly contribute to the ongoing ecocritical discourse within the developing ecological tradition of Latin America/Abya Yala. Ultimately, by centering the *Primer Nueva Crónica y Buen Gobierno* in contemporary times, we are elevating Guamán Poma's ecocentric ethos for a multispecies society, thus emphasizing the centrality of plants and animals in both academic and public debates.[24]

Notes

1. All the quotations in Spanish for this chapter come from the edition of the Biblioteca del Perú. Unless otherwise noted, the translations to English are based on Roland Hamilton's translation, *The First New Chronicle and Good Government.* The images from the autograph manuscript (GKS 2232-4) are obtained from the digitization by the Royal Danish Library, hosted on The Guamán Poma Website.

2. For further exploration of challenging anthropocentrism by centering plants and animals, see Vieira and McHugh. Regarding the concept of animal and plant agencies, Tortorici and Few remind us of the importance of not imposing the human notion of agency onto nonhuman entities, "especially given that the notion of agency arises in a secular Western culture and is itself saturated with Western humanist beliefs" (14). While it is impossible to fully comprehend the perspectives of plants and animals from our human standpoint, one strategy to avoid reducing them entirely to anthropocentrically driven desires and anxieties is to identify instances where plants and animals appear to act to resist harm, preserve their lives, or obtain benefits (Tortorici and Few

15). In any case, centering plants and animals should involve a deliberate plan "to de-center the human" (Whitehead 330).

3. For a series of articles discussing Indigenous coexistence with the natural environment in a global and comparative context, see Larsen and Johnson, *Being.*

4. As Claudia Berrios-Campos has shown, arguably the most emblematic act of defending the home or *wasi* is depicted in Guamán Poma's powerful narrative of his pilgrimage to Lima at the age of 80; there, he personally delivered the copy of the *Primer nueva corónica* into the hands of the viceroy, which ultimately made its way to Spain: "pero su llegada a Lima termina en el peor desamparo, sin comida, sin bestias, sin dinero, fuera de un zaguán, sin casa, sin wasi, sin familia, sin piedad, sin justicia" (however, his arrival in Lima ends in the worst abandonment, without food, without beasts, without money, outside a vestibule, without a home, without *wasi,* without family, without mercy, without justice; 206).

5. I borrowed the notion of "Colonialocene" from Echazú Böschemeier et al., who take up Donna Haraway's call to find a new and powerful name to describe our current society in its state of climate emergency (162). The Colonialocene can be defined as an anthropological framework that explicitly recognizes "the ecological effects of European colonialism" as a defining period within the geological history of the planet Earth (Milanez et al. 96). Thus, the term highlights the continued destructive impact of colonialism through extractivist global capitalism, social inequalities, and the transfer of materials and goods between geographies, shaping the discourse on the human species as a geological force.

6. Silvia Rivera Cusicanqui defines Guamán Poma as "teórico de la condición colonial" (theorist of the colonial condition; *Ch'ixinakax* 27). Mignolo highlights Guamán Poma as "the equivalent of Aristotle and Plato for the Western construction of the idea of Western thinking and Western Civilization" (López-Calvo 186), suggesting that he could be regarded as the earliest figure associated with the decolonial perspective, given the absence of conditions conducive to decolonial challenges before the sixteenth century due to the absence of coloniality. However, Mignolo emphasizes that the focus should not be solely on Guamán Poma's chronological precedence, critiquing the Western inclination toward privileging foundational figures within teleological temporal identifications (López-Calvo 185). The reclamation of the *Primer nueva corónica* also takes place in academic praxis: Echazú Böschemeier et al. propose a reclamation of Guamán Poma within the context of the Brazilian project "ReCânone," a "refundação étnica, racial e epistêmica das universidades brasileiras" (racial, ethnic, and epistemic re-foundation of Brazilian universities; 160). Mariangela Ugarelli has tackled other "instances of appropriation" in a markedly different manner, examining the *Primer nueva corónica* as a hypertext within contemporary Peruvian popular culture (75).

7. As Cecilia Lisa Eliceche has synthesized, "'Terracide' is a term coined by Weichafe

Moira Ivana Millán to denote the destruction of the visible and invisible forces, the tangible and intangible beings, that share territory with us" (Moira in Eliceche 543). Terracide integrates feminicide, transfeminicide, and travesticide, as well as epistemicide, genocide, and ecocide (543–544).

8. For an overview of the extractivist mindset imposed upon Latin America since colonial times, see Fornoff.

9. Ecocentrism, in this sense, is not antihuman; rather, "an ecocentric worldview follows naturally from our evolution-derived, empathetic and aesthetic capacities" (Washington et al. 40).

10. For an in-depth analysis of the environmental consequences resulting from the colonization of Huamanga, the region where Guamán Poma resided for the majority of his life, see Cushman.

11. "Abya Yala" roughly translates to "land in its full maturity" or "land of vital blood" in the Kuna language. For insights into the term "Abya Yala" and its significance in referring to the entire American continent, particularly in asserting Indigenous ancestral connections to the land and challenging colonial perspectives, see Porto Gonçalves.

12. In this and the following instances, translations are my own, as Hamilton's translation is limited to the first half of the *First New Chronicle.*

13. For a cultural history of animal domestication in colonial Latin America, see Norton.

14. For the *uywanakuy,* a Southern Andean ritual of mutual upbringing between humans and nonhumans, see Torres Lezama.

15. It is important to note that while his name centers animality, Guamán Poma's gesture with the monogram of his initials is rather intriguing: he transforms the "F" of "Felipe" into a lowercase "f," presumably to liken it to the cross of Christ's crucifixion. This tension between the textual representation of the word and the iconographic visuality of the monogram—influenced by both Christian and Indigenous symbolism—will be further explored in the analysis of both text and image in the subsequent sections of my chapter.

16. Although I refer to the *Primer nueva corónica* as a manifesto, "its knowledgeable and creative manipulation of European literary modes, Western Christian iconographic traditions, and Andean forms of signification render inadequate any single generic classification that might be proposed to describe it" (Adorno, "Contextualizing" xiv).

17. For the notion of coexistence, see Larsen and Johnson, "Introduction."

18. See Anderson for the challenge of how to problematize the nature/culture divide.

19. Newson demonstrates that "Spanish colonialism was disastrous for the Indian population of America [because] by the end of the colonial period, all Indian groups who had come into contact with Europeans were less than half of the size they had

been on the eve of Spanish conquest, and some had become extinct" (41). She also notes that the Spanish population experienced steady growth during the colonial period (66). This demographic shift likely contributed to Guamán Poma's perception that the tragic loss of Indian lives was being replaced by an increasing number of Spaniards.

20. See López-Baralt and Adorno, *Guaman*. Adorno examines Guamán Poma's *mapamundi*, with Cuzco positioned at its center, to extend her conclusions to the other drawings, presenting compelling arguments (*Guaman* 121). According to Adorno, Guamán Poma shares this symbolic representation with other Andean chroniclers, including Juan de Santa Cruz Pachacuti Yamqui Salcamayhua (*Guaman* 123).

21. For a sociolinguistic and ethno-historical analysis of the two sections of Guamán Poma's work in which he associates colonial functionaries as threats to Indigenous peoples, see Dedenbach-Salazar Sáenz.

22. An exploration of the reasons behind the historical discrediting of the *Primer nueva corónica* until recently can be found in Quispe-Agnoli. She also explores the potential of Guamán Poma's chronicle as a "pluriversal text," offering alternative perspectives on thinking and living.

23. For an analysis of Guamán Poma's advocacy for the rights of Black people in Peru as free citizens, see Styles.

24. As scholars, it is important that we embrace this approach. An exceptional example of a work that utilizes the urgency of contemporary crises to effectively engage with a Mayan text is *Emergency: Reading the Popol Vuh in a Time of Crisis*, by Edgar Garcia.

Works Cited

Adorno, Rolena. "Contextualizing the *Nueva Crónica y Buen Gobierno*." *Guamán Poma: Writing and Resistance in Colonial Peru*. 2nd ed., University of Texas Press, 2000, pp. xi–lxi.

Adorno, Rolena. *Guamán Poma: Literatura de resistencia en el Perú colonial*. Siglo XXI, 1991.

Anderson, Mark. "Multinaturalism/Nonhuman Representation." *Handbook of Latin American Environmental Aesthetics*, edited by Jens Andermann et al., De Gruyter, 2023, pp. 67–89.

Araníbar, Carlos. "Presentación." *Nueva Crónica y Buen Gobierno*, by Felipe Guamán Poma de Ayala, vol. 1, Biblioteca del Perú, 2015, pp. 7–30.

Berríos-Campos, Claudia. "El camino del ostracismo: La justicia en el mundo andino y la negación de la reciprocidad en Guamán Poma de Ayala." *Letras-Lima*, vol. 91, no. 131, 2020, pp. 187–210.

Cadena, Marisol de. "Asumir la política indígena en sus propios términos requiere un análisis más allá de lo político." *Crónicas Urbanas*, vol. 13, 2008, pp. 98–117.

Ceballos, Gerardo, et al. "Accelerated Modern Human-Induced Species Losses: Entering the Sixth Mass Extinction." *Science Advances,* vol. 1, no. 5, 2015, pp. 1–5.

Cushman, Gregory T. "The Environmental Contexts of Guamán Poma: Interethnic Conflict over Forest Resources and Place in Huamanga (Peru), 1540–1600." *Unlocking the Doors to the Worlds of Guamán Poma and His Nueva Corónica,* edited by Rolena Adorno and Ivan Boserup, Museum Tusculanum Press, 2015, pp. 87–140.

Dedenbach-Salazar Sáenz, Sabine. "The Corregidor as Dragon and the Encomendero as Lion: Symbolic Language to Depict Antisocial Behavior in Guamán Poma's Andean Colonial World." *STUF—Language Typology and Universals,* vol. 67, no. 2, 2014, pp. 149–173.

Echazú Böschemeier, Ana Gretel, et al. "Waman Poma de Ayala, Um Autor Indígena Do Século XVII." *TECCOGS: Revista Digital de Tecnologias Cognitivas,* vol. 24, 2021, pp. 157–182.

Eliceche, Cecilia Elisa. "Notes on Spiritual Extractivism: A Choreography." *Critical Times,* vol. 6, 2023, pp. 540–559.

Fornoff, Carolyn. "Extractivism." *Handbook of Latin American Environmental Aesthetics,* edited by Jens Andermann et al., De Gruyter, 2023, pp. 45–66.

Garcia, Edgar. *Emergency: Reading the Popol Vuh in a Time of Crisis.* University Press of Chicago, 2022.

Guamán Poma de Ayala, Felipe. *El primer Nueva Crónica y Buen Gobierno.* 1615. GKS 2232-4, *Royal Library, Denmark,* The Guamán Poma Website, https://poma.kb.dk/permalink/2006/poma/info/en/frontpage.htm

Guamán Poma de Ayala, Felipe. *Nueva Crónica y Buen Gobierno.* Biblioteca del Perú, 2015.

Guamán Poma de Ayala, Felipe. *The First New Chronicle and Good Government: On the History of the World and the Incas up to 1615.* Edited & translated by Roland Hamilton, University of Texas Press, 2009.

Hamilton, Roland. "Introduction." *The First New Chronicle and Good Government: On the History of the World and the Incas up to 1615,* by Felipe Guamán Poma de Ayala, University of Texas Press, 2009, pp. xvii–xxiv.

Heffes, Gisela. "Introducción. Para una ecocrítica latinoamericana: entre la postulación de un ecocentrismo crítico y la crítica de un antropocentrismo hegemónico." *Revista de Crítica Literaria Latinoamericana,* vol. 40, no. 79, 2014, pp. 11–34.

Larsen, Soren C., and Jay T. Johnson. "Introduction: Being Together in Place." *Being Together in Place,* edited by Soren C. Larsen and Jay T. Johnson, University of Minnesota Press, 2017, pp. 1–22.

Larsen, Soren C., and Jay T. Johnson, editors. *Being Together in Place: Indigenous Coexistence in a More Than Human World.* University of Minnesota Press, 2017.

López-Baralt, Mercedes. "'Escribirlo es llorar': La crónica visual de Felipe Guamán Poma de Ayala." *Literatura y cultura en el Virreinato del Perú: apropiación y diferen-*

cia, edited by Raquel Chang-Rodríguez and Carlos García-Bedoya, Pontificia Universidad Católica del Perú, 2017, pp. 405–437.

López-Calvo, Ignacio. "'Coloniality Is Not Over, It's All Over': Interview with Dr. Walter Mignolo (Nov. 2014, Part II)." *Transmodernity: Journal of Peripheral Cultural Production of the Luso-Hispanic World,* vol. 6, no. 2, 2016, pp. 171–196.

Milanez, Felipe, et al. "Epistemological Justice: Decoloniality, Climate Change, and Ecological Conditions for Future Generations." *IDS Bulletin,* vol. 53, no. 4, 2022, pp. 86–100.

Newson, Linda A. "Indian Population Patterns in Colonial Spanish America." *Latin American Research Review,* vol. 20, no. 3, 1985, pp. 41–74.

Norton, Marcy. *The Tame and the Wild: People and Animals after 1492.* Harvard University Press, 2024.

Onions, Charles T. *The Oxford Dictionary of English Etymology.* Clarendon Press, 1966.

Porto Gonçalves, Carlos Walter. "Abya Yala, el descubrimiento de América." *Bicentenarios (otros), transiciones y resistencias,* edited by Norma Giarracca, translated by Javier Lorca and Jorge Montenegro, Una Ventana, 2011, pp. 39–46.

Quispe-Agnoli, Rocío. "Habitando en las fronteras: Insinuaciones pluriversales en la *Nueva Crónica y Buen Gobierno.*" *RECIAL,* vol. 13, no. 22, 2022, pp. 161–182.

Rivera Cusicanqui, Silvia. *Ch'ixinakax utxiwa. Una reflexión sobre prácticas y discursos descolonizadores.* Tinta Limón, 2010.

Rivera Cusicanqui, Silvia. "Pensando desde el Nayrapacha: Una reflexión sobre los lenguajes simbólicos como práctica teórica." *Sociología de la imagen: Miradas ch'ixi desde la historia andina,* by Silvia Rivera Cusicanqui, Tinta Limón, 2015, pp. 205–219.

Schmidt, Elmar. "Latin American Environmental Discourses, Indigenous Ecological Consciousness and the Problem of 'Authentic' Native Identities." *Handbook of Ecocriticism and Cultural Ecology,* edited by Hubert Zapf, De Gruyter, 2016, pp. 413–437.

Styles, Monica. "'Tanbién son ellos de carne y güeso': Guamán Poma de Ayala's Radical Abolitionism." *The Past Awakened: Cultural Reimagination in the Global Hispanophone,* special issue edited by Víctor Sierra Matute. *Arizona Journal of Hispanic Cultural Studies,* vol. 29, 2025.

Torres Lezama, Vicente. "Uywanakuy. Ritual y crianza mutua entre humanos y no humanos en el sur andino de Perú." *Iberoforum: Revista de Ciencias Sociales de la Universidad Iberoamericana,* vol. 15, no. 29, 2020, pp. 135–179.

Tortorici, Zeb. "'In the Name of the Father and the Mother of All Dogs': Canine Baptisms, Weddings, and Funerals in Bourbon México." *Centering Animals in Latin American History,* edited by Martha Few and Zeb Tortorici, Duke University Press, 2013, pp. 93–119.

Tortorici, Zeb, and Martha Few. "Introduction: Writing Animal Histories." *Centering Animals in Latin American History,* edited by Martha Few and Zeb Tortorici, Duke University Press, 2013, pp. 1–27.

Ugarelli, Mariangela. "La tentación de la imagen: El hipertexto de la *Nueva Crónica y Buen Gobierno* de Guamán Poma de Ayala en el imaginario gráfico del Perú contemporáneo." *Latin American Literary Review*, vol. 48, no. 97, pp. 75–87.

Vieira, Patrícia, and Susan McHugh. "Why Plants and Animals?" *Peter Lang Publishing Blog*, 2022, https://medium.com/peter-lang/why-plants-and-animals-a17cdd872bbe

Washington, Haydn, et al. "Why Ecocentrism Is the Key Pathway to Sustainability." *The Ecological Citizen*, vol. 1, 2017, pp. 35–41.

Whitehead, Neil L. "Conclusion: Loving, Being, Killing Animals." *Centering Animals in Latin American History*, edited by Martha Few and Zeb Tortorici, Duke University Press, 2013, pp. 329–345.

11

Migration and Stasis in *Xilase qui rié di' sicasi rié nisa guiigu' / La nostalgia no se marcha como el agua de los ríos* by Irma Pineda

EMILY CELESTE VÁZQUEZ ENRÍQUEZ

Written in Spanish and Diidxazá by Irma Pineda, a Binnizá/Isthmus Zapotec poet and translator from Juchitán Oaxaca, *Xilase qui rié di' sicasi rié nisa guiigu' / La nostalgia no se marcha como el agua de los ríos* (2007), tells a story about migration from two points of view. Translated into English by Wendy Call with the title *Nostalgia Doesn't Flow Away Like Riverwater* (2024), the poetry book portrays the voice of a person about to migrate, juxtaposed with that of their partner, who stays home. Interwoven within both narratives are the anxiety, heartbreak, and hope that often accompany every step of the migration process, from the initial decision to leave to the dreams of eventual return. The book is divided into three sections. Section one, titled "Chupa ladxidua'/Dos es mi corazón" (My Heart in Two),[1] revolves around the displacement, fear of transculturation, and profound anguish experienced by the couple in the face of imminent departure. The second section, "Lu neza/Sobre el camino" (On the Path), encapsulates the effects of the migration journey on the lovers, and is marked by sensations of absence, emptiness, and fragmentation. The third and final section, "Zedandá ti dxi/Un día llegará" (The Day Will Come), evokes a blend of sadness, longing, and hopefulness born from the experience of separation and the yearning for reunification.

Various nonhuman figures emerge throughout the poems, functioning as central elements that underscore the complexity and context of the portrayed events. Among these figures are different animals and plants that reflect the scale and temporality of the dynamics surrounding the migration journey and emphasize the effects of the resulting dislocation. When it comes to animals, Pineda depicts various species confronting existential challenges similar to those faced by humans, as ecological crises drive both into displacement. This approach frames migration as a process often shared by human and nonhuman beings. In her portrayal of plants, the author often uses vegetal life to highlight the persistent strength of its inhabitants' bond with the land, despite the harm. Through the depiction of both animals and plants, Pineda foregrounds the key environmental and social dynamics of the region where the poems are set.

In the context of migration from Mexico to the United States, Pineda's poetry references the historic and place-based lasting effects of colonial practices in a region mainly inhabited by Indigenous people. These effects are evident in the references to environmental harm, intensified by global inequities in climate impact, and shaped by marginalization and systemic racial disparities. Indeed, as highlighted in Pineda's work, the racial hierarchies entrenched in colonial frameworks have resulted in an uneven distribution of climate vulnerability. This disparity often compels those in the communities shouldering the heaviest burden of climate change and other forms of environmental catastrophe to migrate as their only resource left to survive. That is the context surrounding the migration journey in Pineda's poems, which illustrate a region disproportionately affected by social and climate hazards.

As stated by Wendy Call in the introduction to the translated version of the collection, the poems "alternate between two fictional voices based in Pineda's hometown: someone who has migrated to the United States as an undocumented worker and their partner, who has to stay in Juchitán" (xiii). The lovers in the collection are part of the Binnizá (Isthmus Zapotec) people, speakers of Diidxazá (Zapotec of the coastal plain or Isthmus Zapotec), a language spoken primarily in Tehuantepec and Juchitán, the author's birthplace. Juchitán is located in the state of Oaxaca in southern Mexico, connected to the Pacific Ocean through its southernmost regions. This is the most diverse state within the Mexican territory, with seven out of ten people identifying as Indigenous (Pareja Amador 5), and more than a third of the total population being speakers of an Indigenous language. These Native communities often experience economic hardship and face significant barriers to accessing education, healthcare, and housing (López

Santiago and Barajas Gómez 11), a framework that relates to the high levels of migration from the state. Lourdes Gutiérrez Nájera and Kornita Maldonado observe that states such as California are "marked by the presence of Indigenous migrants, the majority hailing from the state of Oaxaca" (813). Because Juchitán is close to the sea, in addition to relying on agriculture and livestock farming, its inhabitants have long depended on the fishing industry for sustenance (Gobierno de México 2020). Pineda's collection addresses the environmental decline of both land and water, making apparent the connections between their degradation and the mass migration of the Binnizá, who can no longer depend on the ecological features of the territory to make a living. These migrations not only affect social ties between migrants and those left behind, as conveyed through the separation of the lovers, but may also disrupt their connection to the land.

Following the notions of deterritorialization and reterritorialization in the context of migration, geography studies scholar Fátima Velez de Castro notes that when individuals migrate, they experience a loss of the land where they were once rooted, engaged, and integrated, with new relations gradually formed with the territory they arrive in (2). This dynamic is often linked to processes stemming from modernization and globalization, including transnational social networks, economic disparities from uneven regional development, global labor demand, and environmental crises. In the case of the lovers described in Pineda's book, the possibility that this experience of loss might occur looms not only over the individual who migrates but also over the person left behind, who must grapple with a newfound reality in which the lived space is emptier. As Wendy Call asserts, "the tangled emotions of border-crossing are all bound up in [Pineda's] book" (xv), here exemplified by the dislocation experienced by the person who leaves and the person who stays. While migration can weaken ties to one's homeland and give rise to different relations with unfamiliar places, migrants may also shape other outcomes. This occurs not only in the sense that, as Velez de Castro contends, "the migrant manages to synthesize in [themselves] several spatial dimensions, combining territories of experience, such as the place of origin and migratory destination" (4), but more specifically when, instead of severing or seeing their connection to their homeland decline or merge with another, migrants strengthen it. In the process, people who migrate assert agency by opposing the expected impact of the colonial forces that intervened in their departure. An example of this is conveyed in Pineda's collection, as displacement does not sever the connection to the homeland, even if a sense of grief lingers.

As I propose in this chapter, this is made possible by the prominent role of the plants and animals in the book, which not only shape the migration experience of one of the speakers but also actively participate in it, often embodying mobility and stasis.

In *Nostalgia Doesn't Flow Away Like Riverwater,* nonhuman entities take on various roles that broaden and reshape common understandings of migration. On the one hand, the plants inhabiting the lovers' homeland play a significant role in helping the migrant preserve their connection to the land, as the memory of some of their main physical features communicates a strong sense of rootedness that offers solace and possibility in the experience of departure. On the other hand, the animals serve as central figures through which the collection emphasizes that migration movements are undertaken by different species facing similar environmental pressures, highlighting both the overt and subtle connections between the migratory flows of human and nonhuman beings and emphasizing that animals have complex stories of migration too.

Human and Animal Mobility

Whereas the depiction of animals in cultural production often positions them as allegorical figures working as affective extensions of the human characters or mediums to emphasize human attributes, as Gabriel Giorgi contends, animal life "ya no se deja someter a las prescripciones de la metáfora y, en general, del lenguaje figurativo, sino que empieza a funcionar en un contínuum orgánico, afectivo, material y político con lo humano" (Kindle). This is particularly relevant in a poetry book about migration where animal figures are imbricated in some of the most distressing moments of a feared journey. If as Glenda R. Carpio identifies, "migration needs to be understood as a global phenomenon, one that, much like global warming, is produced by the actions of institutions that permeate every level of society" (8), in *Nostalgia Doesn't Flow Away Like Riverwater,* the nonhuman entities are fundamental to uncover the hidden presence of a set colonial dynamics affecting different species. Indeed, as I contend in this section, the incorporation of animals within the collection calls attention to some of the main contextual instances surrounding multispecies migrations, holds accountable the colonial schemes behind many of these instances, and emphasizes migrant agency.

In the first poem, titled "Ni chineu'/El Equipaje" (Your Suitcase), the voice of the person whose partner is about to migrate, advises: "Don't forget to take

/ the gift of the jaguar / . . . / the gift of the eagle / . . ." (3). From the very first poem, the prominence of animals takes center stage. In the previous stanzas, animal life is deployed as a source of strength and inspiration for the human who has to face the physical challenges associated with undocumented migration journeys. Their partner asks them to take the *dones*, or gifts, of two animals with them to aid in the process of crossing unknown borders: the tiger's strength to confront the challenges of the journey and the eagle's vision and agility to evade detection and capture. However, beyond offering encouragement, the speaker's emphasis on the movement of these figures reminds us that forced migration is increasingly becoming a necessity across species. When the lover who remains in the homeland requests that the migrant carries with them the attributes of physical motion of two different animals, a tiger, and an eagle, lyrical imagery full of human and nonhuman mobility is expressed. About this juncture, legal studies scholar Charlotte Blattner asserts:

> Humans have long believed that their own migrations and other animal migrations must be understood separately, but the long-term, sustained trend of change in the earth's climate is ruthlessly testing this notion. Global warming, heat waves, rising sea levels, and mounting environmental disasters will pressure millions of humans and nonhumans to seek new homes. (183)

Pineda's collection underscores how the forces driving human migration often prompt the migration of other species as well. The journey of migration is driven largely by the consequences of environmental devastation. In an untitled poem, the speaker recalls leaving the south, where parched, exhausted cornfields and "one ox thin and one dead," reflect the land's inability to sustain them. By the shore, a once-prized fishing boat lies abandoned, no longer a source of sustenance. The sea, once teeming with fish, now "vomits rusted cans," a haunting manifestation of vanished livelihoods and a world in decline (65). As Wendy Call asserts, this poem addresses the key reasons that prompted the decision to migrate, as when the sea was so polluted that it was no longer able to house fish, it "[triggered] the migrant's decision to head north" (xv). Thus, a parched field, a deceased animal—and another one in its bones, on the brink of death—coupled with a sea so polluted that it no longer carries fish and so sick that it vomits trash, are elements that paint the difficult environmental reality faced by the couple. The previous stanzas also make clear that humans are not the only ones impacted by the environmental conditions described in the poem, referencing that depleted food sources and hunger affect multiple species at the same time, as is exemplified by the dying ox. Thereby, the situations described in the poem echo the multispecies connections highlighted by Blattner.

Food insecurity emerges as a central theme throughout the collection. The impact of hunger is depicted not only in overt imagery, such as the reference to the ox's body, but also in the underlying motivations that drive one of the lovers to migrate. This is evident in the poem "Ni cudxi'badu/La siembra" (Sowing): "How can we return to our land / . . . / not a drop of honey left in its belly / to sweeten our homeplace" (130). These verses hint at the land's lost ability to offer nourishment, conveying the impossibility of relying on it for survival. In another poem, the speaker underscores that the primary reason for the land's barren state is the absence of rain: "If only my tears could serve / to water fields / and coax new life / to bloom" (107). The illustration of an emaciated ox and the allusion to the absent fish show how the collection reflects on the impacts of environmental degradation on human and nonhuman beings. By stressing that these species either perished because they couldn't survive on the land or left due to a lack of sustenance, Pineda's poetry resonates with Blattner's assertion that "human and nonhuman animal migrants are often on the move for similar reasons . . . yet we treat them as if they have nothing to do with each other" (183). The collection challenges this misconception, reframing migration as an interspecies phenomenon driven by shared needs and heightened vulnerabilities, particularly in the face of climate change and other forms of ecological decline.

The depiction of a starving ox, the mention of fish disappearing due to habitat pollution, and the reasons behind one lover's migration all point to how environmental degradation endangers life across species boundaries. This is especially evident when environmental crises drive migration, and needless to say, also occurs in the wake of war and other forms of systemic violence that disrupt human and nonhuman habitats. Such connections offer compelling grounds for understanding migration as a multispecies experience. Although it may seem evident that both human and nonhuman entities often migrate for similar reasons, this reality is frequently overlooked or ignored. In Western thought, migration is typically viewed through an anthropocentric lens. Conversely, when nonhuman beings are considered, the human dimension is often excluded. Challenging this separation, Pineda's poetry reveals the inescapable connections between species confronting ecological hurdles within a shared environment. Blattner also references this dynamic:

> [Human-nonhuman] compartmentalization and siloization is rapidly losing validity thanks to climate change, which poses unprecedented challenges for all humans and animals, including loss of habitat caused by global warming of the atmosphere, sea level rise, and mounting disasters (184).

Pineda situates various of those unprecedented ecological challenges within the context of a rural community, emphasizing how, in the words of Samoan spoken word poet Terisa Tinei Siagatonu: "Everyone is affected by climate change but some are affected first" (3:25). When considering that the human speakers of *Nostalgia Doesn't Flow Away Like Riverwater* are Indigenous, the text's focus on the racialized dimension of forced migration becomes evident. Concerning this social dynamic, Alicia Barabas describes: "La mayoría de los 570 municipios que [integran Oaxaca] son de fuerte expulsión y los migrantes salen principalmente de los pueblos mixtecos, zapotecos, triquis, mixes, chatinos, mazatecos y chinantecos" (78). Despite reductions in poverty levels in recent years, as of 2022, Oaxaca remained among the top three states with the highest poverty indexes across Mexico (Almanza). As previously mentioned, a large part of Oaxaca's inhabitants identify as Indigenous, and the book contains a direct mention of how racial and racist frameworks affect the migrant: "No one looks into my black eyes / . . . / is my brown skin transparent?" (81). This reality, combined with recent data on poverty levels in the state and the escalating impacts of climate change, indicates that Indigenous communities in Oaxaca disproportionately bear the weight of precarious environmental conditions. Often, they are compelled to migrate despite a deep-rooted desire to stay, as Pineda's work suggests. In one of the poems, the person about to undertake the perilous journey north briefly contemplates remaining behind to spare their family from the unbearable pain that will result from the separation. Yet, they soon realize: "poverty's dark night / hurts more" (31). This portrayal serves as a reminder of how, as Mary Louise Pratt observes: "Migration is often an effective response by communities, families, and individuals to the extremely uneven distribution of economic and social opportunity across the globe" (84). While forced migration impacts marginalized communities at a planetary level, Pineda's work remains deeply anchored in a specific temporal and geographical context. This grounding is expressed not only through the dialogues of human voices and the integration of poems in the Diidxazá language—a feature that evokes the region in which the poem is set—but also through the deliberate and careful inclusion of specific nonhuman entities, which further solidify aspects of spatiality and temporality.

The speaker, who remains in the homeland, reflects on the river once called "of nutrias," known for its river dogs. As they think of this river, they describe with sadness its lost vitality, once a lively place and now empty: "One day there were so many of us / that the nutrias went away / like our men leave now" (69). By referencing El Río Las Nutrias, the author reinforces the geographical setting of the poems within the specific boundaries of Juchitán. Furthermore, once again, the poem refers to how need-based migration occurs across species. Within this context, this untitled poem emphasizes that while parallels can be drawn between the migration needs of humans and nonhumans, as depicted through the portrayal of river otters and people who had to leave the same geographic region, it also alludes to significant differences that stress the specificity of each species. Whereas humans have to migrate due to food insecurity, the book asserts that in this particular case, nutrias had no alternative but to depart from their aquatic habitat due to the increasing presence of humans. Given that the author employs the phrasing "we were," she recognizes how the human speakers of the book might often participate in the context of dispossession endured by others, particularly nonhuman animals. This element is crucial for highlighting key parallels between human and nonhuman migration and acknowledging important differences that must be recognized to avoid essentialization. The author steers clear of romanticized portrayals of Indigenous people, instead depicting them as complex individuals who may engage with the reality of nonhuman dispossession. This perspective is elucidated through the voice of the lover left behind, who understands the effects of their community on the ecology of the river.

If, as Blattner asserts, climate change renders everyone vulnerable (233), Pineda's work illustrates how this vulnerability is experienced on multiple levels, with racially marginalized communities bearing the brunt of its impact due to the unequal distribution of economic opportunities, as Pratt argues. Furthermore, while the preceding poem places Indigenous people in a higher hierarchy relative to animals—especially concerning the nonhuman inhabitants of El Río Las Nutrias—at the same time:

> Animals have traditionally been regarded as the lowest anchor of worthiness, and metaphorical and literal boundary work that presumes their low status is evident in public discourse, media, and politics where contempt

for animals is used to de-humanize and legitimate the oppression of all unwanted others, including unwanted humans (184).

Therefore, *Nostalgia Doesn't Flow Away Like Riverwater* acknowledges differences across species while simultaneously highlighting significant elements that underscore their shared vulnerability. That vulnerability is particularly evident in the current context of environmental chaos. Whereas the poetry book is populated with harrowing scenes depicting the anguish and loss stemming from human and nonhuman displacement, the author refrains from portraying multispecies migration as solely the outcome of unseen forces that may lurk behind ecological despair. Instead, the articulation of the impact of colonial dynamics on the environment is quietly pervasive and deeply significant. This is evident, for instance, in the poem describing how the sea, once home to fish, has become filled with metal cans instead. Such a portrayal resonates with Michif-settler scholar Max Liboiron, who frames pollution not merely as a byproduct of colonialism, but as "an enactment of ongoing colonial relations to Land" (6). According to Liboiron, the presence of pollution points to the colonial "relations that make Land available for pollution in the first place. [Underscoring the] place of stolen Land in colonizers' and settlers' ability to create sinks for pollution" (15). In terms of Liboiron's argument, the severe contamination of the sea is an enactment of colonial dynamics. The imagery of overflowing trash reflects global capitalist forces that have eroded one of the Binnizá's primary sources of sustenance. Pineda's work is thus in dialogue with what Glenda Carpio denominates "migrant aesthetics," in the sense it "shift[s] the focus away from the migrant as a sympathetic creature upon whom feelings can be projected and toward migration as a phenomenon that involves us all, albeit from diverging perspectives" (4). The depiction of the polluted sea may prompt readers to reflect on their own complicity within the anthropocentric structures of colonialism that have endangered human and nonhuman habitats, compelling their inhabitants to migrate.

At this point, I would like to revisit the opening poem of the collection, where the lover remaining in the homeland requests the migrant to carry with them the cherished attributes of two different animals: a tiger and an eagle. This request achieves at least two results within the collection. As I mentioned earlier, it deploys lyrical imagery full of human and nonhuman mobility. Placing the image of a human migrant alongside one of a tiger with the strength to face the journey and of an eagle who has the power to keep going without being captured helps us to think of migration as a multispecies endeavor. Because this poem is followed by depictions of other animals facing existential threats that have led them to either perish or migrate, as is the case of the oxen, the fish, the river otters, and others such as "birds [who] have gone away" (77), the collection emphasizes that just as humans, animals migrate due to necessity and vulnerability. This approach is particularly significant to conceptualize migration as multispecies:

> When we think of migrating animals, we often presume that animals migrate voluntarily and that there is something "natural" and "necessary" about their move. People are less likely to think of animals as subjects of displacement, say through storms, high winds, swift currents, or droughts. (67–68)

Moreover, in addition to highlighting that animals also experience dispossession and may migrate for reasons beyond their natural patterns, drawing parallels between human and nonhuman migration can help support human rights as well. Recognizing this parallel creates an opportunity to contribute to the decriminalization of human cross-border movement, as it reinforces the view of migration as both a necessity and a right—often a crucial response to survival, especially in the context of environmental devastation.

Vegetal Stasis

Whereas *Nostalgia Doesn't Flow Away Like Riverwater* depicts multiple animals, many of whom are directly relevant to emphasize the interconnectedness that brings human and nonhuman migration into proximity, the poetry book does not include as many allusions to plants. Moreover, when plants appear, they sometimes do so to reflect the hopes and desires of the human speakers. One example can be found in the poem "Ti guiichi/Una espina" (Thorn), in which the person who is about to migrate, states: "A thorn deep in my flesh / is pain itself / . . . I will return with flowers" (7). In these verses, it is possible to see plant life, present through the figures of thorns and flowers, as the vehicle through which the migrant expresses their lived pain and hopes. In contrast to the depicted animals, which frequently embody the distinctive traits and challenges of their specific species, plants are sometimes tethered to the emotions and experiences of human speakers. This literary configuration resonates with Emanuele Coccia's premises regarding how zoocentric perspectives tend to assume that plants are "[beings] without personality and without dignity, [that do] not seem to deserve any spontaneous empathy" (4). However, contrary to what an initial reading might suggest, Pineda avoids a zoocentric bias by giving plants a subtle yet significant role. She presents them as active agents in shaping the migration journey of one of the human speakers, and as living beings who experience environmental harm on their own terms. This twofold configuration is grounded on notions of stasis, as plants remain rooted in a distressed landscape where development and growth are uncertain.

In the poem "Laanu/Nosotros" (Us), the migrant states: "we are children of the trees," who, they assert, will provide shade along their journey (23). Here, the imagery of trees functions not as mere metaphors reflecting the emotions of the human speakers, but as a grounding force through which the displaced migrant affirms a tangible connection to their homeland. The endurance of trees, manifest in their unrelenting attachment to the land despite the environmental catastrophe that surrounds them, becomes a source of solace for the migrant, who perceives their steadfastness as nurturing. The plant's resolute connection to the land is not symbolic; it is a tangible source of strength that helps the migrant navigate their journey, seeing how it is possible to remain connected to the land despite a framework of despair and environmental harm. Furthermore, by emphasizing kinship with the trees that populate their native land, the migrant recognizes and reaffirms their deep bond with the territory. This theme is especially significant in a subsequent poem, where the speaker, now far from their homeland and reflecting on their journey, declares that it has been a long time "since I yanked my feet / from southern lands" (81). The poem captures the act of uprooting oneself, with the image of tearing the feet away from the soil. By using the word *yank*, the speaker evokes a plant-like connection to the land, suggesting that they were forcibly torn from their place by external forces. If, as the migrant states, their feet were torn from the soil, it is because that is where they firmly assert they belonged, and because, as they clearly express, it was a place they never wanted to leave—and one they long to return to.

In the preceding verses, the evocation of plants serves multiple roles: in one poem, their lingering image—offering the memory of their shade as a gesture of care and their permanence as a source of inspiration—becomes a comforting presence, while in another, they exemplify the uprooting that accompanies the migration process and at the same time, the possibility to establish enduring connections with the land despite the dynamics that might threaten to sever them. Through sensuous memories, the migrant finds solace and companions throughout the arduous journey, as it is in the understanding of the plants' rootedness and a sense of kinship with them that they make sense of and ease the consequences of the separation. By refusing to accept territorial loss—which, as noted earlier, is often regarded as an inevitable, almost preordained consequence of migration—the migrant asserts their agency.

Thus, Pineda's treatment of plants is not a limitation in the book; rather, their presence—albeit often nonspecific—shapes the experience of migration and emphasizes some of the most defining characteristics of vegetal life: its permanence and how it asserts belonging. Whereas plants do migrate through different means, the collection tends to focus on the elements of plant life that remain grounded to the land. For instance, in the poem "Guendaredasilú/Recuerdos" (Recollections), the lover of the migrant advises: "Take the sweet recollections that lighten memory / . . . / the scent of frangipani and isthmus jasmine" (11). In this poem, the speaker identifies specific elements of the land that may provide solace to the migrant throughout the journey. Alongside the sounds and movements of laughing children and cawing birds, the speaker evokes the scent of two flower species native to the land. Named using their Binnizá denomination, these flowering plants are positioned on equal footing with other human and nonhuman beings, sharing in the migrant's experience of departure and conveying the interconnection between all forms of life within the depicted territory. The laughter and games of the children, along with the cawing of birds, contrast with the serene presence of flowers, which assert themselves quietly but firmly through their scent. However, the fact that the flowers appear as part of a memory, which, as the lover suggests, might offer some ease along the journey, also alludes to the endangerment of plant life in a territory where sustaining living beings becomes increasingly impossible. In this sense, the flowers remain in a state of stasis, placed in a suspended existence where growth is halted. Their presence endures through the certainty of a scent so deeply intertwined with the landscape that, in the speaker's mind, the two become inseparable. This is one example of how plants, in this case flowering plants, are deeply rooted in the land.

While the previous example illustrates the interconnectedness of plants, animals, and people in shaping memories of the homeland, another untitled poem shifts the temporal focus, expressing a strong belief that the future will be better. In this poem, the speaker not only hopes for the day of their lover's return, but also emphasizes that when they do, they both will be surrounded by "only green fields," also firmly believing they will once again witness "the nutrias playing in the river / and the fish leaping at the delta" (153). The contrast between plant and animal life is emphasized once more, without implying a hierarchy. Instead, their interdependence in shaping a future where the migrant can return without fear of being displaced again, and where the region's nonhuman inhabitants can thrive, is made clear. This possibility is reinforced by a plant-like determination to persist even if it remains in a state of stasis.

In one of the most celebrated poems of the collection, titled "Qui zuuyu naa gate'/No me verás morir," (You Will Not See Me Die), the migrant encapsulates into one single voice the resolve of a community affected by mass displacement: "You will not see me die / you won't forget me / I am your mother / your father / your grandfather's old stories / our age-old traditions / the tear welling from an ancient willow / the saddest branch" (124). As Wendy Call maintains, this poem "asserts the survival of the Binnizá and their unbreakable connection to the land that sustains them—even when they leave it" (xvii). Alongside revered figures that emphasize ancestry and belonging such as a mother, a father, the wisdom of a grandparent, and the inescapable presence of time, communicating the continuation and multiplicity of Binnizá voices, the poem evokes the image of a willow tree. This inclusion affirms that even amid longing and melancholy—expressed by the speaker through their embodiment of a weeping tree and a hidden, sorrowful branch—the Binnizá remain deeply rooted in the land. Furthermore, through the image of the tree, the collection foregrounds a multispecies belonging to the territory, in which human and nonhuman roots survive. Indeed, while the willow tree serves as a channel for the speaker to illustrate that their connection to the land endures despite grieving it from afar, it also emphasizes specific characteristics of the nonhuman entity being named—its longevity, the mournful shape of its branches, and the sap that falls like tears—creating an image of a tree that, like the Binnizá, belongs to the land and remains rooted there even amid a context of existential dread. In this sense, the migrant is not only conveying the sorrow of displaced people but also attempting to encapsulate the distress of the nonhuman, here personified in the figure of an ancient tree whose roots firmly cling onto a wounded landscape. However, as asserted by the speaker, neither distance, sorrow, nor wounds can sever the ancestral connection to the land established by the Binnizá and their nonhuman companions.

Through the depiction of various animal species such as tigers, eagles, otters, and birds whose movements inspire or echo those of the migrant speaker, and whose reasons for departure align with those of humans, Irma Pineda accentuates that migration is a multispecies endeavor. In *Nostalgia Doesn't Flow Away Like Riverwater,* Pineda's approach to humans and animals in movement due to environmental degradation expresses a cross-species experience of displacement.

Though it may seem evident that animals also migrate because of environmental pressures, this reality is often overlooked, as migration is typically framed within human-centric points of view. By incorporating imagery of animals in motion, on the verge of death due to hunger as their habitats can no longer sustain them, or displaced by ecological catastrophes, Pineda emphasizes the interconnectedness of all life in confronting existential crises. Additionally, the depiction of animal life sheds light on the planetary dynamics surrounding forced migration movements, while highlighting geographic, temporal, and species-specific nuances pertinent to human and nonhuman entities alike.

Furthermore, through references to various plants, the author underscores how their stasis, made manifest in the form of a radical connection to a soil that is increasingly unable to nourish them, serves as a counterpoint to the displacement experienced by the human migrant. By invoking the ability of plants to remain grounded in the land, even when the conditions of the environment might lead them to suspended growth, the migrant in Pineda's collection finds the strength and inspiration to maintain their connection to the territory. This also consolidates as an act of refusal to conform with one of the effects of the colonial forces that contributed to the deterioration that made them leave—losing one's territory—and in turn, through the evocation of plant life, the deployment of migrant agency. The connection to the land of plants—exemplified, for instance, by the enduring presence of trees and the assiduous scent of local flowers that persist in an afflicted landscape—offers a sense of continuity and belonging amid large-scale multispecies migrations, suggesting that rootedness is still possible even within frameworks of displacement and environmental harm.

Note

1. In this chapter, I reference the 2024 trilingual edition, which features Wendy Call's English translations of the poems. Therefore, all English translations are drawn from Call's work.

Works Cited

Almanza, Lucero. "¿Cuáles son los estados del país con el mayor nivel de pobreza en 2022?" *Alcaldes de México,* 10 Aug. 2023, https://www.alcaldesdemexico.com/notas-principales/cuales-son-los-estados-del-pais-con-el-mayor-nivel-de-pobreza-en-2022/

Blattner, Charlotte. "Global Migration Crises, Nonhuman Animals, and the Role of Law." *Like an Animal: Critical Animal Studies Approaches to Borders, Displacement, and Othering*, edited by Núria Almiron and Natalie Khazaal, Brill, 2021.

Call, Wendy. "Translator's note." Pineda, *Nostalgia*, xi–xviii.

Carpio, Glenda. *Migrant Aesthetics*. Columbia University Press, 2023.

Coccia, Emanuele. *The Life of Plants: A Metaphysics of Mixture*. Polity, 2018.

Giorgi, Gabriel. *Formas comunes: Animalidad, cultura, biopolítica*. Eterna Cadencia, Kindle Edition.

Gobierno de México. "Juchitán de Zaragoza." https://www.economia.gob.mx/datamexico/es/profile/geo/heroica-ciudad-de-juchitan-de-zaragoza

Gutiérrez Nájera, Lourdes and Kornita Maldonado. "Transnational Settler Colonial Formations and Global Capital: A Consideration of Indigenous Mexican Migrants." *American Quarterly* 69, vol. 69, no. 4, Dec. 2017, pp. 809-821. https://www.jstor.org/stable/26794699.

Liborion, Max. *Pollution is Colonialism*. Duke University Press, 2021.

López Santiago, Noemí and Barajas Gómez, Verónica. "Identidad y desarrollo: El caso de la subregión alta mixe de Oaxaca." *Península*, vol. VIII, no. 2, 2013, pp. 9-37 https://www.scielo.org.mx/pdf/peni/v8n2/v8n2a1.pdf

Pareja Amador. "Editorial." *Población Indígena*. Dirección General de Población de Oaxaca, 2018. https://productosdigepo.oaxaca.gob.mx/recursos/revistas/revista41.pdf

Pineda, Irma. *Xilase qui rié di' sicasi rié nisa guiigu' / La nostalgia no se marcha como el agua de los ríos*. Escritores en Lenguas Indígenas, 2007.

Pineda, Irma. *Nostalgia Doesn't Flow Away Like Riverwater*. Translated by Wendy Call, Phoneme Media, an imprint of Deep Vellum Publishing, 2024.

Pratt, Mary Louise. *Planetary Longings (Dissident Acts)*. Duke University Press, Kindle Edition.

Velez de Castro, Fátima. "Constructing Territories of Deterritorialization—Reterritorialization in Clarice Lispector Novels." *Social Sciences*, vol. 11, no. 12, 2022, pp. 1–13.

Tinei Siagatonu, Terisa. "Layers." *Global Call for Climate Action*, 2015, https://www.youtube.com/watch?v=XgXYP6zqzJk

12

El árbol del chicle

Plant Life and Racialization in Luis Rosado Vega's Poema de la selva trágica *(1938) and Yulene Olaizola's* Selva trágica *(2021)*

JORGE QUINTANA NAVARRETE

This chapter explores the interrelation between racialized bodies and plant life by analyzing representations of chicle extraction in Mexico. Chicle is a natural latex extracted from the *chicozapote* tree, which historically served as the preferred base for the manufacture of chewing gum. The latex was harvested by making zigzag cuts in the tree's bark so that the milky fluid would run down the trunk. This white fluid was then collected and boiled until it reached the appropriate thickness and could be transported to the United States, where the chewing gum industry was developing rapidly. At the turn of the twentieth century, the increase in chewing gum consumption in the United States led to intensive exploitation both of the *chicozapote* trees—found mainly in the Yucatán Peninsula—and of local Maya and mestizo laborers.

The intensification of chicle extraction largely coincided in time with the Amazon rubber boom (1850–1920), both industries sharing similar harvesting methods and socioecological repercussions. In contrast to well-known novels about the rubber boom such as José Eustasio Rivera's *La vorágine* (1924), the literary corpus created by Mexican authors about chicle extraction has received little scholarly attention.[1] Recently, even though synthetic material had supplanted natural latex in the manufacture of chewing gum by the 1970s (Mathews 64–65), the history of chicle extraction has remained a compelling issue and has reappeared in Mexican cultural productions.[2]

How has the artistic approach to this once-profitable activity changed or remained consistent from the postrevolutionary period to the twenty-first century? Specifically, how has the analogy between racialized bodies and plant life been established as a trope in this cultural production? And how does this trope provide insights into the interdependence of chicle extraction, structures of colonialism, and extractive capitalism in Mexico? To answer these questions, I analyze Luis Rosado Vega's long poem *Poema de la selva trágica* (1938) and Yulene Olaizola's film *Selva trágica* (2021) to show how they engage in related ways with the history of chicle extraction. In these works, both racialized bodies and forest flora are simultaneously and paradoxically depicted as radically passive, vulnerable objects and as cruel, brutally violent agents. I argue that this contradictory representation—which stems from a long-standing perspective on tropical nature—plays a different role in each of these works. Written at the height of the Lázaro Cárdenas populist administration, *Poema de la selva trágica* strives to condemn the violence and injustices involved in chicle extraction by establishing a close, *biological* relationship between Indigenous people and the *chicozapote* trees, insofar as both are vulnerable victims destined to surrender their "blood." Rosado Vega acknowledges, but ultimately downplays, the agentic capacities of both plants and Indigenous populations in the Quintana Roo forest. For its part, *Selva trágica*—which, as its name suggests, was inspired by Rosado Vega's poem and other postrevolutionary sources—is a film that similarly posits a racialization of the forest based on the alleged intimacy between racialized bodies and plant life. However, as I argue, in Olaizola's film, this analogy serves the function of highlighting the active rebellion of plants and racialized bodies against various forms of environmental and colonialist oppression.

Poema de la selva trágica

In 1937, one year before the publication of *Poema de la selva trágica,* writer and intellectual Luis Rosado Vega spearheaded a scientific expedition organized by the Lázaro Cárdenas administration to explore the eastern part of the Yucatán Peninsula. Since colonial times, the territory that would become the state of Quintana Roo was considered a sort of frontier region where the viceroyalty of New Spain exercised limited control due to the self-determination of the local

Maya people. In the nineteenth century, the Maya rebelled against Yucatec and Mexican intervention during the Caste War (1847–1901); they launched an armed revolt that effectively established Maya autonomy for more than fifty years. In 1901, the Porfirio Díaz regime took control of the territory with the aim of upholding state sovereignty over the so-called barbaric races, paving the way for exploiting the region's natural resources, including abundant *chicozapote* forests (Martínez-Reyes 51–52). By the 1930s, when Rosado Vega was leading his scientific expedition, Quintana Roo was still considered an isolated region that needed to be politically and economically incorporated into the Mexican state. As Cárdenas himself put it in 1936, it was necessary to "suscitar un estado de cosas en que ellos (Baja California and Quintana Roo) cuenten con población mexicana más numerosa, disfruten de protección más efectiva, vivan con el ritmo económico y social de nuestra nacionalidad, y mantengan y afirmen las características de la cultura patria" (create a state of affairs in which they [Baja California and Quintana Roo] can rely on a more numerous Mexican population, enjoy more effective protection, live with the economic and social rhythm of our nationality, and maintain and affirm the characteristics of our national culture) (Cárdenas 4).

The 1937 scientific expedition to Quintana Roo was firmly embedded in this Cardenista project. Rosado Vega, then director of the Museo Arqueológico e Histórico de Yucatán, and his team of scientists, artists, and other federal officials set out to explore and map the sparsely populated region, discover pre-Hispanic archaeological sites, and suggest policies to promote economic development. All in all, the scientific expedition strove to strengthen the political control of the Mexican state both by producing knowledge that was indispensable to governmentality and by creating an image of the region closely associated with the former splendor of the Maya civilization, an image that could easily be integrated into the Indigenistas' construction of national identity (González Vázquez 8–9). Thus, the expedition spearheaded by Rosado Vega was instrumental in upholding the "colonialismo interno" (internal colonialism) (González Casanova 186) practiced by the Mexican state since the nineteenth century to control the Maya population. While at the turn of the twentieth century the Porfirio Díaz regime endeavored to oppress or even exterminate the Maya population to facilitate the expansion of capital accumulation and state sovereignty, by the 1930s the Cárdenas regime articulated its engagement with the Maya people as a way of "civilizing" them by incorporating them into modern society. This entailed the enactment of a series of top-down social reforms, such as the establishment of *ejidos* or work cooperatives, which would allegedly promote economic development and social progress in the region, but in fact represented a restriction of the autonomy exercised by the Maya in the past and a transformation of their traditional ways of relating to the land (Martínez-Reyes 58, 60).

As a product of his journey through Quintana Roo, Rosado Vega published two literary works—the novel *Claudio Martín. Vida de un chiclero* (1938) and the long poem *Poema de la selva trágica* (1938)—that are infused with the socioeconomic and political agendas of the Cárdenas administration. Both works contain a denunciation of the inhumane working conditions of the chicle harvesters witnessed by Rosado Vega, and his hope that the social reforms put in place by the Cárdenas regime would "redeem" the Indigenous workers. *Poema de la selva trágica* is composed of fourteen chapters or "jornadas" (journeys) representing each day of a trek through the forest, but also implicitly suggesting a historical progression that culminates with the redemption of the Maya in the present day of the 1930s. The narrative starts with a few chapters that set the stage by depicting the flora and fauna of the Quintana Roo forest, goes on to portray the human drama that takes place in this setting by describing the extraction of chicle and mahogany, and concludes with praise for the social transformations brought about by the Revolution in the region. Throughout the poem, as I will show, both the forest and the Maya people are depicted with an exoticizing perspective that corresponds to Rosado Vega's own perspective as a white *letrado* from the city.

The first chapters of the poem introduce the idea of the Quintana Roo forest as a dramatic space full of contradictions that simultaneously embodies vitality, death, beauty, pain, and madness. *Poema de la selva trágica* celebrates the wide variety of flora and fauna that thrive in this fertile land, while also underscoring their appealing and aesthetically pleasing qualities. But the forest is far from being an idyllic, peaceful place because Rosado Vega emphasizes its cruel and menacing aspects, including the pervasive competition between species that results in extensive death and pain. For humans specifically, entering the forest entails the risks of being attacked by wild beasts, falling ill with climate-borne diseases, or even losing their minds as a result of haunting ghosts and hallucinatory visions. The forest is presented, in sum, as a living entity that permanently oscillates between giving life and taking it violently, between fostering diverse species and threatening their existence. This representation of the forest serves the function of foregrounding the overpowering character of the forest, allegedly felt particularly by the Maya people due to their supposed intimacy with nature. Such representation has a long-standing history and was common among early twentieth-century

Latin American narratives set in tropical forests, such as José Eustasio Rivera's *La vorágine* (1924) and Rómulo Gallegos's *Canaima* (1935) (Rogers 3–20).

In fact, Rosado Vega strives to draw a close correspondence between the forest flora, specifically trees, and the Maya people who allegedly existed from times immemorial. While the poem depicts some species of plants as active entities—such as the liana that climbs and entangles to build a tight web—trees are exclusively portrayed as passive, ancient beings, making them more akin to Indigenous people in Rosado Vega's view. For instance, when he is listing the diverse tree species living in the forest, Rosado Vega concludes with the following words: "y otros (árboles) más, y otros más, habitantes / de tal mundo de bárbara traza / que en siglos distantes / fuera albergue del indio y su raza" (and other [trees], and still more, inhabitants / of such a world of barbaric appearance / that in ancient centuries / was home to the Indian and his race) (34–35). The poem suggests an affinity between the Maya and the forest flora, particularly the ceiba tree, which "a su sombra a todos sus hijos cobija, / a todos sus hijos, los indios, aquellos / que injusto destino sin cesar asedia, / de faz bronca, de hirsutos cabellos / y de alma en tragedia" (in its shadow all its children are sheltered, / all its children, the Indians, those / who unjust destiny endlessly besieges, / with rough faces, with shaggy hair / and souls in tragedy) (31–32). Here, Rosado Vega represents the relationship between trees and the Maya as a close relationship based on sharing the same "unjust destiny" and "souls in tragedy," that is, a sort of inherent predisposition to being affected by stronger natural or human forces. Significantly, Indigenous bodies are not recurrently compared to animals as they are to trees, probably because forest fauna, such as jaguars, insects, or serpents, are considered mobile, active beings that are able to attack, defend themselves, or at least flee from danger.

Later in *Poema de la selva trágica,* the same fundamental analogy between trees and racialized bodies lies at the core of the chapter "El árbol de la sangre blanca," in which Rosado Vega describes in a dramatic manner the brutal process of chicle extraction. In botanical terms, the *chicozapote* tree exudes white latex as a defensive mechanism when it is injured or attacked by insects. The natural latex "forms a protective layer over the damaged area" (Mathews 6), deterring further insect attacks or microbial infection. Thus, this defensive reaction plays a part in the "intrinsic language" of *chicozapote* trees; that is, the "modes of communication and articulation used by vegetal specimens to negotiate ecologically with their biotic and abiotic environments" (Gagliano xvii–xviii). Rather than attuning to the *chicozapote* tree's particular modes of agency, Rosado Vega portrays them as completely passive victims that are sacrificed in the name of economic profit:

"Árbol de tormento, / árbol de suplicio / que es bárbaro y lento / el chicozapote muere en sacrificio; / muere en holocausto / de un delirio fiero / de riqueza y fasto / amasados en sangre y dinero" (Tree of torment, / tree of torture / brutal and slow / the sapodilla dies in sacrifice; / dies in a holocaust / of a fierce delirium / of wealth and splendor / amassed in blood and money) (105). To accentuate the dramatic traits of the scene, Rosado Vega presents an anthropomorphized tree whose veins are forcefully ruptured to let their white blood run down in a slow, tortuous process: "le parten las venas, zajando, zajando / hasta que desangre, / y así poco a poco se le irá escapando / la vida en el hilo de su blanca sangre; / se le va matando lenta, lentamente, / en tormento inequívoco y franco" (They slice its veins, cutting, cutting / until it bleeds dry, / and thus little by little / life will escape in the thread of its white blood; / they kill it slowly, slowly, / in a torment unmistakable and frank) (106, 107).

Poema de la selva trágica makes clear that the painful torture trees are subjected to is analogous to the agony suffered by the chicle extractors themselves. The poem underscores the excruciating working and living conditions in which the Indigenous laborers must perform their job. For starters, Rosado Vega describes how the laborers must venture into the forest in small groups—supervised by an exploitative foreman—suffering all the inherent risks of this threatening environment. Then, the laborers live in small, unsanitary huts in the middle of the forest for the duration of the extraction season, consuming unhealthy food and water and working long hours. In addition to these precarious conditions, chicle extraction is an inherently hazardous labor because it entails climbing up tall trees using only a rope to make cuts in the bark with a machete. This activity often results in fatal accidents when careless laborers fall from the top of the tree (Mediz Bolio 108). Thus, in the process of chicle extraction, as Rosado Vega suggests, "se juntan / y enredan con trazas iguales / dos sangres distintas" (they come together / and mix in equal traces / two different bloods) (110); that is, the *chicozapote*'s white blood and the Maya people's red blood are mixed together to produce economic benefit for the American capitalist and a product of consumption for the masses.

The poem symbolizes this close interrelation between the two kinds of blood by switching abruptly between the two. For example, in a crucial scene Rosado Vega condenses the brutality of chicle extraction by imagining that the chewing gum transforms into a human being while being chewed by a consumer: "y que a nadie asombre, / cuando alguien el chicle masca, masca y masca / quizá está mascando la vida de un hombre" (and let it be a surprise to no one, / when someone chews gum, chews and chews / he perhaps is chewing the life of a man) (107). This scene seems to have inspired the book cover, which shows the head of a Black man with a grotesque facial expression chewing a naked Indigenous man. The physical traits of the Black man—wide open eyes, protruding cheekbones, thick lips, large ears and nose—are in line with the racial stereotypes pervasive in late nineteenth- and early twentieth-century visual culture, which typically included the depiction of an exaggerated grimace and picturesque gestures (Nadell 16–25). In addition, the act of chewing gum was generally considered a "bad habit" during this time: an indecent, even lewd activity associated with popular or marginalized social classes, as Rosado Vega himself suggests in the preface (Segrave 97–120; Rosado Vega 12). Thus, by choosing to depict a close relationship between Black and Indigenous bodies through the act of chewing gum, the book cover is putting forth a racialization of chicle extraction and consumption, suggesting that racialized bodies are the primary victims of the capitalist drive for profit. While Indigenous peoples are exploited in the labor of chicle extraction, Black consumers in the United States commit "indecent" acts that allegedly demoralize them by chewing chicle.

As Daniel Nemser has recently argued, the close analogy between plants and racialized peoples as radically vulnerable bodies—implicitly contrasting them to the self-determined, rational white subject—was systematized and raised to a "scientific" principle by Spanish imperial botany during the eighteenth century. In this context, botanical expeditions endeavored to study and classify American plants with the aim of extracting and transporting them alive across broad geographical, climatic differences to the Iberian Peninsula, where these exotic plants became economic resources. In order to do so, botanists required a comprehension not only of the physical features and morphology of plants, but also of their environmental living conditions. Spanish imperial botany developed thus an understanding of the inextricable relationship between local plants and their environment, which was also mobilized to shed light on the alleged intimate connection of native people to their natural surroundings. In this way, as Nemser puts it, the "subject's mastery over colonial nature slips easily into a parallel mastery over colonized humanity, defined by its analogous relation to 'savage' vegetation" (162).

In contrast with Spanish imperial botany, Rosado Vega employs the colonialist analogy between plants and Indigenous bodies with the opposite objective in mind: his intention in *Poema de la selva trágica* is to condemn the brutal exploitation suffered by both plants and the Maya as vulnerable biological bodies.

However, even though Rosado Vega strives to denounce the neocolonial power of foreign corporations, he still endeavors to bolster the internal colonialism of the Mexican state. By this means, the long-standing analogy between plant life and racialized bodies seems to revert to its colonialist meaning in spite of Rosado Vega's explicit intention of dismantling the oppression of the Maya. In the end, according to *Poema de la selva trágica*, the social and environmental impacts of chicle extraction are due primarily to foreign capitalist greed, and the taking over of this industry by the postrevolutionary regime would allegedly solve this problem once and for all.

This state-centered narrative—based on the analogy between plants and Indigenous populations as passive, vulnerable bodies—disregards the Maya people's own knowledge and perspective, which may be better understood by turning our attention to the work of anthropologist Alfonso Villa Rojas.[3] In *The Maya of East Central Quintana Roo* (1945), Villa Rojas not only describes the Maya's disapproving reaction to the land reform established by the Cárdenas regime, but also provides a description of their extensive and complex relationship with plants in a variety of economic, religious, and cultural ways. Rather than considering plant life as passive, vulnerable bodies awaiting economic extraction, the Maya in Tusik acknowledged and engaged with the agency of plants, particularly maize, which Villa Rojas calls "the center of social and religious life" (59). The Maya believed that maize reacted according to the religious behavior of the people, so that its abundance or scarcity was determined by compliance with religious agricultural ceremonies. Apparently, this kind of decisive importance was not attributed to the *chicozapote* trees, whose value according to Villa Rojas was "entirely commercial" (59). But even if the *chicozapote* tree was not woven into the social fabric as profoundly as maize, chicle extraction was still conducted under the general approach to the natural world prescribed by the Maya people, which underscored the importance of seeking permission and help from the gods to exploit natural resources, as well as thanking them accordingly for granting their goods. This close interrelationship with nature disallowed the possibility of the exclusively instrumental, extractive relation with the forest that was promoted by both the global chewing gum industry and the Mexican state.

Selva trágica

Long after the chicle industry has lost its economic importance in the Yucatán Peninsula, the processes of extractive capitalism and the state's internal colonialism in the region have morphed to remain relevant in the twenty-first century. The tourism industry, attracted by the archaeological sites and splendid natural features of the so-called Riviera Maya, has gradually supplanted chicle extraction as one of the most profitable economic activities in the region, resuming the legacy of social and environmental impacts on the forest and its Indigenous and mestizo inhabitants. The most recent endeavor in this respect is the so-called Tren Maya, a massive state-funded project involving the construction of a railway that will connect popular tourist destinations and archaeological sites in the Yucatán Peninsula. Since it was officially announced in 2018, Indigenous communities and social organizations, such as the Ejército Zapatista de Liberación Nacional, have condemned this ambitious project for encroaching on the rights to their land (Castellanos). Notwithstanding the widespread controversy and diverse protests against the project, the Andrés Manuel López Obrador administration began construction of the railway in 2020 and inaugurated the first section in late 2023. In March 2023, the International Rights of Nature Tribunal convened a meeting in Valladolid, Yucatán, to gather information and assess the social and environmental repercussions of the Tren Maya. After surveying the construction sites and listening to Indigenous communities' testimonies in the region, the Tribunal, presided over by Argentine anthropologist Maristella Svampa, reached the conclusion that the project has violated the rights of nature and the rights of the Maya people ("Comunicado de prensa").

In this context, the reemergence of chicle extraction as a topic of cultural production has a special significance and relevancy. One can address this issue by focusing on the award-winning film *Selva trágica* (dir. Yulene Olaizola, 2021), which was shot in the Quintana Roo forest the same year that the Tren Maya construction began. Set during the 1920s on the Quintana Roo–British Honduras (present-day Belize) border, Olaizola's film follows Agnes (Indira Rubie Andrewin), a young Black woman who encounters a group of Maya and mestizo chicle extractors after fleeing from an arranged marriage to a violent white landowner (Dale Carley). The all-male group of workers forcibly takes Agnes with them, fearing that she is a member of a competing British crew of chicle harvesters. One by one, in hopes of possessing the enigmatic, beautiful Agnes, all the workers are lured and ultimately led by her to a physical or emotional demise. The only surviving worker is Jacinto (Mariano Tun Xool), who escapes through the forest before Agnes lures her final victim and finishes him off in the last scene of the film. Jacinto also plays the part of the narrator who, throughout the film, intercalates his musings in Maya about the forest and finally asserts that Agnes is the embodiment of the mythical Xtabay, a woman who is said to spellbind and kill men who lust after her. Heightened by Sofia Oggioni's superb cinematography and Alejandro Otaola's eerie musical score, *Selva trágica* compels viewers to place themselves in the thick of the Quintana Roo forest and its natural and supernatural dangers.

As the filmmaker herself has confirmed, the film draws heavily from the postrevolutionary corpus on chicle extraction and other sources (Garibay). As a non-Indigenous woman from an urban background, Olaizola embarked on a long process of intermittently living on location, researching the region's history and culture, interviewing, and hearing stories from local people to gather material for her film. *Selva trágica* draws on the notion—pervasive, as I showed above, in *Poema de la selva trágica* and other works from the time—of the Quintana Roo forest as a space that is remote, enigmatic, extremely violent, and full of life at the same time. As the character guiding Agnes away from the landowner suggests, paraphrasing Ramón Beteta's *Tierra del chicle* (1937): "Here, everything has the same color. Everything seems to be . . . the same. Hiding from our eyes. The butterflies, the palm trees, the vines . . . Everything seems to be waiting patiently for the enemy to come" (13:30–14:05; Beteta 12). All the environmental risks underscored by Beteta, Rosado Vega, and others—including precarious living conditions, menacing beasts, and debilitating diseases—appear prominently in Olaizola's film and play a vital role in establishing the threatening character of the forest. Furthermore, *Selva trágica* also depicts the deplorable social conditions of chicle extraction at the time, marked by the over-tapping of natural resources, labor exploitation, and fatal work-related accidents.

The first sequence of the film sets the tone by capturing the array of environmental and social dangers involved in chicle extraction, as well as its close relationship with the Maya people. The first shot shows in documentary style the base of a *chicozapote* tree—in the middle of lush vegetation—with zigzag marks transporting white liquid to a bag on the ground. The viewer hears off-screen noises of diverse animal species and the sounds of machetes chopping wood; but at first, the chicle extractor at the top of the tree is not visible. This seems to suggest that the natural latex, as a valuable commodity in the capitalist economy, constitutes the main objective of this activity at the expense of the workers themselves. These laborers are visually and socially alienated from the product of their labor—and from nature that has become a reserve of resources for economic profit. After the first shot, the film shows various scenes documenting the process of chicle extraction. A medium shot encompassing Jacinto and the *chicozapote* tree establishes a close interrelation between both agents, followed by a close-up of the tree bark being slashed by a machete that suggests the environmental harm caused by the chicle industry. Subsequently, the film conveys the hazardous working conditions by showing a high-angle shot of Jacinto, who is tenuously clinging to the tree at a high altitude from the ground.

In addition to all the environmental and social risks suggested in the first sequence, perhaps the most important factor contributing to the "tragic" quality of the setting in Olaizola's film is the supernatural, haunting nature of the forest, which as seen above was also explored by Rosado Vega's poem. *Selva trágica* puts forward these mystic features by incorporating the Maya legend of Xtabay as recounted by Indigenista writer Antonio Mediz Bolio in *La tierra del faisán y el venado* (1922).[4] In fact, Jacinto's voice-over is an adaptation and translation into Maya of chapter 6 of the work. In contrast with other versions of the legend, Mediz Bolio's account presents Xtabay as an evil being who appears in the forest to lure and punish men who are unable to control their sexual desire (Rosado Avilés). Mediz Bolio suggests that Xtabay, instead of appealing to mature prudent men, chooses to put a spell on lustful young men who easily surrender to their passions. Thus, this version of the legend contains a lesson of the importance of self-constraint and a related warning to men who fail to command their primary instincts. Mediz Bolio and Jacinto's voice-over directly address these concupiscent men, the most probable victims of Xtabay, warning them against the fatal consequences by repeatedly interjecting, "¡pobre de ti!" (Poor you!) (Mediz Bolio 189). As Jacinto puts it, closely following Mediz Bolio's account, "Quiera tu suerte que la que temes y deseas no aparezca ante ti. Porque la mujer Xtabay ya conoce el camino que recorres" (You are lucky that she whom you fear and desire does not appear before you. Because the woman Xtabay already knows the path you are on) (22:50–23:28).

In Olaizola's film the legend of Xtabay serves the function of embodying the pernicious repercussions of both human and nonhuman natural instincts. Along with sexuality's destructive force, Xtabay also represents the overpowering nature of the forest itself with its contradictory, disturbing features: beauty, violence, madness, vitality, and death. Several scenes establish a close analogy between Xtabay's racialized, feminine body and the forest. After encountering the chicle workers and leading a couple of them to their downfall in mysterious circumstances, Agnes/Xtabay lures her next victim to an enormous *ceiba* tree in the middle of the forest to engage in deadly sexual intercourse. *Ceibas*—considered sacred by the Maya people—play an important role in diverse versions of the Xtabay legend, which asserts that she either was born from it, embodies it, or takes her victims to these trees because she knows about Maya's cosmology (Rosado Avilés). Olaizola's film creates a sense of intimacy between racialized bodies and the *ceiba* tree through a medium shot of Agnes/Xtabay with her back against the *ceiba* trunk and the worker's naked back in front of her. The dim lighting of the scene helps create an effective visual conflation between human skin and tree bark. Additionally, the enigmatic, suspenseful score evokes a sensation of a supernatural occurrence taking place in the forest.

The last scene of the film similarly reinforces the inextricable relationship between Agnes/Xtabay and the forest by showing her suddenly emerging from the river, enticing her last victim, and finally submerging back into the river to disappear with him in her arms. Thus, *Selva trágica* suggests that Xtabay constitutes a vengeful, supernatural reaction against the "various forms of exploitation (environmental, patriarchal, and colonial)" (García) depicted in the film. Ultimately, Xtabay exclusively punishes men who exercise systemic violence against trees, women, and racialized peoples to exploit them in various ways. As a racialized, feminine body with an intimate relationship with plant life, Xtabay manifests a violent rebellion against the effects of a colonialist, patriarchal, capitalist, and environmentally irresponsible system. This avenging nature of Xtabay is the expression of the violent, menacing facets of the forest itself, which were already suggested in Rosado Vega's poem and other postrevolutionary works. However, while in *Poema de la selva trágica* the forest seems to unleash its violent retaliation indiscriminately—often inflicting pain on the already victimized Indigenous population—in *Selva trágica* the single target of the forest's punishment is exploitative men who give in to patriarchal lust and capitalist greed.

It is essential to note that, by attributing the forest's revenge to a racialized, overtly sexualized character, the film runs the risk of reproducing harmful stereotypes of Black women. As I mentioned before, the representation of dangerous, violent sexuality was already present in some versions of the Xtabay legend, but Olaizola's choice of placing this luring sexuality on a Black body is problematic. In a sense, the film does little to counteract and even reinforces the view of Black women as exoticized, sexually lewd subjects that has a long colonial tradition and modern iterations in the Americas. Furthermore, as a non-Indigenous director who releases films for international audiences, Olaizola runs the risk of appealing to "the viewer's romantic yearning for accessible, authentic exoticism" (102), as Debra Castillo has argued for the case of Jayro Bustamante's *Ixcanul*, a film which similarly has a racialized, highly sexualized protagonist. The portrayal of Black femininity in *Selva trágica* positions Agnes/Xtabay as an object both of fetishization for male characters within the film and of exoticism for urban, international audiences outside the film.

Thus, it is natural to wonder if Olaizola's film, in a similar fashion as Rosado Vega's poem, reverts back to a colonialist framework in spite of its own intentions of denouncing diverse forms of exploitation. While it is clear that Agnes/Xtabay embodies racist and sexist tropes, I argue that the end of the film suggests the possibility of a non-exploitative relationship with trees, women, and racialized peoples. After the demise of nearly all workers, Jacinto—whose voice-over has issued a reasonable warning throughout the film—is the sole survivor of Xtabay's vengeance. He has seen throughout the plot how Xtabay has led men to their doom, but he has not succumbed to lust. As his narration suggests, "Pero ella [Xtabay] no llama a quien no la seguirá. Aquel que se ha armado con una coraza de cuero endurecido" (But she [Xtabay] does not call to him who will not follow her. He who has armed himself with a breastplate of hardened leather) (1:17:50–1:18:03). Significantly, Jacinto is the only character who is opposed to or at least hesitant to partake in the diverse forms of violence and exploitation taking place in the Quintana Roo forest. The viewer last sees Jacinto as he is fleeing by himself through the forest, staring at the impenetrable vegetation and being flooded by the overwhelming sounds of animals. Jacinto's final escape through the forest signals a line of flight away from the instrumentalization of nature, women, and racialized peoples. While Rosado Vega's work attributed the emancipation of the Indigenous population to the political reforms of the postrevolutionary regime, Olaizola's film implicitly suggests that the self-determination of the Maya people in alliance with plant life represents the way out of this unjust, oppressive system.

All in all, Rosado Vega's poem and Olaizola's film engage in related, diverging ways with the history of chicle extraction in the Yucatán Peninsula and its connection with enduring colonialist, extractive structures. Both works mobilize a depiction of the Quintana Roo forest as a dramatic, "tragic" space and aim to shed light on the oppression suffered by both plant life and racialized bodies. Rosado Vega reinforces an analogy between the blood of the *chicozapote* tree and the Maya people based on their alleged similarity as biological, vulnerable bodies. By portraying them as passive victims in need of an external source of emancipation, Rosado Vega downplays their ability to make an impact on the world around them and to actively shape it. Likewise, Olaizola draws on the perspective of Rosado Vega and other postrevolutionary sources to recreate and immerse the viewer in this environment of brutal colonial and extractive exploitation. Olaizola similarly establishes a visual conflation between racialized bodies and forest plants to highlight their shared destiny in this system. Nevertheless, in contrast with Rosado Vega's poem, Olaizola's film suggests in implicit terms the possibility of an escape of Indigenous population from these forms of destructive exploitation. Even if the problematic portrayal of Black femineity undermines its efficacy, *Selva trágica* advances the fate of Jacinto as the promise of a new, non-exploitative socioecological order. Taken together, Rosado Vega's poem and Olaizola's film illustrate how non-Indigenous artists have varyingly taken up the colonial analogy between racialized bodies and plant life with the hope of refashioning it in line with critical perspectives.

Notes

1. This corpus includes *Tierra del chicle* (1937) by Ramón Beteta, *Imágenes de Quintana Roo* (1938) by César Lizardi Ramos, *Claudio Martín. Vida de un chiclero* (1938), and *Poema de la selva trágica* (1938) by Luis Rosado Vega. Later cases are *Chicle: ensayo de novela del trópico mexicano* (1951) by Enrique Vázquez and *Caribal: el infierno verde* (1954) by Rafael Bernal.

2. See, for example, the literary work *U k'a'ajsajil u ts'u' noj k'áax/Recuerdos del corazón de la montaña* (2005) by Ana Patricia Martínez Huchim, and the film *Selva trágica* (2021), directed by Yulene Olaizola.

3. Villa Rojas was a Yucatecan rural teacher who studied anthropology at the University of Chicago and conducted pioneering ethnographic research in the region. In 1936, two years before Rosado Vega spearheaded his scientific expedition, Villa Rojas began carrying out fieldwork in Tusik, Quintana Roo, where he was able to gather information about the Mayas' socioeconomic, political, and cultural organization. The results of this research were published in a few articles in Spanish and in the major work *The Maya of East Central Quintana Roo* (1945).

4. The collection and translation into Spanish of Maya legends was a well-established cultural trend in postrevolutionary times. Antonio Mediz Bolio is perhaps the most well-known Mayanista (Indigenista intellectual interested in Maya culture) of the time, but Rosado Vega also published two books of Maya stories: *El alma misteriosa del Mayab* (1934) and *Amerindmaya* (1938).

Works Cited

Beteta, Ramón. *Tierra del chicle.* DAPP, 1937.

Cárdenas, Lázaro. *El problema de los territorios federales. Un llamamiento al patrio-*

tismo y al sentido de responsabilidad del pueblo mexicano. Talleres Gráficos de la Nación, 1936.

Castellanos, Laura. "La guerra de los pueblos indígenas contra el Tren Maya ya comenzó en México." *Washington Post,* 16 Dec. 2019, https://www.washingtonpost.com/es/post-opinion/2019/12/16/la-guerra-de-los-pueblos-indigenas-contra-el-tren-maya-ya-comenzo-en-mexico/. Accessed 1 Dec. 2023.

Castillo, Debra. "Trafficked Babies, Exploded Futures: Jayro Bustamante's Ixcanul." *Indigenous Interfaces: Spaces, Technology and Social Networks in Mexico and Central America,* edited by Jennifer Gómez Menjívar and Gloria Chacón, University of Arizona Press, 2019.

"Comunicado de prensa. Tribunal pide la suspensión inmediata del megaproyecto del Tren Maya ante la alerta de ecocidio y etnocidio," https://www.rightsofnaturetribunal.org/wp-content/uploads/2023/03/Comunicado-de-prensa-Tribunal-Tren-Maya-FINAL.pdf?fbclid=IwAR3Ig-bQLxCtmsPyKWRvOlgFg9aYnT2IwHgr5A6gxoe2-sfdpYR-O_Iyq2s. Accessed 1 Dec. 2023.

Gagliano, Monica, et al. "Introduction." *The Language of Plants,* edited by Monica Gagliano et al., University of Minnesota Press, 2017, pp. VII–XXXIII.

García, Lawrence. "Tragic Jungle's Plunge into the Heart of Darkness Lacks the Wildness of Herzog." *AV Club,* 9 June 2021, https://www.avclub.com/tragic-jungle-s-plunge-into-the-heart-of-darkness-lacks-1847047791. Accessed 1 Dec. 2023.

Garibay, Arturo. "Sobrevivir a la selva trágica. Una entrevista con Yulene Olaizola." *Top Cinema,* 8 Dec. 2020, https://topcinema.com.mx/2776/sobrevivir-a-la-selva-tragica-una-entrevista-con-yulene-olaizola/entrevistas/. Accessed 1 Dec. 2023.

González Casanova, Pablo. "El colonialismo interno" (Internal Colonialism). *Sociología de la explotación.* CLACSO, 2006.

González Vázquez, David Anuar. *La expedición científica Mexicana al territorio de Quintana Roo (1936–1938): Prácticas científicas y relaciones políticas en la formación del estado-nación.* 2018. MA Thesis, Centro de Investigaciones y Estudios Superiores en Antropología Social.

Martínez-Reyes, José E. *Moral Ecology of a Forest: The Nature Industry and Maya Post-Conservation.* University of Arizona Press, 2016.

Mathews, Jennifer P. *Chicle: The Chewing Gum of the Americas, from the Ancient Maya to William Wrigley.* University of Arizona Press, 2009.

Mediz Bolio, Antonio. *La tierra del faisán y el venado.* Contreras y Sanz, 1922.

Nadell, Martha Jane. *Enter the New Negroes: Images of Race in American Culture.* Harvard University Press, 2004.

Nemser, Daniel. *Infrastructures of Race. Concentration and Biopolitics in Colonial Mexico.* University of Texas Press, 2017.

Olaizola, Yulene, director. *Selva trágica.* Malacosa Cine, Varios Lobos, Manny Films, 2020.

Rogers, Charlotte. *Jungle Fever: Exploring Madness and Medicine in Twentieth-Century Tropical Narratives.* Vanderbilt University Press, 2012.

Rosado Avilés, Cecilia, and Georgina Rosado Rosado. "La Xtabay. Mujer, sensualidad y poder en un mito Maya. Un acercamiento a los arquetipos femeninos." *Yucatán. Identidad y cultura maya,* https://www.mayas.uady.mx/articulos/art_02.html. Accessed 1 Dec. 2023.

Rosado Vega, Luis. *Poema de la selva trágica.* Edición SCOP, 1938.

Segrave, Kerry. *Chewing Gum in America, 1850–1920: The Rise of an Industry.* McFarland & Company, 2015.

Villa Rojas, Alfonso. *The Maya of East Central Quintana Roo.* Carnegie Institution of Washington, 1945.

IV

The Politics of Plant and Animal Life

13

Of Paddocks, Plants, and Cattle

Security and Burden in the Caribbean Age of Sugar

NIALL A. PEACH

Sugar (*Saccharum officinarum*) has come to dominate our understanding of the agribiopolitical[1] relations realized through monoculture on and through the plantation in the nineteenth and twentieth centuries in the Caribbean. Although by no means the only crop produced through monoculture, it enjoys an outsized influence in cultural production, shaping the region's literary history: as backdrop to anti-slavery literature and as protagonist in Caribbean telluric narratives otherwise known as *novelas de la caña* (sugarcane novels). In fact, sugar no longer solely represents the vegetal.[2] Under the moniker *Doña Azúcar,*[3] it encompasses a host of death-producing or necrotic extractivist practices[4] synonymous with the sociocultural and political regulation of life as precarious and unlivable. Through deforestation, chattel slavery, displacement, and the violent reordering of interspecies relations, sugar frames life as precarious. Bénédicte Boisseron's *Afro-Dog* has addressed this reorganization of life through the commensal relation of Haitians to the creole dog. In this, she argues that underneath this current relation of human to nonhuman animal there exists a history of punishment and dehumanization that highlights the animalization of blackness and the violent use of the dog as punishment on the sugar plantation. The same was true of the Spanish-speaking Caribbean. This shift in relation speaks to the organization of human/nonhuman entanglements in sites of environmental transformation, such as the plantation, or, as Franklin Ginn states, how lives become stuck and unstuck (see "Sticky Lives").[5] While sugar and the violence it engendered has dominated academic and cultural imaginaries as the principal narrative of the plantation in the Caribbean, various vegetal, human, and animal entanglements existed on this site and sites related to it, such as the *conuco* (subsistence plot). Sylvia Wynter's expansive work on the human and the overrepresentation of Man has been instrumental in engaging the *conuco* as a site that forms part of the plantation's geography but represents the other "plots" of monoculture's monolithic narrative (see "Novel and History").[6] For Wynter, the *conuco* rejects the plantation's exchange value, in favor of a use-value system of self-sufficiency and, therefore, a different relation to the vegetal than the one available through sugar's monoculture ("Novel and History").

In considering the theoretical entanglements of plants and animals under monoculture, I turn to the *potrero* (paddock), an understudied site that, likewise, challenges the plantation's narrative. With this, I engage the interrelationality of cattle (primarily oxen), guinea grass (*Megathyrsus maximus*),[7] alfalfa (*Medicago sativa*), and Black subjects in Cuba and the Dominican Republic. Within a transnational context, the paddock's presence increased in Cuba as the plantation economy declined following the nineteenth-century Independence Wars, and in the Dominican Republic, early-twentieth-century US neoimperial interest saw sugar's expansion and the paddock's decline. In both geographies, the paddock is framed as paradisical site against the violence of sugar. On this site the abovementioned actors are engaged in the construction of security against sugar and to achieve this become stuck and unstuck in multiple entanglements. As becoming stuck in entanglements brings about security, conversely the dissolution of relations as tactic for security results in individuated burden and vulnerability.[8] For this, I draw on a range of writings on the paddock, but focus on the as-of-yet unstudied paddock narrative *El potrero paraíso: Agricultura y zootécnica* (1888) (*Paradise Paddock: Agriculture and Zootechnics*) by Cuban agriculturalist Juan Bautista Jiménez (1837–1906) and the sugarcane novel *Cañas y bueyes* (1936) (*Sugarcane and Oxen*) by Dominican writer Francisco Moscoso Puello (1885–1959).

Security and Paradisical Paddocks

In both Cuba and the Dominican Republic, cattle have played a significant role in economic and political development. In the former, oxen provided labor and movement on the plantation. In the latter, goats and wild boars were hunted for sustenance and, alongside cattle, were used "as a foil to the crony capitalist model of development under Trujillo" (Derby 313). In fact, as a point of difference from Cuban economic development, for centuries Dominicans relied on swidden farming before sugar's arrival toward the end of the nineteenth century with US investment (Derby 304, 311). But, in both Cuba and the Dominican Republic, the *potrero*, a site often contiguous to the plantation, enabled the economic instrumentalization of cattle, oxen in particular, and was central to agri-cultural discourse on security and well-being in the context of sugar.

Dominican novel *Cañas y bueyes* (*Sugarcane and Oxen*) (1936), by Francisco Moscoso Puello, is an archetypal sugarcane novel and early twentieth-century narrative, focused on exposing monoculture's ills. Its narrative centers on the establishment of the island's first sugar estate in Macorís, called Inocencia, the promise of sugar, and the corrupt (legal) practices of the US-based "Compañía Nacional de Inversiones Territoriales" (National Company for Territorial Investment) and its head, Franklin Harrison (Puello 37).[9] In this retelling of Dominican history, sugar's geography of terror[10] produces the gradual displacement of the characters who embrace it as a future facing crop. As an example, Don Marcial, Inocencia's owner, comes into land on which he builds his estate only through the arrival of a new administration and the seeming falsification of documents that leaves the land's original owner, Don José, with a third of his property. Don José is one of many people affected by the arrival of sugar through his exposure to the insecurity produced by monoculture's mechanisms (loss of land, income, and so on). But, fitting with the novel's title, alongside the misappropriation of land, sugar's arrival transforms the landscape, its paddocks, leaving nowhere for his oxen to remain.

At its beginning, the landscape of *Cañas y bueyes* is mostly untouched idyll with glimpses of paddocks that figure in retrospective mention throughout the novel. This blended aesthetic of the pastoral and paradisical signals the harmonious cohabitation of the human and other-than-human that equates the cultivating, transformative work of the paddock to that of untouched environments, constructing a web of harmonious multispecies engagements that include the human. In an expected extractivist turn with the establishment of Inocencia, the sugar estate's expansion disturbs this harmony as the countryside cedes space for it: "Las hachas abatieron aquel monte y el fuego lo redujo todo a carbones y cenizas" (axes felled the forest and fire reduced everything to charcoal and ash) (Puello 11). Forest succumbs to fire and extractivism replaces the multispecies practices that undergirded life.

In what follows, the destruction of multispecies entanglements is accompanied by the willful abandonment of land as many of the novel's characters are attracted by the promise of security and economic gain through sugar cultivation and working for a US-based company. Of several examples given, the narrator cites Baldomero Rubert, a supposedly crazy man or "un loco" (Puello 40). Baldomero sold his paddock that lay on the proposed railway line for the transportation of cane, displacing his cattle with no mention of what happens to them. The narrator explains his decision, saying "no le faltaría algo que hacer a él o a sus hijos, aunque fuera tumbar algunos de esos montes que había vendido o sembrar caña o encargarse de algún tiro de bueyes" (he and his children would always have work, even if it meant felling the forest he had sold or sowing cane or becoming an ox-driver) (Puello 40). The irony that transportation limited to the plantation takes the place of free movement is compounded by the conditioning of the relation of ox to human, wherein both actors are subsumed into the movement they provide to cane: ox and ox driver. Yet, despite the supposed eventuality of joint labor (ox and ox driver), the effect of Baldomero's decision on the oxen goes untold. In a narrative with characters concerned about land and cattle, wherein pivotal narrative arcs for Don Marcial and Don José revolve around the ownership of oxen and debts over their purchase, the omission of the oxen's fate is peculiar. As if the form of the cane novel had in a narrative sense come to dominate what was accountable, colonizing the language used, the absence of Baldomero's oxen and a focus on his children's future represents an absolute detachment of the human from the animal. The case of Baldomero acts against the use of cattle in securing right to place, such as that seen at the end of the nineteenth century in Cuba.[11] As such, the dissolution of ties to place and subsistence, through ceding of land and the abandonment of oxen to a fate so far unknown, leads to Baldomero's own misfortune on the plantation and is suggestive of the perpetual displacement of the human and animal.

Sugar's consumption of land through monoculture produces an insecure landscape in the narrative with displacement and threats of violence made by the bandits now inhabiting the area against the remaining paddocks, and the animals and plants in them. The violence against plants and animals is notable. One witness describes that "cientos de matas de plátano [fueron] arrancadas" (hundreds of banana trees [were] ripped out) and the bandits "se introducen en los potreros y roban vacas, penetran en los conucos y desraciman los platanares" (enter into the pastures and steal cows, penetrating the plots and uprooting the bananas trees) (Puello 12: 114). The violent eroticism of invasion that leads to subsistence devastation is mimicked, likewise, by the sugar that surpasses the borders of José Prieto's paddock. Replete with foreboding for José and his family, his friend Antonio's workers have begun to plant sugarcane "en el patio y en la misma puerta de su casa" (on the patio and the front door of his house) (Puello 41). The encroachment of sugar into the private space of the pasture ensures the loss of his home and paddock, as part of what the narrator calls the "despojo violento" (violent removal) that includes the loss of his forty cows, the theft of his pigs and his daughters' loss of house, land, and future (Puello 41).

As sugar surpasses its own materiality to encompass its abstraction as political vegetal presence in the narrative, recalling Kregg Hetherington's work on soy as hyperobject and character of the Anthropocene, it facilitates the reordering of life in Macorís toward the unsticking of animal, plant, and human relations present before it. The advancement of cane, its homogenization of sites, and the degradation of soil is a degrading of boundary markers that identify (economic, territorial, food) security for the people, plants, and cattle that inhabit the area. For the vegetal, this is ever truer when considering that the paddock is an agglomeration of vegetal presences that provides a defined site of security. In *Cañas y bueyes* the paddock and its relations are replaced by the plantation, acting merely as futile safeguard against sugar. But, in the previous century in Cuba, the paddock was a tool of the plantation to ensure the security of oxen.

From the end of the eighteenth century onward, the number of *potreros* in Cuba increased, solving what Baltasar de Sotolongo in 1783 called the "crises de la ganadería" (cattle crises)—sparked by limited space on which to rear and feed cattle (Funes Monzote, "Un arcoíris," "Especialización" 112–113). Identifying the paddock as a solution to issues of cattle-rearing and well-being points initially to the site's role in a geography of welfare but, moreover, the crisis in which it intervened highlights the centrality of cattle to sugar production. Oxen provided movement; they propelled the mill's grinding mechanisms and transported cane across the plantation guided by their enslaved or freed *carreteros* (drivers). Even after the arrival of mechanization—such as the steam engine in the 1830s—the ox still performed high volumes of labor given its favorably cheap costs and the decreased availability of enslaved labor (Funes Monzote, "Animal Labor" 213–214). It is estimated that one hour of ox labor was equivalent to 3.8 hours of human labor (Funes Monzote, "Facetas" 92). The burden placed on oxen was great, and the value of their labor supposed an increased exposure to risk; long hours under the sun without water or sustenance led to death during harvest periods or *zafra* (Funes Monzote, "Animal Labor" 215). The paddock was intended then as a panacea, creating a defined site on and adjacent to the plantation for oxen to rest, eat, and regain their strength during periods of downtime. Throughout the nineteenth century the rhetoric of crisis that had sparked the paddock's proliferation was buttressed by commentary on the ox's well-being and dangers to it outside the paddock on the plantation. Such societal concern for oxen reflected the rise of animal protection societies in Europe and the solidification of pro-animal protection movements in the Caribbean. In fact, in 1882 La Sociedad Protectora de los Animales y las Plantas (Society for the Protection of Animals and Plants) was founded in Havana.[12] Appearing four years before slavery's formal abolition in 1886, such calls to protect animals and plants emerged from a broader movement to readdress the ethical treatment of humans (Funes Monzote, "Facetas" 95–96). Despite the comparative ethical thought that grounded animal and plants' rights movements in a human-oriented ethics, a historic distrust of enslaved Black subjects and their entanglements with cattle had long informed agri-cultural discourse on oxen.

With a relation forged through the shared labor of moving the cart—one guiding and the other pulling—enslaved peoples and oxen formed the fabric of the sugar economy (Freyre 14). While they represent an important entanglement because of the shared burden of their labor or rather the subsuming of both into a single laboring unit, this becomes undone as each is subject to nuanced and differentiated burden underneath the plantation's exchange-value economy (Wynter 95–96, 100). Writing in 1863, Galician naturalist Ramón de la Sagra y Peris (1798–1871) discussed abuses on the plantation, stating for the ox that:

> La raza es bella, fuerte, corpulenta, pero poco dócil. Semejante defecto procede del carácter los negros que dirigen este excelente animal, apreciador del buen trato y que se presta con mansedumbre á todas las tareas, mientras que no se le castiga con severidad. El Buey es hijo de la educación, pero de la educación calculada y racional, no caprichosa y violenta: y el negro esclavo, frecuentemente maltratado, se venga de las injusticias que sufre sobre el inocente animal á quien domina
>
> (The race is beautiful, strong, stocky, but not very docile. There is a similar defect in the character of the Black people who lead this excellent animal, that, appreciative of good treatment, servilely lends its efforts to all kinds of work so long as it is not punished severely. The ox is a child of education, but only education that is rational and well thought out and not vio-

> lent or whimsical. The slave, who is frequently mistreated, takes vengeance against the injustices they suffer through mistreatment of the innocent animal over which they are master) (vol. III, 22)

Contrasting with the histories of racial violence surrounding blackness, the abuse of oxen shows the limits of acceptable forms of violence on the plantation. Just as Sagra y Peris begins to make possible a comparative view of a shared burden of unjust treatment, the point retracts behind the master/slave rhetoric which places at its center animal innocence and mistrust of enslaved subjects. What is more, while the vengeful action Sagra y Peris highlights above is a targeted form of violence, any injury to oxen caused by a worker—enslaved, freed, or salaried—was severely punished (Funes Monzote, "Facetas" 91). What follows is a call to reallocate responsibilities of care for oxen, no longer entrusting ox-drivers to supply food and water because of a so-called self-interest toward their own needs and the care of their pigs (Funes Monzote, "Animal Labor" 215). Sagra y Peris's description of how the plantation composes Black life with that of the ox infers to an extent what animal studies has defined as the role of the liminal animal: animals that exist within interstices of human geographies and framed as "nuisances because, unlike domesticated animals, they do not return the favor of being fed by humans" through ceding their bodies for human consumption (Boisseron 92–93). The ox is never meant for human consumption, or rather the enslaved workers have no claim to consume the animal based on their care of it. To be clear, the ox is consumed by the plantation through its labor. However, due to the impossibility of reciprocal action, or repaying the *carretero* for care, the relationship that undergirds plantation labor becomes a source of insecurity for the ox. However, as Sagra y Peris considers the ox burdened by its role as vehicle for restorative justice, he does so without reference to the conditions endured by oxen as part of their labor. Intentionally or not, then, Sagra y Peris rhetorically extends the exceptional treatment to which the ox is subject on the paddock to the plantation writ large. This is to say that he centers the ox's well-being against vulnerabilities to its security, and in doing so places the burden of increased insecurity, framed as mistrust, onto the enslaved. The paddock functioned as a measure of security for cattle against the plantation's inherent insecurities (of labor, life, and well-being), or its geography of terror, as part of a series of cultivated and cultivatable parcels of land—*prados artificiales* (artificial pastures). As Sagra y Peris's redescribing of Black and animal life on the plantation decoupled the ox driver from ox, advocating for a redistribution of responsibilities of care, the paddock, and other *prados artificiales*, imagined a resticking or recomposition of animal-vegetal life for security.

At the mid-nineteenth century in Cuba, paddocks occupied more territory than any other singular agricultural unit, and by the century's end paddocks began to prevail in rural areas affected by the Ten Years War (1868–1878): Cienfuegos had the most sites dedicated to pasture, followed by Trinidad, Cartagena, and La Esperanza (Gallego Jiménez 74). As part of the recomposition of life for security through the paddock, cultural discourse had framed the site as a paradise. The Sociedad de los Amigos del País (Society of the Friends of the Country)—an organization dedicated to progress through science and agriculture, declared in 1841: "Los bosques artificiales que deben ocupar la mitad de la extensión de cada potrero parecen como el arcoíris en medio de las tempestades; las cercas también contribuirán en gran parte a precaver los funestos efectos de la devastación de los montes de esta Isla" (the artificial forests that should occupy half the extension of the paddock appear to be like a rainbow in the middle of a storm; the fences around it should contribute greatly to battling the terrible effects of the devastation of the hills on the island) (Funes Monzote, "Un arcoíris").[13] While in part this passage signals the Edenic discourse of colonial Spanish American writing on Cuba, the paradisical paddock represents a sanctuary that protects those inside it from the horrors of deforestation, abuse, death, and devastation—the storm that rages outside. Discursively, the association of paddock to paradise is reflected in Juan Bautista Jiménez's novel *El potrero paraíso: Agricultura y zootécnica* (*Paradise Paddock: Agriculture and Zootechnics*) published in 1888. In total, Bautista Jiménez—a member of the *Sociedad de los Amigos del País*—published four novels between 1883 and 1894, with each critiquing a key aspect of plantation agri-culture: from degraded soil composition, to deforestation, and the lack of economic investment in viable alternatives to the plantation. As the title *The Paradise Paddock* suggests, the novel imagines the paddock as a paradise away from sugar. Here the balance of vegetal and nonhuman animal life is key to mutual flourishing, benefiting, by extension, the human lives connected to it: the novel's protagonist, D. Plácido, and his family, particularly his daughter, whom he educates about the paddock. Yet, the vegetal is not only the rainbow that makes the sanctuary-paddock. Given the paddock's artificiality—or its creation—the set of relations engendered in the sanctuary, which ensure security, point obliquely to the regulation of life and to the irreconcilable contradiction that critical animal studies have attributed to the contemporary sanctuary farm:

the greenwashing of animal abuse under the marker of sanctuary.[14] As such, while the vegetal facilitates sanctuary, it is also consumed by and in the paddock. This dual function raises the question of the vegetal's capacity for reciprocity and liminality—like the ox—and it moreover signals an entry point for addressing the vegetal's deployment in the control of the animal.

Vegetal Forces: Inside the Paddock

In constituting a compostist view of the paddock's relations—from the soil up—*El potrero paraíso* features myriad plants, which D. Plácido explains have specific roles. First, he cites alfalfa (*Medicago sativa*), claiming it as an excellent Leguminosae because of its "extraordinario impulso vejetativo" (extraordinary vegetal force) (Jiménez 15). Citing alfalfa's capacity for infinite growth and, in turn, infinite sustenance and increased animal productivity, D. Plácido begins to dialogue with the vegetal's infinite growth or what plant philosopher Michael Marder has termed the "'bad infinity' of vegetal temporality" (Marder 12). While there is reference to a vegetal "impulso" (force) throughout the narrative, for D. Plácido alfalfa's vigor should be instilled in the animal "transformando de ese modo las materias vegetales—yerbas—en materias animales, carne y sebo" (transforming vegetal material—grasses—into animal material, meat and fat) (Jiménez 507). Talking about the transformation of vegetal to animal and the favorable exchange value of animal products in comparison with plants, D. Plácido declares "¡Este es nuestro negocio!" (This is our business!) (Jiménez 507). While the "carne" (meat), which for D. Plácido is the result of the plant's absorption by the animal, is indicative of the commodification of the animal for consumption as food and in plantation work, the vegetal protects the animal and is consumed by it. Drawing on the nonreciprocal relation of ox to ox-driver and the latter's construction as vehicle for vengeance and liminal animal, alfalfa certainly is not configured as a "nuisance" as the liminal animal is. Existing as principal food source, alfalfa nourishes the ox. In return the latter feeds the former through fertilization—a practice that had drawn criticism for not being available for the benefit of the paddock in the mid-nineteenth century (Sagra y Peris, vol. I, 229). In fact, D. Plácido uses the need for fertilizer as an argument to justify placing animals into the paddock and not into stables; a practice his future son-in-law decries as being like "prisión" (prison) (Jiménez 266).[15] D. Plácido does not state explicitly the need for fertilizer to replace consumed vegetal force, but thinking of the reciprocal and mutualistic relationship of cattle and the paddock, the exchange of force becomes reason for ensuring the security of the animal away from the stable. However, the response of the vegetal in this exchange is intimately tied to use of the paddock to bolster the ox's strength to withstand abusive labor as the narrative features pages of measurements detailing energetic output and the correlative quantity of plant life needed to sustain activity (Jiménez 225–230).

This same vegetal force is present elsewhere in *El potrero paraíso* to different effect. As D. Plácido elevates alfalfa and other Leguminosae, he pits these against the Gramineae in the paddock. Notably he focuses on guinea grass or *yerba de guinea*. The same advantageous vegetal growth shown by alfalfa becomes a point of tension for guinea grass. Despite admitting that there are paddocks dedicated to its cultivation and that its force can be used not only to hold back the invasion of sugar or the storm outside the paddock, but also the untamed forest, he states that guinea grass offers nonoptimal, watery feed to the cattle (Jiménez 354, 338, 233, 360–362).[16] Moreover, the use of its force to regulate other vegetal life is revisited upon the farmer as D. Plácido claims it invades with the slightest ease the field and savanna where it is left unattended, not respecting "los terrenos defendidos por las contínuas labores" (the terrains defended by continual work) (Jiménez 339). D. Plácido's opinions about guinea grass serve to warn those farmers who might attempt to cultivate it, and even those farmers who do not, that its appearance signals a longer-term struggle they cannot win.

The appearance of guinea grass and its capacity to resist removal from the paddock, taking over space and other vegetal presences, displaces the needs of the cattle that inhabit the paradisical paddock by depriving them of the conditions needed to thrive away from the plantation. Interestingly, D. Plácido's descriptions of this Gramineae contrast with those from earlier in the nineteenth century in Cuba. In 1828 Ramón de Arozarena and Pedro Bauduy considered guinea grass and sugarcane a duad of plants, with the former necessary to the success of the latter, due to the use of guinea grass as cattle feed (Funes Monzote, "Animal Labor" 88). The relationship between these two plants is made further curious by their almost indistinguishable similarity in appearance while growing (Cole). Even as it was declared a weed in Cuba in 1977 and a danger to sugarcane,[17] eighty-nine years prior, *El potrero paraíso* claimed its presence to be just as threatening for the paddock's borders and, consequently, its security.

The conversation around borders occupies a large portion of the narrative and concerns a distinction between live and dead borders (Jiménez 427). On one hand, D. Plácido argues that if the fence is not a "cerca viva" (live fence) composed of trees, the animals will see other paddocks and begin to disdain the ground and grasses they have trodden to the detriment of their own health (Jiménez 427). But the damage occasioned by unwanted vegetal growth is greater than the threat of trodden grasses and envious animal gazes. Guinea grass, alongside another Gramineae, Para grass or *yerba bruja* (*Panicum purpurescens*),[18] invades the pineapple fences common in Cuba. D. Plácido describes them as "los enemigos más poderosos, por lo que invaden y destruyen las cercas de piña" (the most powerful enemies because they invade and destroy the pineapple fences) (Jiménez 430). So much so that there exists an instrument designed by D. José Benito Pérez able to remove these grasses (Jiménez 430). The potentiality for destruction attributed to these grasses produces an aperture in the paradisical paddock to the dangers outside, affecting the animal just as in *Cañas y bueyes* with sugarcane. After the grasses' destruction of the fence, bandits or "rateros" can enter and steal cattle, guided easily out of the pasture field through the gaps in the fence (Jiménez 416–418).[19]

The relationship of guinea grass to the paddock is complex. It appears in *Cañas y bueyes* in the paddock around José Prieto's house as a crop that stops the encroaching sugar planted by his friend, Antonio, ensuring his cattle's safety (Puello 74). Yet, its presence in the Caribbean points to imperial and colonial histories that see it transported from West Africa via chattel slavery, and, therefore, associated with changing historical representations of blackness. In its ruderality, guinea grass's presence reminds us that the Caribbean is a site of enslavement and itself a geography of terror, tied to chattel slavery. As such, its disruption of the paddock's borders—the limits of security—also recalls the mistrust of Afro-descendant peoples, in particular *cimarrones* or runaway enslaved people, as dangers to the safety of the plantation, its border sites, and its cattle.[20] In other words, the vegetal becomes receptacle for the historical mistrust of Black subjects in their dealings with cattle. While the emergence of guinea grass opens possibilities to engage the hidden narratives of the vegetal that sugar forecloses, its presence also opens up a necessary rethinking of a critical approach to the relationship between the plant's biological imperative for exponential, infinite growth, the role of cattle, and the relation of both of these to enslaved African subjects and freed Afro-Cubans and Afro-Dominicans. With this I mean to highlight the importance of addressing the perceived security undermined by guinea grass in *El potrero paraíso* and how this relates both to the broader burden placed on the vegetal, human, and nonhuman animal communities tied to the paddock and plantation site.

If on the one hand vegetal agency is enacted through (violent) violation of secure spaces, leaving them and their cattle inhabitants exposed to increased threat, the plant shoulders burden in the form of its eradication and regulation within the agricultural site. Ultimately, this speaks to the capacity of the vegetal to act against any ostensible passivity interpreted through passive consumption by the human and nonhuman animal. In returning to the question of reciprocity within the paddock in each novel, guinea grass feeds and supports the larger system within which it functions, ensuring the work of the cattle and their safety, as much as it is also a disruptor of this same site. In fact, it is with the destruction of the border that ensures the security of oxen that it engages in a reordering of exchange-value relations on the plantation. Just as the vegetal force of the plants within the paddock helped bolster its positioning as paradise or sanctuary for the ox to escape multiple (potential) violences, the infinite "bad growth" of guinea grass highlights the fragility of a system meant to facilitate both vegetal and animal consumption. What is more, while the ox was framed as a liminal animal for Black subjects on the plantation, so too were Black subjects and guinea grass conceived in this relation as nuisance to the oxen's well-being due to vengeance, nonoptimal nutrition, and exposure to threats via border destruction. All of this led to the plantation's inability to "consume" the ox. It is through this reformulation of life, and the undoing of the paddock, that the vegetal begins to alter then what is possible for the ox on the plantation. To reconsider monoculture's agribiopolitical regulation of the vegetal, nonhuman animal, and human lives that concern the paddock points to security-making and burden. In other words, the regulation of life shows the (undue) burden shared by these actors, how their lives are entangled or stuck, and how they are disentangled or unstuck within sites of (ambiguous) protection or security-making related to the plantation.

Notes

1. In *The Government of Beans,* Kregg Hetherington employs the term "agribiopolitics" to discuss "regulatory assemblages and to contrast the Soy State with the Government of Beans [. . . and] how [agribiopolitics] organizes the health and welfare of communities of people and of plants" (160).

2. Throughout the chapter I draw on Hetherington's work on soy in Paraguay as part of the neoliberal monocropping movement. Following Morton's concept of the hyperobject, "a massively distributed thing that defies anyone's ability to know it but nonetheless remains present, exerting an agency beyond human control," Hetherington claims that soy represents the processes involved in its cultivation and the environmental, social, political, and economic issues it foregrounds (6–7).

3. In Fernando Ortiz's 1940 *Contrapunteo cubano del tabaco y el azúcar* (*Cuban Counterpoint of tobacco and sugar*) he constructs a social history of monoculture in Cuba around the figures of Don Tabaco (Sir Tobacco) and Doña Azúcar (Lady Sugar).

4. Sugar's necrotic influence speaks to the (capitalist) practices of monoculture that, drawing on Achille Mbembe's work *Necropolitics* and that of extractivist aesthetics, produce unlivable landscapes of death as exercise of political power.

5. Franklin Ginn bases this language of entanglement on the slug's existence in the garden.

6. See "Novel and History, Plot and Plantation" wherein Wynter counterposes the plantation's monolithic history creation with the subsistence plot as site of alternative narrative creation.

7. Until 2003 guinea grass carried the Latin name *Panicum maximum* when it was renamed *Megathyrsus maximus*. See Bendarrahim and Elfalleh for more information.

8. I address burden as byproduct of security-making in response to Christina Fredengren's question of "who carries the heaviest burden in time- and site-specific entanglements" (17).

9. The Compañía Nacional de Inversiones Territoriales began paying local officials to expropriate land from its owners as officials declared that most deeds were falsified (Puello 37–38).

10. I have adopted this term from work in Afro-Latin American and Black Geographical Studies through the work of Yilver Mosquera-Vallejo and by extension Ulrich Oslender—from whom Mosquera-Vallejo draws in her own work. Geographies of terror constitute those spaces fundamentally altered and scared by the material and symbolic usage of terror as a form of social control. In other words, "the terms by which we apprehend the world, since it emerges in the contest of a series of massacres, forced displacements, selective assassinations, and threats" (Mosquera-Vallejo 120).

11. Rebecca Scott's work on the case of Gregoria Ciriaco and her mule at the end of the nineteenth century in Cienfuegos, Cuba, shows how Afro-Cubans used cattle to negotiate remaining in place after the territorial insecurity of the independence war from 1895 to 1898 (see Scott).

12. For more information on the rise of these societies in Europe in the nineteenth century, see Funes Monzote, "Un arcoíris" 93–94.

13. Originally found in "Agricultura. Cartilla rústica. Diálogo de un Labrador y su hijo" t. XII, pp. 245–258 from the *Memorias de la Sociedad Económica de la Habana,* I pull this quote from Funes Monzote's article "Un arcoíris."

14. See "Sanctuary" by Timothy Pachiray and "Ecological Biopower" by Jonathan Clark. The former addresses the agritourism of farm sanctuaries in Indiana, USA, and the latter the exercising of ecological biopower over pigs.

15. D. Plácido suggests the stable be used in conjunction with the pasture field and

should occupy those abandoned sites on the plantation such as "vastos barracones, extensas casas de purga abandonadas" (the vast enslaved villages, the extensive, abandoned purging sites) (Jiménez 271).

16. Guinea grass was one of several grasses from Africa used for cattle feed, contributing to the Africanization of the Caribbean's landscape (Carney 166).

17. See Cole's work on guinea grass in contemporary Cuba, p. 69.

18. Fiallo has documented the use of plants such as *yerba bruja* in common Cuban sayings: "yerba bruja no engaña al buey" (105).

19. This is also the main throughline in the intercalated narrative wherein Pancho Meneses attempts to discover the location of the missing (presumed stolen) cows that keep disappearing from D. Celestino Mejías's paddock. Pancho Meneses discovers that they are being led through holes in the fence (that is not a living but a "dead fence" [cerca muerta] made of stone) and killed for the benefit of the surrounding neighbors (Jiménez 416–418, 427).

20. Such was the fear of runaway slaves or *cimarrones* entering the plantation to recruit enslaved people or steal cattle or supplies, walls were erected around enslaved villages (see Singleton; Funes Monzote, "Especialización" 114).

Works Cited

Benabdarrahim, Mohamed Ali, and Walid Elfalleh. "Forage Potential of Non-Native Guinea Grass in North African Agroecosystems: Genetic, Agronomic, and Adaptive Traits." *Agronomy*, vol. 11, no. 6, 2021, https://doi.org/10.3390/agronomy11061071. Accessed Jan. 2024.

Boisseron, Bénédicte. *Afro-Dog: Blackness and the Animal Question.* Columbia University Press, 2018.

Carney, Judith. *In the Shadow of Slavery: Africa's Botanical Legacy in the Atlantic World.* University of California Press, 2011.

Clark, Jonathan. "Ecological Biopower, Environmental Violence Against Animals, and the 'Greening' of the Factory Farm." *Journal for Critical Animal Studies*, vol. 10, no. 4, 2012, pp. 109–129.

Cole, Hannah Rachel. "Plant of the Month: Guinea Grass." *JSTOR*, https://daily.jstor.org/plant-of-the-month-guinea-grass/. Accessed Oct. 2023.

Derby, Lauren. "Trujillo, the Goat: Of Beasts, Men, and Politics in the Dominican Republic." *Centering Animals in Latin American History*, edited by Martha Few and Zeb Tortorici, Duke University Press, 2013, pp. 302–328.

Fiallo, Víctor R. Fuentes. "Las Plantas En El Habla Popular En Cuba." *Revista Del Jardín Botánico Nacional*, vol. 21, no. 1, 2000, pp. 103–108.

Fredengren, Christina. "Beyond Entanglement." *Current Swedish Archaeology*, vol. 29, 2021, pp. 11–33.

Freyre, Gilberto. *Nordeste: Aspectos da influencia da cana sobre a vida e a paisagem do nordeste do Brasil.* Global Editora, 2004.

Funes Monzote, Reinaldo. "Un arcoíris en medio de la tempestad: Visiones del potrero cubano en el silo XIX." *Mundo Agrario,* vol. 21, no. 46, 2020.

Funes Monzote, Reinaldo. "Animal Labor and Protection in Cuba: Changes in Relationships with Animals in the Nineteenth Century." Translated by Alex Hidalgo and Zeb Tortorici. *Centering Animals in Latin American History,* edited by Martha Few and Zeb Tortorici. Duke University Press, 2013, pp. 209–241.

Funes Monzote, Reinaldo. "Especialización azucarera y crisis de la ganadería en Cuba, 1790–1886." *Historia Agraria,* no. 57, 2012, pp. 105–134.

Funes Monzote, Reinaldo. "Facetas de la interacción con los animales en Cuba durante el siglo xix: los bueyes en la plantación esclavista y la Sociedad Protectora de Animales y Plantas." *Signos históricos,* no. 16, 2006, pp. 80–110.

Gallego Jiménez, José Joaquín. *El bandolerismo en la provincia de Santa Clara de Cuba y su represión durante el gobierno del Capitán General Camilo García de Polavieja (1890–1892).* 2019. Universidad Pablo de Olavide, PhD dissertation.

Ginn, Franklin. "Sticky Lives: Slugs, Detachment, and More-than-human Ethics in the Garden." *Royal Geographical Society,* vol. 39, 2014, pp. 532–544.

Hetherington, Kregg. *The Government of Beans: Regulating Life in the Age of Monocrops.* Duke University Press, 2020.

Jiménez, Juan B. *El potrero paraíso: Agricultura y zootécnica.* Santa Clara, 1888.

Marder, Michael. *Plant-Thinking: A Philosophy of Vegetal Life.* Columbia University Press, 2013.

Mosquera-Vallejo, Yilver. "Afro-Latin American Geography." *Routledge Handbook of Afro-Latin American Studies,* edited by Bernd Reiter and John Antón Sánchez, Routledge, 2023, pp. 119–126.

Ortiz, Fernando. *Contrapunteo cubano del tabaco y el azúcar.* Edited by Enrico Mario Santí. *Cátedra,* 2002.

Pachiray, Timothy. "Sanctuary." *Critical Terms for Animal Studies,* edited by Lori Gruen, University of Chicago Press, 2018, pp. 337–354.

Puello, Francisco Moscoso. *Cañas y bueyes.* ABC Editorial, Santo Domingo, 2004.

Rodríguez Orrega, Vero Edilio. "Juan Bautista Jiménez: Ciencia agrícola y 'nunca matar al viejo,'" https://www.5septiembre.cu/juan-bautista-jimenez-ciencia-agricola-y-nunca-matar-al-viejo/#_edn2 (written 29 Aug. 2023). Accessed Oct. 2023.

Sagra y Peris, Ramón de la. *Historia física, política y natural de la isla de Cuba.* Paris, 1842. 12 vols. https://bdh-rd.bne.es/viewer.vm?id=0000177406&page=1. Accessed 18 April 2019.

Scott, Rebecca. "Reclaiming Gregoria's Mule: The Meanings of Freedom in the Arimao and Caunao Valleys, Cienfuegos, Cuba, 1880-1899." *Past & Present,* no. 170, 2001, pp. 181–216.

Singleton, Theresa. "Slavery and Spatial Dialectics on Cuban Coffee Plantations." *World Archaeology*, vol. 33, no. 1, 2001, pp. 98–114.

Wynter, Sylvia. "Novel and History, Plot and Plantation." *Savacou*, vol. 5, no. 1, 1971, pp. 95–102.

14

"There's Nothing Better than Giving Life"

Freeing the "Plant" from the "Plantation" in Recent Latin American Narratives about Coffee

MAURICIO ESPINOZA

In his short story "Han vuelto las aves" (2015), Guatemalan author Eduardo Halfon chronicles the redemption story of a group of small coffee growers from his home country's southwestern highlands.[1] While doing so, Halfon also manages to reconstruct the history of peasant exploitation, violence, and resistance that have characterized Guatemala's coffee industry since its development in the mid-1800s (Cambranes 15–19; Pendergrast 28–36). Proud of the local campesinos' efforts to form a cooperative, achieve a fair price for their premium-quality product, and reintroduce sustainable agricultural practices into their land, farmer Juan Martínez exclaims: "Y es que no hay nada, señor Halfon, como dar vida. Pero dar vida no solo a unas matas de café y unos árboles, sino a la montaña misma" (And there's nothing better, Señor Halfon, than giving life. Giving life not just to coffee plants and trees, but to the mountain itself) (Halfon 70). For Mr. Martínez and the other farmers of the Esquipulas Cooperative in La Libertad, a town in the state of Huehuetenango near the Mexican border, this *giving life to the mountain itself* has involved a process of switching from an intensive farming model (which required clearing the mountain for planting corn and coffee as well as for securing firewood) to a more sustainable model (based on shade-grown coffee and reforestation). The environmental benefits don't stop there. While touring his farm, Mr. Martínez proudly tells Halfon's namesake narrator: "Han vuelto las aves. Han vuelto las ardillas. Han vuelto los micoleones [. . .] Ya no se veían aves, señor Halfon, ya no se veían animales. Antes este cerro estaba pelado" (The birds are back. The squirrels are back. The kinkajous are back [. . .] We'd stopped seeing birds, Señor Halfon. We'd stopped seeing animals. The hillside was all bare) (Halfon 69–70). As this passage and the short story's title indicate, the farmers' new agroecological approach has also resulted in the restoration of natural ecosystems that now provide a habitat for the return of birds and other native fauna. At the heart of this remarkable transformation is one plant: coffee.

In this chapter, I explore the representation of coffee in twenty-first-century Central American and Caribbean narratives. Alongside Halfon's "Han vuelto las aves," I analyze the eco-parable *A Cafecito Story* (2001) by Dominican-American author Julia Alvarez—which focuses on the effort to keep small, sustainable coffee farms from being turned into agrochemical-reliant, monocultural plantations in the Dominican Republic. I chose these stories for two main reasons. First, they are based on real-life events and people. Alvarez's story mirrors her and her husband Bill Eichner's experience developing an organic coffee farm in the Dominican Republic and working with neighboring farmers to preserve sustainable agricultural practices, beginning in the 1990s (Hickman 70). Meanwhile, Halfon (known for his autofictional writing) was commissioned by the Inter-American Investment Corporation to visit the town of La Libertad and write about the Esquipulas Cooperative (Halfon, *Signor Hoffman* front matter). Although clearly fictionalized, it is important that both narratives depict real challenges faced by real coffee farmers in real contemporary contexts—and the solutions these individuals were able to put into practice. In other words, these narratives show the possibility of a literature that engages in a sort of activism by uplifting the struggles and agency of marginalized communities and endangered ecosystems. Second, a closer reading of these stories reveals how they also center the agency and power of plants—coffee but also trees—to restore degraded land, protect existing agroecosystems, and even establish affective relationships with humans. The synergy created in these narratives allows plants to thrive alongside humans and nonhuman animals (particularly birds) in mixed-use landscapes where all living beings interact with and depend on each other.

With these considerations in mind, I propose a reading of *A Cafecito Story* and "Han vuelto las aves" that focuses on the ways in which they manage to liberate the "plant" from the "plantation." By this I mean that coffee in these stories is given (or rather, it reclaims) its own agency as a living organism that can coexist with other species in human-altered landscapes—rejecting, in the process, its colonial legacy of monocultural extractivism and its capitalist imposition as a "cash crop."[2] In order to conduct such a reading, I draw from the concepts of plant agency and reciprocity, establishing a dialogue with other concepts from ecocriticism and decolonial studies that allow me to problematize the historical relationship between *coffee as a plant* and *coffee as a plantation* in the Latin American context. After all, coffee is much more than a popular drink infused with a multiplicity of social and cultural meanings. It is an imported, once-exotic plant that has become an integral part of the rural and economic landscape in many Latin American countries. It is plant that has anchored diverse agroecosystems in Central American and Caribbean highland communities such as the one described in Alvarez's and Halfon's stories. It is a plant that carries with it a long history of colonial and neocolonial exploitation, not just in Latin America but everywhere it is grown along the tropics. And it is—without any other labels or histories attached to it—a plant, a living being that has adapted to a variety of growing conditions around the globe, but which also still exists in the wild in its native East Africa.

Dark Brew, Dark History: Coffee and Power from Arabia to the Americas

Coffee is big business. It is the second most-popular drink on the planet (after tea) and one of the world's most valuable agricultural commodities (Pendergrast xv). And while coffee provides a livelihood for some 100 million people globally, most of the profits end up in the pockets of the wealthy landowners, exporters, intermediaries, and global corporations that control the trade and set prices paid to farmers (Pendergrast xv–xvi). But how did the dark, stimulating brew concocted from *Coffea arabica* gain so much power and popularity worldwide? Since its beginning, the history of coffee has been linked to the history of trade, conquest, and colonial expansion. Native to Ethiopia, the plant was first developed as a commercial crop across the Red Sea in Yemen. An exclusively Arab delicacy at first, coffee soon spread throughout the Islamic world in North Africa, Turkey, and Persia. Not long after it also caught the attention of French and Venetian merchants, thus becoming an increasingly popular drink among Europeans in the late 1500s and early 1600s. Realizing its economic potential, in 1616 the Dutch managed to smuggle a single coffee plant from Yemen, where the Ottoman Turks fiercely guarded their monopoly on the crop. Eventually, the Dutch were able to grow coffee in their colonies in the East Indies beginning in the mid-1600s (Pendergrast 3–20).

It was this colonial drive that brought coffee to the Americas in the early 1720s, as the French introduced the exotic plant to the island of Martinique from where it expanded throughout the Caribbean, South America, Central America, and Mexico in the 1700s and 1800s (Roseberry et al. 2–3). The introduction of coffee into the New World soon changed the worldwide dynamics of production. From Mocha in the Middle East and Java in Southeast Asia, the coffee epicenters shifted to the Caribbean and South America—by 1788, the French colony of Haiti supplied half of the world's coffee fix (Pendergrast 17); and by 1820, Brazil was responsible for half of global production (Roseberry et al. 3). Since then, Latin America has been the world's coffee powerhouse. Today, the region grows more than 55 percent of the beans savored everywhere on the planet, and four of its countries (Brazil, Colombia, Mexico, and Honduras) are among the top ten global producers (Bilen et al.).

Like sugarcane and other agricultural imports before it, coffee was introduced into Latin American colonies to become an export-driven, plantation cash crop. This extractivist model did not change following independence on the continent during the early 1800s. In fact, such an export-dependent, land-and-labor–intensive development system intensified as the new republics sought to consolidate their fragile economies during an arduous process of nation-building throughout the nineteenth century. And all along, the old European colonial powers—now joined by a new emerging economic and geopolitical power, the United States—engaged in all manner of neocolonial and neo-imperialist ventures in these newly autonomous but still heavily dependent nations. Large plantations of native crops—such as rubber trees in the Amazon region, promoted by US corporations—further contributed to environmental destruction, displacement of Indigenous populations, and exploitation of labor, all caused by foreign crops introduced during the colonial period (Wylie, "Green Power" 1–3).

In Brazil, for instance, coffee growers copied the large *fazenda* model implemented by sugarcane production. Together, the two crops were responsible for large-scale deforestation of the Atlantic region forests and an increase in the number of enslaved people in Brazil—more than a million by 1828, or nearly a third of the country's population (Pendergrast 22–23). As Mark Pendergrast summarizes, "Coffee made modern Brazil, but at an enormous human and environmental cost" (22). The same is true for other countries where coffee became the main economic engine during the 1800s and early 1900s, such as Colombia and the small nations of Central America—which became "'dependent' on a single export crop, suffering the same reverses and enjoying the same booms" (Roseberry et al. 3). Coffee elites in these countries not only controlled the local economies, but also wielded significant political power. As a result, coffee production shaped many of the economic, labor, sociopolitical, cultural, and ecological structures that became ingrained in the historical fabric of these nations during the twentieth century—even persisting through today.

Despite its historical significance in the region, coffee has never inspired a memorable narrative within Latin America's literary tradition, the way that other monocultures have. Let us think, for instance, of José Eustasio Rivera's rubber boom saga *La vorágine* (1924); Carlos Luis Fallas's *Mamita Yunai* (1941) and Miguel Ángel Asturias' banana trilogy (1950–1960), about the United Fruit Co.'s operations in Central America; or, more recently, Samanta Schweblin's eco-gothic novel *Distancia de rescate* (2014), about the expansion and nefarious effects of genetically modified, agrochemical-dependent soybean plantations in Argentina. Narratives focused solely on coffee such as *A Cafecito Story* and "Han vuelto las aves" are beginning to fill this void, highlighting the new realities of coffee production in Central America and the Caribbean while weaving the region's long history of colonial and neocolonial exploitation into their plots. In the analysis that follows, I concentrate on the various types of agency that can be found in the two stories—from human to nonhuman—and what that means for understanding the role of *Coffea arabica* within these narratives. Next, I look at the ways in which these types of agency facilitate relationships of reciprocity between humans, nonhuman animals and plants in the agroecosystems described in the stories.

"The shaded coffee will put that song inside you": From Human to Plant Agency

The plots of Alvarez's and Halfon's narratives have striking parallels, which helps to explain why the relationships between human and nonhuman agency develop in similar ways in both of them. In the two stories, small coffee growers face internal and external threats not only to their lands and livelihood, but also to their sense of identity. The farmers of the town of Manabao, in the Dominican Republic's interior mountains, find themselves having to decide between renting their parcels to a greedy company that's expanding agrochemically intensive, higher-yielding coffee production in the area or possibly losing them to the stiff competition. Meanwhile, the farmers of La Libertad have for decades endured a series of challenges: pressure from large landowners, violence during Guatemala's long civil war (1960–1996), unfair international commodity prices, the international coffee crisis of 2001–2002, and an Italian scam artist who promised to sell the farmers' coffee at a premium price in Europe but pocketed most of the profits. Additionally, the two farming communities struggle with the consequences of deforestation from unsustainable agricultural practices. In Manabao, Alvarez's narrator describes "brown mountainsides, ravaged and deforested, riddled with gullies" (12), while Mr. Martínez explains that the mountains in La Libertad had been completely deforested to plant corn and secure firewood (Halfon 70).

Finally, the solutions implemented by the armers to deal with their economic and environmental challenges are identical in both stories. First, they band together and form cooperatives, which allow them to hold on to their land and to negotiate better prices for their high-quality beans. Second, they choose to rely on environmentally friendly agricultural practices. In the case of the Dominican growers, they reject the company's intensive model and retain their traditional shade-grown, organic coffee farming methods.[3] The *caficultores* of La Libertad, meanwhile, turned to shade-grown coffee and reforestations practices, as Mr. Martínez relates: "Ahora que la cooperativa está funcionando, el mismo café nos da dinero para comprar nuestro maíz, y pues ya no necesitamos sembrar milpa. Ahora nuestras mismas matas de café nos dan suficiente leña para el comal, y ya no necesitamos talar árboles. Ahora sembramos árboles" (Now that the co-op is up and running, coffee brings us enough money to buy our maize, so we don't have to plant it. Now our own coffee plants and our shade trees, when we prune them, give us enough wood for the comal, so we don't need to cut down any other trees. Now we plant trees) (Halfon 70).

The hurdles faced by small coffee farmers to preserve their land and ways of life in these two highland towns are not just effective textual catalysts of conflicts that help move the plots forward and create tension within the narratives. They also exemplify the larger historical context of exploitation and violence inflicted upon peasants, Indigenous people, other marginalized communities, and nature in Central America and the Caribbean. In fact, the campesinos of Manabao and La Libertad find themselves fully imbricated into what Peruvian sociologist Aníbal Quijano has called coloniality of power, a concept that helps to explain the concentration of resources and power into the hands of a minority of "dominadores europeos 'occidentales' y sus descendientes euro-norteamericanos"

("Western" European dominators and their Euro-North American descendants), ensuring the continuation of a model rooted in colonial domination that is now more violent and global ("Colonialidad y modernidad" 11). It is important to remember that the economic, social, cultural, and environmental domination that characterizes *coloniality of power* originated with European colonialism in the Americas in the form of extractive industries (mining and plantations), where both people of color and natural resources were subjected to dispossession, violence, and commodification (Quijano, "Colonialidad y modernidad" 11–13; "Colonialidad del poder" 785). Five centuries later, the farmers in *A Cafecito Story* and "Han vuelto las aves" are still suffering the consequences of coloniality. These include various forms of violence, from direct harm inflicted by armed conflict to slow violence[4] that threatens their environment and ways of life; the loss of their land, livelihood, and sense of community; and their affective or spiritual connection with plants and nonhuman animals in their natural milieu.

While Alvarez and Halfon make a point to highlight the effects of violence and the lingering colonial legacies that impinge upon their characters' lives, their stories are ultimately narratives of redemption. Up against a myriad obstacles and structural injustice, the farmers nonetheless find ways to gain and exercise agency. As I indicated before, there are different types of agency that appear in these stories. Human agency is the most commonly found, as the narratives favor the actions of two groups of farmers who seek to assert their autonomy within a hostile, neoliberal capitalist system that views both people and nature as resources to be exploited for profit. I identify two ways in which human agency is represented in these stories. The first follows the anthropocentric logic of humans altering their environments and manipulating plants for their benefit. This utilitarianism is evident in the way forests have been cleared to plant corn in "Han vuelto las aves." In *A Cafecito Story,* not only forests but also shaded coffee farms have been assailed by "la compañía's" commercial farming methods. When Joe, a 40-year-old American teacher disenchanted with his life, arrives in Manabao on vacation, the first thing he notices are deforested mountainsides that suddenly "turn a crisp, metallic green. A new variety of coffee grown under full sun, the old man beside him explains" (Alvarez 12–13). Later, "Joe finds Miguel's farm. You can't miss it. In the midst of the green desert, Miguel's land is filled with trees. Tall ones tower over a spreading canopy of smaller ones. Everywhere there are bromeliads and birdsongs. A soft light falls on the thriving coffee plants" (Alvarez 13).

With the above examples, the authors offer a stark differentiation between formerly bare hillsides and reforested mountains brimming with new life in La Libertad; and between the company's monocultural coffee plantations (whose green uniformity is described as lacking life) and the shaded coffee plots full of trees, flowers, and birds in Manabao. This contrast underscores the fact that not all human agency over nature for agricultural purposes is intrinsically destructive—even if it inevitably leads to disruptions in natural ecosystems and changes to the plants themselves, for example, through selection of desirable traits or domestication. This complex and nuanced relationship between humans and plants—even those grown as crops for subsistence or profit—helps to explain the fallout resulting from the Anthropocene as a way to conceptualize the significant global impact that human activities have had on terrestrial ecosystems. In particular, scholars and activists from the Global South have widely criticized the assumption that environmental damage has been perpetrated by a generalized human collective without distinctions of race, class, gender, or geography (Fornoff and Heffes 4), rather than by "the actions of a minority of colonialists, capitalists, and patriarchs" (Varanasi).

According to Lesley Wylie, in pre-conquest Latin America "plants were not only an important source of food across the continent, but key to Indigenous healing practices and religious life"—an understanding that endured well beyond the conquest among Indigenous people and other racialized communities (*Poetics* 8–9). This non-utilitarian, intimate connection with plants is present in the two narratives through the farmers' efforts to protect their healthy agroecosystems or to reforest degraded land. It is also evidenced by the careful way in which the farmers (who include mestizos as well as Indigenous Maya people) tend to their coffee plants to help them grow: "Don Juan Martínez estaba acuclillado junto a una de sus matas de café. Mientras hablaba, sus manos parecían trabajar solas: quitando hojarasca del suelo, arrancando hierbas y pasto y hojas enfermas" (Don Juan Martínez was squatting beside one of his plants. As he spoke, his hands seemed to work autonomously: gathering dry leaves from the ground, pulling out grass and weeds and sickly twigs) (Halfon 69). Meanwhile, in *A Cafecito Story,* Miguel often equates the healthy growth of coffee plants in shaded farms with the healthy growth of children: "When a bird sings to the cherries as they are ripening, it is like a mother singing to her child in the womb. The baby is born with a happy soul" (Alvarez 15).

Another manifestation of human agency in these two stories highlights the agency of marginalized individuals struggling against the agentic actions of the "colonialists, capitalists and patriarchs" behind the Anthropocene's devastation of earth's ecosystems. As mentioned above, the small farmers featured in these narratives are mainly mestizos, including Miguel and the Martínez family—but there are also Indigenous people in the case of "Han vuelto las aves." Halfon's narrator makes it a point to establish the ethnic background of one of the cooperative's members whom he meets later on in the story: Cruz Pérez Pablo, who drove four hours from the village of Chanjón in Todos Santos Cuchumatán (a municipality in Huehuetenango where the majority of residents are Mam-speaking Mayas) to meet with him. The narrator introduces Mr. Pablo as a man dressed in the colorful traditional clothing from his region, which was "símbolo inequívoco y orgulloso de su identidad" (such a proud and unequivocal symbol of his identity) (Halfon 68). The Esquipulas Cooperative was founded in 1965 with the help of US missionaries, who later had to flee Guatemala due to the violence enacted against priests and nuns who aided poor folks in the country during the civil war period. As Mr. Martínez recalls, "En los años difíciles decir cooperativa era casi como decir una mala palabra" (In the difficult years, saying the word co-op was almost like saying a bad word) (Halfon 58), referring to the risks faced by peasant and Indigenous communities if they were suspected of being associated with leftist ideas or movements during the war years. Mr. Martínez also explains that the point of forming the cooperative was to bring the poor farmers together to be able to compete against the rich ones (Halfon 57). While the value of class solidarity is obvious in this statement, the diverse ethnic/racial composition of the cooperative's membership is extremely significant in the context of Guatemala—a country with high levels of racism and violence inflicted against its large Indigenous population since the time of Spanish conquest, and especially during "the difficult years."

The cooperative in *A Cafecito Story* also originated in an act of solidarity—across class and racial divides. Joe (the American middle-class teacher with a farming background in Nebraska) buys a parcel next to Miguel's land and convinces his new friend to keep farming the traditional way with him. Their relationship is reciprocal: Miguel teaches Joe the ins-and-outs of growing coffee, while Joe teaches Miguel and his family how to read and write. Within three years, Joe collects his first harvest; meanwhile, Miguel and his wife Carmen can now read a whole book (Alvarez 23–25). In the end, many of the small impoverished farmers join Miguel and Joe, form a cooperative and build their own small *beneficio* (mill). Joe's literacy efforts allow the farmers to read the contracts from potential buyers by themselves and to negotiate better terms, which in the end helps to boost their income (Alvarez 25). Finally, it is crucial to underscore the agency of women in agricultural activities that have traditionally been dominated by men—as patriarchy is as much a factor in anthropocentric environmental destruction as it is a pillar of the colonial matrix of power. While in *A Cafecito Story* most of the human agency revolves around the two male protagonists, Joe and Miguel, "Han vuelto las aves" centers the crucial role of Iliana—one of five daughters of Mr. Martínez and his wife, Ernestina. When the Esquipulas Cooperative was on the brink of bankruptcy, Iliana came back home from Huehuetenango's namesake capital city where she had been attending university. Becoming its first female general manager, Iliana secured financing, brought in experts to teach growers about international trade and how to produce a better-quality coffee, modernized the entire operation by installing micro-mills at each farm, and began selling their prized coffee directly to buyers abroad. As a result, Mr. Martínez explains, "Ahora, finalmente, vendemos nuestro café al precio que realmente vale. No al precio que nos imponen los de Nueva York" (Now, at last, we sell our coffee at the price it's truly worth. Not at the price imposed on us by New York) (Halfon 62). Consequently, the agency exercised by these small farmers through their resistance against exploitation and violence and through their cross-ethnic solidarity, is made even stronger by the empowerment of women through the centrality of Iliana's leadership role within the cooperative.

While human agency over nature dominates these two narratives, reading the texts through the lens of environmental humanities helps to identify several instances of agency by nonhuman actors that are present in them. The concept of *plant agency* is central to plant studies, as it has sought to remedy the conventional belief that plants are automatons or voiceless objects (Plumwood 11, 12) or organisms that lack intelligence, consciousness, and behavior (Hall 12, 25–27). Rather, plant agency "moves agency away from human exceptionalism toward a perspective that adopts a subject-subject orientation, [actively embracing] the potential agency of plant life within studies of human culture" (Ardren and Miller 1). Instead of focusing on how humans *act upon plants*, scholars such as John Charles Ryan ask us to consider how plants *act upon humans*, "contributing to the co-generation of our cultural practices, values, perceptions, relations, artifacts, and all else through their volitions in the *umwelt* of which all living beings are part" (104). Independently from their role in the study of human culture and their association with socioecological milieus such as agriculture, plants as living beings are also agents on their own account as they "are perhaps the most fundamental form of life, providing sustenance, and thus enabling the existence of all animals, including us humans" (Gagliano et al. vii).

This agency of plants operates at two levels in *A Cafecito Story* and "Han vuelto las aves." First, the main types of plants featured in these stories—coffee and trees—are fundamental to the constitution of the agroecosystems described in them and upon which their farming communities depend for subsistence and a sense of identity. Trees play a crucial role in the ecologically friendly farming practices implemented by the growers of Manabao and La Libertad. They prevent erosion, feed the soil, regulate temperatures, filter the sun and the rain, and create an overall better growing environment for coffee plants. Beyond their agricultural services, they also attract "birds that come to sing over the cherries" (Alvarez 15) and create an inviting habitat for other nonhuman animals such as squirrels and kinkajous to live in (Halfon 69–70). The direct impact of trees on the configuration of these ecosystems is evidenced not only through their presence, but especially in their absence: the deforested hillsides or the "green deserts" growing only coffee with the help of poisonous agrochemicals lack any biological diversity and are viewed negatively by the farmers who care about their land, their families, and their communities. While it is true that the agency of humans in choosing whether to plant or to cut down trees impinges on their presence or lack thereof in these narratives, it is also true that once established in the landscape, trees exercise their own agency—by reproducing, by adapting to their particular environments, and by interacting with other living organisms and meteorological phenomena. Meanwhile, coffee's agency is exemplified through the ways in which it helps to provide a livelihood to the farmers and to sustain their sense of identity as agriculturalists and small landowners. Coffee plants also have a life of their own: they interact with the soil, other plants and organisms in their growing environment, meteorological phenomena, diseases, pests, and the humans who engage with them through their "cultivation." They get sick (as portrayed in the section of "Han vuelto las aves" where Mr. Martínez removes sickly twigs from a plant) and also rejoice in the other forms of co-dependent life that dwell among them—as when the narrator of *A Cafecito Story* declares that "It is amazing how much better coffee grows when sung to by birds" (Alvarez 25).

The second level of plant agency present in these two narratives highlights reciprocity. In *Braiding Sweetgrass: Indigenous Wisdom, Scientific Knowledge and the Teachings of Plants* (2013), Robin Wall Kimmerer proposes that plants "weave a web of reciprocity, of giving and taking" through which all living organisms are connected and from which they all benefit (20). While plants freely shower us with gifts "literally giving themselves so that we can live," their generosity must be reciprocated in order for the "circle of life making life" to continue

(Kimmerer 20). We can see this "circle of life making life" at play in the quote from *A Cafecito Story* referenced above. The coffee plants are said to grow much better when they hear birds singing to them. Whether we consider this passage literally or metaphorically, reciprocity helps to explain its significance in the story. The birds are able to sing to the coffee plants because first there were trees on the farm that provided them a habitat, and the coffee grows healthy because of the shaded environment made possible by trees. In other words, the birds' song is but another type of nourishment that ultimately originated from the trees, which provide everything the coffee plants and the birds need for thriving. It is a symbiotic system from which the humans also benefit, receiving the gift of the coffee harvest for their livelihood but also the gift of nature for their spiritual sustenance. This is particularly relevant in the case of Joe, who feels a lack of purpose in his life until he starts growing coffee alongside Miguel and rediscovers the joy that birds on his family's farm back in the Midwest used to give him. Early on in the story, Miguel tells Joe that "The shaded coffee will put that song inside you" (Alvarez 15). A few pages later, we witness how Joe starts to grow and flourish in his new life just as the coffee plants he is learning to care for: under the shade of trees and in the poison-free soil, listening to the birds' songs once again. Of course, the success of the cooperative formed by Joe and Miguel is possible only because the farmers reciprocate the gifts they receive from the plants and the birds by protecting the land from commercial farming.

In "Han vuelto las aves" there is another example of reciprocity between plants and humans that foregrounds plant agency in unexpected ways. Toward the end of the story, Mr. Martínez and Iliana are giving the narrator a tour of their farm. Suddenly, nature (birds and coffee plants) appears to take over the narrative, the landscape and the human elements in it: "Don Juan se puso de pie y continuamos caminando en silencio entre las matas del cafetal, recorriendo el terreno quebrado y resbaladizo. Escuchamos el grito lejano de un halcón, luego el trino dulce y metálico de un guardabarrancos, luego el jolgorio en el cielo de una parvada de pericas" (Don Juan stood and we continued walking in silence among the coffee plants, traversing the slippery, uneven terrain. We heard the distant cry of a falcon, then the sweet metallic thrill of a motmot, then the joyous cackling of a flock of parakeets) (Halfon 71–72). Next, the three humans arrive at a place where they find the remains of an abandoned chicken coop. We learn from Iliana that the coop belonged to Osmundo, her only brother, who was murdered three years prior. Osmundo's death is a topic the Martínezes avoid throughout the story, so we are left to speculate about what happened to him.[5]

Amid the rotting structures of the chicken coop (which nature has begun to reclaim), there lies a single large old coffee plant.

Oblivious to the narrator's questions about the chicken coop, Mr. Martínez approaches and "enters" the plant, "Como escondiéndose entre las hojas verdes. Como buscando algo entre las hojas verdes. Como queriendo que la vieja mata lo protegiera" (As though hiding among its green leaves, searching for something among its green leaves. As though wishing the old plant would protect them) (Halfon 72). He then proceeds to tenderly pick the ripe fruits and drop them on the ground, which turns red around his feet. The narrator points out that the farmer appears to grow smaller the more he enters the plant, being finally swallowed in the story's last sentence: "Siguió adentrándose en el follaje de la vieja mata, adentrándose en el verdor de tantas hojas y ramas de la vieja mata, hasta que todo él desapareció por completo" (He kept entering the foliage of the old plant, the greenery of the leaves and branches, until the whole of him disappeared entirely) (Halfon 72). I see two possible interpretations for this passage. One is that the coming together of man and plant to the point of becoming indistinguishable from one another illustrates the strong connection that has developed between them and the reciprocity of their connection—the coffee plant giving away its fruits and offering protection in exchange for the care provided by Mr. Martínez. The second explanation accounts for the dead son, whose presence is still felt on the farm through the remains of his chicken coop—which even three years later continues to feed the old coffee plant as it disintegrates into the soil. If a part of Osmundo has indeed been absorbed by these natural elements, Mr. Martínez's intimate communion with the coffee plant might represent the only way he can reconnect with his son. In either case, the agency given in the narrative to this single coffee plant is remarkable. And the fact that the story ends with an act of deep reciprocity between human life and plant life may signal the possibility of a more sustainable future in Central America and the Caribbean—through agroecological practices such as the ones described in Alvarez's and Halfon's texts.

Notes

1. "Han vuelto las aves" first appeared in the anthology *Hacer la América: Historias de un continente en construcción* (Tusquets, 2014) and was later included in Halfon's short story collection *Signor Hoffman* (Libros del Asteroide, 2015). It was published in English as "The Birds Are Back" in the collection titled *Monastery* (Bellevue Literary

Press, 2014), with translation by Lisa Dillman and Daniel Hahn; translations of passages from "Han vuelto las aves" used in this chapter are from this collection.

2. Developed by Latin American scholars to describe the region's insertion into the world economy through the removal and export of raw materials, extractivism also refers to the exploitative appropriation of nonhuman nature and human labor (Gudynas 10–11). For a historical overview of this practice in Latin America, see Carolyn Fornoff's entry "Extractivism" in *Handbook of Latin American Environmental Aesthetics.*

3. According to Daniel Jaffe, "researchers have catalogued the extraordinary biodiversity that is found in traditional shade-coffee plantations. These plots often contain much of the diversity of the original forest, with dozens of plant species, hundreds of insect species, and a great diversity of soil organisms found in a single small plot [. . .] Traditional coffee plots can also provide a vital sanctuary for many bird species" (135).

4. According to Rob Nixon, slow violence is "a violence that occurs gradually and out of sight, a violence of delayed destruction that is dispersed across time and space" and which little by little wreaks havoc on the environment, disproportionately harming the poorest and most vulnerable people on the planet (2).

5. At the beginning of the story, the narrator mentions that drug trafficking has been a major source of violence in La Libertad in recent years (Halfon 50). This may help explain the reluctance on the part of the Martínez family to talk about Osmundo's passing.

Works Cited

Alvarez, Julia. *A Cafecito Story.* Chelsea Green, 2001.

Ardren, Traci, and Stephanie Miller. "Household garden plant agency in the creation of Classic Maya social identities." *Journal of Anthropological Archaeology,* vol. 60, 2020, pp. 1–10.

Bilen, Christine, et al. "A Systematic Review on the Impacts of Climate Change on Coffee Agrosystems." *Plants,* vol. 12, no. 1, 2023, https://doi.org/10.3390/plants12010102

Cambranes, J. C. *Coffee and Peasants in Guatemala.* Universidad de San Carlos, 1985.

Fornoff, Carolyn. "Extractivism." *Handbook of Latin American Environmental Aesthetics,* edited by Jens Andermann et al., De Gruyter, 2023, pp. 45–65.

Fornoff, Carolyn, and Gisela Heffes. "Introduction: Latin American Cinema beyond the Human." *Pushing Past the Human in Latin American Cinema,* edited by Carolyn Fornoff and Gisela Heffes, SUNY Press, 2021, pp. 1–16.

Gagliano, Monica, et al. "Introduction." *The Language of Plants: Science, Philosophy, Literature,* edited by Monica Gagliano et al., Minnesota University Press, 2019, pp. vii–xxxiii.

Gudynas, Eduardo. *Extractivismos: Ecología, economía y política de un modo de entender el desarrollo y la Naturaleza.* CEDIB, 2015.

Halfon, Eduardo. *Monastery.* Translated by Lisa Dillman and Daniel Hahn, Bellevue Literary Press, 2014.

Halfon, Eduardo. *Signor Hoffman.* Libros del Asteroide, 2015.

Hall, Matthew. *Plants as Persons: A Philosophical Botany.* SUNY Press, 2011.

Hickman, Trenton. "Coffee and Colonialism in Julia Alvarez's *A Cafecito Story.*" *Caribbean Literature and the Environment,* edited by Elizabeth DeLoughrey et al., University of Virginia Press, 2005, pp. 70–82.

Jaffe, Daniel. *Brewing Justice: Fair Trade Coffee, Sustainability, and Survival.* University of California Press, 2007.

Kimmerer, Robin Wall. *Braiding Sweetgrass: Indigenous Wisdom, Scientific Knowledge and the Teachings of Plants.* Milkweed Editions, 2013.

Nixon, Rob. *Slow Violence and the Environmentalism of the Poor.* Harvard University Press, 2011.

Pendergrast, Mark. *Uncommon Grounds: The History of Coffee and How It Transformed Our World.* Basic Books, 2019.

Plumwood, Val. *Environmental Culture: The Ecological Crisis of Reason.* Routledge, 2002.

Quijano, Aníbal. "Colonialidad del poder, eurocentrismo y América Latina." *Cuestiones y horizontes: de la dependencia histórico-estructural a la colonialidad/descolonialidad del poder,* CLACSO, 2014, pp. 777–832.

Quijano, Aníbal. "Colonialidad y modernidad/racionalidad." *Perú Indígena,* vol. 13, no. 29, 1992, pp. 11–20.

Roseberry, William, et al. *Coffee, Society and Power in Latin America.* Johns Hopkins University Press, 1995.

Ryan, John Charles. "Passive Flora? Reconsidering Nature's Agency through Human-Plant Studies (HPS)." *Societies,* no. 2, 2012, pp. 101–121.

Varanasi, Anuradha. "How Colonialism Spawned and Continues to Exacerbate the Climate Crisis." Columbia Climate School, 21 Sept. 2022, https://news.climate.columbia.edu/2022/09/21/how-colonialism-spawned-and-continues-to-exacerbate-the-climate-crisis/. Accessed 28 Jan. 2024.

Wylie, Lesley. "Introduction. Green Power: Plants in the American Tropics." *Understories: Plants and Culture in the American Tropics,* edited by Lesley Wylie, Liverpool University Press, 2023, pp. 1–16.

Wylie, Lesley. *The Poetics of Plants in Spanish American Literature.* University of Pittsburgh Press, 2020.

15

Captivity and Pride in the Yerba Mate World

A Bond for Survival under Persistent Coloniality

JONATHAN MULKI

Our modern inability to recognize plants as living agents, often reducing them to mere backdrops in scenes dominated by humans and animals—a condition termed "plant blindness" (Laist 9)—finds a poignant example in yerba mate. For five centuries, yerba mate has been extracted, consumed for its caffeine, revered, used as a tool of empire, and praised as a national symbol (Sarreal 14). Yet, most contemporary consumers overlook yerba mate's Indigenous roots and its ongoing colonial production dynamics.

In Argentina, yerba mate is romanticized as a symbol of gaucho culture and the Pampas, yet this portrayal obscures its true origins in the Paranaense Jungle and erases key elements of its ecological and cultural identity. This "speciesism"—which transforms yerba into a symbol of whitewashed nationalism—conceals the Indigenous roots and ongoing colonial exploitation underlying its production. As a case where plant blindness and colonialism intersect, yerba mate reveals how drink-fetishism and cultural whitewashing uphold hidden colonial labor systems (Folch 8), especially in Argentina, a "white nation" that obscures its colonial legacy in rural areas. This chapter tells the story of a delicate yet powerful tree that has silently organized the social life of Southern Cone population.

Yerba mate, or simply "yerba," thrives in the distinctive red soils of the Paranaense region along the borders of Argentina, Brazil, and Paraguay. Known for its energizing properties akin to coffee and tea, its leaves are rich in antioxidants and aid in digestion. Initially chewed by the Kaingang, yerba was later adapted by the Guaraní, who perfected the process of toasting leaves and adding hot water—an Indigenous practice that persisted through Spanish colonization and endures today (Pite 20). To prepare mate, a gourd and metal straw are used with hot water just below boiling, creating a communal ritual that is passed down generationally. In Southern Cone societies, mate drinking is a daily ritual for most people, often shared in groups, fostering social bonds and conversation.

For more than five centuries, yerba mate has shaped social practices and conflicts. The Guaraní revered it as both currency and a sacred plant, while Spanish colonizers first banned and then embraced it, adopting Indigenous consumption habits through mestizaje. Yerba soon became a cross-cultural beverage that dissolved social divides—unlike tea, coffee, or chocolate (Sarreal 39). As demand surged, however, it became known as "green gold," prompting an extractive system that endures today. Spanish encomenderos established a coercive labor regime, forcing Indigenous workers on often brutal expeditions. This colonial extractivism persists as modernized debt bondage in cultivated yerbales, with grueling labor and low wages sustaining a regime that endures today.

Due to yerba mate's fragile branches and unique structures, mechanization remains impractical, underscoring the critical role of manual harvesters—*tareferos*—whose work sustains the entire yerba mate economy. Currently, yerba is cultivated and harvested manually before the trees exceed an average human height. This colonial legacy in contemporary yerba mate production remains one of the most grueling forms of rural labor in the region, with tareferos frequently perceived as emblematic of exploitation in the Southern Cone (Gómez Lende 44).

In the plantation system, tareferos spend hours gathering leaves, yet only the initial harvest guarantees their daily wages; the remainder of their labor generates surplus value for contractors, drying facilities, mills, and retailers (Gortari 21). Typically, tareferos manually harvest between 70 and 100 kilograms of leaves and branches per round, placing them in a bag called a *raído*, which they carry on their backs to the weighing station at the end of the line in the yerbal. To secure their economic survival, tareferos may complete between five and ten of these rounds in a single day, leading to considerable physical strain. Another pressing issue is child labor within tarefero communities in rural Misiones, Argentina, driven by poverty and entrenched cultural meanings. Children often work to help their families meet daily needs, entering the yerba mate system from a young age and perpetuating cycles of captivity (Roa, "Estar-en-el-yerbal" 228).

In a context where most consumers remain ignorant of these realities, *Raídos* (2016) by Diego Marcone, an ethnographic documentary, provides a rare visual window into the lives of tareferos in the Alto Paraná along the Misiones-Paraguay border. Through this chapter, I analyze *Raídos* alongside the Gómez family—an Afro-Argentine tarefero family living near the Misiones and Río Grande do Sul, Brazil, border. By engaging in a co-creative viewing of *Raídos*, the Gómez family participates in analyzing a cultural representation of themselves, exploring their lives and labor through a collaborative, participatory lens. This chapter thus becomes an inquiry into coloniality and its ongoing mechanisms, uncovering an inhumane regime centered on a plant essential to the physical, mental, and social fabric of the Southern Cone.

This chapter examines the complex relationship between tareferos and yerba mate—a bond defined by captivity, survival, and paradoxical pride. While the colonial system profoundly impacts tareferos' physical health and subjects them to dehumanizing stigmatization within their communities, this chapter seeks to reveal how, through their intimate relationship with yerba, tareferos foster a sense of pride that reaffirms their often-undermined identities. This survival bond offers a perspective overlooked in the predominantly anthropocentric view presented in *Raídos*, positioning pride as an emotional counter-colonial landscape.

Raídos (2016): A Visual Ethnography

The documentary, available on YouTube and based on the three-year ethnography of María Luz Roa, vividly portrays the modus vivendi of contemporary tarefero families in the Alto Paraná. With a narrative driven by the rhythm of the harvest season, the film forgoes a traditional narrator or interviewer, instead relying on the immersive power of the camera to observe the unselfconscious tareferos at work and in conversation with each other, whether in the yerbal or at their homes—the two main locations where tarefero life unfolds. However, this observational approach also reveals a significant blind spot: yerba mate itself is depicted solely as an inanimate commodity—a drink or a backdrop for human action—never as a living being with its own agency or significance. While the documentary succeeds in humanizing the tareferos, it leaves out the equally important narrative of the plant as an active participant in this interspecies relationship.

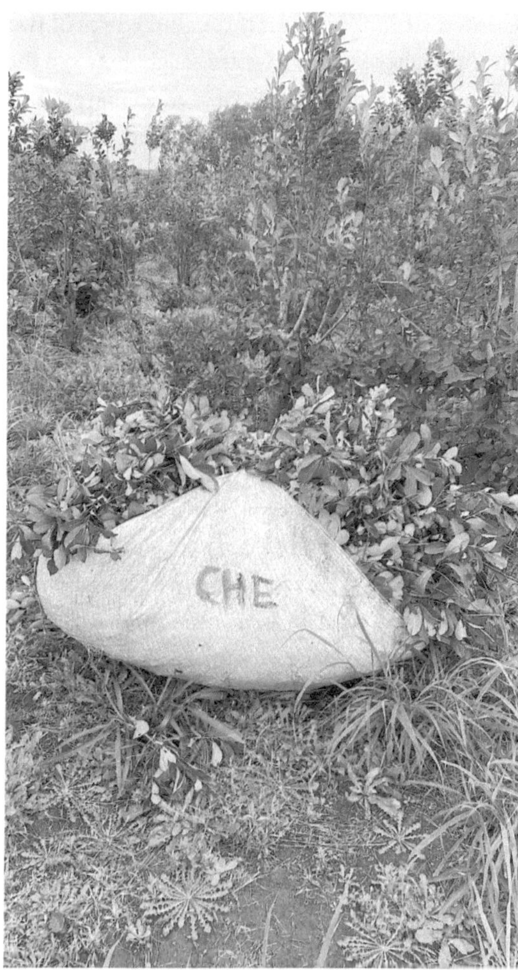

FIGURE 15.1. Yerba mate plants and a raído full of recently harvested green leaves and branches. Credit: Author.

Raídos opens with tareferos recounting the age at which they left school, underscoring child labor as a central issue. From the start, the film exposes harsh living conditions: no running water, families in makeshift wooden shelters, and subsistence on simple foods like reviro (flour, salt, water). Everyday scenes, often silent, unfold over one to two minutes. Even though their homes are kilometers away from the yerbal, their daily lives are inextricably linked to it. While working there, every aspect of life is geared toward surviving the yerbal. There is no excess—neither economic nor bodily energy—for any pursuits outside this cycle (Gómez Lende 58).

In this context, *Raídos* presents a striking contrast through the lives of two young tarefero brothers, Darío and Walter Lemos, who are caught between the demands of harvesting and their pursuit of education. Formal education appears as a rare escape from the yerbal, yet the film highlights how prevalent child labor leads to high dropout rates (Re 222). The tension between child labor and formal education is palpable throughout the entire piece, as we see both the difficulties Walter faces in finding time and space to study, and the physical and mental toll that manual harvest takes on Darío. This contrast between the brothers underscores the systemic barriers that child labor creates for educational attainment and personal growth, further complicating their futures.

Toward the end of *Raídos,* a pivotal moment unfolds as we witness Walter Lemos successfully graduating and securing a job outside the tarefero world in Iguazú. The documentary culminates with his family and neighbors emotionally bidding him farewell. His mother, with tears streaming down her face, utters: "Ya te vas, buscás un futuro" (You leave, you go look for a future). This scene encapsulates the notion that "having a future" is synonymous with leaving the yerbal, a feat achievable only at an early age through formal education—a luxury and immensely challenging goal in a context of dispossession and child labor. Contrasting with feature films like *Prisioneros de la tierra* (1939) and *Las aguas bajan turbias* (1952), classic social films depicting yerba mate harvesters' living conditions and culminating in violent revolts against bosses, emblematic of collective action and trade-unionist aspirations, *Raídos* portrays a yerba mate world devoid of the possibility of collective salvation. Despite being filmed during a period of social mobilization among tarefero communities, the documentary reveals no avenues for collective action, focusing instead on individual narratives of overcoming adversity through personal effort. This portrayal reflects the neoliberal realities intertwined with the colonial system, where structural change is sidelined, and salvation is presented as attainable only through isolated, individual achievement, contingent upon access to minimal education. This reinforces a logic of personal responsibility over collective empowerment, while ignoring the broader systemic forces that continue to marginalize the tarefero communities.

Apart from the opening scene featuring a wet *yerba mate* leaf, and despite the documentary's merits in depicting the harsh living conditions of *tarefero* people, the plants themselves are conspicuously absent as subjects throughout *Raídos*—a surprising omission given that the film is set in a plantation. The plants appear only fragmentarily, in shots capturing the high-speed harvesting process: leaves being plucked, branches being cut, and a vast green backdrop of blurry plants where human stories unfold. *Yerba* plants are visually present several times, yet they are never the focus of conversation or inquiry, nor is there any exploration of the personal relationships the *tareferos* may have with the plants—despite these plants being constant companions throughout lives spent mostly in the *yerbal.* No agency or narrative seems able to emanate from the plant itself. As the collaborative analysis with the Gómez family will later reveal, despite *Raídos*' merits in depicting the contemporary struggles of *tarefero* people, this lack of acknowledgment of *yerba mate* as a living entity hinders a deeper understanding not only of the plant but also of the *tarefero* people themselves.

Watching *Raídos* with the Gómez Family

THE GÓMEZ: A TAREFERO MODUS VIVENDI

Yerbales are typically inaccessible to outsiders due to their geographical remoteness and the proprietors' reluctance to expose the working conditions of tarefero people. My attempt to connect with a tarefero community for fieldwork was met with cautionary advice from local urban residents, who warned me about the tareferos' distinct lifestyle, their unique dialect that might challenge my understanding, and prevailing stereotypes labeling them as irresponsible and lazy. After a year of conversing and introducing myself to local actors, the Gómez family graciously welcomed me to stay at their home during the 2023 harvest season. The family consists of Laura and Adrián Gómez,[1] both Afro-descendant tareferos, and their five children, three of whom have secured jobs outside the yerbal by completing high school.

The Gómez house, along with the entire neighborhood, is built on public land. Despite living there for two generations since their grandparents fled from Brazil, they continue to struggle for official land ownership recognition from local authorities. The village is surrounded by a vast yerbal owned by a white Argentine, known locally as El Polaco ("the Polish"), who sells the green leaves to large yerba mate companies. All the neighbors, who are Afro-descendant Argentines, work exclusively for El Polaco. Unlike typical tarefero dwellings, the Gómez family's brick house has running water, a fridge, and a TV, made possible by their three children's employment outside the yerbal.

My first encounter upon arriving at the community—and the initial scene I observed in the yerbal—was child labor. Children aged 10 to 14 assisted their parents in harvesting green leaves and managing the raído, a task that demands considerable physical strength. To my surprise, these children were the first to teach me the proper techniques of yerba harvest. Since I visited during winter break, they weren't attending the local school but instead were fully immersed in the rhythms and demands of the yerbal.

Tareferos, both young and old, work with plants that, while delicate and vulnerable to environmental stress, can outlive even the harvesters themselves. Many plants do not survive cultivation, yet those that do can thrive for decades. Because yerba mate plants are so sensitive, their harvest requires careful, selective handling. After days in the yerbal, I learned that tareferos do much more than simply remove branches; their hands move quickly yet carefully, assessing each plant's unique branching structure to preserve its vitality. Just as no two humans share the same DNA, no two yerba mate plants share the same branch structure. This individuality demands a selective method that leaves key branches intact to shield the plant's core from intense sun and frost, supporting growth for the following year. In the yerbal's extreme environment, with intense sunlight, humid rains, and cold spells, this careful handling is crucial to keep the plants thriving. As Adrián explained, such selectivity allows the plants to "feed" and flourish. A single mistake—removing the wrong branch—can prevent a plant from sprouting again, threatening both its survival and the tareferos' future livelihood. This delicate process is tailored to each plant, requiring tareferos to adapt their approach swiftly from one plant to the next, which takes a physical toll on their hands, knees, and backs. Such individualized care also makes the yerba mate resistant to mechanized, uniform harvesting; no machine can replicate the plant-specific handling required for a sustainable yield.

Living with the Gómez family revealed that their food habits are shaped by yerba itself and by gendered survival strategies for coping with scarcity. They drink yerba mate almost nonstop from morning until late at night to suppress hunger, while only the men eat at night to have the strength to harvest as much as possible early the next morning. Night after night, I witnessed women and children going to bed without dinner in a form of imposed intermittent fasting. When I asked about it, Laura repeatedly explained they "weren't used to" eating at night, that meals felt too "heavy"—a discursive adaptation that reflects a survival mindset shaped by the demands of yerba harvesting.

My goal during fieldwork was not to conduct formal interviews or traditional ethnographic work, but rather to create opportunities for tareferos themselves to engage in knowledge production. After spending several days living with the Gómez family, I realized that the most effective way to foster this engagement was to share parts of my doctoral research corpus, which focuses on cultural representations of yerba mate. When I noticed the family's TV in the living room, I proposed screening a portion of my audiovisual materials. Raídos was an ideal starting point, as it depicted a reality very similar to what I was observing. Laura and Adrián welcomed the idea, inviting neighbors to join us for a shared meal and film screening.

This approach aimed to move beyond text-based knowledge, creating an environment where their responses—judgment, surprise, laughter, or reflection—could contribute equally to understanding the world of yerba mate from their perspective. This aligns with recent methodological developments conduct by scholars, such as Roa ("De la etnografía"), who moved from ethnography to theater, as an effort to integrate subaltern groups in the production of knowledge. The screening was intended not only to document reactions but also to position the tareferos as active participants in critiquing and interpreting representations of themselves. This created a space for knowledge to emerge in shared, conversational moments, setting the stage for a collaborative analysis of Raídos and paving the way for a participatory approach in uncovering the complex reality of yerba mate production.

THE AUDIOVISUAL PERFORMANCE

The day of the screening arrived. The Gómez family invited six tarefero neighbors, bringing our group to eleven, including children and myself. We chose a rainy day that would keep the Gómez family from working in the yerbal, ensuring they wouldn't lose a day's pay by participating. We gathered around the TV in the Gómez family's living room, where I introduced *Raídos* as a documentary depicting real tarefero families. This prompted laughter and joyful comments from the Gómez family, who were excited to see people like themselves represented on screen for the first time. The scenes from *Raídos* resonated deeply with their own life experiences, creating a unique space where the film's narrative and the family's reality intertwined. In my analysis, I focus on scenes and dialogues that reveal the complex, intertwined relationship between the tareferos and yerba mate.

The opening scenes of *Raídos* are intense, capturing the journey to the yerbal, the communal harvest, and stories of child labor. A particularly striking scene reveals the dynamic interaction between tareferos and the yerba mate plants, set against the rustling sounds of branches, bird calls, and encouraging voices, forming a natural symphony. Meeting daily quotas of 700–1000 kg requires high-paced, exhausting labor, driven not by any external force but by the internalized pressure of debt and meager earnings.

Even as they sat eating, the Gómez family was visibly drawn in by the scenes, laughing and shifting in their seats as memories surfaced. On screen, the tarefero crew's rapid, loud conversation created a communal rhythm of motivation:

> ¡Tengo hambre de yerba!
> (I am hungry for yerba!).
> ¡La viruta no alcanza para pagar la cuenta!
> (The harvest isn't enough to pay the bill!).
> La cuenta es lo que apura
> (The bill is what hastens).
> La cuenta nadie se hace cargo
> (No one takes responsibility for the bill).

Then, someone in the room suddenly exclaimed, "¡Son paraguayos!" ("They are Paraguayans!"), as Adrián and others recognized the tareferos on screen as Guaraní from near the Paraguayan border, contrasting with their own Afro-descendant identity from the Brazilian border. The atmosphere shifted as the men began to inspect the harvesting skills of their Guaraní counterparts, assessing each move with the same focus as one might watch a sports match, pointing out technical details of the manual harvest.

Throughout the screening, the group's reactions shifted between laughter, commentary, and moments of intense silence, particularly during scenes of tareferos receiving pay, weighing harvests, or discussing wages. These silences often gave way to anxious exclamations: "¡Ahí está! ¡Ahí le está robando El Polaco!"—recognizing their own patron in the on-screen employer.

Another recurring theme was child labor and education. Whenever adult tareferos recalled leaving school or Raídos depicted speeches on education, Laura would echo the documentary's words with a reprimanding tone for those present, saying "¡dejó la escuela!" ("he left school!"), and "¡claro que se va a arrepentir!" ("of course he'll regret it!"). These comments would hush the group, and Laura would share examples from her own life. "Me acuerdo cuando El Pipi quería la platita para ir al baile y yo le decía que no fuera a tarefear, que fuera a estudiar" ("I remember when Pipi wanted some money to go to the dance, and I would tell him not to go to the yerbal, but to study"). Laura would press on the importance

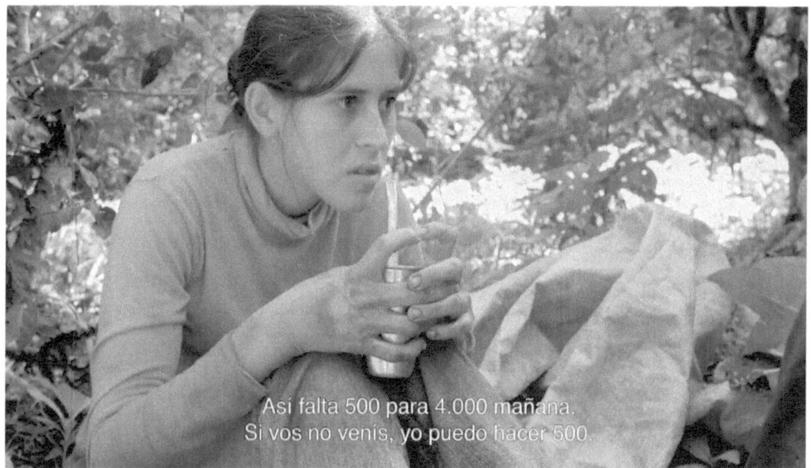

FIGURE 15.2. A still from the film *Raídos* of a tarefero woman resting in the yerbal, drinking tereré (cold yerba mate). Credit: *Raídos,* directed by Diego Marcone.

of schooling, recalling how her sons grew angry at her for this—anger she had to absorb and resist.

I could see that Laura was using the documentary as a way to negotiate values within her community. Just days before, she had shared the years-long struggle to convince local authorities to invest in a single-room public school where children of all ages could study together. For her, this classroom symbolized a rare chance for transformation. It was through this opportunity that her three children first accessed education and then secured jobs away from the yerbal, mirroring Walter Lemos's journey in the documentary. The men in the room remained silent as she spoke, reflecting—as *Raídos* does—how the struggle for education among tareferos often rests on the shoulders of the women. This maternal determination to secure education for their children is a quiet but powerful counter-colonial act.

By the seventeenth minute, *Raídos* delves into a scene set in the yerbal, where a tarefero couple, taking a respite to drink mate, is surrounded by the lush yerba mate plants, forming a green wall that carves out a space for intimacy. This scene reveals the physical toll of tarefero life, evident in the transformation of their bodies. A striking moment occurs as the young tarefero woman removes her gloves, revealing hands altered in size and shape from relentless branch harvesting (see fig. 15.2).

The camera shifts to her feet, her shoes engulfed by red mud, creating a stark contrast between her youthful face and her overgrown hands. As she massages her pinkie, gazing into the green expanse of the yerbal, an intense dialogue ignites in the Gómez's living room. Someone exclaims, "¡Mirá sus manos!" ("Look at her hands!"). In quick response, Laura says, "Me recuerda al abuelo Raúl" ("It reminds me of Grandpa Raúl"). Suddenly, the scene on the screen halts as the internet connection falters due to the ongoing storm. Quickly shifting back to conversation, Laura shares a memory of Adrián's father, Raúl, a lifelong tarefero whose hands, heavily deformed from years of labor, felt peculiar during embraces in his later years. Struggling to find the right words to describe this sensation, Laura decides to demonstrate. I stand and move toward her.

Laura explains, "Así te hacía el abuelo Raúl" ("This is what Grandpa Raúl would do"), as she wraps her arms around me. Instead of feeling the flat of her palms, I am met with pointed, finger-like protrusions pressing into my back, evoking the sense of being touched by an object rather than a hand. The sensation is akin to the pressure of a rack. Adrián adds, "Te quería abrazar con toda la mano, pero te clavaba los dedos" ("He wanted to hug you with his whole hand, but you felt only his fingers poking"). This moment of physical connection lingers with me, vividly illustrating the profound and lasting transformation that tareferos experience—a reshaping that extends beyond work to permeate even the most intimate aspects of their lives, altering basic human interactions. At the same time, it portrays a transgenerational and spectral yerba agency preserved in tactile memory.

Yet in the yerba mate world, hands can also portray dynamics of power and coercion. Before screening *Raídos,* we needed food for the invited neighbors, which meant driving to town. On our way back, Adrián's truck ran out of gasoline, and, to my surprise, the only place to refill was at El Polaco's garage—the owner of the yerbal and, in this colonial landscape, the provider and holder of debt for the tareferos. This was my first encounter with him, and he seemed eager to meet me. While Adrián refueled his truck, one of El Polaco's foremen greeted me with an aggressive handshake, one that cracked my knuckles, leaving my hand numb—a clear signal that I was not welcome in the area. Back at the house, Laura and Adrián checked if my hand was injured. They explained:

> Así te saludan los patrones acá, te aprietan la mano hasta casi rompértela, para ver de qué estás hecho. Si la mano se te dobla, como se te dobló a vos, ellos dicen: ¡ah, este no vale nada!
>
> (That's how the bosses greet you here. They squeeze your hand until it al-

most breaks, to see what you're made of. If your hand bends, like yours did, they say, Ah, this one's worth nothing!).

While in my case it was a warning to an outsider, the Gómezes explained that landowners like *El Polaco* often assess a tarefero's harvesting capacity through a firm handshake, evaluating the shape and endurance of their hands. These hands are expected to serve for a lifetime, passed down across generations as marks of labor and submission, until they no longer feel fully human, even in moments of tenderness—like Raúl's, remembered in the bodies of his family and now in mine.

A Bond for Survival

The tarefero experience reveals a profound, complex relationship with the yerba mate plant, encompassing captivity, companionship, and vital sustenance. As the audiovisual performance and testimonies reveal, the colonial forces underlying the yerba harvesting system reshape tareferos' bodies, with material and symbolic repercussions. Locally, these bodily transformations reinforce their captivity. Yet, to my surprise, the Gómez family and their neighbors, despite viewing the plants as "green shackles," do not resent the yerba; rather, they find in this relationship a subtle means to rehumanize themselves, complicating the notion of their bond with the plant.

Tarefero bodily changes stem from intense biospheric friction, where the plant's agency leaves visible marks on flesh and bones. The grueling work often leaves tareferos covered in mud and dirt, or *yaré* in Guaraní. During *Raídos,* Adrián Gómez remarked, "El tarefero es espalda-sucia" ("The tarefero is dirty-back"). Notably, he used "is" rather than "has," implying that this is part of their identity. These changes also evoke animalistic metaphors to depict the tarefero experience, frequently expressed by tareferos themselves and reinforced by writers like Rafael Barrett and Alfredo Varela, who compare harvesters to "pigs in the mud" or "burden donkeys" to highlight the dehumanizing effects of colonialism. This narrative is echoed in *Raídos,* where, around the fiftieth-minute mark, an elder tarefero likens their condition to being "left like pigs" in mud. Over time, tareferos internalize these physical changes, embedding them within personal narratives as unique expressions of their subjectivities, as demonstrated by the example of Grandpa Raúl's hands.

At the same time, these bodily transformations serve as stigmatizing markers within local communities, especially among non-tarefero eyes, who establish

FIGURE 15.3. The hands of a ten-year-old tarefero child in the yerbal. Credit: Author.

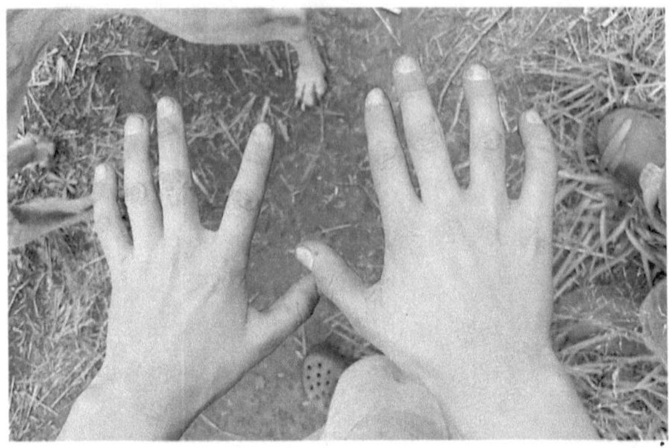

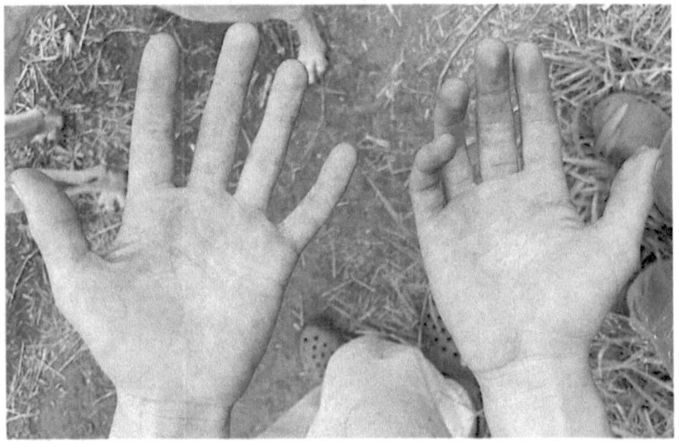

social distance by reinforcing the tareferos' status as an "other" through the identification of these visible markers. As anthropologist Diana Haugg notes, these markers cause tareferos to be "seen from afar," resulting in stigmatization and social exclusion ("Cuerpos" 56). Labels like "dirty," "drunk," "indians," and "negros" ("La cosecha" 98) further entrench this stigmatization, embedding colonial hierarchies within social structures and hindering interclass solidarity that could challenge the colonial system. As I learned from casual conversations in Misiones and Paraguay—be it with drivers, hotel staff, or restaurant workers—stigmatizing responses were naturalized when they discovered my interest in meeting tareferos. This stigmatization operates subtly, normalizing the dehumanization of colonized bodies in ways that allow coloniality to endure unchallenged. These yerbal markings become lifelong symbols of captivity, limiting tareferos' opportunities to seek livelihoods beyond the yerbal. Child labor intensifies this captivity, marking children's bodies, specially hands, with the plant's agency before they even reach adolescence (see fig. 15.3).

In this context, the tarefero bond with the plant is imbued with conflicting emotions, symbolism, and even mysticism. Laura shared her perspective: "Como decía mi padre, la yerba mate es una planta maldita, porque mientras cosecha la planta, el tarefero se pela a sí mismo" ("As my father used to say, yerba mate is a cursed plant, because while peeling the plant, tarefero peel themselves"). This metaphor, absent from *Raídos,* reflects a painful bond with yerba trees. When I asked Laura to elaborate, she explained, "El tarefero se queda sin nada" ("the tarefero is left with nothing"), as though the dispossession endured by tareferos were an expression of the yerba's mystical agency itself.

Yet despite this notion of yerba as a "cursed" entity, a sacred dimension persists within tarefero culture. The Guaraní revere yerba as a divine gift from Ñamandú, a belief sustained within their communities. This reverence is shared by tareferos, albeit with a pragmatic focus. As Adrián explained, they acknowledge yerba mate's evergreen nature, recognizing it as a lifeline for their survival. This duality speaks to the complex ontology of yerba mate among tareferos, where seemingly opposing views coexist without contradiction. Above these cursed and sacred perceptions lies a bond grounded in mutual survival. Tareferos recognize the plant as a living entity needing care, establishing a relationship based on interdependent survival. Although the plant's demands tether them, this labor-based care transforms suffering into compassion for their "green shackles," allowing them to perceive the plant as a fellow being and helping them endure structural oppression.

This bond is not merely about survival; it has also become a profound source of pride. For tareferos, pride is vital in resisting both coloniality and dehumanization, affirming their identity and irreplaceable skills. Walking through the yerbal with Adrián, I asked about the roots of this pride, and his response was unequivocal: "Nunca han podido reemplazarnos, no hay máquina que pueda hacer nuestro trabajo" ("They have never been able to replace us; no machine can do our work"). His words resonated with a contagious compassion and the conviction that only they truly understand and relate to yerba—a plant fundamental to the everyday life of millions across southern South America.

This approach embodies a complex interspecies partnership where yerba mate is both a source of captivity and a means of survival, intertwining tareferos' livelihoods with the well-being of the plant itself. The fact that they must nurture the very "shackles" that bind them to the yerbal for much of their lives stands as a testament to their resilience. Harvesting alongside family and friends, tareferos cultivate not only a unique plant-human bond but also a resilient community within the yerbal. These shared experiences create moments of pride and communal strength, sublimating their captivity into a collective sense of affirmed identity within the plantation. For the tareferos, yerba mate is central to their lives—a relationship of dependency and meaning that many articulate simply: without yerba mate, there is nothing here.

Conclusion

This chapter *endeavors* to demonstrate that understanding human life in the yerbal *must include* the role of the plant itself. *Raídos*, while valuable in documenting the sociological and interpersonal dimensions of tarefero life, unintentionally *reproduces* yerba blindness. By capturing tareferos without acknowledging their interspecies bond with yerba mate, it *risks reinforcing* a disconnect that *limits* the depth of our understanding. Yerba mate is more than a backdrop; it is an agent of resilience, *helping* tareferos *resist* dehumanization and *cultivate* a source of pride that *affirms* their identity in the face of enduring colonial constraints. This labor *sustains* not only tarefero families but also the daily social rituals of the Southern Cone, where yerba mate is a national staple.

Just as material inequalities persist in the yerbal, intellectual inequalities shape who participates in the production of knowledge. This chapter's effort to make the yerba mate plant visible also seeks to bring tareferos into the conversation, counteracting the epistemic marginalization they face. The shared viewing of Raídos with the Gómez family thus becomes a collaborative space, allowing for alternative forms of understanding beyond text—an audiovisual performance of collective memory.

Further, this work explores the complex issue of child labor within tarefero communities, complicating the dichotomy of labor versus education. For yerba ethnographers, child labor remains challenging to document directly due to the remoteness of the yerbales and the coercive oversight of landowners. As this chapter shows, however, child labor persists in the territory, highlighting the enduring colonial structures within the yerba mate industry, where systemic exploitation continues across generations. Children join the harvest not out of compulsion but to help meet their families' immediate needs. In these contexts, education and child labor often coexist, creating a precarious balance that threatens future school retention. As our focus on plant agency reveals, children assisting in the yerba harvest face relentless biospheric friction, imprinting early physical markers that, over time, perpetuate a cycle of captivity.

In conclusion, the distance we maintain between the human and vegetal worlds limits not only our understanding of plants like yerba mate but also our comprehension of the laborers who cultivate them. This distance is emblematic of a broader cultural blindness that not only hinders social change but also sustains colonial structures in the yerbal, where tareferos remain caught between survival and systemic exclusion—a pattern that could easily replicate in other geographies, with different plants yet similar coercive regimes.

Note

1. The Gómez family authorized me to share information about their lives in this chapter. To prevent any possible repercussions from employers and local authorities, their names—as well as the name El Polaco—have been changed.

Works Cited

Aguilar Carrasco, Pilar. "El cine, una mirada cómplice en la violencia contra las mujeres." *El sustrato cultural de la violencia de género,* coordinated by Ángeles de la Concha, Sintesis, 2010, pp. 241–276.

Barrett, Rafael. *Lo que son los yerbales paraguayos.* Capital Intelectual, 2010.

Burgos, Angela María, and Ricardo D. Medina. "Origen e historia." *Yerba Mate: Reseña Histórica y Estadística. Producción e Industrialización en el siglo XXI,* edited by Pablo Capellari, Consejo Federal de Inversiones, 2017.

Delistraty, Cody. "The Intelligence of Plants." *Paris Review,* Sept. 2019.

Folch, Christine. *The Book of Yerba Mate: A Stimulating History.* Princeton University Press, 2024.

Gómez Lende, Sebastián. "De la acumulación primitiva a la acumulación por desposesión: superexplotación laboral en la cosecha de yerba mate del nordeste argentino (1870–2018)." *Espacio y desarrollo,* no. 35, 2020, pp. 39–69.

Gortari, Javier. *De la tierra sin mal al tractorazo. Hacia una economía política de la yerba mate.* Sudamericana, 2007.

Hall, Matthew. *Plants as Persons: A Philosophical Botany.* SUNY Press, 2011.

Haugg, Diana E. "Cuerpos del trabajo: 'Yo me crié en la tarefa, no sé hacer otra cosa de trabajo, cuando me di cuenta, ya era tarefera.'" *ETNICEX,* no. 8, 2016, pp. 51–60.

Haugg, Diana E. "La cosecha de yerba mate en Misiones (Argentina): una actividad laboral -tarefa- con marcas de desigualdad de género." *La Manzana de la Discordia,* vol. 15, no. 1, 2020, pp. 91–120.

Laist, Randy, editor. *Plants and Literature: Essays in Critical Plant Studies.* Rodopi, 2013.

Magan, María Victoria. "Dos crisis yerbateras: similitudes y diferencias en las circunstancias que llevaron a la creación de la CRYM (1935) y la INYM (2002)." IX Encuentro de Cátedras de Ciencias Sociales y Humanísticas para las Ciencias Económicas, 6–7 Jun. 2002, Mar del Plata.

Malnatti, Daniel. "Diez días como un yerbatero: la vida de los cosechadores." *Todo Noticias,* 26 Mar. 2022.

Marcone, Diego, director. *Raídos.* La Marmota Contenidos, 2016.

Marder, Michael. *Plant-thinking: A Philosophy of Vegetal Life.* Stanford University Press, 2013.

Montagnini, F., et al. "Organic Yerba Mate: An Environmentally, Socially, and Financially Suitable Agroforestry System." *Bois et Forêts des Tropiques,* vol. 308, no. 2, 2011, pp. 59–74.

Navajas, Pau. *Caá Porã. El Espíritu de la yerba mate.* Tienda Las Marías, 2013.

Pite, Rebekah E. *Sharing Yerba Mate.* University of North Carolina Press, 2023.

Rau, Victor H. *Cosechando yerba mate: Estructuras sociales de un mercado laboral agrario en el Nordeste argentino.* Ciccus, 2012.

Re, Daniel A. "La ayuda infantil en la tarefa de yerba mate. Cultura, mercado y legislación." *Revista Conflicto Social,* vol. 8, no. 14, 2015.

Roa, María Luz. "Estar-en-el-yerbal. La conformación de subjetividades tareferas." XI Congreso de Antropología Social, 2014, Rosario, Santa Fe, Argentina.

Roa, María Luz. "De la etnografía al teatro: caminos metodológicos de una performance-investigación colaborativa con cosecheros/as de yerba mate en Misiones, Argentina." *Cuadernos de Música, Artes Visuales y Artes Escénicas,* vol. 18, no. 1, 2023.

Rodríguez, Lisandro R. "Producción y comercialización cooperativa yerbatera en los márgenes. La provincia argentina de Misiones (1991–2014)." *Revista Iberoamericana de Viticultura, Agroindustria y Ruralidad,* vol. 3, no. 9, 2016, pp. 50–74.

Sarreal, Julia. *Yerba Mate: The Drink that Shaped a Nation.* University of California Press, 2023.

Varela, Alfredo. *¡También en la Argentina hay esclavos blancos!.* Omnívora, 2020.

Woodward, Wendy, and Erika Lemmer. "Introduction: Critical Plant Studies." *Journal of Literary Studies,* vol. 35, no. 4, 2019, pp. 23–27.

Zang, Laura M. "Yerba Mate as a Settler Crop: From the Decline of Old-Growth Trees to the Rise of Plantations." *Apuntes,* no. 87, 2020.

16

Return to Nature

The Politics of Animals and Plants in Two Turn-of-the-Twentieth-Century Latin American Vegetarian Cookbooks

VANESA MISERES

Vegetarianism and reflections on animal-free diets in Latin America are not recent phenomena or mere trends. While the Western world traces vegetarian practices back to classical Athens with figures like Pythagoras, traditions of plant-based diets also have long roots in other parts of the world, particularly in Asia, where religious and ethical beliefs fostered vegetarianism for centuries. By the early twentieth century, European vegetarianism, tied to naturism, had merged with political activism—especially among anarchists who opposed capitalist exploitation symbolized by meat and alcohol.[1]

In Latin America, this movement also has deep roots yet remains understudied in the context of nineteenth- and early twentieth-century culture. This essay explores Latin American vegetarianism through two cookbooks: Antonio Valeta's *El régimen vegetariano: 250 platos de comida sin carne* (The Vegetarian Diet: 250 Meatless Dishes) from Uruguay, and Antonio Blandina Torres's *La cocinera vegetariana* (The Vegetarian Woman Cook) from Mexico. Using food studies, critical animal and plant studies, and feminist theory, I examine how these texts frame the relationship between animals, plants, and humans, highlighting the ethical and political dimensions of vegetarianism. In his prologue to *La cocinera vegetariana*, Mexican writer Amado Nervo noted the widening gap between "nature and civilized man," calling for a "re-education" by nature. These cookbooks position vegetarianism as a path to personal health and social emancipation, responding to the industrial and urban pressures that were seen as "antinatural" forces corrupting both body and soul.

El régimen vegetariano (1915): Plants, Animals, and Politics in the Rio de la Plata Region

All diets are political. But during the first two decades of the twentieth century, that statement seemed more radical than in any other time. This was a period of utopias and, in Latin America in particular, a time in which political forces were searching for a project that could surpass the national experiences and imageries built in the previous era (Laborde). Socialism and anarchism emerged as strong forces against a capitalist economy and the control of state.[2] And they paid particular attention to diet and biopolitics in general as a path to individual improvement and in pursuit of the common good. These interests were also a response to the State's eugenics practices and their desire for population control that brought politics and health together in order to improve the overall well-being of the population, prevent the spread of diseases (tuberculosis, typhus), and create a stronger and more productive labor force.[3] While the State conceived the family and individual as the source of unhealthy habits, anarchists and socialists put the responsibility on the unfavorable environment in which they were condemned to live.

Within the political conception of an individual free from the yoke of the state and capitalism, several anarchists embraced vegetarianism. In South America, this was a challenging move, with countries such as Argentina and Uruguay holding some of the world's largest meat consumption rates per capita. As Gustavo Laborde explains, meat was usually perceived in nineteenth-century Latin America as an enabler of civilization (Laborde), a European inherited habit in opposition to the mostly vegetarian Indigenous diet. In Clorinda Matto's *indigenista* novel *Aves sin nido* (Torn from the nest, 1889), for instance, the city character of Fernando Marín cogitate about the Indigenous people's lack of intellectual capacity and its connection to a vegetarian diet based on beans and quinoa (58). In Argentina, Esteban Echeverría wrote *Apología del matambre* (Apology of the matambre, 1837), a satirical essay in which he refers to the carnivorous citizens of Buenos Aires, the *carnívoros porteños*, and their love for this cut of meat, the *matambre*, as the source of the physical and political strength that gave them independence at the beginning of the century: "con matambre se alimentan los que . . . con hierro ensangrentado escribieron: *Independencia, Libertad*" (those who . . . with bloody iron wrote: Independence, Freedom are fed with matambre) (no pagination). Last, the gaucho culture of meat consumption, which was previously condemned as a sign of backwardness by intellectuals like Domingo F. Sarmiento, was celebrated at the end of the nineteenth century. The return to the values of the Argentine gaucho represented a xenophobic and nationalistic response to modernity (Delaney 435). Vegetarianism, in fact, was perceived by several conservative sectors as an eccentric and anti-Argentine practice, just as anarchism and just as the Rural Society gauchos continued to express during the 2019 conflict with vegan activists. The dramatic standoff at the Rural Exposition, where protesters were chased out of the arena by gauchos on horseback, revealed enduring cultural tensions between traditional livestock practices and emerging critiques of animal exploitation that challenge national culinary and rural identities.

Nevertheless, in Chile, Simón Rodríguez Rozas published *La Carpofagia* (vol. 1, 1901 and vol. 2, 1903); the book was reviewed by Rudolf Franck in the German vegetarian magazine *Vegetarische Warte* in 1903 and announced as the first book on vegetarianism written in Spanish (Koeder). In 1909, Venezuelan author and vegetarianism activist Carlos Brandt published *El vegetarismo* (Vegetarianism), influenced by his education in Germany, where he became familiar with naturism and the ideas of Leo Tolstoy in his article "The Morals of Diet," which advocates for vegetarianism and discusses anarchism and pacifism as related political standpoints. That same year, Catalan anarchist and naturist José Fernando Carbonell published *El vegetarianismo teórico y práctico* (Vegetarianism in Theory and Practice) in Uruguay, where he emigrated at an early age. This work is a treatise on the science and art of vegetarian nutrition and contains an extensive number of recipes for broths, soups, stews, salads, and desserts (Zubillaga no pagination). Journals and magazines echoed the surge of vegetarian publications and activities and, in the River Plate region, anarchists' periodicals were particularly interested in the subject (Stavisky, "El vegetarianismo" 10). A 1913 article in *La acción obrera*, for example, mentioned the vegetarian diet as key to the anarchist formula, and *La protesta* became a regular platform for the promotion of vegetarian meetings and restaurants (Prado).[4]

Antonio Valeta's *El régimen vegetariano* is a significant example of the political and anarchist roots of vegetarianism in Latin America. Valeta (1882–1945) was an anarchist and naturist doctor who opposed human and animal exploitation, considering them part of the same kin.[5] Anarchism held a moral view on modern life and considered that current social problems including war, alcoholism, prostitution, and high infant mortality rates, among others, were the result of immoral decisions influenced, as mentioned above, by a harmful social environment. They attacked the bourgeoisie for appropriating surplus value and causing overcrowding and unsanitary conditions for the workers (Laborde). Valeta's cookbook adheres to these ideas and also follows the anarchist interest in reaching and transforming the consciousness of the working class through popular genres like the pamphlet and the recipe. That is, formats that could easily circulate at home and in the factory. For this reason, the book is structured in two sections. One consists of a series of brochures with concise but repetitive statements about health and nutrition and with social and political commentaries against carnivorism. This section presents vegetarianism as the best diet for working-class men and women. The second part is composed of recipes for a plant-based diet, with additional information on the properties and health benefits of vegetables and fruits.[6] Valeta emphasizes that, perhaps to compensate for the resistance felt by locals to vegetarianism, the recipes have been carefully adapted to the *criollo* culture (5).

The first part of *El régimen vegetariano* portrays animals persuasively. They are seen in conviviality with humans and, as previously mentioned, as part of the same kind: "no hay motivo para poner al hombre en un orden especial del reino animal" (there is no reason to place man in a special order of the animal kingdom) (8). The similarities between people and apes, moreover, serve Valeta to argue that fruits and vegetables are the natural humans' food.[7] The author not only establishes this similarity to convince the readership of the ethical need for a vegetarian diet, but also highlights a larger point. As Donna Haraway explains, apes were mostly associated with colonial exchange and the possession of animals, but Valeta, as well as other vegetarians, saw them as sources of rationality from which to learn a healthier way of life (Haraway 11). It is interesting to note that on this point, he quotes Ignacio Albarracin (1850–1926), president of the Argentine Animal Protection Society, who opposed cruelty in slaughtering animals and in cock and bull fighting. In *El Zoófilo Argentino* (The Argentine Zoophile), Albarracin affirmed that when not being exploited by the civilized man, animals live a prolonged and healthy life, since they do not adulterate the natural state of their food. As a consequence, they benefit from living free of the "tormentosos dolores que son de moda en los racionales" (tormenting pains which are fashionable in rational people) (Valeta 9). Building on Albarracin's argument, *El régimen vegetariano* challenged the traditional perception of nature / culture. It questioned the idea that individuals differentiate or affirm their cultural identity through food transformation, as proposed by the anthropologist Claude Lévi-Strauss (2008) or, more recently, by the historian Felipe Fernández Armesto (2002). Valeta, on the other hand, condemns cooking as an attempt to hide the irrationality and violence associated with eating meat.[8] Cooking, in sum, separates "the meat eater from the animal and the animal from the product," as veganism activist and scholar Carol Adams argues. Through being cooked, animals become what Adams calls the "absent referent," that is, meat is turned into a "free-floating" image, detached from the original referent (the animal) so that people can dispose of them in any way they wish (13). Conversely, Valeta not only recovers animals' lives but also argues that animals possess a form of nonverbal intelligence, which allows them to make informed decisions about their diet based on the effects it has on their bodies (Derrida 375–377). Animals' intelligence destabilizes human reason and highlights their superior understanding of the natural world.

In Valeta's cookbook, plants dominate the second section. While the parallel with animals might suggest a biological basis for human-animal connections, the human-plant relationship is rooted in symbolism. The cookbook suggests that plants, like animals, have a language: they communicate through a nonverbal medium that humans must learn. This understanding doesn't come from medical prescriptions but rather through an intuitive connection, following "los sanos preceptos de nuestra madre común" (the wholesome precepts of our common mother) (59). Recipes with vegetables, legumes, and fruits, then, can be read as an archive of what Monica Gagliano understands as plant knowledge, "always available to those who listen" (20). Like Gagliano, we can think of Valeta's ideas on plants' intelligence and voices as a reciprocal revelation (Gagliano 38), since he affirms that knowing how plants grow, how they are cultivated, and how we should eat them is a form of understanding ourselves, our bodies, and health. For this reason, Valeta proposes eliminating unnecessary and harmful intermediaries to directly engage with plants and their nutritious properties. Cooking, again, is perceived as a human intervention, an artifact that corrupts this link between humans, and fruits, for instance, are advised to be consumed raw. Fruit juices, on the other hand, could replace meat broth, made of animals that had to be "asesinados sin compasión" (mercilessly murdered) (11).

Additionally, Valeta establishes a metaphorical connection between human bodies and plants, suggesting that diseases can "brotar de nuevo como las malas yerbas que bordean las flores exquisitas de un jardín que se abandonó" (sprout again like the weeds that border the exquisite flowers of an abandoned garden) (56). This metaphor not only underscores the shared fragility of plants and humans, requiring vigilance and care, but also aligns with a plant studies perspective that sees plants and humans as sharing similar growth and development processes. In this way, Valeta challenges the idea of plants' passiveness—a point that thinkers like Stefano Mancuso (2020) have also supported. Instead of anthropomorphizing plants, Valeta suggests that by understanding our bodies in plant-like terms, we can reconnect with our "green" origins and confront human tendencies toward rationalism and exploitation.

However, this perspective on plants and health in Valeta's work also takes on a moralistic and nearly eugenistic tone. Vegetarianism is presented as conferring a physical and ethical superiority over meat-eating, an implication that hints at a form of purification or discipline. Such moments in *El régimen vegetariano* reveal eugenistic and statist undertones, highlighting an impulse to shape healthier, morally "better" populations. Ironically, while the book promotes anarchist ideals, its language around health and purity aligns with statist ambitions for managing the well-being of the citizenry. This duality—of liberation and control—reflects the broader tensions within Latin American anarchism and feminism (addressed toward the end of the chapter), where political ideals for personal freedom can intersect with visions of idealized, disciplined bodies for the collective good.

Although cooking is stripped of its artistic and creative dimension, Valeta still offers a wide variety of recipes that he will continue to promote in future works such as *La cocina con plantas silvestres* (Cooking with wild plants) (1939). He suggests vegetarian dishes from the local cultures like the corn *mazamorra,* a pudding-like dessert of South American Indigenous roots, or vegetarian versions of criollo dishes like the "puchero sin carne" (meatless stew) (108). The vegetarianization is also marked with the addition of "a la vegetariana" to other international dishes like ravioli or incorporating nonnative ingredients like rhubarb to traditional local recipes such as *alfajores,* a South American sandwich cookie (113, 112). Last, a recipe like the "sopa económica," containing three ingredients only—lettuce, butter, and stale bread—reveals that *El régimen vegetariano* promotes an alternative approach to human life and its environment that is class-conscious and distanced from what anarchists understood as an exploitative system perpetrated by capitalism and the owners of means of production, who saw nature as radically separated from humans (115).

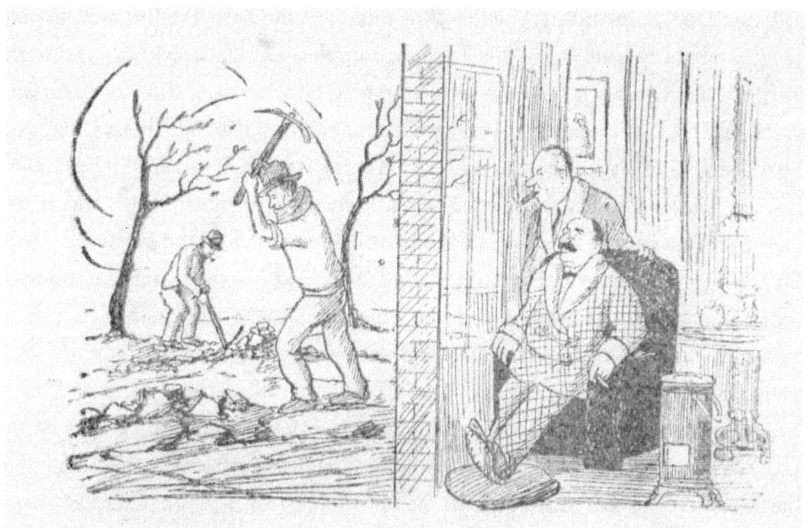

FIGURE 16.1. "Practical demonstration of the different physiological needs." Antonio Valeta, *El régimen vegetariano*, 1929, p. 84. While this image tries to convey that people should follow different diets according to their needs and work, it also contains a clear political message. While the fit persons are workers, represented outdoors and doing manual agricultural labor, the two men on the right are portrayed as urban people, inactive, and obese, in an enclosed and dark room and smoking, a vice that vegetarian anarchists associated with a carnivorous diet. Reproduced from the original held by the Department of Special Collections of the Hesburgh Libraries of the University of Notre Dame.

La cocinera vegetariana (1918): Gender Roles and the Global Locality of Naturism

La cocinera vegetariana was edited and published in Mexico by Antonio Blandina Torres, a Spanish naturist doctor who served as consul in Mexico and about whom there is limited information. While it contains less political content than Valeta's cookbook, the book still highlights the political transnational networks of naturism and the importance of Latin American authors and naturism activists within this global movement. The list is surprisingly robust, and it incorporates mentions of Mexican and Cuban naturist centers, libraries, and restaurants, naturist periodicals such as "Pro-Vida," founded in Havana by the Catalan socialist, publicist, and librarian Adrián del Valle (1872–1945), and a wide variety of books and cookbooks, including Valeta's *El régimen vegetariano*, which is announced as "una obra bastante completa" (a quite complete work) on criollo vegetarian cuisine (58). The last section on recommended books for the study of naturism mentions other titles such as *Vegetarianism and Occultism* by Charles Webster Leadbeater (1854–1934), and *Naturismo práctico*, published in Yucatán by Cuban novelist Carlos Loveira (1882–1928), while Mexican revolutionary Venustiano Carranza placed him in charge of the Labor Department of the said state (156). *La cocinera vegetariana*, then, built an archive of Latin American naturism that reinforced the locality of the movement while, at the same, time put the continent in a transnational dialogue focused on an approach to humans, animals, and plants beyond national borders and detached from official medical approaches.[9] In fact, naturism, and *La cocinera vegetariana* in particular, promoted a vegetarian diet as a physiological need to reestablish humans' "full satisfaction and harmony with the environment" (8). As the quote by Dr. Terieux states, naturism was perceived as "la ciencia de vivir felices" (the science of living happily) (81).

Although in this cookbook vegetarianism is almost exclusively embedded in this alternative view of health and medicine and political forces like anarchism are barely mentioned, the book connects vegetarianism with political activism, for instance, when it mentions pacifism:

> Los individuos de las sociedades de pacifismo, temperancia, protectoras de animales, etc. Que a su vez no sean vegetarianos, sus hábitos están en contra posición [sic] de los mencionados principios. Teniendo presente, pues, que la propaganda más eficaz es el ejemplo; mal proteje a los animales quien se los come.
>
> (Pacifist, temperant, animal protection society members, etc., who are not vegetarians violate these principles. Bearing in mind, then, that the most effective propaganda is by example; those who eat animals do not protect them well.) (98)

Suggesting a link between vegetarianism and pacifism highlights the importance of personal food choices in the pursuit of a nonviolent world. It proposes that by choosing vegetarianism, individuals make a statement against both the political violence of war and other forms of human aggressiveness (including gender violence) and cruelty toward animals. The quote also works as an appeal for a more peaceful and compassionate world, since killing animals, the cookbook states, also kills sensibility (102).

Blandina Torres similarly intercalates vegetarian recipes with small graphic and text vignettes that put his cookbook in dialogue with the works of other European naturist doctors and renowned figures in the Western political and cultural world such as Hippocrates, Jean Jacques Rousseau, or the German physician Johann Heinrich Lahmann (1860–1905). Vignettes, moreover, include vegetarian dietary maxims on how to run the kitchen, health benefits of fruits and vegetables, and a clear ethical message about animal consumption, as mentioned. One vignette includes a quote by Leo Tolstoy in which the Russian novelist argues about carnivorism's inappropriateness in contemporary society (91). The eighty menus available reflect, on the other hand, the educational and practical purpose of this publication. It calls for a need for re-educating Mexican citizens on eating vegetarian food as well as educating foreign readers on Mexican food. Thus, the menus include local terms for ingredients and utensils such as "jitomate" for tomato, "chícharos" for peas, and "comal" for iron griddle. At the same time, a local recipe like *quesadilla* is explained in a distant tone, presumably addressing non-Mexican readers. Instead of asking for *tortillas,* the recipe requires "tortitas delgadas de maíz" (thin corn pancakes) (76). Apart from this brief mention, the cookbook's omission of tortillas—a staple in both Mayan and Aztec diets—is surprising.

Sarah Back-Geller observes that nineteenth-century liberal thinking on Indigenous foodscapes was still shaped by Enlightenment medical discourse, which viewed digestion as central to preventing and curing most ailments. Thus, many Indigenous dishes, especially the tortilla (made from unleavened dough), were deemed incompatible with "healthy" digestion (91). *La cocinera vegetariana* calls for a rational dietary shift to "combatir la tremenda epidemia gastrointestinal" (fight the tremendous gastrointestinal epidemic) responsible for 60 percent of diseases in Mexico (2). As a result, wheat and other flours were favored over corn, with recommendations for consuming fruits with bread and recipes such as "potato bread" from Holland and Germany, and "panecitos económicos" (cheap bread rolls) (12, 21, 35). These examples illustrate that, although naturist vegetarianism was promoted as an alternative to mainstream medicine, it still reflected Western biases by downplaying traditional Mesoamerican diets, which were largely plant-based or pescatarian. Before European contact, Mesoamerican cuisine was primarily vegetarian, with no access to large domesticated livestock other than the turkey, yet it was diverse and nutritionally balanced.

Consequently, the return to nature proposed by Amado Nervo in the prologue to this cookbook is mediated by Western culture and disassociated from native practices that were inherently in harmony with what the land had available. That is to say, it implies a *de-nativization* of local foodways and a racial hierarchization of food under which some ingredients such as *chiles* are considered unhealthy stimulants for the organism, or preparations like *pulque* (fermented drink made of the agave plant) are rejected for the same reason (93). In the repertoire of recipes, readers learn how to treat chiles poblanos to "quitarles su mal sano picoso" (remove their unhealthy spiciness), and, with the argument of considering a non-Mexican audience, one can find the "enchiladas sin chile" (chili-free *enchiladas*) (62, 28). The erasure of local habits and foodstuff is reinforced by the organization of eating under the European structure of a four-course meal plus a dessert.

But what is certainly prominent in Blandina Torres's cookbook is the discussion of vegetarianism in gender terms. First of all, the title explicitly indicates that its targeted audience is the "vegetarian woman" who cooks or, better yet, she who wants to learn more about vegetarian foodways. Second, the cover includes the dedication to "la abnegada mujer mexicana" (the self-sacrificing Mexican woman) (2). It is possible to find at least two initial and somewhat contradictory arguments for women's association with vegetarian diet. One lies in the cultural conceptions and symbolizations of women in the Western world, which have historically associated the female body, mainly understood in its procreative functions, with nature's life cycles, unlike men, who have been identified with culture (68–87). Under the ideal of separate gender spheres, nature has likewise been seen as the embodiment of all the characteristics that women possess such as domesticity, pureness, simplicity, and beauty. On the contrary, men have been seen as rational, assertive, and in control of nature and, therefore, of women. The other one is based on the fact that during the nineteenth century, the link between women and nature was also manifested in the encouragement women received to work with plants. Following the popularity of Swedish botanist Carl Linnaeus's *Systema Naturae* (1735) and its taxonomy of the natural world, botany became a common and fashionable activity among women from Europe and the Americas. Together with drawing and collecting plants and flowers, women also delved into gardening and gained both scientific and practical knowledge of the vegetable world. Consequently, both a traditional understanding of women's roles and advocacy for the expansion of women's education were initially linked to women's inclination to nature and, more specifically, to plants. Blandina Torres's introduction to *La cocinera Mexicana* condenses these perspectives in the following passage:

> A la Mujer Mexicana, en quien, como antes indicamos, entraña especial característica de elevadas dotes y abnegados principios; y que su práctica

moral y material en la vida cotidiana, esencialmente hablando, puede sintetizarse la más elevada aspiración del movimiento femenil moderno mundial, es con quien tengo mayor esperanza para cimentar en nuestras habituales costumbres el uso de la alimentación que propagamos.

(To the Mexican Woman, in whom, as we indicated before, entails a special characteristic of elevated gifts and self-sacrificing principles; and whose moral and material practice in daily life, essentially speaking, can be synthesized the highest aspiration of the world's modern feminine movement, is on whom I have greater hope to cement in our habits the implementation of the feeding system that we propagate.) (5)

Rooted in a stereotypical perception of Mexican women in their role as caregivers, paradoxically, the author expresses optimism about the potential for implementing vegetarianism as an emerging habit among them. As mothers, women are more inclined, the quote seems to suggest, to more compassionate ways of connecting with nature. Therefore, they are more open to nonviolent foodscapes. *La cocinera vegetariana* shares feminist vegan activists' and scholars' argument that women are not the subject but the object, together with nonhuman animals, of men's possessive desire and violence. There is a clear indication of the latter in Amado Nervo's cookbook prologue: "La tristeza mana siempre de la carne, y cuando se ha dicho que la carne es triste, acaso no se ha querido hablar de la mujer, que, es, en suma, la menos triste de las carnes" (Sadness always springs from the flesh, and when it was said that the flesh is sad, it was not meant to speak of the woman, who, in short, is the least sad of the meats) (XVI).

Women are thus portrayed in the cookbook in parallel with meat itself, as victims of both carnivorism and patriarchy—an association that predates Carol Adams's arguments in *The Sexual Politics of Meat.* Blandina Torres explicitly illustrates this parallel later in the cookbook, using two contrasting images: one of a woman consuming meat and another on a vegetarian diet. While one is described as deteriorating, with a miserable aspect, the other one possesses a healthy facial expression (50, 9). Patriarchal foodscapes, which perpetuate and normalize animal product consumption, can limit women's dietary choices and place them in unhealthy conditions, including violence against themselves, as the book shows in other sections associating meat consumption with alcoholism, and gender violence as a consequence of both. The book expands this assertion to a more political dimension by including a vignette with a quote by Cuban naturist doctor Ramón Suárez, who affirms that vegetarianism would only be

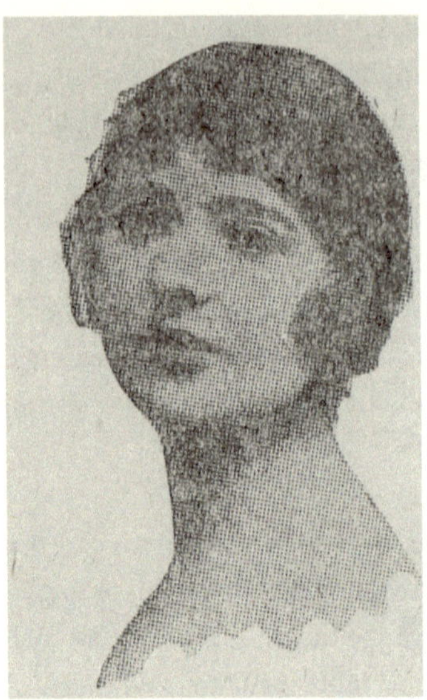

FIGURE 16.2. "Healthy expression of a vegetarian woman." Antonio Blandina Torres, *La cocinera vegetariana*, Centro Naturista de México, 1918, p. 9. Reproduced from the original held by the Department of Special Collections of the Hesburgh Libraries of the University of Notre Dame.

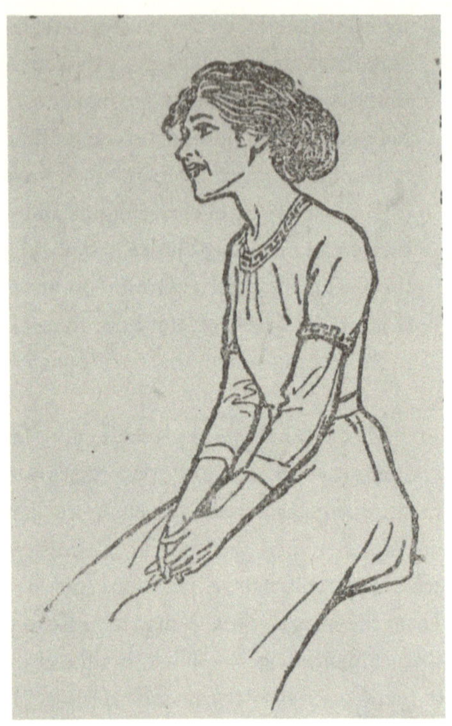

FIGURE 16.3. "Here is a miserable aspect of a woman for not eating well. The impoverishment of organisms is very general with meat foods." Antonio Blandina Torres, *La cocinera vegetariana,* México City: Centro Naturista de México, 1918, pp. 9, 50. Reproduced from the original held by the Department of Special Collections of the Hesburgh Libraries of the University of Notre Dame.

fully implemented when society gives a woman "el completo de los derechos que le corresponden" (the full rights to which she is entitled).[10] Women are, then, inherently inclined to vegetarianism at the same time that vegetarianism depends on the status of women's social and political emancipation.

Turning to Valeta's *El régimen vegetariano,* we find a similar feminist engagement.[11] The final section of the cookbook includes endorsements from prominent feminist voices in Uruguay, who praised the book for its contributions to women's and children's health. Early twentieth-century feminists in Uruguay, many of whom were medical professionals, were deeply invested in advancing healthcare and improving nutrition as part of broader social reform. As scholars like Asunción Lavrin and Graciela Sapriza have shown, these feminists often advocated for science and education as vehicles for activism. Nutrition, seen as vital to public health and social improvement, was a key focus of feminist programs in areas like puericulture, domestic science, and home medicine. Vegetarianism, in this context, aligned with their vision of a society made healthier through improved diets, and several of these women shared Valeta's socialist ideals, as well as a commitment to pacifism and anti-oppression.

Among the supporters of *El régimen vegetariano,* feminist physician Paulina Luisi, heralded as the "apostle of feminism" in Uruguay, commended Valeta's contribution to public health and the "difusión popular de los principios de higiene" (popular dissemination of hygiene principles) (150). Nylia Molinari Calleros, a nutritionist and president of the Uruguayan League Against Women Trafficking, echoed Valeta's emphasis on children's natural preference for fruits over "el canasto del carnicero" (the butcher's basket). Another endorsement came from pediatrician Sara Rayola (151). Although not directly involved with Valeta, the Puerto Rican feminist Luisa Capetillo—who, in 1919, established one of the first vegetarian restaurants in New York—also championed vegetarianism as a path to social reform. Like Nervo, Capetillo viewed nutrition and hygiene as essential elements of modernity, linking them to specific routines, including meatless diet, bathing, and calisthenics (XXVI). In both cookbooks, vegetarianism is thus framed not only as a dietary choice but also as a vision of social progress intimately connected with feminist ideals of health, social equity, and nonviolence.

Finally, another noteworthy figure linking feminism and diet is Fernando Carbonell, who in his essay *Feminismo y marimachismo* (1900), explores how cooking perpetuates forms of servitude when it involves the subjugation of either human workers (domestic servants) or nonhuman animals (consumed meat). He argues:

> El vegetarianismo . . . embellece y dignifica la cocina. Destierra la horrible sangre, la grasa fétida y, por ende, el jabón corrosivo que arruga y quema la epidermis. La vegetariana, aun cuando se dedique á las faenas culinarias, no perderá el albor y la tersura de sus manos; no llevará á los salones unas "manos de cocinera."

(Vegetarianism . . . beautifies and dignifies the kitchen. It banishes the horrible blood, the fetid fat and, therefore, the corrosive soap that wrinkles and burns the epidermis. The vegetarian woman, even when she devotes herself to culinary tasks, will not lose the luster and smoothness of her hands; she will not bring "cook's hands" to the salons.) (6)

Unlike Valeta, who framed vegetarianism as a departure from culinary labor, Carbonell sees it as a way to enhance the kitchen itself, elevating the experience by eliminating animal products and, thus, elements he considers degrading. For him, vegetarianism transforms cooking from a form of servitude into an aesthetically pleasing, dignified activity. This shift aligns with suffragette feminism's desire to break from associations of cooking with subjugation, manual labor, and violence.

Carbonell's view on vegetarianism also resonates with two opposing perspectives found in *La cocinera vegetariana* regarding women's relationship to food preparation and diet. On one hand, it appeals to feminist sectors critical of women's relegation to the kitchen; on the other, it preserves a traditional view of women's "natural" goodness and inherent beauty. Carbonell suggests that a woman's inclination toward a plant-based diet is both a "gift" and a "gift of love," emphasizing her "natural" frugivorous disposition as an ideal feminine quality: "para la mujer . . . es un don y un don de amor de ser frugívera" (for the woman . . . it is a gift and a gift of love to be frugivorous) (124). This complex intersection of vegetarianism, feminism, and culinary labor—spanning the writings of Valeta, Torres, and Carbonell—ultimately reflects both progressive and traditional views on gender, food ethics, and women's roles in society at the turn of the century.

Conclusion

Cookbooks promoting a plant-based diet represent more than a collection of recipes; they constitute a pedagogical and political tool that vegetarians with a diverse political background that includes anarchism and naturism used to express their ideas on Latin American modernized societies, according to the relationship that people established with plants and animals. In their own particular ways and through a collection of recipes and reflections on positive and negative everyday consumption habits, *El régimen vegetariano* and *La cocinera vegetariana* adhere to the idea of "return to nature" as a human reconciliation with its environment.[12] Following the principles of what was known in Europe as the *Lebensreform* movement,[13] these texts strived for the state of nature, conceived humans in a nonhierarchical animal kin and animal consumption as a form of body contamination, and found in plants and vegetables the source of a nonviolent and healthy subsistence. In their formulation of their ideals of human reconnection to nature, the authors bring politics and gender relations into discussion, combining a view of the local ecosystem with the transnational nature of vegetarianism. These debates show us that their "return to nature" utopia may also result in uncompassionate attitudes toward those deemed hopelessly degenerate (again, the absence of Indigenous subjects and diets highlights this point).

Exploring the animal and plant politics of Latin American vegetarian cookbooks, which I have shown to be a rich yet largely unexplored cultural archive, offers a unique perspective to integrate animal and plant studies while positioning humans in ecological terms, as Val Plumwood suggests. This approach encourages us to understand and historicize human attempts to view themselves as part of a network of respectful, equitable relationships with other beings (78). While these cookbooks reveal contradictions in their notions of equality and nonhierarchical environmental views, they challenge the human/nature dualism that often shaped studies of Latin American culture, literature, and politics at the turn of the century. Through recipes, vegetarian cookbooks connect humans with nonhuman animals and the animated plant world. In these texts, plants and animals are not silent, passive entities waiting to be consumed; rather, they play an active role in envisioning alternative paths to modernity. Finally, these cookbooks illuminate Latin American food politics within a deep interspecies entanglement, resonating with concerns over ecological balance in the Anthropocene.

Notes

1. See Gregerson, Spencer, and Notaker.

2. See Leandro Delgado.

3. See Nancy Stepan (1991) and Diego Armus (2016).

4. Other Latin American vegetarian publications include the magazines *Vida y Natura* (1915) and *Vida Nueva* (1926) from Rosario, Argentina, and *Manual de cocina vegetariana chilena* (1931) by Chilean cookbook writer Lucía Vergara.

5. Antonio Valeta (1882–1945) founded the Naturist Studies Center "Hygiene and Health" in Montevideo in 1911, and published the magazine with the same name in 1914. In 1910, he published his first successful book, *Manual Práctico del naturismo y el vegetarianismo*. He also founded the Popular League Against Alcoholism and directed the journals *Fisiocultura* and *Regeneración*. He continued publishing books like *El na-*

turismo en el hogar, Botánica práctica, arte de comer y nutrición, and *Estragos del alcoholismo* as well as brochures containing the rules for the sports he invented.

6. My descriptions and analysis are based on the 8th edition of Valeta's cookbook, the only one I was able to consult.

7. A similar argument is made in Simón B. Rodríguez's *La Carpofagia,* Manuel Lezaeta Acharán's *La medicina natural al alcance de todos,* and Carlos Brandt's *El vegetarismo.*

8. Like most of the vegetarian publications of the period, his cookbook presented "any preparation involving heat, such as boiling or frying," as reductors of the nutritional value of foodstuffs (Notaker 231). For instance, U.S. naturist Ella Kellogg in *Science in the Kitchen* (1893) affirmed that "the use of condiments is unquestionably a strong auxiliary to the formation of a habit of using intoxicating drinks" (31).

9. The transatlantic dialogue within this network is noteworthy. Spanish-born authors like Valeta and Blandina Torres promote the work of fellow Spaniards, such as Catalan writers Ignacio Domenech, R. P. Sansón, and Francisco Carbonell, among others. For more on naturism in Spain, see Josep Maria Roselló.

10. The perceptions of women in relation to vegetarianism are contrasting. A review of Chilean Simón B. Rodríguez's *La Carpofagia* by Rudolf Franck, for the German vegetarian magazine, *Vegetarische Warte* (no. 4, February 23, 1903), refers instead to women as needing to be trained and educated in a modern and healthy (vegetarian) way of cooking. The review follows Friedrich Nietzsche's argument about women and their lack of understanding of food's profound meanings. For the German philosopher, it is "bad female cooks" who have delayed human development (*Beyond Good and Evil: Our Virtues,* Aphorism no. 234).

11. The feminist-vegetarian connection is first mentioned in critical studies on vegetarianism in Sheri Lucas's response to Kathryn Paxton George's book *Animal, Vegetable, or Woman?: A Feminist Critique of Ethical Vegetarianism* (2000). Numerous scholars, including Josephine Donovan and Kathryn Paxton George, have extensively analyzed this connection since 1990.

12. See John Bellamy Foster and Henry Notaker.

13. See the special issue "The Nature of German Environmental History," *German History,* vol. 27, no. 1, 2009, pp. 113–130, https://doi.org/10.1093/gerhis/ghn079

Works Cited

AA.VV. "The Nature of German Environmental History," *German History,* vol. 27, no. 1, 2009, pp. 113–130, https://doi.org/10.1093/gerhis/ghn079

Acharán, Manuel Lezaeta. *La medicina natural al alcance de todos.* Boletín Comercial, 1929.

Adams, Carol. *The Sexual Politics of Meat.* Continuum, 2010.

Armus, Diego. "Eugenesia en Buenos Aires: discursos, prácticas, historiografía," *História, Ciências, Saúde—Manguinhos,* vol. 23, 2016, pp. 149–169.

Back-Geller, Sarah. "Comida, civilización y república. El pensamiento de Rousseauen la conformación de una dieta patriótica en México." *Rousseau En Iberoamérica: Lecturas e Interpretaciones Entre Monarquía y Revolución,* edited by Gabriel Entin and José Ma Portillo Valdés. Coloquio "Rousseau en Iberoamérica: del reformismo borbónico a las revoluciones de independencia," Ciudad Autónoma de Buenos Aires, Argentina: SB, 2018, pp. 87–106.

Bellamy Foster, John. *The Return of Nature: Socialism and Ecology.* New York University Press, 2020.

Blandina Torres, Antonio. *La cocinera vegetariana.* Centro Naturista de México, 1918.

Brandt, Carlos. *El vegetarismo.* Tipografía Mercantil, 1909.

Carbonell, Fernando. *Feminismo y marimachismo.* Centro Natura, 1900.

Delaney, Jeane. "Making Sense of Modernity: Changing Attitudes toward the Immigrant and the Gaucho in Turn-of-the-Century Argentina." *Comparative Studies in Society and History,* vol. 38, no. 3, 1996, pp. 434–459.

Delgado, Leandro. *Anarquismo en el novecientos rioplatense: Cultura, literatura y escritura.* Estuario Editora, 2017.

Derrida, Jacques. "The Animal that Therefore I Am (More to Follow)." *Critical Inquiry,* vol. 28, no. 2, 2002, pp. 375–377.

Donovan, Josephine. "Feminism and the Treatment of Animals: From Care to Dialogue." *Signs,* vol. 31, no. 2, 2006, pp. 305–329.

Echeverría, Esteban. "Apología del matambre," 1837. https://www.produccion-animal.com.ar/informacion_tecnica/carne_y_subproductos/74-apologia_del_matambre.pdf.

Fernández Armesto, Felipe. *Near a Thousand Tables. A History of Food.* The Free Press, 2002.

Frayne, Carl Tobias. "The Anarchist Diet: Vegetarianism and Individualist Anarchism in Early 20th-Century France." *Journal of Animal Ethics,* vol. 11, 2021, pp. 83–96.

Gagliano, Monica. *Thus Spoke the Plant: A Remarkable Journey of Groundbreaking Scientific Discoveries and Personal Encounters with Plants.* North Atlantic Books, 2018.

Gregerson, Jon. *Vegetarianism: A History.* Jain Publishing Company, 1994.

Haraway, Donna. *Primate Visions: Gender, Race, and Nature in the World of Modern Science.* Routledge, 1989.

Hau, Michael. *The Cult of Health and Beauty in Germany: A Social History, 1890-1930.* University of Chicago Press, 2003.

Kellogg, Ella. *Science in the Kitchen.* Modern Medicine Publishing Co., 1893.

Koeder, Christian. "El vegetarianismo en América del Sur ~1900," https://www.christiankoeder.com/2021/08/Carpofagia.html.

Laborde, Gustavo. Recetarios Uruguayos, episode 7 "Vegetarianos y anarcos unidos en Uruguay en la primera mitad del siglo XX," podcast audio, date unknown, https://delsol.uy/recetarios

Lavrin, Asunción. *Women, Feminism, and Social Change in Argentina, Chile, and Uruguay, 1890–1940.* University of Nebraska Press, 1998.

Lévi-Strauss, Claude. "The Culinary Triangle." *Food and Culture: A Reader,* edited by Carole Counihan and Penny Van Esterik, Routledge, 2008, pp. 36–45.

Lucas, Sheri. "A Defense of the Feminist-Vegetarian Connection." *Hypatia,* vol. 20, no. 1, 2005, pp. 150–77.

Mancuso, Stefano. *The Incredible Journey of Plants.* Other Press, 2020.

Matto de Turner, Clorinda. *Aves sin nido.* Stockcero, 2004.

Molinari Calleros, Nylia. "El problema de la nutrición." *Boletín de la Oficina Sanitaria Panamericana (OSP),* vol. 9, no. 11, 1930. https://iris.paho.org/handle/10665.2/11119.

Nervo, Amado. "Confidencias del natural (a modo de prólogo)." *La cocinera vegetariana,* edited by Antonio Blandina Torres, XI–XVI, Centro Naturista de México, 1918.

Notaker, Henry. *A History of Cookbooks: From Kitchen to Page over Seven Centuries.* University of California Press, 2017.

Ortner, Sherry B. "Is female to male as nature is to culture?" *Woman, Culture, and Society,* edited by M. Z. Rosaldo and L. Lamphere, Stanford University Press, 1974, pp. 68–87.

Paxton George, Kathryn. *Animal, Vegetable, or Woman?: A Feminist Critique of Ethical Vegetarianism.* SUNY Press, 2000.

Plumwood, Val. "Animals and ecology: Towards a better integration." *The Eye of the Crocodile,* edited by Lorraine Shannon, ANU Press, 2012, pp. 77–90.

Prado, Silvano. "La fórmula comunista anárquica." *La acción obrera* (January–June) 1913, https://archive.org/details/accionobreraarg1913-I/1913-06-07/page/n1/mode/2up?q=vegetariano.

Rodríguez , Simón B. *La Carpofagia.* El Globo, 1901.

Roselló, Josep Maria. *La vuelta a la naturaleza: El pensamiento naturista hispano (1890–2000).* Virus, 2003.

Sapriza, Graciela. "Ciencia, política y reforma social. Esperanzas y conflictos de la primera médica del Uruguay: Paulina Luisi (1875–1950)." *Género y ciencia en América Latina: mujeres en la academia y en la clínica (siglos XIX–XXI),* edited by Lizete Jacinto and Eugenia Scarzanella, Iberoamericana, 2011, pp. 53–76.

Shaffer, Kirwin R. *Anarchist Cuba: Countercultural Politics in the Early Twentieth Century.* PM Press, 2019.

Spencer, Colin. *The Heretic's Feast.* University Press of New England, 1995.

Stavisky, Sebastián. "El vegetarianismo en la prensa anarquista rioplatense." *Quinto Sol,* vol. 27, no. 2, 2023, pp. 1–17.

Stavisky, Sebastián. "Médicos de sí mismos. Medicina naturista, revolución social y éxodo de la ciudad en el anarquismo de Buenos Aires a comienzos del siglo XX." *Ecopolítica,* vol. 16, 2016, pp. 2–25.

Stepan, Nancy. *The Hour of Eugenics: Race, Gender, and Nation in Latin America.* Cornell University Press, 1991.

Stuart, Tristram. *The Bloodless Revolution: A Cultural History of Vegetarianism from 1600 to Modern Times.* 1st American edition, W. W. Norton, 2007.

Valeta, Antonio. *Botánica práctica, arte de comer y Nutrición.* Higiene y Salud, 1940.

Valeta, Antonio. *Cocina con plantas silvestres.* Higiene y Salud, 1939.

Valeta, Antonio. *Estragos del alcoholismo.* La Rural, 1913.

Vergara, Lucía. *Manual de cocina vegetariana chilena.* Imprenta Gutenberg, 1931.

Valeta, Antonio. *Manual Práctico del naturismo y el vegetarianismo.* Higiene y Salud, 1910.

Valeta, Antonio. *El naturismo en el hogar.* Imp. Latina, 1915.

Valeta, Antonio. *El régimen vegetariano,* 8th ed. Higiene y Salud, 1929.

Walker, Lara. *Absolute Equality. An Early Feminist Perspective / Influencias de las ideas modernas.* Arte Público Press, 2008.

Zubillaga, Carlos. "Carbonell y Vila, José Fernando." *Diccionario biográfico de las izquierdas latinoamericanas,* http://diccionario.cedinci.org

Afterword

A Latin American Mélange of Existence

PATRÍCIA VIEIRA

I read the *Small Encyclopedia of Common Beings* (*Pequena Enciclopédia de Seres Comuns,* 2021), a book by my friend Maria Esther Maciel, in a state of wonder. In this half-literary, half-literal selective encyclopedia, commonplace Brazilian plants and animals stand in friendly proximity, grouped not by kingdom, geographical provenance, or human use, but rather by the likenesses of their everyday names. In the first section, "Marys," we encounter "Noisy-Mary," a restless brown-orange bird, "Stinky-Mary," a bug that releases an unpleasant smell when under attack, or "Shameless-Mary," a weed with beautiful red, pink, orange, or white flowers that favors humid locations.[1] Under "Johns" we find "Liquor-John," a nocturnal, carnivorous fish, "Milk-John," a large tree with sweet-smelling light green flowers, or "Crazy-John," a reddish Amazonian beetle. The "Widows and Small Widows" section introduces the reader to the "Happy-Widow," a bird with white feathers and a boisterous behavior, the "Tightly-Grabbed-Love-Small-Widow," a bindweed with heart-shaped leaves, and the "Human-Widow," a sad, solitary human being. And the final section, "Hybrids," comprises a collection of names that involve plant-animal assemblages, including the "Zebra-Bromelia," a plant with dark green leaves adorned with white and pale yellow stripes, the yellow-tailed "Banana-Fish," found in tumultuous river waters, or the singing "Goat-Tree-Frog."

Browsing through such an extraordinary gathering of beings, I was reminded of the ties that bind the living beyond species boundaries and Linnean taxonomic divides. This unorthodox encyclopedia highlights the grassroots wisdom of popular nomenclature that foregrounds the similarities between disparate forms of life in their variegated colors, shapes, and temperament. Plants that adopt animal characteristics, animals that mix vegetal and beastly traits, reptiles that look like birds, fish similar to felines, bushes that imitate insects are all part of a lively mélange of existence.

It is not by chance that, for human communities who live in close contact with a wide diversity of more than humans, such as the peoples of the Amazon River Basin, transformation is central to their understanding of reality. A common trait of Amazonian cosmovisions is a former state of indistinction between different entities that only later acquired their current, stable identities (Viveiros de Castro, "Cosmological Deixis" 471). The memory of past fluidity between beings leaves indelible traces in present life forms and fuels constant transmutations of one entity into another, turning metamorphosis into a structuring feature of the Amazonian imaginary. Amazonian peoples realize something readers also discover in Maciel's remarkable encyclopedia: that the intricacies of existence are grounded on unexpected alliances, feuds, and collaborations between disparate beings, which cannot be completely grasped by neat scientific or academic categories.

The *Small Encyclopedia* also underlines the entanglement of humans and more than humans. The plant and animal Marys and Johns, widows and small widows in the book not only have human designations but also display structures of feeling usually attributed only to humanity. They have friends and foes, suffer from anger and greed, laugh and show wisdom. To be sure, one might accuse the author of giving in to anthropocentrism in her descriptions. But these beings' proximity to humankind can be read as more than an unethical projection of *Homo sapiens'* way of being in the world, imposing incongruous categories onto others. Rather, the anthropomorphism—and the *anthropopathos,* the human sensitivity—of the plants and animals in the book points to oft-overlooked affinities, bringing together otherwise dissimilar beings: for instance, the color orange, found in the flowers of a plant, the hair of some humans, the body of an insect, and the feathers of a bird; solitary behavior displayed by a fish, a lizard, and an increasing portion of humanity; or the intelligence to solve pressing issues of existence that binds all forms of life. Maciel's short encyclopedic-like texts are a literary rejoinder to recent scholarship (Bennett; Karlsson; Ryan) calling for an understanding of anthropomorphism as a way of emphasizing the analogies between humans and other beings and of undoing baseless assumptions of human exceptionality. Plants and animals are human-like, in the same way as humans are plant- and animal-like. Riffing on the dry language of science and the austere structure of discreet encyclopedia entries, Maciel's writing reminds us that life is complex, entangled, and playful in its multifarious instantiations.

The present collection brought Maciel's *Small Encyclopedia* to mind in that both works, one using literary license and the other the tools of literary, film, and art criticism, question ready-made assumptions about plants, animals, and humans and highlight the porous boundaries between species. Pardo Porto and Pérez's edited book bridges critical plant and animal studies to offer an encompassing analysis of the key role played by more-than-human beings in cultural life. Latin American texts, film, and artworks overflow the confines of Western, scientific kingdoms and can only be fully appreciated by resorting to theoretical frameworks capacious enough to comprehend the multiple ties that bind all forms of existence. Such an encompassing approach is both a scholarly and a sociopolitical statement. It takes a stance against the compartmentalization of research at a time when academic work is increasingly fragmented, focusing on narrow specializations that often thwart an understanding of broader cultural, geographic, and ecological contexts.

The focus of the volume in more-than-human languages and epistemologies shows that articulation and intelligence are not perquisites of humanity alone and highlights the pitfalls of anthropocentrism. The book's inclusive take on more-than-human existence honors previously marginalized Indigenous, African, and other place-bound—*campesino*, riverine—traditions of Latin American thought, where the frontiers between forms of life are ever shifting. By emphasizing the ravages of extractivism and the resistance to this predatory practice, the chapters in the collection point toward the rights of plants and animals beyond their commodification by humans.

Hailing from the same Latin American country as Maciel, but drawing on a distinct tradition of thought, Brazilian, Yanomami shaman Davi Kopenawa also reminds his readers of the links between all forms of life and of the dangers of extractivism in his magnum opus *The Falling Sky: Words of a Yanomami Shaman* (*A Queda do céu: palavras de uma xamã Yanomami*, 2010), written in partnership with his lifelong associate, French anthropologist Bruce Albert. Kopenawa details the various steps in the long process of becoming a shaman, a central part of which is learning how to see the *xapiri*, a word often translated as "spirits" (Kopenawa and Albert, 63). As anthropologist Viveiros de Castro explains in his preface to the book, the *xapiri* are "'spiritual' images of the world" and its "invisible guardians," "countless living beings" that are the "sufficient reason and efficient cause of what we call Nature" (13).[2]

For Kopenawa, the *xapiri* are images of animals considered to be the ancestors of humans: "A long time ago, when the forest was still young, our ancestors, who were human with animal names, metamorphosed into animals to be hunted. [. . .] It is therefore those ancestors turned others that we hunt and eat nowadays. The images we make descend and dance as *xapiri* [. . .] are their forms as ghosts" (Kopenawa and Albert, 117). The Yanomami are fully cognizant of their proximity to the animals they hunt and eat: "no matter how much meat from hunting we eat, we still know full well that these are human ancestors turned animals. They are inhabitants of the forest as much as we are. [. . .] They are not different. Today, we give ourselves the name of humans, but we are identical to them" (117–118). If humans know that animals are their relatives, the *xapiri,* by the same token, "consider animals as ancestors, similar to them, and so they name them" (117). Dichotomies such as those separating matter and soul, creatureliness and spirit, bestiality and reason collapse in Yanomami thought, in that animals, humans, and the *xapiri* recognize one another as members of the same extended family. While animal in origin, the bodily shape of the *xapiri* is human-like (111). Combining human and animal features, these spiritual beings are the protectors of their human kin. They sing and dance in a cosmic performance that sustains the balance of the rainforest and allows for the continued existence of all its inhabitants.

The songs of the *xapiri* originate in age-old trees planted by the main Yanomami deity, Omama, at the edge of the forest, where the land ends and the foundations of the sky are grounded. These trees have singing lips from which the *xapiri* learn the countless songs that enable them to sing and dance, and, when shamans sing, they reproduce these chants (Kopenawa and Albert 114). In *The Falling Sky,* it becomes clear that human wisdom, centered around the figure of the shaman, has more-than-human origins. Shamans are taught their healing songs and dances by the animal-ancestor images of the *xapiri,* who have, in turn, acquired them from trees. Vegetal life is the source of all knowledge, which is then passed on from the *xapiri* to the shamans and then to the larger human community. This process of knowledge transfer displays clear similarities to the transmission of energy from the sugar produced by plants through photosynthesis to the bodies of plant-eating animals and then to the humans who hunt these animals. Physical and spiritual sustenance follow the same path that connects all life, emphasizing the dependence of humans on plant and animal existence. Far from regarding themselves as the pinnacle of Creation, as reason-endowed beings superior to all other forms of life, the Yanomami are keenly aware of their indebtedness to plants and animals for nourishment and knowledge. It is thanks to the wisdom acquired from more-than-human beings that shamans can go on performing their songs and dances, which prevent the sky from falling.

Kopenawa's reflections in *The Falling Sky* find echo in the chapters of the present volume that emphasize the indebtedness of human biocultural life to all the other beings with whom humanity shares the planet. Several chapters analyze the agency of plants—grass, palm trees, coffee, chicle, etc.—their entanglement with nonhuman and human animals and their resistance to capitalist, monocultural exploitation. Other articles shed a critical light upon the reduction of animals to cattle in the Anthropocene. Similar to Kopenawa's text, the essays in the volume denounce the consequences of unbridled extractivism applied to plant and animal life and tease out the ethical and political corollaries of heeding plant and animal languages and ontologies.

Maciel's *Small Encyclopedia* and Kopenawa and Albert's *The Falling Sky* are hybrids, the former a literary pastiche of scientific language and the latter straddling the genres of (auto)biography, philosophical treatise, and cosmological narrative. By occupying a liminal space between different languages and categories, both texts stage a fruitful dialogue between Western modes of thought—taxonomic and encyclopedic classifications, in the former; anthropological language in the latter case—and homegrown Latin American discourses on more-than-human beings. Likewise, the four sections of *Plants and Animals in Latin American Cultures* point to the cultural hybridity of Latin America as a continent at the crossroads between extractivist colonialism and internal/neocolonialism, on the one hand, and local traditions, movements, and ways of relating to the natural environment, on the other. The plethora of topics discussed in Pardo Porto and Pérez's volume—from different languages and knowledges beyond the human, through a move away from anthropocentrism and analyses of Indigenous, multispecies responses to colonialism, to the legal framework of the rights of nature to fight against predatory, extractivist practices—reveals the wealth of Latin American culture in its engagement with the more-than-human world.

Drawing on the core methods of literary, film, and art criticism, cultural studies, historiography, and anthropology and touching upon cultural productions as varied as poetry and cookbooks, early chronicles and New Wave films, painting and photography on plant and animal life, the research methodologies and topics discussed in this book showcase the contribution of Latin American cultures to contemporary discussions on environmental crisis, anthropogenic species extinction, and, more broadly, the role of *Home sapiens* within the web of existence. In the wake of *Small Encyclopedia* and *The Falling Sky,* the current book underscores the vitality of Latin American human and more-than-human cultures, grounded on the coexistence and shared sociality of plants, animals, humans, and all other entities.

Acknowledgments

This text is part of the ECO project, funded by the European Research Council (ERC) under the European Union's Horizon 2020 research and innovation program (grant agreement no. 101002359).

Notes

1. All quotes from books in a language other than English are rendered in my translation.

2. The notion of "shaman" and of "*xapiri*" are very close in Yanomami, since the term for shaman literally translates as "spirit-people" (Viveiros de Castro, "Prefácio," 18, note **)

Works Cited

Bennett, Jane. *Vibrant Matter: A Political Ecology of Things.* Duke University Press, 2010.

Karlsson, Frederik. "Critical Anthropomorphism and Animal Ethics." *Journal of Agricultural and Environmental Ethics,* vol. 25, 2012, pp. 707–720.

Kopenawa, Davi, and Bruce Albert. *A Queda do céu: palavras de uma xamã Yanomami.* Companhia das Letras, 2015.

Maciel, Maria Esther. *Pequena Enciclopédia de Seres Comuns.* Todavia, 2021.

Ryan, John. "Writing the Lives of Plants: Phytography and the Botanical Imagination." *a/b Auto/Biographical Studies,* vol. 35, 2020, pp. 97–122.

Viveiros de Castro, Eduardo. "Cosmological Deixis and Amerindian Perspectivism." *Royal Anthropological Institute of Great Britain and Ireland,* vol. 4, no. 3, 1998, pp. 469–488.

Viveiros de Castro, Eduardo. "Prefácio—o recado da mata." Kopenawa and Albert, pp. 11–41.

CONTRIBUTORS

THOMAZ AMANCIO is a teaching fellow in the Humanities at the University of Chicago. His research explores how field research in the plantation and the cattle frontier shaped literary and sociological writing in Brazil. His writing has appeared in the *Journal of Lusophone Studies*, *PHILIA*, and *Porto Alegre* reviews.

ANA CAROLINA CARMONA-RIBEIRO is an architect and professor at the School of Architecture and Urbanism of the Federal Institute of São Paulo (IFSP), Brazil. Her research focuses on the relations between plants, art, and landscape architecture. She is the author of *The Guidebook of Modernist Botany* (2020), which discusses the meanings and representations of vegetation (and related categories, such as landscape and nature) in the São Paulo–based modernism of the 1920s and 1930s.

BRIAN T. CHANDLER is professor of Spanish at the University of North Carolina Wilmington. His research focuses on contemporary Latin American narrative, poetry, and theater with a particular focus on the relationship between science and literature. His book *Science Fusion in Contemporary Mexican Literature* (Bucknell UP, 2024) examines how Mexican authors fuse science and literature to offer fresh perspectives on topics in biopolitics, historiography, metaphysics, ethics, and ecological crisis in the age of the Anthropocene.

MAURICIO ESPINOZA is associate professor of Spanish and affiliate faculty in the School of Environment and Sustainability at the University of Cincinnati. His areas of research are Central American literary and cultural studies, Latinx popular culture, migration, food studies, and translation. He is coeditor of *Central American Migrations in the Twenty-First Century* (Arizona UP, 2023) and *The Rise of Central American Film in the Twenty-First Century* (UP of Florida, 2023).

PILAR ESPITIA is assistant professor at the Department of Literature in the Pontificia Universidad Javeriana (Colombia). Her research focuses on medieval, early modern, and colonial literatures. Espitia's research has appeared in *Revista Medieval Haereticus* and *Cuadernos de Literatura,* and she is currently coordinating the research project "Constelaciones estéticas de la naturaleza en la literatura: perspectivas pre-modernas y post-modernas."

MICAH MCKAY is associate professor of Spanish at the University of Alabama who works within an environmental humanities framework to study twentieth- and twenty-first-century Latin American literatures and cultures. He is the author of *Trash and Limits in Latin American Culture* (University of Florida Press, 2024) and coeditor of *Environmental Cultural Studies Through Time: The Luso-Hispanic World* (Hispanic Issues On Line, 2019).

VANESA MISERES is associate professor of Spanish at the University of Notre Dame. She specializes in nineteenth- and twentieth-century Latin America. She is the author of *Mujeres en tránsito: viaje, identidad y escritura en Sudamérica (1830–1910)* (North Carolina Studies in the Romance Languages and Literatures, 2017), *Gender Battles: Latin American Women, War, and Feminism* (U of Toronto Press, 2025), and coeditor of *Food Studies in Latin America: Perspectives on the Gastronarrative* (U of Arkansas P, 2021). Miseres is preparing a manuscript on the cultural history of vegetarianism in Latin America from the 1900s onward, as well as a study on gender and science in Latin America (1850–1950), focusing on women's uses of botany, horticulture, and domestic science.

JONATHAN MULKI is a PhD candidate in the Department of Spanish and Portuguese at the University of California, Davis. He pursues the recently created Designated Emphasis (DE) in environmental humanities. His dissertation examines representations of yerba mate in literature and film, with a focus on Argentina.

KATE OSTROM is a lecturer in the Department of Romance Languages and Literatures at the University of Michigan at Ann Arbor. She holds a PhD in Hispanic and Latin American languages, literatures, and linguistics and the environmental humanities from Wayne State University. Her current project analyzes the US-Mexico border through an environmental humanities approach, tracing the multi-being losses that occur in borderscapes. Kate was a 2023–2024 and 2024–2025 Wayne State Rumble Fellow.

CRISTINA E. PARDO PORTO is assistant professor of Latin American and Latinx visual cultures at Syracuse University. Her research examines the intersection of visuality and coloniality in the Americas, with an emphasis on the global diasporic networks of Central America and the Caribbean. Pardo Porto has coedited two special issues of *Istmo*, both titled *Photography in, on, and from Central America*, and curated the exhibition *Joiri Minaya: Unseeing the Tropics at the Museum* at the Syracuse University Art Museum. Her contributions extend to published and forthcoming articles in journals including *Art Journal, Hispanic Review, MLN, Romance Quarterly*, and *Letras hispanas*, among others.

NIALL A. PEACH is a visiting assistant professor of Spanish at the University of Cincinnati. With his work, he engages the relationship among environment, race (Blackness and Indigeneity), and (neo-)imperialism in nineteenth- to twenty-first-century Mexico and the Caribbean. Through a plant studies and blue humanities lens he contends with questions of belonging, re-existence, flourishing, and survivability of human/nonhuman entanglements in the face of destruction on and around the plantation. He is coeditor of *Alexander von Humboldt: Perceiving the World* (Purdue UP, 2023), and his monograph *The Garden State: A Politics of (Up)Rooting in 19th century Latin America* is forthcoming.

OSCAR A. PÉREZ is an educator and researcher of Spanish language and Hispanic studies. His work extends to fields that include the environmental humanities, science and technology studies, posthumanism, medical humanities, and languages for specific purposes. He has published in various critical volumes and academic journals, including *Ecozon@, Hispanic Issues On Line, Hispanic Studies Review*, and *Latin American Literary Review*. He is the author of *Medicine, Power, and the Authoritarian Regime in Hispanic Literature* (Routledge, 2022).

JORGE QUINTANA NAVARRETE is associate professor of Spanish at Dartmouth College. His research interests include Mexican culture (nineteenth and twentieth centuries), utopian studies, environmental humanities, and posthuman theory. His peer-reviewed articles have appeared in *Hispanic Review, Journal of Latin American Cultural Studies, Revista Hispánica Moderna, Revista Canadiense de Estudios Hispánicos*, among others. His book *Biocosmism: Vitality and the Utopian Imagination in Postrevolutionary Mexico* (Vanderbilt University Press 2024) traces the intellectual constellation of biocosmism in Mexico: the study of universal life understood as the vital vibrancy that animates everything in the cosmos from inorganic matter to living organisms to outer space.

BEATRIZ RIVERA-BARNES is associate professor of Spanish at Penn State University. She is the coauthor with Jerry Hoeg of *Reading and Writing the Latin American Landscape* (Palgrave Macmillan) and the author of *The Nature of Hate and the Hatred of Nature in Hispanic Literatures* (Lexington Books). She is also the author of numerous articles on Hispanic ecocriticism published in academic journals and of five novels and a collection of short stories.

VÍCTOR SIERRA MATUTE is assistant professor of Spanish and comparative literature at Baruch College, CUNY. His research areas include material culture, affect theory, transoceanic studies, and the history of the senses and emotions. He is the editor of the volume *Soundscapes of the Early Modern Hispanophone and Lusophone Worlds* (2025) and has published articles in journals such as *Bulletin of Hispanic Studies, Romanic Review, Romance Studies, Latin American Research Review,* and *Bulletin of Spanish Visual Studies,* among others.

EMILY CELESTE VÁZQUEZ ENRÍQUEZ is assistant professor in the Department of Spanish and Portuguese at the University of California, Davis. Her book, *Border Biomes: Ecological Imaginaries of Mexico's Edges* (Vanderbilt University Press, 2025), puts into dialogue the fields of border and migration studies with the environmental humanities. Her research has appeared in *Revista de la Universidad de México, Symposium, iMex, Romance Quarterly, Latin American Literary Review, Ciberletras,* among others.

PATRÍCIA VIEIRA is research professor at the Center for Social Studies of the University of Coimbra. Her fields of expertise are Latin American and Iberian literatures and cultures, Portuguese and Brazilian cinema, utopian studies, and the environmental humanities. Her most recent book is the edited collection *The Environment in Brazilian Culture: Literature, Cinema and the Arts* (Florida UP, 2025). She currently coordinates the European Research Council Consolidator project "ECO–Animals and Plants in Cultural Productions about the Amazon River Basin" and co-coordinates the Gerda Henkel Foundation funded project "Resilient Forest Cities: Utopia and Development in the Modern Amazon." For more information: www.patriciavieira.net

INDEX

Page numbers in *italics* refer to illustrations.

www.ingramcontent.com/pod-product-compliance
Lightning Source LLC
LaVergne TN
LVHW041111080826
845145LV00007B/1769